The Politics of Social Protest

Social Movements, Protest, and Contention

Series Editor: Bert Klandermans, Free University, Amsterdam

Associate Editors: Sidney G. Tarrow, Cornell University
                      Verta A. Taylor, Ohio State University

The Politics of Social Protest

Comparative Perspectives on States
and Social Movements

**J. Craig Jenkins and
Bert Klandermans, editors**

UCL
PRESS

British Library Cataloging-in-Publication Data
A catalogue record for this publication is available from the British Library.

ISBN: 1-85728-296-5 HB
      1-85728-297-3 PB

Cover design by Dawn Mathers

Contents

Part IV. The State and Movement Outcomes: System Transformations and Political Reform

Part I

Introduction

Chapter 1

The Politics of Social Protest

J. Craig Jenkins and Bert Klandermans

Surprisingly little attention has been paid to the interaction between social movements and the state. This is all the more surprising given the central importance of social movements as forces for political change in the contemporary world and the importance of the state in shaping political change. Whether we look at the interaction between social protesters and party politics in the United States or Western Europe or at the democratization struggles in Eastern Europe, China, or Latin America, the nature and development of social movements cannot be understood without reference to the central role of the state. As the institutionalized center for the legitimate monopoly on the means of violence, the state is the ultimate arbiter for the allocation of socially valued goods. The state is therefore simultaneously target, sponsor, and antagonist for social movements as well as the organizer of the political system and the arbiter of victory. As organizer of the political system, the state shapes the relationships between social movements and the institutionalized interest representation system. In the Western democracies, the central relationship is that between social movements and political parties and the governmental institutions that regulate the relationships between citizens and the state. Social movements that aim to alter social institutions and practices have to come into contact with the state, if only to consolidate their claims.

This volume brings the interaction between social movements and the state to center stage. Because it is primarily concerned with the politics of social protest movements in the Western democracies, it focuses on the four-way interaction between citizens, social movements, the political representation system, and the state. The primary focus is the three-way struggle between social movements, political parties, and the state, looking at the opportunities that electoral politics present to social movements, the impact of social protest on political parties and electoral processes, and, finally, the implications that these relationships have for the modern democratic state. The volume traces the emergence of the modern social movement out of changes in the conception of political representation that occurred during the construction of the liberal democratic state in the nineteenth century through to its contemporary impact on the late-twentieth century state. Because movement-state relations cannot be fully understood except through broad-ranging comparative analysis, the essays range from nineteenth-century France to the left-libertarian or "new social movements" of Western Europe to contemporary protest in Israel, Peru, and the Western democracies to the post-communist transformation of Eastern Europe. A central theme woven throughout the volume is that *political opportunities* are central to the emergence and development of social movements and that these opportunities are primarily structured by the organization of the state, the cohesion and alignments among political elites, and the structure, ideology, and composition of political parties. In this sense, the state shapes the *conflict and alliance systems* that shape social movement emergence and development. At the same time, social movements are also agents of political change. They act upon these opportunities, and their actions in turn often help to generate new opportunities. Any thorough discussion of the state and social movements must focus on both sides of this relationship.

We propose as an organizing device for thinking about the interaction between social movements and the state a diamond scheme (Figure 1). In this scheme, we assume the existence of an institutionalized political representation system based on mass parties and interest associations. In other words, this scheme is most useful for mapping movement-state relations in the Western democracies. It would have to be modified radically to deal with nondemocratic contexts. In chapter 2, "Social Movements, Political Representation, and the State," we discuss how to revise this scheme to deal with nondemocracies.

The diamond outlines the different relations that need to be addressed in discussing movement-state relations in liberal democracies. The left side of the diamond (arrows *a* and *d*) refers to the relationship of citizens to the political representation system, chiefly mass parties and formal interest associations, and the state. This is the traditional subject matter of political science. Our primary emphasis will be on the center and right side of the diamond (arrows *b, c*, and *e*)—on the impact of social protest and movement efforts on the

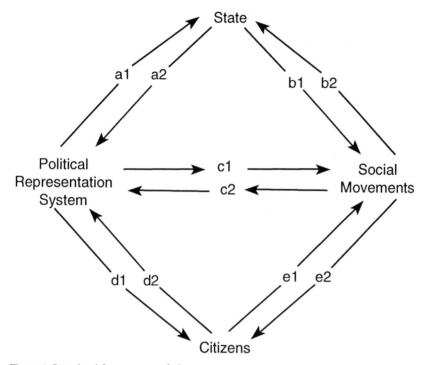

Figure 1. State/social movement relations

political system and the impact, in turn, of the political system back on social movements.

First, some definitions. By *state*, we mean the institutionalized system for claiming a legitimate monopoly over the means of violence over a specified territory. This ensures the ability to make and enforce binding decisions and thus places the state at the center of political conflicts. By *political representation system*, we mean the institutionalized set of organizations that claim to represent and aggregate the interests of various social interests. This places political parties, interest associations, and various social institutions claiming to represent broad constituencies at the center of the interface between the state and civil society. These groups have institutionalized access to centers of political decision making and are thus, in Charles Tilly's (1978) phrase, "polity members." By *social movement*, we mean a sustained series of interactions between the state and challenging groups (Tilly 1984). Social movements, then, constitute a potential rival to the political representation system and can play a major role in restructuring the relationship between the state and civil society. By speaking of *social protest*, we point to the collective action of social movements that are attempting to alter the representation system, public policies, or the general relationships between citizens and the state. We refer to the *political system* as this entire complex of relations.

The key themes that concern us throughout this volume relate to various combinations of arrows in the diamond scheme. First and perhaps foremost, we are concerned with *political opportunities*, that is, the impact of the state and the political representation system on social movements (arrows *b1* and *c1* in the diamond). How do political opportunities shape the emergence and development of social movements? How are movement goals and tactics shaped by the ideology, strategies, and policy styles of state managers and party leaders? Has neocorporatism closed off the normal channels of political access, thus forcing movements into disorderly protest, or has it worked to regulate conflict, thus reducing the pressure for protest? Do state repression and other controls undermine movements or do they mobilize new supporters?

Second, we are concerned with the impact of social movements back on the state (arrow *b2*). In terms of direct movement-state relations, we are concerned with questions of the political goals of contemporary movements and their ability to alter state institutions. Are the "new social movements" oppositional in the classic sense, are they apolitical, as some critics aver, or are they pursuing a program of "self-limited radicalism" (Offe 1985b)? Are social movements central agents of political change? What, after all, do we mean by social movement "success"? Do we gauge this by looking at the specific goals and agendas of activists or at the impact of their actions? Building on the now classic scheme that William Gamson devised in his *Strategy of Social Protest* (1975), we look at questions of political access and agenda setting (or "acceptance") as well as specific policy gains (or "new benefits"). We also need to expand this framework to incorporate structural change in the state system itself as well as alterations in the political system as a whole.

Third, we deal with the impact of social movements on the political representation system (arrow *c2*). We know that social movements often generate the issues and ideas that political parties adopt and eventually introduce into public policy, but we know relatively little about how this process works. Does this vary on the basis of movement strategies, party orientations, and electoral coalitions? Does intense party competition or voter volatility condition this effect? A classic story is that of the social movement that finally "went to Washington" and became part of the political establishment. Does this facilitate movement success? What are the circumstances that facilitate political incorporation?

Fourth and finally, social movements can have indirect effects on the political system by shaping the attitudes and actions of citizens (arrows *e1* and *e2*). Here the question has to do with the ability of social movements to mobilize and alter citizen orientations. More than three decades ago, Rudolf Heberle (1951) argued that social movements were the primary crucible of new political identities, generating the new ideas and loyalties that eventually transform the political system. Some social movements become third parties while others permeate the existing parties, operating as "special interests" within party chambers. In either case, the central avenue is through altering the attitudes and actions of the average citizen. A related measure is the generation of new styles of political action or repertoires. Samuel Barnes and Max Kaase in their celebrated *Political Action* (1979) made the forceful point that social movements create the new action repertoires, thus altering the relations of citizens to the state and to the party system.

We have organized the essays in this volume into three major themes as defined by our diamond scheme. The first theme—the *origins of social protest* —examines how social protest develops and operates as a complement or an alternative to political parties and interest associations. In addition to and in competition with these institutionalized vehicles for representing political interests, social movements have emerged to create new identities and press ignored claims, thereby preventing political parties and interest associations from monopolizing the intermediary relationship between citizens and the state. The second theme—*political opportunities*—elaborates on the impact of the state and the electoral system on social movements. Social movements develop in a context defined by the state and the representation system, which afford opportunities for mobilization and set limits on the effectiveness of movement strategies. Social movements also operate in this context, setting in motion changes that often create new opportunities for further action. Hence opportunities both *exist* and are *made*. The third theme—*system transformations and outcomes*—investigates the impact of social movements on the state and the representation system. Here the primary concern is the ability of movements to bring about political and social change as well as to alter specific policies and governmental practices.

The essays in this book move beyond existing social movement theories by examining the role of states in social movement development. Although resource mobilization and new social movement theories saw social protest as inherently political and offered many useful ideas about the politics of social protest, they did not develop a comparative analysis of the relationships between states and social movements. Nor did they examine the interests and structures of the state itself. They also underestimated the political origins of social protest, resource mobilization theory by neglecting questions of ideology and consciousness and new social movement theory by overemphasizing the apolitical goals of contemporary protesters. By building on theories of the state, we begin at the center point of modern politics: the structure of power and the struggle of new groups and actors to secure a political voice.

Our discussions begin with an attempt by J. Craig Jenkins to develop an agenda and comparative framework for the analysis of movement-state interaction. He argues that discussions of the state ought to bear on the study of social protest because social protest is inherently a political act, because the state regulates the political environment within which protesters operate, and because social protest is, at least implicitly, a claim for political representation. Although traditionally the question of social movements has been secondary in the study of the state, Jenkins shows how dominant approaches to the study of the state have implicitly contained an approach to the study of social movements and their political impact. He also points to various refinements of state theory that need to be incorporated so that we can deal with the politics of social protest in authoritarian settings.

The discussion continues with the origins of protest. Social protest has traditionally been defined as an alternative to electoral action. Ronald Aminzade argues that this dichotomy is actually a historic product of political struggles in the nineteenth century over the concept of political representation. Drawing on a historical analysis of nineteenth-century France, he contrasts two modes of representation: a "mandate" model and a "trustee" model. Aminzade argues that the mandate model preceded the modern trustee conception and encouraged a fusion of protest and voting, demanding that representatives act at the behest of citizens. The trustee conception was a major foundation of the modern bourgeois republic, splitting protest from voting by requiring that citizens retire to the sidelines once the voting was over. Much later in the twentieth century this model gave rise to the "elite" or pluralist theory of liberal democracy in which direct voice and protest were regarded as dysfunctional to democratic rule. As we look at contemporary protests, this distinction poses in fresh terms the question of the legitimacy of different relationships between citizens and the state.

A second focus is the mainsprings of protest action. Karl-Dieter Opp, Steven Finkel, Edward Muller, Gadi Wolfsfeld, Henry Dietz, and Jerrold Green address the question, How is political ideology related to protest? Drawing on a rational choice theory, they compare the relationship between political self-placement and protest potential in three contemporary democracies: West Germany, Israel, and Peru. Ideological incentives are critical to protest activism and, as the authors show, the configuration of ideological incentives varies significantly between these three polities. Supporting a variant of the "extremism" hypothesis that those at the ends of the political spectrum are more politically committed and therefore more likely to engage in "direct action," they find that rightists are as likely to protest as leftists in Israel and Peru, while the middle-of-the-roaders remain on the sidelines. Reflecting the post-World War II political reconstruction of West Germany and the various currents of social protest during the 1960s and 1970s, protest there is limited to those on the left of the political spectrum.

Michael Wallace and J. Craig Jenkins take up a similar set of questions in comparing social protest in eight Western democracies. In addition to looking at individual sources of protest, they also use the contrast between these democracies to identify the importance of political institutions in shaping protest. Drawing on the eight Western democracies originally studied by Barnes and Kaase (1979), they examine "new class," postindustrialism, and neocorporatism as images of the mainsprings of social protest. They conclude that the "new class" constitutes a significant source of protest but is overshadowed by the younger generation, men, and the more educated. Religiosity and, at least in predominantly Catholic countries where a confessional party has organized Catholic doctrine into the political system, Catholicism discourage protest. In the Anglo democracies, by contrast, Catholics constitute a dissident minority. In contrast with the idea of "apolitical protest" and the erosion of party identities, Wallace and Jenkins find that protest is strongly rooted in political identifications, especially ideological self-placement and left-party loyalties. Those who are loyal to leftist parties are consistently more supportive of protest. Reinforcing Barnes and Kaase's idea of "political activists," they find that those who are more active in conventional politics are also more active in protests. One of their most significant findings is that a rise in protest potential does not consistently give rise to actual protest. This relation is mediated by the political representation system. Liberal and neocorporatist states have comparable protest potentials, but the latter have experienced considerably less actual protest, indicating that the representation system is a significant constraint on actual protest.

Recent discussions of the political representation system have focused on the question of neocorporatism as a system of institutionalized bargaining between the state and associations of employers and workers. Is this a benign development that promises a more coherent response to social and economic problems? Or does it auger a new form of controlled participation and political exclusion, possibly even more darkly a move toward state corporatism? In their early formulations, Philippe Schmitter (1983) and Gerhard Lehmbruch (1984) emphasized the pacific effects of neocorporatism. Recent observers, however, have contended that it is a highly unstable system and that, by narrowing political access, neocorporate regimes have stirred new protest sentiments (F. Wilson 1990). Michael Nollert casts new light on this question, arguing that neocorporatist regimes are less likely than other regimes to experience protest, primarily as a result of their better economic performance. Distinguishing two dimensions of performance—economic growth and income inequality—he argues that the working and middle classes in neocorporatist systems have a material basis for their consent. A more centralized system of decision making coupled with informal bargaining relations helps consolidate this consent. Hence, in contrast to the neo-Marxists who contend that neocorporatism is a "class trick" and the political exclusion theorists who think it is oppressive, Nollert makes a strong case for seeing political stability as flowing from governmental performance.

Part III focuses on political opportunities and the interplay between protest movements and electoral politics. Building on the schemes advanced by Kitschelt (1986) and Tarrow (1989b), Hanspeter Kriesi argues that political opportunities are the central determinant of social movement development. Developing a scheme based on Kitschelt's ideas about the structure of state capacities and Tarrow's arguments about the configuration of power, he argues that the rules of the electoral system, the informal procedures of elites for dealing with outsiders, and the stance of the organized left (including both political parties and the organization and party ties of organized labor) have decisively shaped the political fortunes of the new social movements. These movements fared better in democracies with integrative elites, a unified left that was out of power, and pluralistic or religiously divided unions. They were more likely to adopt moderate goals and develop an independent constituency and program that ensured sustained mobilization. One of Kriesi's major innovations is distinguishing between the *formal institutions of the state*, which has been the primary focus of past work on political opportunities, and the *informal bargaining procedures of elites*, which shape the way in which elites respond to challengers. These in turn have historic roots in the development of the state and its relationships to various classes, especially the industrial working class. Adding to Kitschelt's (1986) earlier argument about the mixed success of movements in "weak" states, his ideas about the political style or informal procedures of elites in dealing with citizens helps account for the procedural and substantive successes of the new social movements as well as their defeats.

Diarmuid Maguire develops similar arguments about the trajectory of the recent peace movements in Britain and Italy. Emphasizing the tensions that exist between protest and electoral mobilization, he argues that the British Labour Party in the 1980s represented a "catch-all" party par excellence that saw major electoral advantages in co-opting the peace movement. Following a logic of electoral competition, it adopted most of the movement program, but in the process siphoned off the enthusiasms of the movement and exposed it to the hazards of electoral politics. Labor defeat at the polls spelled movement disaster. In Italy, the Communist Party (PCI) has long dominated the left, adopting a tutelary stance toward social movements. It therefore treated the peace movement as a troublesome stepchild that had to be guided into correct channels. The movement adopted a "class conflict" model of opposition but failed to develop an independent constituency and, incorporated into the PCI's ideological program, was eventually blunted. This story follows the lines of David Meyer's (1990, 1993) work on the nuclear freeze movement in the United States. A permeable Democratic Party made it possible for the freeze to set the agenda but, once it was absorbed, it could not shape the actual policy process.

A persistent theme has been the political channeling of movements by the party system. In their analysis of the left-libertarian or "new" social movements in Italy and West Germany, Donatella della Porta and Dieter Rucht argue that the central factor regulating movement development is the supportive or alienating stance of the dominant left party. They broaden the focus to deal with all four of the major new social movements: the student movement, the women's movement, environmentalism, and the new peace movement. Highlighting the shifts in ideology and action, they argue that the central factor was the stance of the major left party. The more confrontational or alienating this left party toward the new movements, the more radical the movements. Movement goals, then, are not fixed by the interests or ideas of supporters but rather are politically emergent or "made" by the interaction between social movements and their political environment. Della Porta and Rucht also build on Bert Klandermans's (1990) distinction between the alliance systems and the conflict systems. Social movements simultaneously confront an environment of potential allies (such as left parties) and opponents (or the conflict system). The movements' goals, tactics, and eventual successes are largely shaped by this complex environment. Della Porta and Rucht also show striking parallels between the movements in these different countries, anchored together by international diffusion of tactics and goals and a common set of international threats. In contrast to Kriesi, these authors contend that the governmental power of the left party is irrelevant. Their argument, in a nutshell, is: if the institutionalized left decides to promote change, it can facilitate a reformist challenge that eventually enjoys modest success.

Part IV centers on the outcomes of social movements, especially their effects on the state and the political representation system. We begin by looking at a broad range of changes that constitute movement success. Paul Burstein, Rachel Einwohner, and Jocelyn Hollander outline a bargaining perspective that emphasizes that when a movement's target is dependent on the movement, the target is willing to concede movement gains. They distinguish six types of movement success: acceptance, agenda access, policy victories, output response (or satisfying the grievances of movement activists), and structural changes. Past work has dealt primarily with only two of these dimensions, access and policy changes, and virtually ignored output response and structural change. Although they largely endorse Gamson's (1975) argument about the virtues of "thinking small," they also argue that we should include broader measures of success that better reflect the aims of movement activists. Ultimately, success is proportional to the dependence of targets on movement activists and thus the political exchanges into which movements can enter.

The message is that movement success is largely a product of the political environment, especially the power and resources of political parties. As a result, social movements often have a hands-off approach toward parties, viewing them with skeptical eyes as sources of entangling alliances. Russell Dalton explores the partisan orientations of the environmental movements of the ten members of the European Community. He identifies three distinct strategies: alliance with one of the existing parties, a third-party strategy, and an antipartisan stance. In general, he finds that the environmental leaders have followed an antipartisan stance. Despite strong leftist leanings, they view partisan alliances as blunting their effectiveness by tying them too closely to the fortunes of particular parties. At the same time, they also maintain strong informal relations with party leaders, typically those of the left-of-center parties. Antipartisanship strengthens their bargaining position, making them appear to be independent and thus to have access regardless of who is in power. In general, environmentalism, like most of the new movement issues, appears to reinforce long-standing trends toward a more fluid, issue-based politics.

Finally, we look at the most profound type of movement-initiated changes, namely, the transformation of political systems. Recent analyses of democratic transitions have typically treated movements as secondary, focusing instead on elite negotiations over a "democratic pact," the economic conditions for "class compromise," or the role of international crisis and intervention. Bronislaw Misztal and J. Craig Jenkins draw our attention to the differential role of protest in the postcommunist transitions. Comparing Poland and Hungary, they argue that protest was more central in Poland, that this stemmed from features of the Polish communist state, and that this protest wave left behind a distinctive political legacy, namely, hyperpoliticization and a weak political center. Although both communist states confronted identical problems—economic crisis, weak legitimacy and popular unrest, and loss of Soviet protection—the Polish state was more politically vulnerable. Private agriculture and an autonomous intelligentsia and church created havens for dissidence that overwhelmed the state. The Hungarian state was stronger but, in an ironic twist of fate, launched a "second economy" that created a new petite bourgeoisie that eventually became oppositional. The transition was driven more by the loss of Soviet protection and, as a result, the postcommunist regime was stronger. Although their skepticism about the long-term prospects for Polish democracy may not prove to be warranted, Misztal and Jenkins make a convincing case that the "movementization" of Polish politics has not been a happy fate.

Chapter 2

Social Movements, Political Representation, and the State: An Agenda and Comparative Framework

J. Craig Jenkins

The global upsurge of social movements over the past few decades has placed the question of the state and its relationship to social movements at the center of the intellectual agenda. In the United States, the social protests of the 1960s and the rise of professional advocacy in the 1970s spurred discussions about the mobilization of resources and the political processes that facilitate social movement success in terms of changing public policies and institutional practices. In Western Europe, the rise of the alternative movements and the Green parties challenged the postwar political consensus, questioning the benefits of economic growth and compromise politics. Drawing on discussions of the political economy of advanced capitalism, students of these "new social movements" traced their emergence to the rise of a "new class," more diffuse forms of social control, and growing technocracy. In the Third World, peasant revolts against corrupt and ineffective governments, nationalist revolutions against the colonial powers, austerity protests against repressive governments and the international bankers, and the democratization struggles against authoritarian regimes have focused attention on the class nature of these states, their repressiveness and institutional weaknesses, and their vulnerabilities to international controls. Dependency ideas about growing poverty and class polarization, world system analyses of "weak states," and state-centered arguments about kleptocracies were advanced to explain this political upsurge. And, most recently, movements fighting for democracy, human rights, pluralism, and a market economy have emerged in Eastern Europe and China, creating a "postcommunist" hybrid between capitalism and socialism and altering the meaning of the political left and right. While no codified theory has yet developed to account for these transformations, the emergence of these postcommunist states poses in fresh terms the question of the relationship of social protest to the state and to societal transformations.

Our concern is the interaction between social movements and the state. By *social movement*, we mean Charles Tilly's (1984) conception of a sustained series of interactions between a challenging group and the state. Our primary concern is with collective actors who are excluded or marginalized in the political order, either organizing new groups or advancing new political claims that have previously been ignored or excluded. In speaking of the *state*, we use Max Weber's (1947) classic conception of the institutionalized claim to a legitimate monopoly over the means of violence within a specified territory. In examining the state, we distinguish between the *state* itself that attempts to enforce these claims, the *regime* or the structure of rule and the legitimizing myths used to sustain that claim, and the *government*, that is, the personnel who actually make authoritative or binding decisions. This allows us to distinguish between social movements that challenge the government and its policies, those directed at the regime and its legitimizing myths, and those that adopt the more radical goal of reorganizing the state and its territorial claims. Intermediating between the state and social movements is the *political representation system*, that is, the set of institutions that claim to represent social interests.

This essay provides a critical assessment of the usefulness of three general approaches to the study of the state—neopluralist, state-centered, and neo-Marxian theories—as explanations of the politics of social movements. We argue that these theories provide a basic orientation for studying the politics of social movements. They constitute paradigms in the sense of general frameworks of analysis with underlying assumptions about the nature of the state and its relationship to society. Yet the relationship between the state and social movements constitutes a major gap in the existing literature. State theorists have largely focused on those who hold and wield power rather than studying their challengers. Social movement scholars have primarily focused on those who are contesting power rather than their relationships with the powerful. The basic premise of this essay is that the state is central to the study of social movements and that theories of the state provide the starting point for an understanding of the politics of social movements.

In studying the politics of social movements, we address three basic issues. First, what accounts for the origins and the goals of social movements? Why do citizens turn to protest or rebellion? Is their aim transforming the system, altering the rules of the political game, or changing specific policies? Second, what accounts for the strategies and tactics of movements? Here we are concerned with the organization of challengers, their relationships to institutional actors such as political parties and interest associations, and their use of disruptive or institutional tactics. Do they attempt to forge coalitions, emphasize protest or institutional tactics like lobbying and litigation, or build centralized organizations? Third, what accounts for the outcome of challenges? Are movements that "think small" in terms of goals and strategies more successful? How do these choices interact with political opportunities? What do we mean by movement success? Before we address these questions, however, we need to know why the state is central to the politics of social movements.

Why the State?

There are three major reasons for bringing discussions of the state to bear on the study of social movements. First and paramount, social movements are inherently political. Whether we adopt a narrow conception of movements centering on acts of mass defiance with an anti-institutional impulse (Piven and Cloward 1977, 1992; Traugott 1978) or a broader one of groups that attempt to bring about change in the distribution of socially valued goods (McCarthy and Zald 1977), social movements are based on demands for social change. Because the state constitutes the legitimate monopoly over the means of violence, it is central to the adjudication of conflicting claims. Even personal change efforts have at some point to deal with the state. Social protesters may demand fundamental changes in the nature of the state itself or they may seek more narrow institutional reforms, including those that are required to support changes in their personal lives, but, if their demands are to prevail and become part of the institutional landscape, the state has to become involved in institutionalizing these claims. Put another way, social changes without the support of the state will not persist. The state is therefore a target for social movements.

Second, the state organizes the political environment within which social movements operate, creating opportunities for action and, alternatively, imposing restrictions on movement activities. Traditionally, the question of political opportunities has been considered in terms of institutional access, especially formal protections for civil and political rights. In fact, the political struggle for these rights has been a central social movement demand. In the contemporary democratization struggles throughout the developing world, these rights have been basic movement demands. Recently, social movement scholars have moved beyond this formal conception of political opportunities by examining three additional dimensions: (1) the institutional structure of the state, especially its centralization and policy-making capacities; (2) the beliefs and ideologies of leaders, including their ideas about their mandate to rule and their strategies for dealing with citizens; and (3) the changing structure of political power. Kitschelt (1986), for example, has argued that decentralized or federal states such as the United States and West Germany are more permeable and yet have fewer policy-making capacities. This allows movements to emerge but prevents challengers from using the state to institutionalize major changes. Discussing elite ideologies in chapter 3, Ronald Aminzade contends that the shift to a trustee conception of political representation among French elites narrowed routine access to voting, thus forcing a sharp split between electoral and protest politics. Hanspeter Kriesi puts forward a similar idea in chapter 7 when he argues that in France and Italy political leaders adopted exclusive strategies with regard to citizens, forcing movements in these countries to adopt oppositional stances. A third focus has been the structure of political power, ranging from the opportunities created by elite divisions (Piven and Cloward 1977; Tilly 1978; McAdam 1982; Jenkins and Brent 1989), to electoral realignments and changes in governing coalitions (Jenkins 1985; Tarrow 1989a; Kriesi in chapter 7 of this volume), to institutional sponsorship for challenges (Gamson 1975; Jenkins and Perrow 1977; McCarthy and Zald 1973). The basic idea is that social movements are largely products of their immediate political environment, especially the alliances that they form in contests for power. This type of political process theory has been especially useful in explaining the policy successes of social movements in the United States and Western Europe.

A third reason for dealing with the state is that social movements constitute a claim for political representation. All modern states entail some system of representing social interests vis-à-vis the state. In communist states, the party claimed to represent the general interests of "the people" as a whole. In liberal democracies, political parties and interest associations claim to represent diverse social groups and, insofar as the system is open to all voices, the people as a whole. A key question is whether social movements constitute a direct form of representation resembling classic conceptions of participatory democracy (Carter 1974), a device for representing the underrepresented and countering entrenched oligarchies (Gamson 1975; Berry 1984; Lawson 1988), or an elitist group of self-appointed advocates (Etzioni-Halevy 1989). In assessing this question, we have to deal with the relationship between citizens and the state as mediated through movements.

Theories of the State and the Study of Social Movements

Theories of the state have traditionally focused on the left half of the diamond scheme of state-movement relations presented in chapter 1. Because of a primary concern with institutionalized power, social movements and their relationships to the rest of the political system have traditionally been ignored or treated as secondary. Classic pluralism and elite theory largely ignored movements, contending that they constituted irrational outbursts with little impact on institutional power. Although classic Marxism provided some useful ideas about movements, it was more concerned with its political vision than with analyzing movements and their relationship to the state. Contemporary work on the state, however, has begun to treat social movements as central political actors in creating new political identities and constituencies (Klein 1984; Dalton and Kuechler 1990), in changing public policies and political representation (Berry 1984; Gelb and Palley 1981), and in altering the structure of the state and the system of rule (Touraine 1981; Valenzuela 1989; Misztal and Jenkins in chapter 12 of this volume). In examining these new perspectives, we briefly trace their emergence from classical state theories and identify underlying assumptions about the nature of the state and its relationship to social movements.

Classic Pluralism and Neopluralism

Building on classical liberal ideas about the moral sovereignty of the individual and the virtues of limited government, early pluralistic theories of democracy were advanced in the immediate post-World War II era to provide a "realistic" conception of liberal democracy based on competing elites; a growing middle class; the rise of a professionalized mass media; the muting of social cleavages with economic affluence and the development of cross-cutting social ties; and the development of extensive linkage institutions in the form of interest associations, nonprofit organizations, nonpartisan expert bodies, and "interest aggregating" political parties (Deutsch 1961; Dahl 1967; Almond and Powell 1966; Lipset 1960). Reflecting the political quiescence of the immediate post-World War II period, this theory argued that economic development had created a differentiated social structure, economic affluence, and an infrastructure of communication networks that moderated social cleavages and encouraged strong ties between elites and masses, thereby deterring irregular or "extremist" actions on either side. Liberal democracies were seen as relatively permeable regimes. As Robert Dahl put it, "Whenever a group of people believe that they are adversely affected by national policies or are about to be, they generally have extensive opportunities for presenting their case and for negotiations that may produce a more acceptable alternative" (1967, p. 23). In these early versions of pluralism, then, social movements were viewed as irrational outbursts to be explained in terms of "short-circuited thinking" and the *Ersatzgemeinschaft* or substitute community sought by socially dislocated and marginalized individuals (Smelser 1963; Kornhauser 1957).

By the late 1960s, these early versions of pluralist theory had come under attack, eventually generating a "neo" version of pluralism. This "neopluralism" had two central components: a *rational choice theory of protest* that explained movement and institutional politics in the same terms; and a *political process theory of political opportunities* that emphasized the political allies supporting challenges. Both of these arguments stemmed from the critique of classic pluralism and yet depended on similar assumptions about state and society relations, thus generating a neopluralism.[1] They also had the distinctive limitation of being confined to liberal democratic capitalism. Let us first look at the critique of classic pluralism.

First, there was mounting evidence that support for social movements was centered among the better organized and more cohesive segments of the population (Oberschall 1973; Halebsky 1976)—not among the dislocated and mentally deranged, but among those who were integrated into co-optable networks. Second, the discontinuity between conventional politics and movement politics was questioned. Protest potential was greater among those who were active in conventional politics, creating a significant group of "activists" or "dualists" who combined electoral and protest politics (Barnes and Kaase 1979; Herring 1989). These two findings encouraged the development of rational choice theories of protest whose key tenet was that movement and institutional politics could be explained in the same terms. Third, challengers secured gains and entered the political representation system through unruliness rather than the peaceful compromise envisioned by classic pluralism (Gamson 1975; Piven and Cloward 1977). Fourth, the liberal democracies were at best an imperfect pluralism in that opportunities were historically variable and powerless groups depended on the support of sponsors and political allies (Gamson 1975; Jenkins and Perrow 1977). These last two insights contributed to a political process theory of political opportunities.

We call the resulting ideas neopluralism in the sense that they accepted the basic state/society model of classic pluralism. Autonomous groups in civil society were the primary source of political demands and the state was seen as an "umpire," that is, an external institution for adjudicating conflicting social interests. In other words, interests were defined by positions in civil society, not by the independent actions of the state. Although the state was only semi-permeable and was opposed to the organization and political access of new groups, it had no distinctive interests of its own, which set this theory off from state-centered ideas. Nor was it an institution of class control, which distinguished it from the Marxian arguments. As in classic pluralism, protest stemmed from state failure, primarily "linkage failure" in terms of oligarchic tendencies and exclusion from the political representation system. Because of its primary concern with problems of expanding political access and organizing the unorganized, it was limited to liberal democratic capitalism.

Let us take first the rational choice theories of protest. The early formulations began with Mancur Olson's (1965) identification of the "free-rider" problem, that is, the likelihood that rational individuals in large groups would attempt to derive collective goods from the contributions of others. Since this was a central problem for organizing movements, it posed a critical dilemma. Building from the assumption that protesters were as rational as conventional actors, several analysts rejected Olson's original "by-product" theory of selective incentives and turned instead to various ideas about collective or social incentives, often called "soft" incentives. Olson had contended that collective action could be induced by offering individual side benefits or "by-products," such as individual honors and material gains. The critics contended that this could not explain protest and movement support, which was motivated instead by solidarity and purposive incentives. People protested because they were committed to overriding goals and emotional bonds. In other words, a rational choice theory had to adopt a broader theory of motivation to account for protest. Solidarity and the formation of consciousness (Fireman and Gamson 1979; Jenkins 1983b) and ideological incentives (Opp 1989 and in chapter 4 of this volume) were the mainsprings. Free riding turned out to be largely a result of problems of availability and information. In the protests against the Three Mile Island nuclear disaster, the majority of potential supporters failed to join rallies because they were unaware of the events or because of family and job commitments (Walsh and Warland 1983). Participation was less than 20 percent of potential supporters in the mass antinuclear demonstrations in the Netherlands in the early 1980s for similar reasons (Klandermans and Oegama 1987). Moreover, turning Olson on his head, Pamela Oliver (1984) has shown in a series of clever experiments that those who were more aware of the free-rider problem were more likely to support collective action.

This rational choice thesis constituted a major advance over the earlier "crowd mind" models of classic pluralism. Still, there were problems. First, what accounted for the formation of interests? In particular, why were protesters often willing to risk their lives for causes that were doomed to failure? Pointing to the democracy protesters who defied armed tanks on the streets of Beijing in the summer of 1989, Calhoun (1991) argued that such high-risk activism required reference to an internalized code of honor that strict rational choice ideas could not explain. The theory needs to be complemented by a theory of interest formation that explains the development of ideological and solidarity commitments. Second, the theory implies that all types of political mobilization are the same. But there is good reason to believe that movement mobilizing and electoral mobilizing are qualitatively different. Not only do the risks differ but, as Schwartz (1976) and Redding (1992) have shown for the American populist movement and Kitschelt and Hellemans (1990) for the contemporary alternative movements in Western Europe, the incentives and the mobilization processes differ. Social movements rely on face-to-face interaction and emphasize the formation of new solidarities and identities. Organizing is group or class specific, centered among a collectivity with a strong sense of grievance and collective fate. Political parties, by contrast, are primarily concerned with controlling public office and hence resort to different tactics, using media images and formalized communications and tapping into preexisting loyalties. The logic of electoral competition also pressures party leaders to adopt an inclusive definition of their constituency. While there are parallels and both can be approached in broad rational choice terms, there are important differences that have to be kept in mind. Social movements attempt to *make* a new historic actor while parties attempt to *rule* in the name of an already constituted actor. At least in liberal democratic contexts, this leads to different logics of mobilization.

The second component of neopluralism was a *political process* theory of opportunities. The general permeability question had been the Achilles heel of classic pluralism. The major innovation was actually fairly simple, namely, recognizing that political opportunities varied. Classical pluralist theory had assumed that liberal democracies guaranteed a basic floor of opportunities. The recognition that opportunities varied over time and for specific groups set off a flurry of studies of the sources and dimensions of opportunities. First there was the recognition that access varied for particular groups, distinguishing polity members from excluded groups (Tilly 1978). Next there was the idea that member-outsider coalitions were vital to the formation and success of movements, including both support groups and left-party allies (McAdam 1982; Jenkins 1985). Then there was evidence that political realignments and crisis periods divided elites and weakened entrenched opponents, thereby making for successful challenges (Gamson 1975; Piven and Cloward 1977; Jenkins and Brent 1989). Finally, there was the cross-national evidence of a U-shaped relationship between formal opportunities in terms of political and civil rights and protest with the mixed systems (chiefly moderate authoritarian and neopatrimonial regimes) creating greater and more intense protest while the liberal democracies and state socialist regimes were less conflict prone (Timberlake and Williams 1984; Gurr 1989). Following up a similar reasoning, Powell (1982) found that among the Western democracies, those with proportional representation systems were more responsive to intense beliefs and hence substituted third parties for protest. Liberal democracy, then, emerged as an institutionalized conflict-regulation system that enforced compromise and bargaining, thereby discouraging militant and radical challenges to the political order.

This political process theory, however, dealt only with groups and institutional rules. Political opportunities were dealt with in terms of the immediate political environment of allies and opponents, what Klandermans (1990) referred to as the alliance and conflict systems. The state was conceived as a biased "umpire" that protected polity members and enforced the rules of the political game. It was not an independent actor with distinctive interests of its own. Nor did it define the processes that create the interests of political actors, including those of social movements. These were treated as a given by the structure of civil society. By conceiving the state as an independent actor pursuing its own interests and allowing it to play a central role in defining political interests, including those of challengers, a state-centered perspective offered a distinctive view of the relation of movements and the state.

Classic Elitism and State-Centered Theory

The basic premise of state-centered approaches is the classic elitist argument that the provision of public order is a good in its own right and that states as such have a distinctive set of interests stemming from their claims to territory and a monopoly on legitimate violence. Extending Thomas Hobbes's classic insights about the moral imperatives of civil order, recent analysts have argued that the chief problem confronting the less-developed countries is the provision of civil order and, specifically, the development of a strong state capable of regulating domestic conflicts and implementing effective policies (Huntington 1968; Higley and Field 1979; Migdal 1988). Similarly, students of neocorporatist regimes have emphasized the state's ability to define political interests and to enforce social compacts that ensure better economic performance and prevent open conflict (Schmitter 1983; Katzenstein 1985; Nollert in chapter 6 of this volume). A second premise pertains to the field of international relations, arguing that states are geopolitical actors that are shaped by their competitive relations with other states. As such, they have a direct stake in the industrial development that fuels their military and fiscal capabilities and thereby tend to align against popular movements that contest such developments. They also have an ideological stake in protecting states with similar worldviews, reinforcing military alliances. States that are internationally weak are likely to experience fiscal and military crises, thus becoming vulnerable to domestic challengers (Skocpol 1979).

The central concept in this elitist tradition is that of *state capacity*.[2] Borrowing on Hintze's (1975) classic conception of the state as a Janus-faced institution that simultaneously faces inward toward domestic groups and outward toward the international arena, the basic idea is that states have varying capacities to control their domestic populations and to protect and enhance their international position vis-à-vis the field of competing states. While domestic capacities are the most directly relevant for understanding social movements, the recent development of global or transnational social movements, such as the peace movement and environmentalism, that draw upon international ties for resources, strategies, and mutual support poses new questions for the international capacities of states (Willets 1982; Alger 1990; Klandermans 1992).

Domestic capacities fall into three categories. First there is ability to maintain domestic order through repression, what Michael Mann (1988) has called "despotic control." The state is able to block concerted opposition and use its effective monopoly on violence to secure quiescence. State repression has a curvilinear or U-shaped relationship to protest, erratic or inconsistent use of force tending to create more militant and larger challenges (Timberlake and Williams 1984). Second is the infrastructural capacity of the state, essentially its ability to mobilize labor and financial resources. Having a strong and vibrant economy feeding off increasing productivity and international trade advantages is a major source of infrastructural power. States also vary in their extractive capacities, especially their ability to raise revenue in the form of direct taxation and to mobilize troops for the military. Cameron (1984) has shown that infrastructurally strong states have less industrial conflict; they use their resources to reduce grievances. Third and most directly relevant for social movements is the administrative and rule-making capacity of the state, especially the structure of the government, the degree of administrative centralization, and the professionalism of the civil service.

These allow states to define political interests and to enforce decisions, thereby controlling protest.

How do these factors affect the development of social protest? In a formulation of this institutionalist argument, Kitschelt (1986) contended that centralized "strong" states created weak oppositions but, paradoxically, because of their strong policy-making capacities, these states were also able to implement major changes. In other words, the movements were weak but, if they happened to prevail, they would win major victories. "Weak" states, such as the United States and West Germany, were decentralized and highly permeable, thus facilitating movement mobilization, but, because of their policy-making weakness, were unable to implement movement gains. This basic idea has since been combined with other aspects of state structure. In chapter 7 of this volume and elsewhere (Kriesi et al. 1992), Hanspeter Kriesi defines the opportunity structures of states in terms of two dimensions: (1) policy capacities based on centralized ruling making and administration; and (2) the control strategy of elites, that is, their use of exclusionary or inclusive approaches to citizens. In this scheme, France is a strong state because it combines a presidential system with a highly centralized administration and weak courts. French elites have also adopted an exclusionary stance, minimizing their contacts with citizens. Together these factors dampen mobilization, but they also generate a radical and centralized opposition. As Birnbaum (1988) argues, French movements have adopted antistatist or anarchist strategies in response to this centralized monolithic state. Protest cycles are infrequent, starting with large explosions that lack organizational staying power, and quickly subside. By contrast, decentralized and inclusive states, such as the United States and Switzerland, are more permeable, creating numerous assimilative movements and more frequent yet gradual protest cycles.[3]

Another policy capacity stems from the strength of linkage institutions. Here state strength comes from the downward controls of the political representation system. In other words, the state uses the political interest system to control the definitions of citizen interests, including those organized by movements. The strongest states are those with centralized and extensive linkage institutions, either neocorporatist or communist regimes, pluralist states like the United States lying in between, and neopatrimonial regimes on the weak end. In the former Soviet Union, for example, centralized party control coupled with state ownership of economic production and strong party-controlled intermediary organizations created a relatively stable political system. In cross-national studies, the Soviet regimes have been the most stable (Hibbs 1973; Gurr 1989). In this vein, Bronislaw Misztal and I argue in chapter 12 of this volume that the Polish state was the most vulnerable link in the Soviet alliance system because it contained a large private farm sector, an independent intelligentsia, and an autonomous church that provided refuge for oppositional groups. Zhou (1993), however, has argued on the basis of Chinese experience that Soviet states also confront a "large numbers" problem in which large numbers of people have similar claims, patterns of interaction, and targets of grievances, thus creating large-scale and sudden spontaneous upheavals. Whether this is a distinctive feature of China with its tradition of centrally launched purification campaigns or a general feature of communist states remains unclear. In the middle, pluralistic states also have significant control over the organization of movements. McCarthy, Britt, and Wolfson (1991), for example, argue that nonprofit law enforces a distinction between political and tax-exempt charitable organizations, thus discouraging alliances between the two. At the weak end of the linkage systems are neopatrimonial regimes that rely on personalized controls and clientele networks. While these autocrats may have significant despotic powers, they lack the administrative capacity to mobilize broader resources and enforce decisions. Goodwin and Skocpol (1989) have therefore argued that neopatrimonial regimes are the most likely settings for Third World revolt.

Social movements are also shaped by the *international capacities* of states, especially their ability to compete militarily in the interstate system and to control international trade. Militarily weak states are unable to defend their territorial claims, draft conscripts, or ensure an orderly supply of resources, creating a greater likelihood of political protest and coups d'état (Russell 1974; Boswell and Dixon 1990; Jenkins and Kposowa 1990). World system theorists have also argued that peripheral Third World states that depend on a limited number of exports, especially agricultural products and raw materials, are economically vulnerable and thereby prone to rebellion (Wallerstein 1979; Boswell and Dixon 1990). International alliances are therefore critical to immunizing states against rebellion. A central feature of the collapse of the communist states was the military weakness of the Soviet Union after its withdrawal from Afghanistan. When the Soviets refused to intervene against challenges in Poland and East Germany, the communist states in Eastern Europe rapidly collapsed.

State strength is also a dynamic property that changes historically in the course of state building. Tilly (1988), for example, has placed state building in the center of his analyses of political rebellion, arguing that rural revolt in France was largely a response to the direct penetration of the political center into peripheral regions, threatening the claims of both landlords and peasants and provoking regional rebellions. Regional resistance movements also varied in response to the political strategy of central elites. Barley (1991) points out that state builders in the Ottoman Empire adopted a divide and conquer strategy based on building regional alliances with local notables and hence reduced the intensity of revolt. In France, a direct control strategy proved far more disruptive, forcing an alliance between the local nobility and peasant communities against the state.

This state-centered approach, however, does not address the social groups that supported state building or particular types of regimes. States reflect the interests of state managers rather than classes or groups in civil society. Conflicts are over who occupies the command posts, not the formula for rule or dominant ideologies. While this approach has the virtue of emphasizing the interests of the state as an actor and its control over social groups, it provides little insight into the historical development of different regimes. These have instead been the central aim of class theories of the state.

Classic Marxism and Neo-Marxism

Classic Marxism is based on the central idea that the state is a class instrument in that it protects the property interests of the upper classes. While Karl Marx and Friedrich Engels never developed a full-scale theory of the state, they did offer several general ideas about the politics of the working-class movement. First, they argued that each ruling class had its own type of regime and that changes in the property system required a revolutionary transformation. Absolutist regimes, for example, reflected a compromise between the declining feudal aristocracy and the rising bourgeoisie. The rise of the bourgeoisie required a revolutionary break and the introduction of a liberal democratic republic. Second, they argued that this liberal or bourgeois state was relatively autonomous in that it mediated the competing interests of different factions of the upper class and simultaneously presented itself as a national or popular state as opposed to representing a specific segment of civil society. This ability to present itself as representing the "general interest" of society while actually protecting ruling-class interests was essential to the ideological function of the state. Third, this liberal democratic state also provided the opportunity for the emergence of an oppositional movement centered in the wretched industrial working class that would transform the system, ushering in a classless society. The working class, then, had an interest in strengthening liberal democracy and might eventually gain power through electoral means.

Several of these prophecies proved erroneous, forcing major revisions in the classic formulation. Not only did the working class fail to become the numerical majority, but in advanced capitalism it reached compromises with its historical antagonists, supporting a welfare state that protected it against the marketplace. In other words, the antagonistic quality of these interests was historically contingent. In many countries, the industrial bourgeoisie supported authoritarian regimes, and the peasantry, which Marx and Engels had viewed with disdain as relics of "rural idiocy," proved to be a major agent in political revolutions. In advanced capitalist countries, a "new class" of salaried professionals and managers emerged as a supporter of a set of "new social movements." In response, neo-Marxists developed class coalition theories of regime transformations, a social democratic explanation of the welfare state and social reform cycles, a "new class" thesis about the new social movements, and class conflict theories of rural revolt.

First let us look at class arguments about the nature of regimes. Drawing on Engels's ideas about the antiliberal stance of the German Junkers and the thesis that a social revolution was necessary for capitalist development, Barrington Moore (1966) developed a historical analysis of the social origins of liberal democracy in France and the United States and of authoritarian capitalism in Germany and Japan. The key to the democratic route was a bourgeois revolution rooted in a political coalition of agrarian capitalists, commercial peasants, and the urban bourgeoisie. "Revolution from above," or fascism, was based on a conservative coalition between commercial landlords who used coercion to control their workers (slavery or serfdom), a strong authoritarian bureaucracy, and a politically dependent industrial bourgeoisie. A third route to the modern world—communist revolution—was a product of institutionally weak bureaucratic empires that succumbed to peasant rebellion. Class struggles, then, were central motors of social change, and the type of regime was fixed by the ruling-class coalition that controlled the path to modernity.

Students of the Third World have extended this scheme to account for the authoritarianism of states that depend on latifundia and plantation agriculture (Paige 1975; Wallerstein 1979) and bureaucratic-authoritarian regimes that have forged a coalition between state bureaucrats, transnational corporations, and a politically dependent national bourgeoisie (O'Donnell 1979; Cardoso and Faletto 1979). Echoing Marx and Engels, the industrial working class has been the central supporter of contemporary democratization movements and has been most successful where it has forged an alliance with small farmers and the urban middle classes (Therborne 1977; Stephens 1989;

Valenzuela 1989). Yet, contrary to classic Marxism, the industrial bourgeoisie has been an indifferent supporter of democracy. As Misztal and I argue in chapter 12 of this volume the postcommunist transitions in Eastern Europe are partially a result of the class conflicts and the relative strength of class-based opposition movements.

Second has been the social democratic thesis on the rise of the welfare state, which builds on the relative autonomy thesis, namely, that for the liberal state to legitimize itself as an independent mediator, it must have sufficient autonomy to construct compromises between conflicting interests. In other words, it cannot be the simple tool of the dominant class but must be responsive to the political demands of the lower classes. At the same time, it is structurally dependent on the capitalist economy to create tax revenues and sufficient prosperity for political stability (Block 1987). One method of legitimation is to promote nationalism and the ideology of individual citizenship (Poulantzas 1973). This isolates individual citizens and displaces class hostilities onto other nations. A second measure is to protect the working class by providing social insurance, public health, and education and using progressive taxation and Keynesian fiscal policies, that is, the welfare state. Working-class protest and an electoral challenge from the working class has been a central force behind the introduction of the welfare state, yet the government that actually instituted these changes has frequently been a liberal capitalist or Christian democratic one (Jenkins and Brent 1989; Esping-Andersen and van Kersbergen 1992). In other words, it has been a concession granted by conservatives rather than a direct victory by the working-class party. Similarly, strong unions and a social democratic party are major sources of the level of social welfare effort (Korpi 1983; Przeworksi and Sprague 1986; Esping-Andersen 1985, 1990). The welfare state, then, constitutes an institutionalized class compromise that provides workers with economic security while also allowing capitalist profitability.

This class compromise thesis also offers a distinctive explanation of social reform cycles. Economic crises are seen as stimulating lower-class protests and simultaneously spurring upper-class rivalries over how best to address economic and social problems. Because the state is not the simple tool of the upper class, rival upper-class groups have to form political blocs that compete electorally for popular support. Jenkins and Brent (1989) argue that hegemonic competition between liberal and conservative power blocs in the 1930s accounted for the rise of the American welfare state. Simultaneously, the state also initiates on its own social reforms designed to promote political stability and economic growth. Relief for the poor, unemployment insurance, and sim-

ilar welfare measures were launched in response to economic crisis and political protest. This produces a social reform cycle in which, first, protest
leads to proworker measures, then demobilization sets in, and, third, ratio-
nalizing reforms are introduced to gear these measures to enhance profitability (Piven and Cloward 1971; Block 1987).

The "new class" thesis claims that the historical antagonism of worker and
capitalist has given way to a new conflict between salaried professionals and
technocracy (Touraine 1969; Gouldner 1979). These knowledge workers face
a contradiction between their work autonomy and the requirements of the
profit system, leading to support for an array of new social movements. There
is mixed evidence for this thesis, however. While the new class does appear
to be a significant supporter of new social movements and related liberal attitudes, it does not appear to be oppositional (Macy 1988), and there is significant movement support for these new movements stemming from other
groups, such as youth, minorities, and residents of large cities (Kriesi 1989a;
Wallace and Jenkins chapter 5 in this volume). Instead of challenging capitalism, these new movements represent a form of "self-limited radicalism" (Offe
1985b) in focusing on the relationship between the state and private life.

Finally, neo-Marxists developed several theories of rural movements that
made the peasantry central to political revolutions. Addressing the historical
movements that opposed the intrusion of capitalist agriculture, Wolf (1969)
developed a "middle peasant" theory of revolt, arguing that semi-autarkic
middle peasants are the major source of rural rebellion. These middle peasants draw on traditional village institutions and independent land claims to
mount a conservative challenge against the intrusion of the capitalist market.
Although their aim is to restore a precapitalist economy, they end up weakening an authoritarian state and creating opportunities for an urban-based revolution. A second theory focuses on anticolonial or nationalist revolts where international capitalism has already been established. Pointing to the intensity
of class conflicts and the degree of lower-class solidarity that flow from particular production systems, Paige (1975) argues that migratory workers in
agricultural export enclaves are the most volatile. Hacienda workers are too
disorganized, and commercial smallholders and wage workers are able to
gain concessions without revolt. Migratory workers are still involved in independent subsistence production, which gives them sufficient cohesion and
autonomy to mount a revolt. Because these estates are based on land-inten-
sive production, class conflict approximates a zero-sum game, with landown-
ers turning to repression and workers to revolutionary challenges to the
state.

This neo-Marxian approach, however, still has limitations. Despite the recognition that class conflicts might be nonantagonistic and that social movements were *made* rather than responses to the immanent requirements of some teleological scheme (Touraine 1981), there is still a tendency to confuse ideological critique with sociological analysis. Some continue to speak of "reactive utopias" (Castells 1983) and imperfect consciousness as if class interests were ethical universals. Others offer inflated claims about the "antisystemic" nature of contemporary movements and reductionist arguments about the interests of ethnic and cultural movements (Arrighi, Hopkins, and Wallerstein 1989; Wallerstein 1979). There is also a failure to deal with the independence of political institutions and processes. The state is treated as a functional part of the economic system (O'Connor 1973) rather than an autonomous arena in which movements and their allies and opponents came into conflict. This approach needs to be supplemented by the types of arguments put forward by the state-centered and political process theories.

Whither Social Movement Theory?

These three theories of the state frame the major arguments about the politics of social movements. As general frameworks for understanding the state and politics, they are rooted in competing political visions of the "good society." In fact, this is more the root of their disagreements than empirical matters. The pluralist tradition is based on the moral sovereignty of the individual, offering a vision of the state that maximizes individual liberty. In terms of social movements, the key question is expanding opportunities for new groups to organize and compete in the political arena. The elitist tradition draws on Thomas Hobbes's classic argument about the moral imperative of political order. The basic issue is the ability of the state to regulate social conflicts, including political challenges mounted by social movements. The Marxian vision is premised on the centrality of community and the injustice of class inequality. Social movements are a vehicle for creating community by attacking social privilege.

The task of sociological analysis is to harness these frameworks as tools for understanding the politics of social movements. Do they help understand the origins of social movements, their strategies, and their outcomes? Alford and Friedland (1985) argue that these theories operate on different levels of analysis with distinct conceptions of interests and power.[4] Neopluralist arguments deal with groups and institutions, accounting for the mobilization and incremental victories of social movements in liberal democratic regimes. Rational choice theories of mobilization and political process arguments about movement development explain specific movements, not the social movement sector as a whole or the nature of regimes. State-centered ideas pick up the thread at this point, building arguments about the social movement sector in different regimes. The strong-state thesis about radical yet weak challengers explains how the social movement sector as a whole is shaped by the institutional structure of the state. It does not, however, explain the origins of regimes or their transformation. At this point, neo-Marxian ideas about class struggles and regime changes become useful. Moore's (1966) argument about the class coalitions behind liberal and authoritarian capitalism and dependency arguments about nationalist revolutions become relevant.

Despite this complementarity, there are significant points of contention. In the neopluralist theories, movements originate from "linkage failures," either political exclusion or oligarchic tendencies. Goals are centered on the benefits of political access, chiefly social protection and symbolic recognition. So long as the polity is permeable, movements will be transitory and their goals incremental. While state-centered theories do not actually address the question of movement origins, they do contend that movement goals are fixed by the state's general approach to dealing with citizens. Exclusionary approaches generate radical or antistatist challenges, not class antagonisms. In Birnbaum's (1988) formulation, exclusionary states stem from state-directed industrialization and strong administrative capacities. This departs from the neo-Marxists, who distinguish antagonistic from nonantagonistic class conflicts. In the former, production is labor intensive and gains can be achieved only through conquest, that is, reducing or abolishing the power of the opponent. Since the state is essentially seen as an instrument of dominant class power, antagonistic relations lead to exclusionary states. Future comparative work should focus on the origins of exclusionary states and their relations with upper classes.

A second point of contention centers on the strategies that make for success. The neopluralists have argued the advantages of "thinking small" by pursuing narrow gains, building alliances while using unruly tactics. As Burstein, Hollander, and Einwohner argue in chapter 10, movement gains stem from the dependence of targets on movement constituencies, which can be best used by maintaining relationships and building up alliances. Several of the essays in this volume, however, make the point that movement alliances with political parties are fraught with dangers. Maguire's comparison of the British and Italian peace movements and della Porta and Rucht's treatment of the alternative movements reinforce Dalton's thesis that movements are better off maintaining a nonpartisan or even an antipartisan stance. Otherwise, they become victims of party losses. Moreover, this argument of "thinking small" is limited to liberal democracies where opportunities are greater. It is also most relevant to movements that frame their goals in terms of political access and incremental policy gains. Outside of liberal democracies, change in the distribution of socially valued goods typically requires changes in the relationship of citizens to the state. Movements that "think big" are more relevant, despite the types of drawbacks Misztal and I identify in our essay on Polish postcommunism. Nor does the argument of "thinking small" address the implications of the "radical flank" effect (Haines 1986) in liberal democracy, namely, that radical challengers are essential for the incremental victories of moderates. We need systematic comparisons of movement strategies in different types of regimes and state systems.

A third source of contention is the durability of political opportunities. Political process arguments have focused on the immediate political environment surrounding particular movements, what Klandermans (1990) has called the conflict and alliance system. State-centered theories have concentrated instead on the institutional structure of the state, using this to explain the entire social movement sector. As Kriesi shows in chapter 7, these theories can be fruitfully synthesized, using institutional arguments to explain the conflict and alliance system. Yet there remains an issue of durability. Discussions of strong states have typically assumed that once set, institutional structures persisted, affecting the state's approach to citizens for decades. In building his argument about the French state, Birnbaum (1988) points to the royal autocratic tradition as well as monarchal attempts to promote military industries. Others have argued that political opportunities are variable and dependent on the actions of specific groups, including efforts by movements to create their own opportunities (Tarrow 1993b). We need a clearer conceptualization of different types of political opportunities and close-grained comparative historical analyses to sort out the durable from the transitory features of political opportunities.

A final gap is one that stands largely outside existing state theory. Social movement scholars have become increasingly aware of the international nature of social movements, not only the diffusion of strategies and tactics but also the existence of common targets and international coordination among movements. As Tarrow (1993b) has noted, social movements have been internationalized at least since the mid-nineteenth century, when the antislavery movement unfolded. Because it had to attack an international institution, opponents found that they had to address slavery as an international problem. In our analysis of postcommunist transitions, Misztal and I argue that the international dependence of the communist states on the Soviet Union created a type of international opportunity structure that triggered the collapse of communism. Similarly, democratization movements in the Third World have been decisively shaped by international events, including the pressure of the United Nations and the Western powers to give in to citizen demands. Observers have long noted that secessionist challenges are rarely successful, in part because of international reinforcement. There is a logic akin to that of polity members that leads states to join ranks against the entry of new contenders. New states might upset the balance of power or call the rules of the system into question. Until recently, the only successful secessionist challenge in the post-World War II period was Bangladesh, in which Indian military intervention was decisive. British and American neutrality, premised on the idea of a region of influence, sanctioned this move. In short, there is strong reason to believe that social movements are not just prisoners of their national boundaries but are profoundly shaped by their international environments. Discussions of political opportunities need to be extended to deal with these international aspects.

How should we proceed? The essays in this volume offer several suggestions. First, our inquiries should be broadly comparative. States constitute distinct systems, making it necessary to treat states as units of observation as well as contexts for study. In order to capture the interaction of states and social movements, it is invaluable to have a basis for comparison. The number of states depends on the argument. Misztal and I deal with two countries, comparing the postcommunist outcomes in Poland and Hungary. This allows us to identify the political processes that transformed these regimes and created different outcomes. Nollert examines the degree of neocorporatism in the eighteen democracies of the Organization for Economic Cooperation and Development and its impact on political protest. This allows him to look at different regime structures, thereby highlighting the mechanisms by which corporatist bargaining reduces protest. Aminzade examines a single case over time, the nineteenth-century French state, to develop a historical interpretation of the formation of ideologies of democratic representation and how this created the modern social movement as a new relationship between citizens and the state. Yet even here, other liberal democracies and historical changes within this one state provide a yardstick.

Such work poses sticky problems of comparability. Does protest potential, for example, have the same meaning in the Netherlands that it does in the slums of Mexico City? Or does participation in ethnic riots have the same determinants in Los Angeles as in Kinshasa or Nairobi? Second, we need to develop a measure for capturing these features. Political opportunity, for example, is a complex construct with multiple dimensions, many of them specific to particular types of regime. Conventional measures, such as the political and economic liberties index (cf. Timberlake and Williams 1984), are at best crude approximations. We have not yet worked out ways of studying divided elites and state capacities in more than a handful of state settings.

Second, studies of social movements and the state need to be sensitive to temporal processes. Although cross-sectional studies are useful so long as the analyst is aware of their limitations, the development of movements and their impact is a process that occurs over time. Traditional historical methods and annualized time-series techniques have been the favored methods to date. Future work will have to draw on more sophisticated methods, such as event history and full panel analyses, that capture temporal processes. They will also need to combine these with conventional narrative history to capture the details of specific contexts and draw out their generality.

Third, the study of social movements needs to address the international aspects of protest. Past conceptualization has treated movements as prisoners of their states, but there is growing evidence that international components are central. International arrangements define targets and political opportunities and create the conflict and alliance systems that shape social movement development. Nor is the old conception of a "society" tightly bounded by a "state" the typical arrangement. Just as "societies" are not always congruent with the boundaries of their "states," so social movements span conventional boundaries, operating at local as well as regional and international levels. As we move toward an increasingly globalized society, social movements become increasingly global.

Fourth, these studies need to draw on ideas developed in other fields. Students of the state, for example, have developed a rich conceptual understanding of the nature of the state and political processes, but have paid little attention to social movements. This volume shows that these ideas can provide major insights on the politics of social movements. Similar gains might also come from drawing on ecological studies of organizations, especially ideas about the sources of organizational creation and survival. Discussions of movement identities and ideologies can also gain from cultural studies of the development of meaning systems. The study of the state and social movements is a relatively newly charted field. Much remains to be done.

Notes

This essay benefited greatly from Bert Klandermans's comments as well as discussions with Sid Tarrow and Kurt Schock.

1. This departs from McAdam (1982, pp. 20–59), who associates resource mobilization arguments with elite theory and political process with neo-Marxian theory. In terms of state theories, this is misleading. Both resource mobilization and political process arguments share the classic pluralist ideas about the relationship between state and society and, in this sense, constitute a revised neopluralist argument. The question is one of paradigmatic assumptions about the nature of the state and its relationship to social relations.

2. This discussion of state capacities draws on Mann (1988), Rueschemeyer and Evans (1985), and Birnbaum (1988) as well as Wallerstein's (1980) discussion of "strong" states. As a complex multidimensional concept, it needs further conceptual clarification as well as better measurement.

3. See also the discussion of movement organization, goals, and tactics in Kriesi, chapter 7 of this volume, and Kriesi et al. (1992).

4. For a similar synthesis of political process and world system theories of political conflict, see Jenkins and Schock (1992).

Part II

The Origins of Social Protest:
Ideology, Regimes, and Oppositions

Chapter 3

Between Movement and Party: The Transformation of Mid-Nineteenth-Century French Republicanism

Ronald Aminzade

Social Movements: Formal Organization, Institutionalization, and Ideology

Scholars disagree about the role of informal and formal organization in the constitution of a social movement. Theories rooted in the collective behavior tradition typically emphasize informality, spontaneity, and emergent norms. In this tradition, social movements, like panics, crazes, and riots, involve relatively unstructured and informally organized behavior. "As a collectivity," write Ralph Turner and Lewis Killian, "a movement is a group with indefinite and shifting membership and with leadership whose position is determined more by the informal response of adherents than by formal procedures for legitimizing authority" (1987, p. 223). Collective behavior theorists typically acknowledge the importance of formal organization only in the later stages of movement development. In contrast, resource mobilization theorists usually distinguish social movements from more spontaneous forms of collective action and emphasize formal organization and planning (Jenkins 1983a, pp. 528–29). While acknowledging a diversity of organizational forms and varying degrees of formal organization across movements, they usually emphasize the importance of formally structured organizations during all phases of movement development. Formal leadership and membership and formalized rules characterize some movements even during their emergent phase (McCarthy and Zald 1973, 1977).

Strategic as well as organizational characteristics have attracted the attention of social movement theorists. A key feature of most definitions of social movements concerns the willingness of movements to adopt unconventional or disruptive actions to bring about (or oppose) change. In contrast to political parties and pressure groups, movements embrace disruptive and unconventional politics. Mark Traugott (1978, p. 45) contends that in seeking to change or replace existing social structures, a movement adopts "an anti-institutional stance" evidenced by resort to "illegal behavior aimed at the reconstitution or overthrow of the structures it attacks" or by a willingness to "engage in or envision acts that when successful bring it into an inevitable confrontation with the existing order." A movement, writes Alberto Melucci, pushes conflict "beyond the limits of compatibility with the system in question, i.e., it breaks the rules of the game, puts forward non-negotiable objectives, questions the legitimacy of power" (1981, p. 176). What distinguishes movements, in these definitions, is a willingness to use unconventional, sometimes illegal or revolutionary, forms of collective action. Lacking institutionalized connections to economic and political elites, social movements embrace disruptive actions rather than work within existing institutional frameworks. Although such definitions do not necessarily imply an incompatibility between movements and institutionalized politics, they do highlight as a defining feature of a social movement the adoption of disruptive or unconventional strategies.

One of the central debates among social movement theorists concerns the relationship between a movement's organizational structure and its strategy. The key questions are: Do social movements necessarily lose their anti-institutional character as they become more formally organized? Does the adoption of strategies emphasizing institutionalized politics necessarily lead to increasingly formal organization? In short, does the internal organizational structure of a movement bear any necessary relationship to its strategy of contending for power?

Following Weber and Michels, some social movement theorists have treated formal organization and anti-institutional politics as antithetical. For example, Piven and Cloward argue that the efforts of leaders of American social movements to build enduring formal organizations "blunted or curbed the disruptive force which lower-class people were sometimes able to mobilize" (1977, p. xii). Their analysis implies that as movements become more formally organized, they will inevitably divert energies from mobilizing mass defiance and become more accommodating of the status quo. Scholars who adopt the evolutionary framework of a "life cycle" approach to social movements (Lang and Lang 1961) typically treat formalization and institutional accommodation as two dimensions of a single process. Other scholars have portrayed these processes as less closely intertwined. They have documented cases in which the development of formal organization did not lead to an abandonment of anti-institutional politics and unconventional or illegal political strategies. Thus, for example, William Gamson's (1975) study of American social movements found that formal organization is compatible with mass defiance and unconventional or unruly strategies of protest. His research suggests that the development of formal organization and institutionalization may not always be complementary processes (see also Jenkins 1977, 1985).

Once we cease to regard institutionalization and formalization as part of a unified process that can be mapped on a single continuum, we can begin to explore their relationship. This reconceptualization suggests that movements and parties may follow different historical trajectories of development as defined by these two processes. By documenting the historical development of mid-nineteenth-century French republicanism from a movement into a party, this essay seeks to clarify the relationship between formalization and institutionalization in a particular historical context. This context was marked by shifting restrictions on voting and associational rights and by conflicting understandings of political representation in the republican political culture of mid-nineteenth-century France.

My historical research addresses the following questions: Did the transformation of French republicanism from a movement into a party entail the development of more formal organizational structures and the simultaneous rejection of anti-institutional politics in favor of electoral politics? Did the organizational and strategic dimensions of French republican politics follow parallel lines of development? For example, was a growing orientation toward more-institutionalized forms of political action, such as elections, accompanied by increasing formalization? Did formalization lead to co-optation and an abandonment of disruptive, or anti-institutional, politics? If formalization and institutionalization were not always closely connected, what were the determinants of each of these processes that help to account for the divergence? More specifically, how did a shifting political opportunity structure and conflicts over the meaning of political representation shape each of these processes?

First I document two key organizational features of mid-nineteenth-century French republicanism, diversity and localism, and argue that these characteristics gave early French republicanism a transitional character, exhibiting features of both a party and a movement but more closely resembling the latter. Next I chart republicans' shifting strategic orientations, arguing that the willingness of republicans to embrace disruptive, nonelectoral forms of collective political action was closely tied to a struggle within French republicanism over alternative participatory and representative visions of democracy. In conclusion I suggest that, in the case of French republicanism, for-malization and institutionalization were not always parallel processes because each was shaped by different factors. Although the shifting political opportu-nity structure—especially changing levels of repression—played a key role in shaping both processes,[1] the localized character of French politics and the rules of the electoral system were criticial determinants of formalization. Regime crises, prior experiences with different strategies, and ideological struggles among republicans over alternative visions of democracy played a more central role in shaping republican strategies of contention for power.

Organizational Features of Mid-Nineteenth-Century French Republicanism: Diversity and Localism

The French Republican Party was not a single organization but a collection of diverse organizations dispersed over a wide area. These organizations were loosely linked by coordinating institutions like Parisian newspapers, traveling spokespersons, and elected parliamentary leaders who traveled to Paris when the legislature was in session. At the local level, the Republican Party was composed of diverse forms rooted in a rich organizational heritage that included the Jacobin clubs of the French Revolution, the secret conspiratorial societies of the Restoration, and informal centers of sociability like *cercles* and cafés (Huard 1978). Local party activists maintained close ties to informal day-to-day centers of sociability. Local republican newspapers typically linked these social networks by establishing a small degree of coordination between dispersed and ostensibly nonpolitical centers of sociability. "The role closest to that of the offices, committees, and headquarters of the twentieth-century political parties," observed Maurice Agulhon, "was played throughout the nineteenth century by the editorial offices of the newspapers" (1983, p. 16).

The importance of different organizational forms varied with changing levels of political repression. Intensified repression typically reinforced the role of secret societies and informal centers of sociability like cafés, vintners, and cabarets. Periods of political liberalization heightened the importance of electoral associations, circles, and popular clubs and increased the possibili-ties for more centralized coordination. During periods of intense repression, when republican militants were more likely to face jail or exile rather than fines or acquittals, and when the survival of local party newspapers was jeop-ardized, informal social networks and clandestine secret societies took on greater importance (Merriman 1978). Secret societies had a very different organizational structure than politicized circles, electoral committees, or clubs. Their clandestine orientation meant an emphasis on military discipline, elaborate rituals, and small cells linked in an authoritarian manner to the top leadership.

Political repression had contradictory consequences. By weakening the national Republican Party and fostering localization, repression impeded formalization, making informal centers of day-to-day sociability and face-to-face contacts a central basis for political mobilization. But repression also fostered formalization at the local level, since formal rules of membership and participation helped republican organizations guard against infiltration by police spies and informers.

Anthony Oberschall's observation that "a still viable network of communal relations can be the foundation and breeding ground for the rapid growth of modern associational networks" (1973, p. 123) is clearly illustrated by the case of French republicanism. This was especially true in regions like Provence and lower Languedoc, where cultural traditions of popular sociability provided a fertile breeding ground for the growth of formal political associations (Huard 1982; Agulhon 1982). The pattern identified by Oberschall is especially evident in France after 1849, when republicans extended their electoral efforts into the French countryside, politicizing traditional communal institutions like the village club (*chambrées*), communal ceremonies like *fêtes* and carnivals, and popular folklore. Republicans used traditions of mutual aid and institutions of popular sociability to forge new patterns of political solidarity.

Mid-nineteenth-century French republican mobilization was based on what social movement theorists have labeled "bloc recruitment." It relied on the incorporation of preexisting workplace and neighborhood groups that already possessed high degrees of group identity and extensive interpersonal ties. "Social and political debate took place in the established locations and institutions of working-class sociability," writes Maurice Agulhon, "because this was convenient, because it was discreet (at least anywhere but in the tavern) and also to exploit a trait . . . : these simple men who looked upon each other as brothers were prone to group reactions and once an idea took hold it was not long before it was accepted by all" (1984, p. 57).

Although it was oriented toward electing candidates, the organization of mid-nineteenth-century republicanism exhibited features of both a movement and a party. Despite an organizational structure that more closely resembles a social movement than a contemporary political party, early French republicans maintained institutionalized linkages to political and economic elites and competed for electoral office, working within institutionalized channels of political participation.

The informal character of French republican organization was in large part a result of its predominantly local orientation prior to 1871. This localism was reinforced by the reality that republican electoral strength was greatest at the level of local urban politics, where republicans won their earliest electoral victories and initially exercised important political functions. Prior to 1848, republicans won elections designating officers of urban National Guard units, which led to their dissolution in Lyon, Grenoble, Marseilles, and Strasbourg in 1834–35. They also won majorities on city councils in a number of large French cities, including Toulouse, Grenoble, and Strasbourg. It was at the local level, where politics involved face-to-face interactions and personal connections, that ordinary people first ventured into politics and gradually accrued political experience. Local parties and governments, which were smaller in scale and less remote than central state institutions, were generally more accessible to working-class interests and more responsive to working-class struggles. They were also less responsive to pressures emanating from national dominant class actors, the exigencies of international relations, and the interests of central state managers.

Republican strength at the local level stemmed in large part from the fact that local politics had been more democratic than national politics since the Revolution of 1830. The electoral law of 1831 enfranchised 20 to 25 percent of all French males over the age of twenty-one for municipal elections, creating fifteen times as many voters in local as in national elections (Vigier 1973, p. 277). Many professionals, shopkeepers, and well-off artisans who did not qualify to vote in national elections because they did not pay over two hundred francs in taxes participated in the election of National Guard leaders and city councilors. Those social groups—artisans, shopkeepers, and professionals—which played a central role in the struggle for suffrage reform in 1846–47 and, more generally, in mid-nineteenth-century republican politics, were initiated into electoral politics at the local level.

Despite efforts at national coordination, which peaked during national electoral campaigns (in 1837, 1839, 1842, and 1846) and then diminished, French republicans did not create a political party in the modern sense of the term prior to 1848. During the July Monarchy (1830–48) there were nationally recognized republican leaders and national republican newspapers, and republicans actively contested elected offices in all regions of France. But there was no national organization that selected candidates and enforced adherence to a consistent political platform. The national party was a loose collection of prominent local leaders of similar political persuasion. National party organization centered around the half-dozen or so prominent republicans in the Chamber of Deputies and around those who gathered at the offices of the two national republican newspapers in Paris, *Le National* and *La Réforme*. The repressive legislation of the July Monarchy, which outlawed even the use of the term *republican*, inhibited the development of a centralized national party organization. A poorly developed national system of transportation and communication also contributed to the party's decentralized and loosely coordinated character.

After the establishment of a republic in 1848, French republicans renewed efforts to create a national party organization capable of coordinating electoral activities across localities. The advent of universal male suffrage and relaxation of restrictions on association, assembly, and the press encouraged republicans to organize on a regional level for purposes of candidate selection, electoral propaganda, and voter mobilization. The shift in electoral rules in 1848, from the *scrutin uninominal d'arrondissement*, in which voters chose a candidate within relatively narrow geographic boundaries, to the *scrutin de liste du département*, in which voters selected an entire list of candidates within a fairly large geographic area, also fostered the growth of political parties. Republicans gradually extended their activities beyond the urban areas to which they had been largely confined prior to 1848, in an effort to win the mass of rural voters away from their traditional allegiances to local notables.

The first nationwide direct election of a president under a regime of universal male suffrage, in December 1848, prompted the formation of a national electoral organization to support the presidential candidacy of Ledru-Rollin, Republican Solidarity. This organization, which had a central committee in Paris, established branches in sixty-two of France's eighty-six departments. It rapidly acquired an estimated total of more than 30,000 members in 353 branches. Concerned not only with winning elections but also with providing administrative leadership for a new government, Republican Solidarity established a shadow cabinet in Paris, with various "ministries," including a Ministry of Workers' and Farmers' Associations (Berenson 1984). Republican Solidarity had a hierarchical and centralized organizational structure, with the General Council initially appointing all local officers, who were subsequently elected by local members and then approved by the council (Latta 1980).

Under the direction of Republican Solidarity, urban-based party organizations began sponsoring electoral committees in rural constituencies where there had not been a republican presence. Republican electoral committees coordinated the campaigns of parliamentary representatives on a regional scale. The organization also provided a closer link between Parisian parliamentary and provincial republican leaders. Despite the party's centralized Jacobin character, the direction of its activities and selection of its candidates still remained localized and centered around provincial newspaper offices. In contrast to "modern" political parties, the national committee did not distribute any campaign funds to local branches or issue papers to card-carrying members. Nor did it enforce party discipline upon the party's legislative personnel.

The effort to create a centralized national republican party quickly succumbed to political repression. In early 1849, the government shut down Republican Solidarity's national headquarters, officially outlawed the organization, and arrested its most prominent leaders. Continuing repression inhibited the development of a centralized party structure. The harsh repression that followed Louis-Napoleon Bonaparte's coup d'état of December 1851 temporarily destroyed what remained of national Republican Party leadership and organization. The persistence of universal male suffrage after the coup stimulated continuing local electoral activities organized by party activists, but these became even more independent of national leadership. The new regime reinstituted the *scrutin uninominal d'arrondissement*, which reduced the size of electoral districts and thus fostered more localized electoral activities. During the 1850s, republicans retreated into the informal social networks of neighborhoods, workplaces, and cafés that had always served as a base for earlier clandestine activities. These informal centers of organization existed alongside weakened formal organizations, which were revived after the inauguration of liberal reforms during the 1860s. It was not until the revival of republican electoral politics during the late 1860s that a national party leadership once again began to coordinate local and regional electoral activities.

The persistence of localism was less the result of ideological commitments than the product of a political opportunity structure marked by geographically small units of electoral representation and periods of intense political repression and by a national economy characterized by a weakly developed system of transportation and communication. Although localism fostered informal organization, a variety of factors stimulated formalization, including the need for coordination when electoral politics moved beyond the local level, the desire to limit the power of local notables in the nomination of electoral candidates, and the threat posed by police spies during periods of intense political repression. In response to these forces, republican organization became more formalized during the middle decades of the century, but this did not mean either a paid staff or formal membership dues. It did mean the development of routinized procedures for selecting candidates, holding them accountable to the party's goals, and organizing elections beyond the local level. Republican socialists typically demanded a more formal process of candidate selection rather than the informal oligarchic control of local bourgeois republican leaders. Republicans shared an appreciation of the need for formal organization in order to mobilize electoral support at a regional and national level. They also understood the need for formal organization during periods of intense repression, when the careful monitoring of the membership and leadership protected against the danger of infiltration by police spies. But this appreciation of the virtues of formalization went hand in hand with a willingness to take to the streets and engage in anti-institutional politics to demand or defend the republic.

Republican Strategies and Meanings of Representation

An understanding of the changing stance of republicans toward strategies of capturing state power requires an analysis of the different understandings of political representation among republicans. French republicans shared a common commitment to a constitutional form of government. This commonality gained importance in the face of staunch opposition to republican government on the part of the powerful members of the property-holding class, most of whom preferred some form of monarchy.[2] Republicans also shared certain common values, including a belief in progress and political rationalism, a hostility to aristocracy and monarchy, and a refusal to accept tradition as a legitimate basis of political authority. Most republicans agreed on a political program that included universal male suffrage, civil liberties, parliamentary government, tax reform, free secular education, and universal obligatory military service, but they differed over what strategy was most appropriate to attain these political goals. These strategic differences were closely tied to alternative understandings of the meaning of political representation.

Republicanism meant the creation of parliamentary institutions staffed by regularly elected representatives. All republicans accepted the legitimacy of such institutions. Most mid-nineteenth-century French socialists regarded them as a necessary prerequisite for socialism. The short-lived republican experiment of 1848–51, however, encouraged some socialists who had supported the republican cause to question representative institutions. Reflecting on his experience as an elected representative in June 1848, Proudhon wrote: "Since I set foot on the parliamentary Sinai, I ceased to be in contact with the masses: absorbed in my legislative work, I completely lost touch with what was happening. One must live in this isolation booth called the National Assembly to understand how those men who are the most completely ignorant of the conditions of a country are almost always those who represent it" (cited in Lequin 1984, p. 68). Despite such reservations on the part of a minority of socialist leaders, parliamentary institutions continued to elicit strong support among the vast majority of socialist workers after 1848. Even those sympathetic to Proudhon's syndicalist vision often showed up at the ballot box on election day during the Second Republic and late Second Empire. But the commitment of republican socialists to parliamentary institutions was based on a participatory understanding of representation and democracy dating back to the Old Regime.

The mid-nineteenth-century republican socialist vision of democracy was based on the notion of the imperative mandate. According to this principle, elected officials were delegates who were obliged to obey the expressed wishes and grievances of their constituents. This idea did not originate with Rousseau, but dated back to the elections of the Estates General of the Old Regime. Delegates to the Estates General were mandated not to deliberate on issues but to accurately present the wishes of their constituents, as expressed in the documents (*cahiers*) drawn up by each order in local and regional deliberative assemblies. Any attempt by delegates to usurp the power of their constituents by exercising initiative and going beyond the explicit mandate eleborated in the *cahiers* was punished by removal from office and, at times, by judicial and financial penalties.[3] Delegates to the Estates General were not chosen in a contested process of election in which candidates offered alternative views of the grievances that should be presented to the king in the Estates *cahier*. They were selected before issues and grievances were even compiled in the *cahiers*, so that the selection of delegates on the basis of their positions on given issues was not possible. The function of the delegates was not to represent the views of competing factions within the Estate or *bailliage* or to deliberate on issues. It was to present their constituents' deliberations to the king, closely following the instructions contained in the *cahier* (see Soule 1962, p. 19; Halevi 1985, p. 98).

During the French Revolution and throughout the early and middle decades of the nineteenth century, the notion that elected officials were mandatories was dominant within republican circles. The sansculottes of the French Revolution adopted this imperative mandate view of representation. The principle was elaborated in the Constitution of 1793 in the statement that the government was the property of the sovereign people and its officials their clerks. This understanding of representation was reflected in republican hostility toward executive power and in the opposition of most republicans to the direct election of a president. It was also expressed in the language of mid-nineteenth-century republican politics, which termed the written platforms of candidates for elected office *mandats*. Republicans did not deny the need for representative institutions in a country as large as France, but they regarded the principle of the imperative mandate as a way in which to ensure popular control of elected officials. The imperative mandate vision of democracy was summarized in radical republican leader Ledru-Rollin's famous statement of 1841: "I am their leader, I must follow them." The republican commitment to the imperative mandate was also evident in 1848, in the numerous popular clubs that arose in the aftermath of the February revolution. Most clubs saw their function as providing a public forum for the discussion of political issues and as vehicles for exerting direct popular pressure upon government officials (on the Parisian club movement, see Amman 1975).

The view of elected officials as delegates with binding obligations to the voters who elected them legitimated anti-institutional strategies of contending for state power. The participatory vision implied the right of citizens to take nonelectoral collective political actions if their elected representatives were not abiding by their mandates. This vision endorsed electoral politics but never renounced the need for revolutionary action under certain circumstances. Socialist republicans did not always respect the boundary between institutionalized and anti-institutional collective action. During times of ferment, when workers were drawn into republican politics, such as the periods following the revolutions of 1830, 1848, and 1870, workers took to the streets and made use of traditional nonelectoral forms of popular protest, including processions, demonstrations, petitions, banquets, political charivaris, and serenades, to chastise or put pressure on government officials. In their view, disruptive nonelectoral tactics complemented rather than undermined electoral politics.

The alternative liberal republican view of representation considered elected officials to be trustees for the nation, not simply delegates of their constituents. This view was elaborated during the French Revolution by the Abbé Sièyes. It was a response to the incompatibility of the notion of the binding mandate with the claims of deputies of the Third Estate to constitute themselves in a National Assembly representing a unitary national will (Baker 1987, p. 480). Liberals regarded elected delegates as representatives of the French nation, not of the constituents in their locality or region. Consequently, liberal republicans advocated granting considerable discretion to representatives in their parliamentary activities. They viewed representation as the process by which an educated and enlightened propertied elite is entrusted with political power.

The Constitution of 1789 proclaimed the liberal notion of representation. It prohibited the imperative mandate, stating that the National Assembly embodied the will of the nation and that "the representatives elected in the departments will not be representatives of a particular department but of the whole nation, and they may not be given any mandate" (Birch 1971, p. 46). The parliamentary monarchy of the liberal Orleanist regime (1830–48) adopted this same principle of representation, proclaiming the independence of elected officials toward the electorate as necessary for "national sovereignty" (Bastid 1954, p. 219). While many republicans criticized the widespread corruption and lack of accountability fostered by this system of representation, liberals argued that the imperative mandate was inapplicable to an electorate of vast numbers and that it would foster popular disorder by encouraging interventions from extraparliamentary bodies. Liberal republicans also contended that direct democracy would lead representatives to put local interests above the national interest. By inhibiting compromise and bargaining among legislators, it would also produce endless parliamentary stalemates, thereby strengthening the power of the executive branch. Liberal republican criticisms of participatory visions of democracy were strengthened by the institutional changes inaugurated by the plebiscitary democracy of Louis-Napoleon Bonaparte during the 1850s and 1860s. Louis-Napoleon successfully used plebiscites and referenda to manage expressions of popular support. The regime also instituted an electoral system based on small geographic units (*le scrutin d'arrondissement*), rather than the larger units (*départements*) favored by liberals who regarded elected officials as representatives of the nation. The corruption and patronage politics encouraged by this system made many republicans less sympathetic toward direct democracy.

Liberal and participatory visions of democracy were both grounded in fraternalist principles and organizations that denied citizenship rights to women.[4] Although equally committed to a fraternalist form of political association that fostered gender inequality, these alternative shared understandings had very different implications for strategies of contention for power. Whereas the imperative mandate notion of representation legitimated disruptive collective action when elected officials were unresponsive to their constituents, the liberal view of the role of elected officials, as representatives with some degree of independence from their constituents, questioned the legitimacy of anti-institutional politics. Liberal republicans insisted on keeping politics firmly implanted within the parliamentary arena. They advocated strategies that emphasized the rule of law and renounced violent, as well as nonelectoral, collective political action.

Shifting Republican Strategies and Political Opportunity Structures

French republicans remained divided throughout the nineteenth century over whether, and when, a revolutionary strategy was legitimate. Republicanism was born amid revolutionary ferment; both the First and Second Republics were installed by violent revolution. The republican Constitution of 1793 guaranteed the right to insurrection "when the government violates the rights of the people" (Soboul 1975, pp. 315–17). During the early 1830s, republican socialists of the Society of the Rights of Man split over the issue of revolutionary violence. A dissident faction condemned the leadership's unwillingness to embrace revolutionary violence. After the repression of 1834–35, many republicans looked to insurrection as the only viable road to a republic and joined secret insurrectionary societies. The abortive Parisian insurrection of 1839, however, marked another turning point, after which republicans increasingly turned toward the ballot box. The amnesties of 1837 and 1840 restored the ranks of republican leadership. The former released imprisoned leaders and the latter allowed republicans to return from exile in England, Belgium, and Switzerland. Imprisonment and exile convinced many republican leaders that insurrectionary violence, which had prompted repression rather than social change, was no longer the way to topple a regime that had remained in power for over a decade.

During the early 1840s, both the liberal wing of the party, represented by the newspaper *Le National*, and the radical and socialist wing, represented by *La Réforme*, rejected insurrectionism. This abandonment of a revolutionary strategy did not mean that republicans were simply content to compete for electoral office in the highly restricted political arena of the July Monarchy (1830–48). Republicans complemented their electoral activities with more-disruptive tactics designed to challenge the legitimacy of existing suffrage restrictions. They mobilized those ineligible to vote via various petition campaigns for suffrage reform, in 1840 and in 1846, and in the banquet campaign for suffrage reform of 1846–48, which culminated in the revolution of February 1848.

The republicans' willingness to abandon revolutionary action in favor of an electoral strategy was rooted in their belief in the power of electoral politics to fundamentally transform the character of their society. During the 1840s, many republicans came to regard universal male suffrage as a panacea that would solve the nation's pressing economic and political problems. This belief in the power of electoral politics was widely shared, even by those on the opposite side of the political spectrum. "Democracy," proclaimed the Legitimist newspaper *Gazette de France* in 1848, "always has communism as its outcome" (cited in Tudesq 1964, p. 1076). This assumption of an incompatibility between democratic politics and capitalism was echoed in Karl Marx's assessment of the constitution of the Second Republic as undermining politically the very social class that it empowered economically. The fear of property owners that free elections would threaten their property and privileges has been carefully documented by Thomas Forstenzer, who observed:

> Having witnessed that, after decades of oligarchy, a single day of street fighting was sufficient to establish political equality among all Frenchmen, a notable might have viewed a similar birth of social equality as a frightening possibility. A perception of the left as strong enough to launch a revolution, win a victory at the polls, or even continue to gain adherents among the lower classes constituted a sufficient threat to traditional values to provoke a desperate social fear among the elites. (1981, p. 22)

Conservatives quickly learned that universal male suffrage could serve as a bulwark against revolution rather than a prelude to socialism. Their fears of democracy were allayed by the election of a conservative majority to the National Assembly in April 1848, the subsequent repression of the June 1848 insurrection, and the election of a nonrepublican president, Louis-Napoleon Bonaparte, in December 1848. These defeats did not deter republican electoral activities. After December 1848, republicans grew steadily in electoral strength and expanded their electoral base from the cities into the countryside. In the May 1849 Legislative Assembly election, republicans captured 180 seats and about one-third of the total vote, making a strong showing in rural areas that had never before voted republican. Many of those who played a key role in organizing the electoral victories of May 1849, including thirty elected deputies, took to the barricades in June 1849, when Louis-Napoleon violated the constitution by invading Rome.

The repression of the 1849 insurrection was followed by new laws restricting club activities (June 19) and the press (July 27). This intensified repression did not lead republicans to abandon an electoral strategy. Republican electoral successes soon prompted a conservative attack on the most fundamental principle of the republic, universal male suffrage. Republican victories

in the by-elections of March 1850, held to replace the republican deputies im-
plicated in the insurrection of June 1849, intensified conservative fears. On
May 31, 1850, the conservative majority of the National Assembly reponded
by passing a new electoral law limiting suffrage rights. The law, which disenfranchised 2.7 million voters, or 28 percent of the country's electorate, revived debate among republicans over the viability of an electoral strategy.
Many socialist workers abandoned electoral politics in favor of secret revolutionary societies and militias. Eighty-four republican deputies defended a
nonviolent parliamentary strategy in response to the law. But twenty-four
deputies created the New Mountain, which was unwilling to renounce revolutionary violence in the absence of universal male suffrage. The New Mountain organized the revolutionary secret societies that proliferated in the
provinces in 1850 and 1851 (Weill 1928, p. 251; Huard 1978, p. 109). Though
committed to the establishment of a parliamentary form of government,
these organizations were also dedicated to the use of revolutionary violence
to defend the republic. Many disenfranchised socialist workers threatened to
show up at the voting booth with a rifle in one hand and a ballot in the other
for the election of 1852. Republican Party leaders repeatedly urged their
working-class and peasant followers to wait patiently for the election of 1852,
in the hope that an electoral triumph would topple the government.

The ambivalence of many republicans toward revolutionary action was
rooted in a key tenet of republicanism, enshrined in constitutions, the principle of majority rule (see Offe 1985a on majority rule as a legitimating principle). This principle had not yet secured widespread legitimacy among mid-
nineteenth-century republicans because the fundamental issue of the
institutional and legal framework within which majority rule should operate
remained contentious. Republicans disagreed over whether actions of
elected officials that violated the elector's mandate by disobeying the principles of the republic, such as the French invasion of Italy in 1849 or the electoral law of 1850, justified resort to violent extraparliamentary action. When
monarchists gained power in the National Assembly during the Second Republic, socialist republicans viewed it as a threat to the very existence of the
republic. They were hesitant to accept electoral defeat because there was no
guarantee that their opponents would accept the institutional foundations of
the republic, which had been inaugurated on the barricades.

The establishment of universal male suffrage in February 1848 did not
mark a sudden triumph of electoral politics as the only legitimate means of
expressing political opinions. Although liberal republicans contended that
the advent of suffrage meant the end of an era of revolution, republican work-

ers were less willing to renounce the barricades for the ballot box. Republican socialists initially demonstrated their willingness to use revolutionary violence in a context of universal male suffrage during the Rouen insurrection of April 1848. When Rouen's socialist workers took to the barricades, after the electoral defeat of the radical republican candidate Frederick Deschamps, they justified their insurrection in terms of the defense of the republic. Given the polarized political atmosphere and the candidacy of former Orleanists and supporters of another Bourbon restoration, Rouen's republican socialists saw the election as a question of the triumph or defeat of a republic that had recently been established via revolutionary action. The insurrection began with a confrontation, on April 27, 1848, between armed National Guardsmen and republican workers who had gathered in front of city hall to hear the announcement of election results (Zevaes 1927; National Archives of France: BB30 365, report of Procureur General Senard, May 5, 1848). Rouen's socialist workers interpreted Deschamps's electoral defeat as a repudiation of the republic, which was in principle constitutionally guaranteed rather than subject to majority rule. Parisian workers who took to the barricades in June 1848 after the conservative Assembly dissolved the National Workshops also thought that they were defending the republic (Gossez 1956, pp. 439–58). When republicans again mounted the barricades in June 1849, they did so in defense of the Constitution. This was also the case in December 1851, when republicans took up arms to resist Louis-Napoleon's coup d'état and defend the Constitution. In the context of mid-nineteenth-century French politics, revolutionary means were compatible with legalistic ends. Insurrectionary violence and democratic constitutionalism are not necessarily antithetical.

Louis-Napoleon's coup of December 1851 was followed by an intense repression that, though preserving universal male suffrage, temporarily destroyed the Republican Party and put an end to the party system of the Second Republic. Although the imperial government revived what many republicans regarded as the cornerstone of democracy, universal male suffrage, it destroyed the competitive party system that gave meaningful content to electoral activities by arresting or exiling opposition party leaders and severely restricting rights of association, assembly, and the press. Louis-Napoleon represented an ambiguous symbol vis-à-vis democracy. As the descendant of Napoleon, he laid claim to the imperial tradition, which had spread republican ideas and institutions to much of Europe. As an heir of revolutionary republicanism, with its claims resting on popular consent, Louis-Napoleon embraced universal male suffrage. Yet he rejected political parties as divisive factions, severely restricted associational rights, and relied on administrative pressures and state patronage, not a party organization, to win carefully managed elections, including nationwide plebiscites in 1852 and 1870.

During the Second Empire (1851–70), the potential impact of universal male suffrage was limited by measures that weakened the parliament and made mayors appointed rather than elected officials. During the 1850s, republican activities were driven underground by a police state apparatus that enforced severe restrictions on association, assembly, and the press (Payne 1966). Secret conspiratorial societies took on a more important role in republican politics. Massive abstentions marked the elections of the 1850s, as urban workers abandoned the ballot box as a solution to their problems. When the political opportunity structure shifted during the 1860s, republicans embraced electoral politics and scored stunning triumphs in municipal elections in a number of France's larger cities. The liberal reforms of the 1860s, loosening restrictions on association, assembly, and the press, made it possible for republicans once again to organize effective electoral campaigns. Workers turned out at the polls in growing numbers to support republican candidates during the elections of the 1860s. Their willingness to use the ballot box did not, however, signal an abandonment of disruptive forms of political protest.

Republican workers' view of institutional politics and unruly political action as complementary rather than antithetical is evident in the electoral activities of the late Second Empire. When the republican candidate at Toulouse, Armand Duportal, was narrowly defeated in the legislative elections of 1869 by rural votes from the surrounding countryside, after winning a sizable majority in the city of Toulouse, socialist workers who had turned out at the polls in large numbers took to the streets in protest. The announcement of election results touched off three days of rioting marked by several confrontations between demonstrators and police and dozens of arrests (National Archives of France: BB18 1766). During the May 1869 election in St.-Etienne, workers gathered in the streets as well as the voting booths to support the republican candidate Frederick Dorian. Although women were not invited and did not attend Dorian's electoral rallies, they stood outside on the street with their children and cheered the republican candidate when he entered and left the building. The police commissioner described the scene outside one electoral rally as "a sort of charivari, with women banging spoons against soup-tureens they had brought to eat their soup on the street." Electoral campaigns had not yet become staid affairs; they provided those excluded from suffrage with opportunities to publicly express their political sentiments in raucous traditional forms of collective action. According to police reports, Republican Party activists were stationed at the exits after Dorian's electoral rallies to remind workers leaving the meetings that they were "men of order" (Municipal Archives of St.-Etienne: 7 K1, Central police commissioner's reports of May 5, 16–18, 1869). During the campaign, republican workers shouted down the royalist candidate Rochetaillé when he appeared in the neighborhood of Montaud and disrupted an electoral gathering of his supporters. This prompted Rochetaillé to cancel a subsequent electoral meeting so as to avoid a violent confrontation. Dorian had campaigned as a "free thinker," attacking the church and clergy and calling for free compulsory secular education. After Dorian won the election, capturing 62 percent of the votes cast, his working-class supporters celebrated their triumph, on the evening of May 24, by attacking the Jesuit college Saint-Michel, breaking several windows and setting fire to the concierge's chamber. For these republican workers, demonstrations and violent street protests were a natural extension of the struggle at the ballot box.

After the French defeat in the Franco-Prussian War in September 1870, revolutionary politics took on increased importance. War defeat and the reestablishment of the republic in a situation of political and economic crisis prompted a renewal of participatory politics and a revival of revolutionary strategies. In a context of war and regime crisis, urban workers in numerous cities seized weapons and forced their way into local National Guard militias that had previously excluded them. Socialist workers formed revolutionary clubs and organized popular demonstrations designed to pressure local authorities into accepting revolutionary measures, including a mass mobilization of the entire population (*levée en masse*) to expel Prussian troops from French soil.[5] The election of a royalist-dominated National Assembly at the beginning of 1870 encouraged republicans to embrace revolutionary action in defense of the republic. In 1871, as in 1848, revolutionary republicans refused to accept any verdict of majority rule that threatened the existence of the republic. Republicans proclaimed insurrectionary communes in March 1871 in France's largest cities, including Paris, Lyon, Marseilles, Nîmes, Toulouse, St.-Etienne, and Narbonne (Gaillard 1971). The communards justified their resort to insurrection as a defense of the new republic, which was threatened by the monarchist-dominated National Assembly at Versailles. Their call to revolution did not, however, imply a rejection of electoral politics. One of the first actions of the Parisian revolutionary communards was to hold municipal elections.

The repression of the revolutionary communes of 1870–71, when more than 25,000 insurgents died (Edwards 1973), marked a decisive turning point in the history of French republicanism. It set the stage for the defeat of socialist elements within the Republican Party, the institutionalization of a conservative republican form of the state, and the triumph of liberal notions of representation and democracy among republicans.[6] The direct democracy of the imperative mandate, embraced by the revolutionary communards, was displaced by the liberal representative vision of democracy, which was enshrined in the republican constitution of 1875 and became dominant within republican circles by the 1880s (Huard 1985, p. 138; Nicolet 1982, pp. 413–15). Following the defeat of the communes, compromises to secure the republic and prevent the reestablishment of either a monarchy or an authoritarian military regime led republicans to reject key elements of the French revolutionary tradition. Many of the political principles that had dominated mid-nineteenth-century republicanism were violated by the republican constitutional provisions of 1875 (Nicolet 1982, pp. 166, 424). Republicans reluctantly accepted institutional arrangements—a strong executive and a bicameral legislature with an upper house—that had been staunchly opposed by the republicans of 1848. The abandonment by French republicans of "anti-institutional" politics set the stage for subsequent socialist and anarchosyndicalist challenges to the limits of liberal democracy and for the formation of a working-class political party during the later decades of the century. Institutionalized politics became firmly accepted among republicans only after republicanism was transformed and severed, ideologically and institutionally, from its previously close connections with participatory visions of democracy and with socialism.

During the middle decades of the nineteenth century, shifting political circumstances, especially the rhythm of repression, shaped the changing attractiveness of alternative strategies, which were the subject of heated conflict among French republicans. But changes in the institutional structure of the state, or in the balance of power among polity members, or in the openness of the polity as evidenced by shifting levels of repression, cannot alone account for the willingness of republicans to risk their lives on the barricades or endure hardships in the hope that their elected representatives would eventually redress their grievances. Ideologies of representation were also critical determinants of strategic choices, for they enabled, or inhibited people from, recognizing and seizing opportunities to act collectively. For example, the toppling of the imperial regime and establishment of a republic in 1870 was not simply the inevitable consequence of an altered political opportunity structure produced by a conjuncture of economic and political crises. It was also the result of a participatory ideology of representation that encouraged people to pursue their hopes, fears, and aspirations in culturally specific ways, by taking to the streets to force reluctant republican elected officials to proclaim the republic.

Conclusion: Organization, Strategy, and Ideology

The historical study of social movements highlights the difficulty of clearly distinguishing between unconventional and institutionalized political behavior, and between social movements and political parties, in historical contexts not marked by the dominance of associationally based politics and a liberal-democratic political culture.[7] In historical contexts in which voting rights are restricted, understandings of representation contested, associational rights fragile, state capacities to grant concessions and institutionalize conflict limited, and local politics communally rather than associationally based, the dichotomies of contemporary political theory are problematic. In mid-nineteenth-century France, distinguishing between movements and parties in terms of electoral and nonelectoral strategies is difficult, since early political parties sometimes ventured outside the electoral arena and combined disruptive collective political action with efforts to elect candidates. In this historical context, the close connection between political protest and electoral politics meant an elusive and fluid, rather than fixed, boundary between social movements and political parties. The mid-nineteenth-century French Republican Party, though contesting electoral office, simultaneously adopted disruptive, unconventional, and sometimes illegal tactics, combining seemingly antithetical forms of collective political action. Only after the establishment of a liberal-democratic political culture and institutional setting during the late nineteenth century did the dichotomies of contemporary political theory—for example, protest versus voting—become widely shared assumptions for French republicans. A historical perspective on social movements makes the boundary separating institutionalized and anti-institutional politics appear not as natural or inevitable but as the historical product of the triumph of a particular organizational form—political parties—and of a particular vision of political representation.

A historical perspective also enables us to identify more clearly just what is new about so-called new social movements and thus to avoid the danger of overstating the novelty of contemporary movements (see Tarrow 1989b; Calhoun 1993). Social movement theorists sometimes view contemporary challenges to the legitimacy of political parties by advocates of participatory democracy as a recent product of new social movements that question the premises of liberal conceptions of representation and democracy. This study of mid-nineteenth-century French republicanism reminds us that such questioning by committed democrats accompanied the creation of liberal-democratic institutions. One branch of the mid-nineteenth-century French republican movement elaborated an alternative participatory vision of democracy that challenged the assumptions of liberal-democratic institutions of representation, including their restrictive definition of politics and their rigid separation of institutionalized and anti-institutional politics.

This study also calls into question the notion that laws of development rooted in organizational dynamics inevitably produce the progressive formalization of movement organizations. The history of French republicanism during the middle decades of the nineteenth century suggests that formalization followed a very uneven path. Prior to 1848 republican organization remained highly informal in character as a result of the localized character of French politics. An orientation toward institutionalized forms of political action, such as elections, did not require high levels of formalization, since republicans could effectively pursue electoral goals using informal centers of popular sociability as vehicles of political mobilization. After 1848 the extension of universal male suffrage and civil liberties as well as a new geography of representation fostered the development of more formal organization. But it was the first direct nationwide election of a president that prompted the initial creation of a highly centralized, formal Republican Party organization. The subsequent repression of 1849–51 destroyed this organization and drove republican activities underground, reinforcing the local, decentralized, and nonhierarchical character of early French republicanism. Despite universal male suffrage, nationwide elections, and the rapid development of transportation and communication infrastructure during the Second Empire (1851–70), republicanism remained rooted in informal local networks of sociability. Throughout the 1850s intense repression drove republican politics underground and temporarily eliminated the remnants of formal national party organization. The relaxation of restrictions on assembly, association, and the press during the 1860s stimulated the development of more formal organization among republicans, especially during the national elections of 1869. In short, throughout the mid-nineteenth century, French republicanism remained informally organized, despite oscillations back and forth between more and less formally organized political activity, largely in response to changing levels of political repression and shifting electoral rules.

An ideological commitment on the part of republican socialists to a participatory vision of democracy privileged local politics and impeded formalization, but organizational developments were a product more of institutional
than of ideological factors. Ideology was not an important factor inhibiting
formalization, since most republicans acknowledged the virtues of more formal organization—a greater ability for coordination across large areas, an enhanced ability to win nonlocal elections, a greater capacity to ensure durable
gains, and an enhanced capacity to resist government infiltration during periods of intense repression. For liberals a strong commitment to the rule of law
translated into sympathy for more formalized organizational rules, while for
socialists a desire for greater popular participation in the nomination of party
candidates encouraged support for formal rules to limit the informal power of
local notables. Localism and organizational diversity, not ideological opposition to the principle of formal rules, impeded formalization. Ideological
conflicts among republicans focused on divisions over strategic rather than
organizational choices.

Republican strategies of contention for power, which alternated between
revolutionary and electoral politics, were closely connected to ideological
conflicts over the meaning of representation and democracy. Though committed to the republic and the electoral process, republican socialists justified
their illegal actions in terms of a participatory democratic ideology that legit-
imized insurrectionary challenges to those who violated their mandates as
representatives of the people. Reform and revolution were not dichotomies
for republican socialists, who simultaneously legitimated both strategies, depending on rapidly changing political circumstances. Shifting republican
strategies of contention for power were shaped by the very same forces that
influenced the process of formalization, including varying levels of political
repression and laws governing elections, but also by the ongoing struggle
among republicans over the meaning of democracy. Republicans shifted their
strategies in accordance with changing political opportunities, especially the
level and likelihood of repression. But shifting political strategies were sensitive to ideological as well as institutional dynamics.

Formalization and institutionalization did not follow parallel trajectories
because of different dynamics propelling the two processes. The intensified
repression that marked shifting political opportunity structures fostered both
informality and anti-institutional politics. Shifts in the direction of greater formalization, however, did not automatically produce institutionalization. Republicanism retained its anti-institutional character, even during periods of
increased formalization, because most republicans did not see electoral activ-

ities and unconventional political actions as necessarily antithetical. For republican socialists, formal organization might offer the possiblity of more effective coordination and durable political gains, but it did not mean a willingness to abandon unconventional or disruptive forms of collective action, justified by a participatory vision of democracy and the notion of the imperative mandate. The adoption of electoral strategies during the 1840s was not the outcome of bureaucratization within the republican movement but a result of choices—of contested strategies chosen by party leaders—based on experiences with previous strategies and ideological commitments.

The adoption of strategies emphasizing electoral (i.e., institutionalized) politics did not lead to increasingly formal organization, with features such as a paid staff, formal membership dues, and formally elected leaders. Even when republicans rejected revolutionary politics in favor of an electoral strategy, they retained their informal, decentralized organizational structure. This structure was determined by a variety of factors, including the persistence of localism and the geography of representation, not just strategic considerations.

In the long run, institutionalization and formalization did go hand in hand, but this connection was not the inevitable product of a developmental logic. It was a result, during the last three decades of the nineteenth century, of the establishment of a liberal-democratic political culture and an institutional setting that embodied a distinctive understanding of the meaning of political representation. The triumph of liberal understandings of democracy among French republicans delegitimized direct forms of collective political action. In this particular historical context, institutionalization rapidly stimulated the formalization of French republicanism. In a liberal-democratic context, there is a necessary link between the pursuit of an electoral strategy and formalization, since the accountability of elected representatives requires formalization, given the absence of mechanisms of popular intervention and control. The relatively recent historical emergence of this context, and its contemporary inapplicability to large parts of the globe, suggests the need to historicize our theories of social movements. This does not mean a historicist denial of the possibility of abstracting across time and place. Rather, it implies the need to ground our theories in time and place and to be more explicit about the dependence of regularities on historical contexts.

Notes

My thanks to Craig Jenkins, Barbara Laslett, Doug McAdam, Sid Tarrow, Charles Tilly, Erik Olin Wright, and Mayer Zald for helpful comments on an earlier draft. This essay also benefited from insightful criticisms provided by participants in the University of Minnesota History and Society Program and the Indiana University Political Economy seminar.

1. Sidney Tarrow (1989b, p. 34) separates the concept of political opportunity structure into four main components: the degree of openness or closure of the polity; the stability or instability of political alignments; the presence or absence of allies or support groups; and divisions within the elite or its tolerance or intolerance of protest. My emphasis is on the first component—the relative openness or closure of the polity, as reflected in the level of political repression.

2. Thoughout the July Monarchy, French property holders consistently supported royalist rather than republican candidates. On the stance of the French bourgeoise toward republicanism and democracy, see Ponteil 1968.

3. The form and content of mandates varied across elections and localities. French historians disagree about the latitude given to deputies by their constituents. See Soule 1968, pp. 76–78, and J. Russell Major 1960, p. 8.

4. Fraternity was not simply a republican expression of community; it was a gendered sociocultural form of solidarity and community that played a central role in the constitution of republican organization. Fraternalism appealed to a particular vision of masculine camaraderie and male authority, allowing republicans to construct cross-class solidarities, based on fictive kinship, via shared definitions of manhood and rituals of male bonding. See the pioneering work of Mary Ann Clawson (1989), who identifies four elements that define fraternalism as a unique social form: corporatism, ritual, masculinity, and proprietorship.

5. The *levée en masse* referred to the precedent of the French Revolution when, in 1792–93, volunteer batallions led by new commanders, not the generals of the Old Regime, drove foreign invaders from France. The revolutionary government that organized the *levée en masse* ended in Robespierre's Committee of Public Safety and the revolutionary armies became agents of the Reign of Terror.

6. Workers continued to embrace the imperative mandate, however, as a way in which to ensure that representatives would remain responsive to workers' grievances. In elections to labor arbitration boards (*conseils de prud'hommes*), for example, union leaders enforced discipline on representatives by insisting that they sign a letter of resignation in advance, to be used in the event that they violated their mandate. In 1891 and 1893, the authorities responded to these efforts to promote class solidarity rather than conciliation by annulling the election of those who had accepted the imperative mandate (Olszak 1987).

7. The fluidity of the boundary between parties and movements is also evident in certain contemporary political contexts where liberal-democratic assumptions remain open to contestation by left-wing political parties. This fluidity is documented in Sidney Tarrow's (1990) study of "new social movements" in Italy, which documents the initial emergence of the social movements of the 1960s and 1970s as insurgencies within the party system: "Beneath the surface appearance of a rigid opposition between the wild, spontaneous, and antipartisan new movements of the 1960s and 1970s, and the staid, tired, conservative institutions of the party system there was . . . a much more complex and interpenetrating set of relations" (p. 271).

Chapter 4

Left-Right Ideology and Collective Political Action: A Comparative Analysis of Germany, Israel, and Peru

Karl-Dieter Opp, Steven E. Finkel, Edward N. Muller,
Gadi Wolfsfeld, Henry A. Dietz, and Jerrold D. Green

Identification with "left" or "right" ideologies often has been hypothesized to play a significant role in motivating individuals to participate in unconventional political activities such as protest or political violence. Yet the limited empirical evidence regarding the strength and nature of the relationship between ideological identification and protest behavior has been inconclusive. Muller (1979), for example, found a relatively strong tendency for ideological "leftists" to participate in "aggressive political behavior" in his analysis of West German national survey data from the 1970s, and this finding subsequently was replicated in later surveys gathered in New York City and among members of environmental groups in the United States (Muller and Godwin 1984). Opp, however, in his analyses of opponents of nuclear power in West Germany and in his reanalysis of the samples analyzed by Muller and Godwin, found a "U-shaped" relationship between ideological identification and political protest, with individuals on either the extreme "left" or "right" participating at higher levels than ideological moderates (Opp 1985, 1989). Finally, the sole cross-national survey analysis of individual participation in protest activities conducted to date, the Barnes-Kaase study of five Western democracies in the 1970s, reported much variation in the relationships between adherence to left or right ideologies and protest behavior in particular countries (Klingemann 1979b, p. 286). In the Netherlands, West Germany, and the United States, ideological leftists were relatively more likely to protest than were those in the center and on the right, while in Austria and Great Britain the relationship between ideology and protest was essentially nonexistent.

In this essay, we attempt to extend and clarify these previous analyses by presenting evidence regarding the relationship between ideological identification and political protest in three countries with widely different political, socioeconomic, and cultural characteristics—Germany, Israel, and Peru. We show first that the relationship between ideological identification and political protest varies significantly across the three countries: in Germany leftists are much more active in protest than individuals in the center or on the right, while in Israel and Peru both leftists and rightists are more active than individuals in the political center. Second, we propose and test two explanations for these divergent patterns, one based on individuals' affiliations with political parties in each country, and the other based on the mix of perceived costs and benefits associated with protest that are theoretically linked to individuals' ideological identifications. We find support for both explanations in our empirical analyses; some unexplained or net effect of ideological identification remains in many of our models, however, and we conclude by offering some possible explanations for these unexpected results.

Left-Right Ideology and Political Protest: Alternative Explanations

Following much previous research, we use as our measure of ideological identification the left-right self-anchoring scale: individuals are presented with a ten-point scale whose endpoints are labeled "left" and "right" and are asked to provide the number on the scale that "best describes" their political views (for some earlier applications, see Arian and Shamir 1983; Finlay, Simon, and Wilson 1974; Inglehart and Klingemann 1976; Kilpatrick and Cantril 1960; Klingemann 1972, 1979c; and Laponce 1970). But why should values on this scale be related to an individual's propensity to participate in political protest? We offer two explanations, a "political parties" explanation and an "expected utility" explanation.

Left-Right Ideology and Party Identification

First, it may be argued that self-placement on the left-right scale refers not to abstract ideological concepts, but rather to individual preferences or attachments to particular political parties. Arian and Shamir (1983, p. 140), for example, argue that in Israel (where their data were drawn), as well as in most other contemporary democracies, "there exists a left-right space, but it is a political space, mainly a party space, and not an ideological space." According to this formulation, most individuals lack the sophistication necessary to conceptualize the political world on the basis of broad ideological categories (cf. Converse 1964); consequently "left and right . . . are political . . . cues given by the political system . . . that are party based and party related" (Arian and

Shamir 1983, p. 140). Inglehart also poses this as a possible explanation for the relationship between ideological identification and political behavior:

> In many European countries (particularly those with multiparty systems) the terms "Left" and "Right" have become stereotypes for specific groups of parties. Through long usage, these labels have become partly assimilated to established party loyalties that owe their origins to religious or social class ties, or to political leanings transmitted from one's parents, rather than to one's response to current issues. . . . Insofar as Left-Right self-placement is contaminated with a party identification component, it would not necessarily be an indicator of one's attitude toward social change, or of one's potential to engage in political protest. (1979, p. 350)

We have shown previously that identification with and integration into particular political parties provide significant motivation for individual participation in these forms of behavior (Finkel and Opp 1991). When the party leadership and organization provide behavioral cues or expectations that promote protest, individuals with strong identifications or affective attachments to the party are likely to be motivated to comply. In Germany, for example, the Green Party leadership and organization long have endorsed protest as a means to attaining specific political ends (Hülsberg 1988; Papadakis 1984), and our earlier empirical analysis showed that Green identifiers in the German mass public were far more likely to participate in protest activities than individuals in other party groups (Finkel and Opp 1991). In Israel, a recent study of protest events since 1946 showed that a full 18 percent were initiated by political parties, and we therefore expect to observe in that country the same pattern of results (Lehman-Wilzig 1990).

To the extent, then, that ideological identification is little more than a surrogate for party affiliation, we would expect the relationship between the left-right scale and political protest in particular countries to depend on (1) the presence or absence of political parties that encourage protest and (2) the extent to which followers of these parties are concentrated at particular points on the self-placement scale. In other words, if parties that are considered "leftist" encourage protest behavior while "rightist" parties do not, then we should see a preponderance of protest among leftist individuals as measured by the self-anchoring scale. If there are both leftist and rightist parties that encourage protest behavior, then a U curve between ideological identification and political protest should emerge. In either case, the overall relationship between self-placement and protest will be spurious as a result of each of these variables' association with party identification.

Left-Right Ideology and Expected Utility

An alternative explanation of the relationship between ideological identification and political protest is provided by expected utility, or expectancy
value, theories of political participation (Ajzen and Fishbein 1980; Feather
1982; Klandermans 1984). Simply put, expectancy value theory posits that individuals will participate in a given form of collective political action if the expected rewards of the outcomes outweigh the negative utilities or costs. Elaboration of a complete expected utility model for political protest will take us
far afield; in this essay we are concerned exclusively with those aspects of the
expected utility framework that are theoretically most closely linked with the
notion of political ideology or ideological identification.[1] We group those aspects into three general categories: public goods motivation, personal normative beliefs, and social network rewards and costs. Each has been found in
previous research to be strongly related to protest behavior, and each has direct relevance for ideological identification as well.

Public Goods Motivation.   The meaning of the terms *left* and *right* certainly
may differ across social and cultural contexts, as these labels come to be associated with different referents in different environments (Conover and
Feldman 1981; Fuchs and Klingemann 1990). But, following Downs's widely
cited definition of ideology as "verbal images of the good society and the chief
means of constructing such a society" (1957, p. 96), we may specify certain
general types of referents that seem to be inherent in the conception of political ideology. "Verbal images of the good society" represent, in fact, generalized social and political values that individuals may wish to see realized in a
given political system (Fuchs and Klingemann 1990, p. 213). These values, in
turn, may give rise to specific views on particular political issues facing national governments, and to more general beliefs about the ability of national
officeholders and the political system to represent or further the values and
preferences of the individual. Consequently, if identification on the left-right
scale is linked to the *content* of political ideology, then individuals who identify themselves as "leftists" will hold different political values, policy preferences, and attitudes about performance of incumbents and the political system than individuals on the right or in the center of the self-anchoring scale.

In the collective action framework that we adopt in this essay, such values
and political views may be characterized as individual preferences for "public
goods," that is, goods that affect or that can be enjoyed by all members of a collectivity, and that cannot feasibly be withheld from any member.[2] Individuals

who desire more "equality" in the political system, or who desire stricter environmental protection, in fact are expressing preferences for particular public goods that could benefit many, if not all, members of the political system. Indeed, we have argued (Finkel, Muller, and Opp 1989; Muller, Dietz, and Finkel 1991) that nearly all the political "grievance" or "discontent" variables that are commonly thought to influence political protest and other forms of political behavior can be viewed as preferences for public goods. This category encompasses dissatisfaction with public policies enacted by government, dissatisfaction with the form of government itself, and even personal feelings of relative deprivation, provided they are then "politicized," or blamed on the political system. Thus, one of our major expectations, translated into collective action terminology, is that different ideological identifiers will have different preferences for public goods and levels of political discontent.

However, precisely because of their status as "public goods," these preferences should play no *direct* role in the individual's calculation of the expected utility of participating in political protest. This is so because of the well-known "free-rider" problem in the provision of public goods: in large groups individuals may have an incentive to abstain and allow others to bear the costs of action to provide the public good, which then cannot be withheld from the nonparticipants (Olson 1965; Tullock 1974). However, preferences for public goods should have a *conditional* effect in the individual's expected utility calculus: individuals with strong preferences for public goods will participate only if they also believe that collective action can be successful and that their own participation is important for the action's success (Finkel, Muller, and Opp 1989; Klandermans 1984; Muller, Dietz, and Finkel 1991). Thus, the influence of public goods preferences on protest (and other forms of collective action) depends on perceptions of group and individual efficacy in achieving the public good through protest activity, and we call the composite construct that we create from all of these variables the individual's *public goods motivation* for political protest.[3]

It is likely that ideological groups will differ significantly on this public goods motivation construct, and these differences may explain to a large degree any observed differences in their participation rates in political protest. Aside from differences in preferences for public goods themselves, differences between "leftists" and "rightists" may exist on perceptions of the most effective means of achieving them. If rightists or other ideological groups in particular countries have achieved success in the past through protest or political violence, then we may expect their perceptions of group efficacy through protest to be relatively high. Since leftists in various contexts often espouse beliefs in principles of "solidarity" (Fuchs and Klingemann 1990), then we may expect their levels of the "importance of personal participation" to be relatively high as well. In general, as the Downsian definition of ideology encompasses "the chief means of constructing" the good society, identification with particular ideological labels should correlate strongly with perceptions of the likely effectiveness of both the group and the individual in achieving desired public goods through various forms of political participation.

Personal Normative Beliefs.   Ideology encompasses not only cognitive beliefs about the effectiveness of various forms of behavior in achieving political goals, but also beliefs about particular behaviors' normative justifiability. That is, ideologies specify appropriate modes of bringing about social change (Fuchs and Klingemann 1990, pp. 213–214) and hence can provide important incentives or disincentives for the individual to participate in a given form of political action. Gurr, for example, argues that one of the main functions of political ideology is to provide "norms about the desirability of political violence" (1970, p. 194), and Coleman links these normative beliefs specifically to the individual's expected utility of engaging in particular forms of behavior:

> If one has come to hold an ideology containing a utopian vision, then working toward the realization of that vision generates internal psychic rewards, independent of the surrounding social capital. . . . If this conjecture about the role of utopian ideology is correct, the importance of such ideology can be great because the benefits it generates depend only on participation, not on success of the revolt or on effectiveness of the individual's participation in bringing about that success. (1990, pp. 494–95)

Thus the incentive value of personal normative beliefs may be distinguished conceptually from incentives related to group and individual efficacy, and these beliefs should be relevant for predicting individual participation in collective protest activities. It is important to note, however, that such norms need not represent only positive incentives for participation; they may proscribe behavior, and hence represent a disincentive or cost to the individual as well. Norms proscribing violence or breaking the law are widespread in many countries, and thus can operate as a deterrent effect on individual protest participation.

Adherence to particular ideologies may lead individuals to adopt quite different norms about the desirability of violence or other forms of behavior. Muller notes that in contemporary Germany:

> The left embraces a social change ideology that condones political aggression when it is necessary in the interests of social reform, [while] by contrast, the

right tends to be more concerned with social control and to feel that rules should be obeyed rather than challenged. (1979, p. 89)

In other countries, at other times, we may observe normative justifications for protest on both the extreme left *and* the extreme right, as the left certainly has no historical monopoly on legitimating violence in the pursuit of political ends (Grundy and Weinstein 1974).

Social Network Rewards and Costs.   In addition to public goods motivation and personal normative beliefs, one other category of incentives may also have strong links to both individual participation in collective political action and ideological identification. Theorists from the so-called resource mobilization school of collective action (McCarthy and Zald 1977; Oberschall 1973) emphasize the importance of group memberships and social networks in the mobilization process. Numerous empirical studies attest to the pattern that participants in social movements and protest activities are far more likely to be integrated into preexisting organizations and friendship or neighborhood networks than less active individuals (Jenkins 1983a; McAdam, McCarthy, and Zald 1988; Oberschall 1973; see Dietz 1980 for particular emphasis on Peru).

From the expected utility perspective, these processes occur as groups and other social networks provide important "solidarity" or "interpersonal" incentives that reduce the likelihood that individuals will free ride on the efforts of other group members who are working to achieve collective goals. Individuals who are highly integrated into groups obviously will be more likely to adhere to the behavioral expectations of the group, as tightly knit groups may be able to identify and impose sanctions on defectors from group actions or free riders. More generally, individuals may be motivated to participate in collective action as a means by which they may "gain or sustain friendships, . . . maintain . . . social standing, and . . . avoid ridicule and ostracism" from significant others in their social or friendship networks (Chong 1991, pp. 34–35). Such "social network" incentives have been identified as relevant for participation within interest groups and other organizations (Clark and Wilson 1961; Knoke 1988), and much recent survey-based research has shown their importance for participation in protest and unconventional political activities as well (Finkel and Opp 1991; Klandermans 1984; Muller and Opp 1986; Muller, Dietz, and Finkel 1991; Opp 1989).

Social network incentives, moreover, may be linked to ideological identification in several significant ways. First, individuals with strong preferences for certain public goods, or "ideological" values in the sense described earlier, should be likely to join groups and otherwise integrate themselves into social networks that attempt to provide those goods to the collectivity. In this sense, obtaining social affiliation or solidarity rewards through collective action depends directly on the prior ideological values of the participants. As Fireman and Gamson note:

> Some selective incentives depend . . . on a consciousness of the movement's worth. If social movements provide constituents with valued friends, esteem, [or] status . . . they facilitate mobilization primarily to the extent that constituents share principles that the movement defends. (1979, p. 34)

Individuals, then, should be likely to seek out groups and social networks that are consistent with their ideological aspirations, and these networks in turn provide incentives for individuals to contribute to the collective goals of the group.

Second, group and social network memberships may also result in the reinforcement of the individual's ideological values or identifications. One of the major means by which groups and other social movement organizations retain the loyalty of their members is through altering or heightening ideological appeals (Snow et al. 1988). Groups "seek to bring the beliefs and attitudes of potential recruits into sync with the ideological frame of the movement" and otherwise "negotiate a reasonable fit between the attitudes of members and the official 'party line' of the . . . organization" (McAdam, McCarthy, and Zald 1988, pp. 725–26). In this way, individuals who are integrated into social networks may be exposed to information and appeals that will heighten their preexisting orientations and ideological identifications. We therefore expect a mutually reinforcing relationship to obtain between identification with particular ideological labels and the memberships that provide individuals with social and solidarity incentives for protest.

The party identification and expected utility models discussed thus far represent two alternative explanations for the relationship between left-right ideology and political protest. To the extent that there is an observed relationship between self-placement on the anchoring scale and protest behavior, we hypothesize that it may be accounted for through their mutual relationship with either party affiliation or the variables that constitute our expected utility model: public goods motivations relating to the goals and likely success of protest behavior, adherence to personal normative beliefs that justify and promote protest, and expectations of social network or affiliation rewards that may be obtained through protest participation. It should be noted that these two explanations are not necessarily competitive; we argued in a previous essay that party identification itself may be correlated with many of these same expected utility variables (Finkel and Opp 1991). These explanations do, however, encompass variables that represent rival direct effects on protest that may account more or less adequately for variations in the rates of protest participation for various ideological groups.

Research Design and Measurement

We test these hypotheses using survey data from three highly disparate nations: (West) Germany, Israel, and Peru. In Germany a representative survey (n = 714) was conducted with respondents age eighteen and older between November 1987 and January 1988.[4] In Israel a total of 1,266 Jewish citizens age eighteen and older were interviewed in a representative national survey in January 1988.[5] The national sample in Peru was conducted in December 1987 and consisted of 1,571 respondents who were eighteen and older.[6] Nine provinces with the largest electoral populations, a total of about 60 percent of the national voting population, were selected.

These countries vary widely in many ways and thus afford an unusually well-suited set of contexts in which to draw general conclusions about political protest and its relationship with ideological identification. The countries differ geographically and in regard to culture and religion; they represent different levels of economic development as measured by gross national product per capita and related variables; they range in the early 1990s between relatively good (Germany), satisfactory (Israel), and extremely poor (Peru) levels of macroeconomic performance as measured by growth rates, inflation, and unemployment. Germany and Israel are relatively egalitarian societies, whereas Peru is an extremely inegalitarian society; and although all three countries are democracies in form, Germany is a consolidated democracy with extensive civil and political liberties, Israel is relatively more repressive because of the problem of the Occupied Territories, while civil and political liberties are least secure in Peru, an emerging democracy with a history of coups and severe repression of dissident social movements.

The countries' recent histories with respect to political protest suggest wide variation in the ideological orientations of the participants as well. Germany throughout the 1980s witnessed intense protests related to nuclear energy, the environment, and disarmament that appeared to be focused on the left of the political spectrum. Israel at the same time saw the simultaneous emergence of protest groups on the left advocating negotiations with Palestinians and right-wing groups advocating increased settlement activities in the Occupied Territories and a general hard-line stance against the Palestinian uprising. In Peru a leftist insurgency initiated by Sendero Luminoso (Shining Path) had escalated since 1980 into a high-intensity rebellion of major proportions resulting in repeated declarations of states of emergency and martial law. The three countries thus afford ideal opportunities for rigorous testing of the processes that link ideological identifications among individuals who participate in collective protest and political violence.

Measurement of Political Protest.   We measured potential for participation in legal and illegal protest according to procedures developed by Muller (1979). The scales represent a multiplicative interaction between past participation ("never," "once," "several times") and future intention regarding each activity (five categories, from "not at all" likely to "very likely"), and are all logged to the base ten. To ensure respondent anonymity, questions regarding protest behavior were asked in the form of a self-administered questionnaire, which the respondent placed in a separate envelope that was sealed and given to the interviewer.

The set of legal protest items in each country included sign a petition; take part in a permitted demonstration; wear a button or a sticker for a political cause; work with a citizen action group; collect signatures for a petition. The illegal items included take part in a demonstration that breaks the law; seize buildings; participate in confrontations with police or other governmental authorities; participate in political activities that may result in property damage; participate in protest activities at the workplace that are against the law; participate in confrontations with other political groups or individuals; seize building sites or land; take part in public disorders. Factor analyses were conducted on the resultant legal and illegal protest items, and in each country two distinct factors corresponding to the legal and illegal behaviors emerged. For more details on the measurement of the dependent variable, see Wolfsfeld et al. (forthcoming).

Measurement of Ideological Identification.   Each respondent was first asked whether she or he had ever heard the terms *left, right,* or *center* "to describe your own or others' political views." Respondents who answered in the affirmative were then presented with the ten-point scale labeled "left" and "right" at the endpoints and asked to select the number of the box that came closest to her or his position. Respondents who could not place themselves on the scale or had not heard of the terms were treated as missing cases, resulting in the loss of 14.7 percent of the sample in Germany, 13.7 percent in Israel, and 15.6 percent in Peru.

Measurement of Party Identification.   Respondents in each country were asked whether there is a political party they "feel close to." Respondents who answered no were classified as nonidentifiers. Respondents who answered yes were then asked to indicate the party. Our measures of party identification are a series of dummy variables corresponding to identification with particular parties in each country, in addition to a dummy variable representing "nonidentification" with any party. In Germany, the parties, arrayed from left to right on the political spectrum, are the Greens, SPD (Social Democratic Party), FDP (Free Democratic Party), and CDU/CSU (Christian Democratic Party/Christian Social Union). In Peru, the parties are IU (United Left), APRA (Popular Alliance for the American Revolution), AP (Popular Action), and PPC (Popular Christian Party). In Israel, the procedure was modified somewhat because of the large number of relatively small political parties, which results in low numbers of valid cases for several party groups. Following Arian's (1985) summary of the parties' programs and their general ideological orientations, we grouped the following parties in a "left parties" category: Ratz, Shinui, Progressive List, and Chadash. We grouped the following parties in a "right parties" category: Thiyah, Tzomet, and Kach. The center-left Labor Party was included as its own category, as was the center-right Likud Party.

A very small number of respondents identified with other parties, such as the Communist Party in Germany or the religiously oriented Agudat Yisrael and NPP in Israel. These respondents were treated as missing cases. The number of valid cases in each country, omitting both identifiers with these small parties and individuals who did not place themselves on the left-right ideological scale, was 601 in Germany, 997 in Israel, and 1,318 in Peru.

Measurement of Public Goods Motivation.   Following Muller, Dietz, and Finkel (1991), we constructed a public goods motivation variable through a relatively complex multiplicative procedure involving several variables. First we constructed a measure of the individual's overall level of political discontent, encompassing dissatisfaction with the performance of government in a variety of issue areas, a measure of overall alienation from the political system, and three separate measures of relative deprivation related to income, general welfare, and the deprivation of groups with which the respondent identifies.[7] This discontent measure was then weighted by the individual's perceptions of the likelihood of group success through legal and through illegal protest, and also by the individual's perceptions of personal influence and the importance of personal participation in legal and illegal protest behaviors.[8] High values on public goods motivation thus indicate strong preferences for certain public goods and beliefs that collective action can be successful in providing those goods and that individual participation is important for the success of the collective movement.

Measurement of Personal Normative Beliefs. We asked one question to measure whether respondents felt that taking part in legal protest actions was morally justifiable: the extent to which they agreed or disagreed that "politics should be left to our elected representatives." The item was transformed to a scale of zero to one (from five response categories), so that high values indicate agreement with the statement and low values indicate disagreement. The item thus measures the normative "cost" to the individual of taking part in legal protest behaviors.

For illegal protest, we combined four items into a similar normative cost-benefit variable. Three items referred to the moral justifiability of violence: "If citizens struggle for important political causes, violating the law may be necessary"; "Violence against property in order to achieve certain political goals is morally justifiable"; and "Violence against persons in order to achieve certain political goals is morally justifiable." The fourth item was a question asking respondents to estimate the likelihood of "feeling guilty" if they took part in illegal actions such as "blocking streets or damaging property." The four items were added and transformed to a zero to one scale, so that high values represent a high normative "cost" of illegal protest participation and low values represent a low normative cost.

We also asked one question to measure the personal normative *benefits* of participation. Individuals were asked to estimate the likelihood (scored on a zero to one scale) of "feeling good for standing up for what I believed in" if they participated in legal and in illegal protest activities.

Measurement of Social Network Incentives. We measured the expectations of others regarding legal and illegal behavior by asking respondents to think of people whose opinion is important to them—their spouses, friends, colleagues—and then asked how those people would react if they were to participate in each type of political action. Respondents could choose between five codes indicating a very negative (-2) to a very positive (2) judgment. Scores in the negative region indicate that the respondent perceives a cost from participation and scores in the positive region indicate a perceived benefit.

We also measured the extent to which respondents were members of groups that encouraged legal and illegal activities. Respondents were requested to report their perceptions of whether any political or social group to which they belonged "encouraged" legal and or illegal protest, "discouraged" these behaviors, or did not care either way. The perceived group encouragement variable is a dummy variable indicating whether or not any membership group "encourages" protest participation.

We measured the extent to which the individual expected to meet people through legal and illegal action by asking respondents about the probability that, if they engaged in that form of action, "I could get to know people with similar interests and views." Responses ranged from "very unlikely" to "very likely" on a zero to one scale.

Results

Ideological Identification and Political Protest

We present first the overall distribution of left-right ideological identification in each country in Figure 1: in all three countries there are few individuals who are at either the extreme left or extreme right, as each distribution appears to be approximately normal. These findings replicate results from previous cross-national studies conducted in the United States and Western Europe (Klingemann 1972; Barnes et al. 1979) and indicate that despite wide variations in ideological conflict at the elite level in these countries, the plurality of mass respondents view themselves as politically "moderate."

Nevertheless, the data still reflect the relatively higher intensity of ideological conflict in Israel and Peru compared to West Germany. In both Israel and Peru, the percentage of ideological extremists is about twice as high as in Germany. In Peru the proportion of extreme leftists is higher than the proportion of extreme rightists, while in Israel there are about twice as many extreme rightists as those on the extreme left. These patterns, we believe, reflect each country's recent political histories: a growing religiously oriented right wing in Israel, and a growing leftist radicalism in Peru rooted in the severe economic and political crises of the 1980s.

Figures 2 and 3 present the mean level of legal and illegal protest, respectively, for individuals in the various ideological groups. Because of the few numbers of cases in individual categories at the extreme ends of the self-

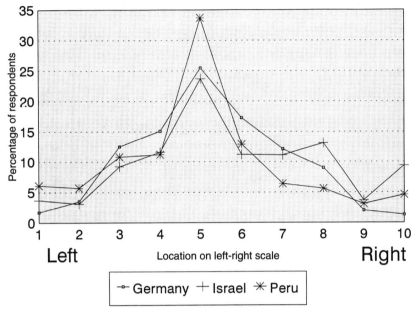

Figure 1. Ideological self-placement in Germany, Israel, and Peru

placement scale, we collapsed the scale into five groupings: extreme left (values 1 and 2); left (values 3 and 4); center (values 5 and 6); right (values 7 and 8); and extreme right (values 9 and 10). This procedure also has the advantage of allowing us easily to test the statistical significance of any curvilinear patterns we may find by using the "center" grouping as the baseline category in dummy variable regression analyses (to be presented in Tables 3 to 5).

The figures show that the overall relationship between the self-placement scale and protest participation is highly variable across the three countries. For legal protest, the German pattern is consistent with previous research in many Western democracies: the relationship between ideological identification and protest is generally linear, with participation potential decreasing relatively consistently from extreme left to right. In both Israel and Peru, on the other hand, the relationship appears to be curvilinear, as both leftists and rightists show higher levels of protest potential than those in the ideological center.[9] In general, however, the differences between the ideological groups are smaller in Israel and Peru than in the Federal Republic.[10]

The results are generally similar for the relationship between the self-placement scale and illegal protest behavior. In Germany, extreme leftists are far more participatory than any other ideological group. There is also a slight

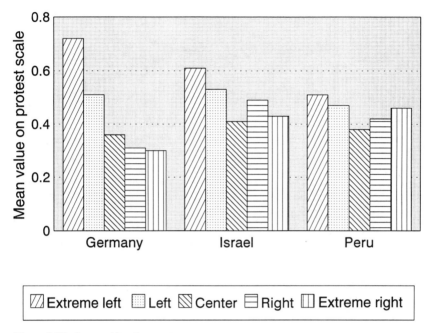

Figure 2. Ideology and legal protest

tendency of extreme rightists to participate more actively than individuals in the simple "right" category, but both right-wing groups are the least participatory in the sample. Again, in Israel and Peru a curvilinear pattern emerges, as extreme rightists in Peru and both rightists and extreme rightists in Israel are more prone to participate in illegal protest actions than those in the center. Nevertheless, the overall strength of the relationship between ideological identification and protest is weaker in both Israel and Peru than in the Federal Republic; that is, differences between the groups as a whole in those countries are less pronounced.[11]

In the next section, we test the extent to which these divergent patterns can be accounted for by the two explanations discussed earlier: party identification and expected utility. We present first the relationship between ideological identification and the variables contained in each of the explanations separately, followed by regression analyses attempting to account for the bivariate relationships between self-placement and protest behavior by controlling for party identification and expected utility variables. For these alternative explanations to account adequately for the patterns seen in Figures 2 and 3, two conditions must hold: first, there must be a relationship between self-

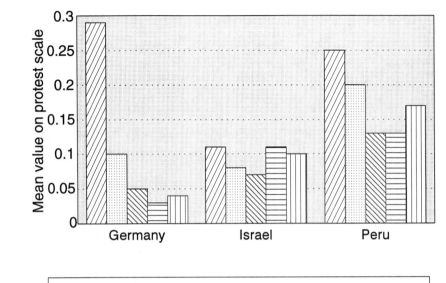

Figure 3. Ideology and illegal protest

placement and the variables in the party identification and expected utility models; and second, those variables themselves must be related to political participation. As we will see, these conditions hold to varying degrees in the three countries.

Ideological Self-Placement and Party Identification

If ideological self-placement simply reflects an individual's general affiliation with a particular political party, then we should observe a relatively high correlation between ideological and partisan identification. Table 1 shows the proportion of individuals within each of the five ideological groups who identify with various political parties in each of the three countries.

The table shows a close, though far from perfect, correspondence between left-right ideology and party identification. The relationship appears to be reasonably strong in Germany, where no leftists identify with either of the two right of center parties, and almost no rightists identify with either of the two left of center parties. Still, within each of the ideological groups in West Germany, at least 30 percent of the respondents profess *no* party identification at all (or at least no party they "feel close to"). Of particular interest in Germany are "left" and "extreme left" individuals, since they exhibit the high-

Table 1. Percentage of ideological groups identifying with various political parties

	Extreme left	Left	Center	Right	Extreme right
Germany					
Greens	39	10	2	0	0
Social Democratic Party (SPD)	32	45	20	6	0
Free Democratic Party (FDP)	0	2	5	6	0
Christian Democratic Party/ Christian Social Union (CDU/CSU)	0	3	10	39	55
No party identification	29	40	64	50	45
N	(31)	(166)	(257)	(127)	(20)
Percent	5	28	43	21	3
Israel					
Left parties	31	20	4	2	1
Labor	47	49	30	13	3
Likud	3	3	17	38	43
Right parties	3	1	3	13	31
No party identification	16	26	45	34	22
N	(68)	(208)	(348)	(242)	(131)
Percent	7	21	35	24	13
Peru					
United Left (IU)	49	34	9	3	5
Popular Alliance for the American Revolution (APRA)	34	36	31	28	37
Popular Action (AP)	1	7	10	20	20
Popular Christian Party (PPC)	1	2	6	21	18
No party identification	15	21	44	28	21
N	(155)	(289)	(614)	(159)	(101)
Percent	12	22	46	12	8

est levels of protest behavior (as shown in Figures 2 and 3). Among the extreme left group, only 40 percent identify with the Greens, the party most closely related programmatically to protest behavior (cf. Finkel and Opp 1991), and among the left group, only 10 percent are Green identifiers. The large number of Social Democratic Party identifiers and unaffiliated individuals among the left groups clearly will limit the ability of party identification to explain the overall ideology-protest relationship in the Federal Republic.

The correspondence between ideology and party identification is slightly less pronounced in Israel than in Germany. Although fewer numbers of individuals profess no party affiliation at all in Israel, not even a plurality of extreme leftists identify with parties to the left of the left-center Labor Party. Similarly, over 40 percent of extreme rightists identify with the moderate-right Likud Party, a greater number than identify with more right-wing, though smaller, parties. Neither Labor nor Likud, the two "establishment" parties in Israel, consistently promotes protest behavior on the part of its members or identifiers, although there has been some relationship between the Labor leadership and peace movement activists (Aronoff 1989, p. 100). Certainly neither party has as strong a tie to protest movements as do smaller parties on the left such as Ratz or Shinui, which have many supporters within the peace movement, and parties on the right such as Tzomet and Thiyah, which have very strong links to Gush Emunim and other settler groups that have engaged in a large variety of legal and illegal acts of protest (Aronoff 1989, pp. 81–85; Sprinszak 1991). Because of this tendency of even extreme ideologues to identify with "nonextremist" parties, we expect that party identification will explain at best only a portion of the overall ideology-protest relationship in Israel as well.

The relationship between ideology and party identification is weakest in Peru, especially among those groups on the right of the ideological spectrum. Both the right and the extreme right appear to divide their loyalties among three parties: the traditional Popular Christian Party (PPC); Popular Action, a party centered largely around former president Fernando Belaunde Terry; and the then-ruling center-left Popular Alliance for the American Revolution (APRA), a historically radical party that "has so changed its image and policies over time that by 1980 it resembled . . . a social democratic party on the Western European model" (Dietz 1986–87, p. 145). Since none of these parties has been strongly oriented toward political protest in the recent past, it seems unlikely that right-wing protest participation in Peru can be accounted for by party affiliation. On the extreme left, however, the table shows a relatively strong concentration of United Left Party (IU) identification, and relatively few numbers of nonidentifiers. Since the IU has some factions that have endorsed political protest in recent decades (CIED 1980), we may expect leftist protest participation to be explained at least partially through this pattern of party affiliation. In general, though, the data reflect a relatively high degree of ideological fragmentation and fractionalization in the Peruvian party system.

Ideological Self-Placement and Expected Utility Variables

An alternative explanation for the relationship between ideological identification and participation emphasizes the costs and benefits perceived by individuals in various ideological groups in relation to protest behavior. We hypothesized specifically that three components of a general expected utility

Table 2. Ideological identification and average values of expected utility variables, Germany

	Extreme left	Center	Extreme right
Legal protest			
Public goods motivation	.48	.38	.34
Standing up for beliefs	.66	.54	.63
Moral norms proscribing protest	.23	.50	.60
Group encouragement	.39	.14	.11
Expectations of others	.48	−.09	−.15
Meet like-minded people	.76	.64	.67
Illegal protest			
Public goods motivation	.16	.06	.03
Standing up for beliefs	.49	.25	.15
Moral norms proscribing protest	.46	.80	.89
Group encouragement	.23	.03	.00
Expectations of others	−.23	−1.45	−1.80
Meet like-minded people	.70	.51	.62

Table 3. Ideological identification and average values of expected utility variables, Israel

	Extreme left	Center	Right
Legal protest			
Public goods motivation	.53	.44	.45
Standing up for beliefs	.69	.61	.62
Moral norms proscribing protest	.32	.48	.53
Group encouragement	.13	.08	.11
Expectations of others	1.03	.49	.63
Meet like-minded people	.68	.59	.63
Illegal protest			
Public goods motivation	.09	.09	.08
Standing up for beliefs	.46	.46	.46
Moral norms proscribing protest	.75	.75	.70
Group encouragement	.01	.01	.01
Expectations of others	−1.34	−1.62	−1.63
Meet like-minded people	.50	.54	.49

model had direct theoretical relevance for ideological identification: public goods motivation, personal normative beliefs, and social network incentives. We show the mean levels of these variables for the different ideological groups in each country in Tables 2–4, and as with the party identification analyses in Table 1, Tables 2–4 show mixed support for the hypothesis that these variables can explain the ideology-protest relationship.

To simplify the presentation of the findings, we show the mean levels of

Table 4. Ideological identification and average values of expected utility variables, Peru

	Extreme left	Center	Extreme right
Legal protest			
Public goods motivation	.43	.40	.41
Standing up for beliefs	.72	.68	.63
Moral norms proscribing protest	.31	.33	.27
Group encouragement	.23	.20	.17
Expectations of others	.21	−.01	.19
Meet like-minded people	.64	.65	.61
Illegal protest			
Public goods motivation	.18	.15	.13
Standing up for beliefs	.66	.60	.57
Moral norms proscribing protest	.61	.66	.63
Group encouragement	.09	.07	.05
Expectations of others	−1.29	−1.44	−1.58
Meet like-minded people	.65	.62	.58

each expected utility variable for three ideological groups in each country: the most active leftist group, the most active rightist group, and the ideological centrists. For Germany and Peru, the most active groups at each end of the ideological spectrum are the extreme left and extreme right, while in Israel the most active groups are the extreme left and the nonextreme right.

Our expectations clearly are confirmed in the Federal Republic of Germany. For every expected utility variable relating to legal and illegal protest, extreme leftists in Germany show the highest levels of perceived benefits and lowest levels of perceived costs, exactly what we would expect since this ideological group is by far the most active in protest behavior. Moreover, the differences between the variables' level for extreme leftists and centrists is typically much larger than the difference between the levels shown for centrists and extreme right-wing respondents. For example, extreme leftists register more than one and one-third times the level of our composite public goods motivation variable for legal and illegal protest as extreme rightists, half the level of perceived normative costs, and three to five times the expected rewards from conforming to the behavioral expectations of important others. Extreme leftists are highly integrated into groups that the respondent perceives to encourage protest behavior as well. Since the perceived group encouragement variable is dichotomous, its value may be interpreted as the proportion of individuals in that ideological group who do belong to a group that is thought to encourage protest. As can be seen, almost 40 percent of extreme leftists belong to a group that is perceived to encourage legal protest, compared to only 10 to 15 percent of the other groups, and close to one-fourth of extreme leftists belong to a group that is perceived to encourage illegal protest, compared to essentially no one in the other ideological grouping. All of these differences are entirely consistent with the differences in participation between these ideological groups shown in Figures 2 and 3. Thus, if the expected utility variables themselves are highly related to participation, they may explain the ideology-protest relationship in Germany.

In Israel, the correspondence between the expected utility-ideology and ideology-participation relationships varies for different ideological group comparisons, and for the two forms of protest behavior. For legal protest, the table shows that extreme leftists perceive significantly higher levels of benefits and lower levels of costs than do ideological centrists, exactly what we should expect from Figure 2. The largest differences are found on perceived personal normative costs, behavioral expectations of important others, and perceived group encouragement. The differences between rightists and centrists on the expected utility variables are less striking, but still generally consistent with the higher levels of protest among rightists shown in Figure 2.

For Israeli illegal protest, however, the results correspond with the patterns in Figure 3 only to a limited extent. While extreme leftists perceive lower levels of disapproval for illegal protest from significant others, on all other variables the level for this group is approximately equal to those observed for ideological centrists. Further, in contrast to our expectation that rightists should show higher values of expected benefits and lower expected costs than centrists, the data indicate that this pattern holds only for expected normative costs; for all variables the levels of the expected utility variables for rightists are either equal to or slightly in the opposite direction from the expectations derived from Figure 3. These patterns suggest that expected utility will have limited effect in explaining the differences in participation rates between these ideological groups.

The results are also mixed for the Peruvian sample. According to Figure 2, we would expect that extreme leftists should show the highest expected utility for both legal and illegal protest, followed by extreme rightists. This expectation is confirmed for extreme leftists on four of the six expected utility variables, and the results for extreme rightists are consistent with expectations on three of the expected utility variables as well. For illegal protest, however, the data clearly disconfirm our expectations regarding extreme right-wing protest behavior: for five of the six variables, extreme rightists show lower levels of expected positive utility than centrists, yet extreme rightist participation is higher than participation in the ideological center. The data do confirm our expectations for extreme leftists for all six variables, indicating that expected utility may be able to account for observed differences in illegal protest between the Peruvian center and left, though not for differences between the center and right.

Explaining the Effects of Left-Right Ideology on Political Protest

Having shown the relationship between left-right ideology, party identification, and expected utility variables in each country, we present in this section regression models predicting legal and illegal protest behavior with these three sets of explanatory variables. The analyses will provide evidence regarding the relative importance of ideology, party, and expected utility in predicting behavior, as well as decisive tests of whether party identification and/or expected utility variables can explain the differences in participation rates for the various ideological groups. If either party identification or expected utility can explain the ideology-participation relationship, then the bivariate effects of ideological identification on protest should be substantially reduced once the other variables are taken into account. Tables 5–10 show the results for legal and illegal protest in Germany, Israel, and Peru.

Each table contains three separate regression models. The first predicts protest behavior with all the dummy ideological identification variables except "center," which serves as the baseline category. The unstandardized coefficients in this model indicate the difference between the given ideological groups' average participation level from centrist individuals. The second model includes dummy variables for the various political parties in each country, with the omitted baseline group being the "nonidentifiers." The unstandardized coefficients for the leftist and rightist groups in this model indicate participation differences between these ideological identifiers that cannot be explained through their party affiliations. The final model adds the expected utility variables, and here the coefficients for ideology indicate the overall net effect of ideological identification on protest, controlling for both party identification and expected utility.

Tables 5 and 6 display the results for the Federal Republic of Germany. Model (1) in both tables indicates that only leftists and extreme leftists differ significantly from centrists in protest participation. Controlling for party identification in model (2) reduces the unstandardized coefficients of the left and extreme left groups by approximately one-third, as many of these individuals (as seen in Table 1) identify with the Green Party, whose adherents exhibit high levels of both legal and illegal protest. Identification with other

Table 5. Regression models predicting legal protest, Germany

	(1)	(2)	(3)
Ideology			
Extreme left	.341*	.220*	.132*
			(.10)
Left	.150*	.118*	.036
			(.05)
Right	−.043	−.044	−.024
			(−.03)
Extreme right	−.081	−.078	−.055
			(−.03)
Party identification			
Greens		.340*	.189*
			(.14)
Social Democratic Party (SPD)		.034	.012
			(.02)
Free Democratic Party (FDP)		.133*	.077
			(.05)
Christian Democratic Party/			
Christian Social Union (CDU/CSU)		.032	.039
			(.05)
Expected utility variables			
Group encouragement LP			.124*
			(.17)
Expectations of others LP			.039*
			(.14)
Meet like-minded people LP			−.017
			(−.02)
Public goods motivation LP			.421*
			(.21)
Standing up for beliefs LP			.084*
			(.09)
Moral norms proscribing LP			−.152*
			(−.18)
Adjusted R^2	.11	.17	.40

Note: Number of cases for all models is 601. Unstandardized coefficients presented for all models; model (3) includes standardized coefficients in parentheses.
* $p < .05$ (two-tailed).

parties is not significantly related to illegal protest, while identifiers with the Free Democratic Party, somewhat unexpectedly, show higher levels of legal protest than nonidentifiers. Controlling for expected utility in model (3) further decreases the direct effects of ideology. Differences between leftists and centrists in both forms of protest are now statistically insignificant, and the effect of extreme left identification is reduced to only one-third of its original magnitude in model (1).

Table 6. Regression models predicting illegal protest, Germany

	(1)	(2)	(3)
Ideology			
Extreme left	.229*	.154*	.067*
			(.11)
Left	.053*	.039*	.013
			(.04)
Right	−.025+	−.019	−.008
			(−.02)
Extreme right	−.011	−.005	.022
			(.03)
Party identification			
Greens		.200*	.112*
			(.18)
Social Democratic Party (SPD)		−.022+	−.016
			(−.05)
Free Democratic Party (FDP)		−.030	−.007
			(−.01)
Christian Democratic Party/			
Christian Social Union (CDU/CSU)		−.019	.002
			(.01)
Expected utility variables			
Group encouragement IP			.088*
			(.13)
Expectations of others IP			.018*
			(.12)
Meet like-minded people IP			−.005
			(−.01)
Public goods motivation IP			.474*
			(.24)
Standing up for beliefs IP			.022
			(.03)
Moral norms proscribing IP			−.086*
			(−.13)
Adjusted R^2	.16	.26	.41

Note: Number of cases for all models is 601. Unstandardized coefficients presented for all models; model (3) includes standardized coefficients in parentheses.
* $p < .05$ (two-tailed).
+ $p < .10$ (two-tailed).

We conclude that in Germany, left and extreme left protest participation results from a combination of partisan identification with the Greens and perceptions on the part of these ideological groups that participation is associated with positive expected utility, that is, perceptions that protest can be effective in achieving political goals, that protest is normatively justifiable, and that protest is perceived to be encouraged by important others and groups to which the individual belongs. The expected utility model is by far the most powerful in terms of explaining individual participation in collective action (as witnessed by its contribution to adjusted R-squared), but in terms of accounting for the ideology-participation relationship, both party affiliation and expected utility play significant roles. Finally, we note that some small direct effect of extreme left ideological identification remains even after controlling for all other variables.

The models in Israel are shown in Tables 7 and 8. For legal protest, all ideological groups except extreme rightists differ significantly from individuals in the center, validating the partial curvilinear relationship between ideology and protest seen in Figure 2. Controlling for party identification shows that individuals in each party group except Likud participate at higher rates than nonidentifiers. These outcomes reduce the magnitude of the ideology coefficients by approximately 25 percent for the leftist groups, but do not affect the effect of rightist identification. The addition of the expected utility variables contributes significantly to the prediction of legal protest, and in combination with party identification explains completely the participation of individuals on both the left and extreme left. Only a small but significant net effect of rightist participation remains in the final model.

For illegal protest in Israel, the results show that the effects of extreme right-wing ideological identification on protest is mediated completely by identification with right-wing political parties, while extreme left-wing protest appears to operate independently of party affiliations. Adding the expected utility variables again results in a better predictive model, and one that explains essentially all protest differences between the ideological groups except for individuals on the extreme left. Although the effect for this group was relatively weak in model (1), almost none of its effect is explained by either party identification or expected utility. We speculate later on some possible reasons for this pattern of results.

The Peruvian results in Tables 9 and 10 exhibit several interesting patterns as well. Initially, there are small but significant effects of all ideological groups on legal protest, and the addition of party identification explains roughly one-fourth to one-third of their magnitude. Of particular interest is the finding that identifiers with all party groups in Peru, except the traditional Christian PPC for illegal behavior, participate in protest at significantly higher levels than nonidentifiers. The addition of the expected utility variables further reduces the effects of left-wing protest, but fails to account for the participation by those on the extreme right. The same holds true for illegal protest, where most of the participation of the left wing, but none of the

Table 7. Regression models predicting legal protest, Israel

	(1)	(2)	(3)
Ideology			
Extreme left	.207*	.145*	.062+
			(.06)
Left	.120*	.079*	.039+
			(.06)
Right	.075*	.077*	.053*
			(.08)
Extreme right	.027	.012	.010
			(.01)
Party identification			
Left parties		.079*	.115*
			(.13)
Labor		.075*	.042*
			(.07)
Likud		.005	−.001
			(−.01)
Right parties		.149*	.070*
			(.07)
Expected utility variables			
Group encouragement LP			.105*
			(.11)
Expectations of others LP			.035*
			(.16)
Meet like-minded people LP			.009
			(.01)
Public goods motivation LP			.647*
			(.29)
Standing up for beliefs LP			.099*
			(.12)
Moral norms proscribing LP			−.097*
			(−.13)
Adjusted R^2	.04	.09	.34

Note: Number of cases for all models is 997. Unstandardized coefficients presented for all models; model (3) includes standardized coefficients in parentheses.
* $p < .05$ (two-tailed).
+ $p < .10$ (two-tailed).

participation by the extreme right, is explained by party identification or by expected utility. Again, expected utility variables contribute by far the most explanatory power in the overall models of protest, yet they do little to account for either legal or illegal protest by those on the extreme right. As in Israel and Germany, some small direct effects of identification with certain ideological labels on political protest remain.

Table 8. Regression models predicting illegal protest, Israel

	(1)	(2)	(3)
Ideology			
Extreme left	.039*	.045*	.036*
			(.07)
Left	.012	.019	.018
			(.06)
Right	.038*	.027*	.019+
			(.06)
Extreme right	.032*	.009	.014
			(.03)
Party identification			
Left parties		.001	−.001
			(.00)
Labor		−.032*	−.025*
			(−.08)
Likud		.006	.007
			(.02)
Right parties		.044*	.024
			(.03)
Expected utility variables			
Group encouragement IP			.077+
			(.05)
Expectations of others IP			.020*
			(.13)
Meet like-minded people IP			.013
			(.04)
Public goods motivation IP			.623*
			(.19)
Standing up for beliefs IP			.024*
			(.07)
Moral norms proscribing IP			−.109*
			(−.15)
Adjusted R^2	.01	.03	.16

Note: Number of cases for all models is 997. Unstandardized coefficients presented for all models; model (3) includes standardized coefficients in parentheses.
* $p < .05$ (two-tailed).
+ $p < .10$ (two-tailed).

Discussion and Conclusions

We have extended previous research on the relationship between ideological identification and political protest in two ways. First, we examined these relationships in the Federal Republic of Germany, as well as in two non-European democracies, Israel and Peru. We found that the traditional pattern of protest being highest on the left and lowest on the right held only in Ger-

Table 9. Regression models predicting legal protest, Peru

	(1)	(2)	(3)
Ideology			
Extreme left	.138*	.087*	.071*
			(.08)
Left	.089*	.052*	.013
			(.02)
Right	.047*	.034	.030
			(.03)
Extreme right	.087*	.064*	.070*
			(.07)
Party identification			
United Left (IU)		.153*	.086*
			(.12)
Popular Alliance for the		.125*	.085*
American Revolution (APRA)			(.14)
Popular Action (AP)		.118*	.063*
			(.07)
Popular Christian Party (PPC)		.093*	.044
			(.04)
Expected utility variables			
Group encouragement LP			.043*
			(.06)
Expectations of others LP			.025*
			(.10)
Meet like-minded people LP			.023
			(.02)
Public goods motivation LP			.785*
			(.37)
Standing up for beliefs LP			.122*
			(.11)
Moral norms proscribing LP			−.016*
			(−.02)
Adjusted R^2	.03	.07	.29

Note: Number of cases for all models is 1318. Unstandardized coefficients presented for all models; model (3) includes standardized coefficients in parentheses.
* $p < .05$ (two-tailed).

many, as rightists and extreme rightists in the other countries were more active than centrists and in some models as active as or more active than those on the nonextreme left. The results suggest that the simple association between ideology and protest behavior can vary widely according to country context.

Second, we tested two models to explain the observed differences between ideological groups in protest behavior and found consistent, though not complete, support for their predictions. We found that the relationship be-

Table 10. Regression models predicting illegal protest, Peru

	(1)	(2)	(3)
Ideology			
Extreme left	.122*	.085*	.061+
			(.10)
Left	.074*	.048*	.019
			(.04)
Right	.007	.004	.017
			(.03)
Extreme right	.041+	.034	.055*
			(.07)
Party identification			
United Left (IU)		.105*	.061*
			(.11)
Popular Alliance for the		.036*	.046*
American Revolution (APRA)			(.10)
Popular Action (AP)		.047*	.019
			(.03)
Popular Christian Party (PPC)		.034	.038+
			(.05)
Expected utility variables			
Group encouragement IP			.050*
			(.06)
Expectations of others IP			.023*
			(.11)
Meet like-minded people IP			.022
			(.03)
Public goods motivation IP			.827*
			(.35)
Standing up for beliefs IP			.033+
			(.05)
Moral norms proscribing IP			−.104*
			(−.10)
Adjusted R²	.04	.06	.27

Note: Number of cases for all models is 1318. Unstandardized coefficients presented for all models; model (3) includes standardized coefficients in parentheses.
* p < .05 (two-tailed).
+ p < .10 (two-tailed).

tween ideological identification and protest is mediated to some degree by political party identification, and the variations in the nature and ideological programs of the parties in each country partially explain the behavioral patterns of individuals who identify with particular ideological labels. However, party identification was limited as a general explanation for the ideology-protest relationship. Ideological and partisan identifications were by no means perfectly related in any country, as many left and right identifiers either identified with centrist parties that do not encourage protest or did not identify with any of the country's political parties. Models that contained ideological and partisan identification as predictors of protest behavior were generally fairly weak in explanatory power.

We proposed an alternative explanation that included variables from previously developed expected utility models that are theoretically linked to ideological identification. We found that in general expected utility variables were the most powerful predictors of protest behavior. These factors also explained to a significant degree the protest behavior of most ideological groupings. That is, individuals in the various ideological groups are generally more or less likely to participate in protest because of the behavior's perceived mix of benefits and costs. In line with our theoretical discussion, we argue that these benefits and costs are inherent to the notion of ideology itself, and thus these effects are entirely understandable. To label oneself, for example, an extreme leftist means precisely to exhibit strong preferences for particular public goods, to adopt certain views of the likely efficacy and moral propriety of various tactics to achieve these goods; it is also likely to mean associating with groups and other individuals who share one's ideological outlook and provide social or solidarity incentives to participate or not in certain forms of behavior. Ideological self-identifications are thus linked directly to the preferences and perceived constraints contained in expected utility models of behavior.

Neither expected utility nor party identification, however, was able to explain fully certain behavioral patterns we observed in the three countries. For both legal and illegal protest in all three countries, significant differences between extreme leftists and centrists remained after controlling for party identification and expected utility, although the magnitude of this net effect was relatively small in all cases. Similarly, in Israel and Peru some net effect of right-wing and extreme right-wing protest, respectively, remained after controlling for other variables as well. While we cannot explain definitively why these patterns exist with our data, we can offer several possible interpretations that may be investigated more fully in future research.

First, our results are consistent with an interpretation of extremist ideological identification as a partially nonrational factor that can operate as an independent motivation for participation in collective political action. While the net effects of ideological identification may result from measurement error or omitted expected utility variables, it is also possible that self-placement at the extremes of the ideological scale represents a motivation for political participation that cannot be explained within the rational action framework. We should note, however, that the magnitude of these net effects is relatively small in all countries for both legal and illegal protest.

Alternatively, it may be the case that our models in general have identified the relevant variables for explaining left-wing protest behavior but have been less successful in explaining right-wing protest actions. In all tests except for illegal protest in Israel, the magnitude of the unstandardized coefficients for the left and extreme left was reduced substantially, if not completely, by controlling for party identification and expected utility. Yet in Israel and Peru the coefficients for right-wing protest were often unchanged after introducing these other variables as controls. It is possible that right-wing activities in these countries—a mixture of vigilante behavior, counterdemonstrations against the left, and nationalistic displays—may be governed by a set of expected utility variables different from those considered here, or perhaps by other factors altogether. Still, we emphasize that in both Israel and Peru the initial magnitude of the right-wing effects was quite small.

Finally, examination of the pattern of effects in all three countries suggests one other possible interpretation. For illegal protest in Israel and Germany, significant effects remained for identification with the extreme left, while in Peru a significant net effect was observed for identification with the extreme right. This pattern may indicate that the relationship between left-right ideology and at least illegal protest may be conditioned by the ideological leanings of the parties that control the government. In Israel and Germany, rightist or center-right coalitions were in power at the time of our surveys, while in Peru the party in power was the moderate left APRA. The net effects for extreme ideological leftists and rightists may then represent residual dissatisfaction with the government or policy that was not measured through our indicators of preferences for public goods. If that is the case, then future cross-national research should include direct measures of incumbent performance and government satisfaction as components of public goods motivation that may lead extreme leftist and rightist self-identifiers to participate in collective action.

Notes

This research is part of an international project supported by grant SES870–9418 from the National Science Foundation (USA) and by a grant from the Volkswagen-Stiftung (Volkswagen-Foundation, FRG). An earlier version of this paper was presented at the Twelfth World Congress of Sociology in Madrid, July 8–14, 1990. Steven Finkel would also like to thank the Committee on Summer Grants at the University of Virginia and the German Academic Exchange Service (DAAD) for additional support of this research.

1. For prior efforts at applying expected utility theory to explain protest behavior, see Finkel, Muller, and Opp (1989); Muller, Dietz, and Finkel (1991); Opp (1989).

2. Public goods are technically *nonexcludable*, that is, they cannot be withheld from any individual regardless of his or her contribution toward their provision; they have *jointness of supply* in that the supply does not change regardless of how many people consume or enjoy the goods (cf. Olson 1965; Oliver and Marwell 1988).

3. More specifically, we hypothesize that the "importance of personal participation" contains three possible factors: a sense of specific personal influence through a given form of behavior; a belief in the strategic principle that contributions from *all* group members are necessary for group success; and an adherence to the principle of "conditional cooperation," or "calculating Kantianism," that says individuals will participate if enough others are doing the same. Any of these variables will promote beliefs in the importance of the individual's contribution to the group's efforts. For evidence regarding the impact of each of these variables on the public goods motivation construct in Germany and Peru, see Finkel, Muller, and Opp (1989); Muller, Dietz, and Finkel (1991).

4. The German data were collected by the Gfm-Getas Survey Research Institute in Hamburg, a firm with expertise in designing and implementing surveys on protest and political participation. Each survey was a probability sample drawn according to the design of the working group of German market research institutes. In this procedure the first step is to select sample points (voting districts). Then the interviewer looks for households according to a random route procedure. Finally, a member of the household is randomly selected to be interviewed.

5. The data in Israel were collected by Mod'in Ezrachi, a professional polling company with a good deal of experience in political surveys. The method for the national sample consisted of a cluster sampling technique similar to the one described in reference to Germany.

6. The survey in Peru was carried out by the APOYO, one of the largest and most experienced research organizations in the country. Each province is divided into twenty-five square blocks that were treated by the National Institute of Statistics in October 1987. From each of the sets of twenty-five blocks, five blocks were selected randomly. Within each block, housing units were selected randomly. Within each housing unit, ten interviews were planned (random selection). In Lima, approximately 400 interviews were conducted, while in the other provinces (Callao, La Libertad, Piura, Junin, Arequipa, Cuzco, Lambayeque, and Loreto), about 150 interviews were conducted.

7. The relevant discontent variables in each country were ascertained through multiple regression analyses predicting legal and illegal protest with the full set of discontent items. The relevant variables for legal protest were: in Germany, dissatisfaction with the government's performance regarding income inequality, environmental pollution, community problems, nuclear power, and perceptions that the group in society that the individual felt closest to was not "getting what it deserved," or "group deprivation"; in Israel, dissatisfaction with the government's performance regarding crime, preserving the Jewish culture in Israel, and preventing another war, as well as politicized "income deprivation," the perception that the individual's income is not as much as he or she deserves and that the state is responsible for this situation; in Peru, income and group deprivation. For illegal protest, the results were: in Germany, all policy dissatisfaction measures mentioned above as well as dissatisfaction with government performance regarding unemployment, group deprivation, and overall alienation from the political system as measured in Muller, Dietz, and Finkel (1991); in Israel, system alienation; and in Peru, income deprivation, group deprivation, and system alienation.

8. The questions corresponding to perceptions of group success, personal influence, and importance of participation may be found in Muller, Dietz, and Finkel (1991, pp. 1271–73).

9. It should be noted again that the national sample drawn in Israel excluded Israeli

Arabs for reasons of costs. Since Israeli Arabs are more likely both to support the political left and to participate in protest activities (Wolfsfeld forthcoming), it is reasonable to assume that their inclusion in the national sample would have strengthened the curvilinear relationship found in Israel between ideological identification and protest behavior.

10. The eta values for the relationship between the entire five-category scale and legal protest are .33 in Germany but only .20 in Israel and .17 in Peru.

11. The eta values for the relationship between the entire five-category scale and illegal protest are .40 in Germany but only .10 in Israel and .20 in Peru.

Chapter 5

The New Class, Postindustrialism, and Neocorporatism: Three Images of Social Protest in the Western Democracies

Michael Wallace and J. Craig Jenkins

The upsurge of social protest in the Western democracies over the past several decades has sparked a wide-ranging discussion about the origins and legitimacy of protest action. What were once seen as marginal or perhaps even deviant modes of political activity have now become a staple of the political system. Where once protest was centered among political outsiders, such as the working classes and ethnic minorities, it is today used by neighborhood associations, antiabortion advocates, supporters of women's rights, and a wide variety of political groups. At least three general interpretations have been advanced to account for this contemporary protest wave: *new class arguments* about the rise of a new group of "knowledge workers" whose position in the social division of labor gives rise to tensions between their work autonomy and the profit system; a *postindustrialism thesis* about the looser social controls and new cultural expectations created by economic affluence, generational change, and the growth of the service economy; and the rise of *neocorporatist policy making* and *party dealignment*, which have reorganized the structure of political representation and, alternatively, created social peace based on a new "social contract" or, by excluding new groups and weakening social controls, created new oppositional movements.

This essay explores these three interpretations by examining the eight Western democracies included in the first wave of the Political Action Project (Barnes and Kaase 1979): the United States, Italy, Britain, West Germany, Switzerland, Finland, the Netherlands, and Austria.[1] These countries exhibit significant variation in political and social institutions in addition to constituting a representative group of Western democracies. We pursue two types of analyses: a macroanalysis that treats these eight countries as political systems, and a microanalysis that looks at individual participation in protest.

Borrowing from Kohn's (1989, pp. 20–23) terminology, we treat countries simultaneously as *units* of analysis and as *contexts*.

First, we look at these democracies in terms of the relationship between class structures, political institutions, and power configurations as they affect the likelihood of protest. The basic idea is that social and political structures—such as the size of the new class, union density, or the degree of neocorporatism—should be associated with the frequency of protest and its potential. Second, we look at individual protest participation in these countries, treating them as contexts for studying the generality of patterns and assessing how particular national characteristics contribute to protest. Do new class locations, leftist commitments, or secular attitudes give rise to protest participation? Are there distinctive patterns, such as religious-secular clashes or left-party traditions, that generate protest in particular countries? While these are complementary methods, they ask different questions. The former looks at macrostructures, asking whether national characteristics create system outcomes, while the latter asks about the sources of individual protest participation and whether they vary across countries. While these methods should complement one another, there is no logical requirement that factors that work at one level will necessarily prevail at the other.

We selected the eight countries in the first wave of the Political Action Project survey, conducted in 1973–76, to ensure significant national variation. Although the second wave is more recent (1979–81), it was restricted to only three countries; we therefore draw on the first wave. The data are somewhat dated, but since the survey was conducted a few years after the protest peak of the late 1960s, it captures the crystallization of support for protest that, judging by the second-wave survey (Jennings and van Deth 1990), persisted through the 1980s. We also look at mass collective action—industrial strikes, protests, riots, political violence—during the same period. Here we draw on data from Taylor and Jodice (1983) and the International Labor Organization (1977). This gives us a comparison between collective protest events and individual participation. It also allows us to compare protests that are focused on the state and political actors as opposed to a broader range of social institutions and practices. We include three countries—Italy, Switzerland, and Finland—that were in the original Political Action Project survey but were not previously analyzed. Italy is generally seen as a contentious system of polarized pluralism with a strong but excluded oppositional left party (Sartori 1976), Switzerland as a culturally pluralistic "peaceful" system organized by concertation among peak associations (Lehmbruch 1984), and Finland as a neocorporatist system with a strong social democratic party. Including these three countries broadens the spectrum of our analysis.

Three Theories of Contemporary Protest

Our three theories point to different sources of social protest.[2] The new class thesis argues that changes in the class structure of the Western democracies have inverted the traditional association between lower class positions and political unrest. Protest now emanates from the well-educated and professionally oriented upper middle class rather than the industrial working class. Postindustrialism arguments look at a broad set of social trends that have created looser social controls and new aspirations, causing protest to be viewed as an extrapolation of routine forms of political action and to be centered among adherents of the affluent "new culture." Neocorporatist and dealignment ideas point to the loosening of traditional party ties and the centralization of policy making in the hands of an elite triad of party leaders, peak associations, and top governmental administrators, forging a new social contract or, alternatively, weakening social controls and creating a new sense of alienation. We contend that these three images are *not* mutually exclusive, but rather each contributes to an understanding of the roots of contemporary protest in the Western democracies.

The key idea in the *new class thesis* is that a growing set of knowledge workers are responding to the tensions between their work autonomy and the profit system by challenging the "old class" of entrepreneurs and top-level managers. These workers have a high sense of self-direction in their work, which puts them in conflict with the bureaucratic routines of the modern corporation and government agency. Their self-direction produces support for "direct action" politics as well as for oppositional political attitudes. There are variants of this new class thesis. In the bolder formulations, the new class is a broad professional-managerial class that is the agent for a new round of class struggle (Ehrenreich and Ehrenreich 1977; Gouldner 1979; Berger 1986); the working class is typically seen as a conservative force opposing these challenges. In other interpretations, the new class consists of salaried professionals, especially those with college degrees (Poulantzas 1975; Ladd 1979; Wright 1985), who support "single-issue" reform movements and liberal social views but are not oppositional (Lipset 1981; Brint 1985). Several studies have supported the second version, showing that credentialed professionals are more supportive of liberal social causes (Brint 1984; Zipp 1986; Macy 1988) and several of the "new" social movements (Kriesi 1989a) and are more

protest prone (Jenkins and Wallace 1995). Does this hold for a range of prot\
activities and for all the Western democracies? What about countries where
working-class organization and protest have historically been prominent?

The *postindustrialism thesis* points to a broad set of social and demographic
changes, arguing that these changes have loosened traditional social controls
and nurtured a new postmaterialist political culture. The growth of the service
sector and higher education, an expanded youth cohort, and the coming of
age of an affluent generation have created greater cognitive mobilization,
broader support for a postmaterialist or "self-fulfillment" ethic, and demands
for direct participation in decision making (Inglehart 1977, 1990a; Jennings
and Niemi 1981). Paralleling these shifts, the changing status of women has altered expectations about work and career and educational aspirations, and
has created new claims on the traditional "male" preserve of political life. In
some formulations, postindustrialism has been linked to a revived status politics thesis that traces the new protest to the spread of modernist culture and
the resulting clash with traditional religious moralities (Bell 1977). In this
vein, the "new social movements" have been traced to the formation of new
collective identities in the context of the looser social controls of postindustrial societies (Melucci 1989). The strongest evidence comes from Inglehart
(1990a, 1990b), who shows the links of affluent backgrounds and generational
change to postmaterialist values and protest. There is also evidence that education leads to greater tolerance for political expression and hence protest
(Hall, Rodeghier, and Useem 1986) and that youth are more protest prone
(Isaac, Mutran, and Stryker 1980; Jennings 1987). There is also evidence that
women with more education and labor force experience are more active in the
feminist movement (Dauphinais, Barkan, and Cohn 1992). We extend this reasoning by exploring the role of life cycle and generational change, women's
status, and religious orientations with regard to protest.

Neocorporatist and dealignment arguments have focused on changes in the
political representation system. Building on the general thesis that protest is
driven by struggles for political access (Gamson 1975; Tilly 1978), several researchers have argued that party dealignment and the transformation of traditional left opposition parties into broad "catch-all" parties have created a
more volatile electorate, more open to political alternatives (Huntington 1982;
Dalton, Beck, and Flanagan 1984). Paralleling the postindustrialism thesis,
the parties have lost their social control capacities, alienating citizens and
leaving them available for new callings. At the same time, the rise of neocorporatist bargaining among business and labor peak associations, top-level bureaucrats, and strong social democratic parties has brought about a consoli-

dation of power. Some have contended that this has created a new "social contract" and strengthened social controls, thereby reducing industrial conflicts and protests (Schmitter 1981; Katzenstein 1985; Nollert chapter 6 in this volume). Others have contended that it has created a more insulated, less accountable policy system and thereby increased alienation and protest (Offe 1981; Panitch 1986), while still others have suggested that it has had no impact (F. L. Wilson 1990). We therefore look at the effects of partisan alignments and neocorporatism.

The Systemic Sources of Protest: A Macroanalysis

Protest involves participation in unconventional or noninstitutionalized political action. While all protests depend on negative sanctions to influence their targets, they vary in their noninstitutionalization. We draw on Kaase's (1990b, p. 395) distinction between *legal unconventional actions* (petitions, boycotts, lawful demonstrations), *civil disobedience*, which is typically illegal and directly challenges authorities (rent and tax strikes, wildcat strikes, painting signs, blocking traffic), and *political violence* (physical damage to property or persons). We also use Taylor and Jodice's (1983) distinctions between public demonstrations and marches, political strikes, riots, and political violence.

There are two basic ways of gauging protest. An *events approach* uses public records such as newspaper accounts or official reports to capture the frequency and characteristics of actual protest events. A *survey approach* looks at the self-reports of protest participation, including approval of and willingness to become involved in protest. Survey data can be used to analyze the individual sources of protest, or they can be aggregated to create country characteristics of protest activity or potential. Our analysis in this essay combines all these approaches.

We also distinguish between *protest potential* based on an expressed willingness to engage in protest actions and actual *protest participation*. While the two are distinct in that the former taps attitudes toward protest and the latter actual behavior (see Budge's 1981 critique of Barnes and Kaase), the question is whether these two dimensions are significantly different in terms of their origins.[3] In parts of our analysis, we combine these two dimensions of protest into a single indicator of protest activity on the basis of empirical evidence that they stem from very similar origins.

Our main concern is whether some countries are more protest prone. Figure 1 charts involvement in and willingness to participate in any of ten types of protest using the Political Action Project data. Throughout this essay, we

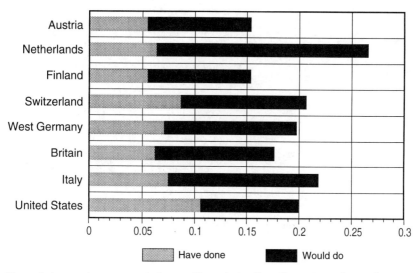

Figure 1. Aggregate responses to ten specific protest actions: Percentage who say they "have done" or "would do" these actions

rank the eight countries according to degree of neocorporatism, ranging from the more pluralistic (the United States, Britain, and Italy) to the more neocorporatist (Finland, the Netherlands, and Austria); countries that show a mixed pattern fall in between (West Germany and Switzerland).[4] In general, the pluralistic polities have slightly higher levels of actual protest yet complementary levels of potential. Between 6 and 10 percent of the respondents in the pluralistic polities have actually participated in protests as compared to only 5 to 8 percent in the neocorporatist states. Protest potential, however, is more widespread and especially high in the Netherlands, a pattern that persisted in the second wave of the Political Action Project study (Kaase 1990a, p. 32). Once potential and actual participation are combined, there is no consistent relationship between neocorporatism and protest. In other words, the total support for protest appears to be similar, yet neocorporatism limits actual protest behavior.

   Table 1 breaks these data down by specific actions, aggregating respondents' claims that they "have done" or "would do" each action. *Legal unconventional actions* (petitions, boycotts, demonstrations) are the most popular: between 30 and 80 percent have been involved or would be willing to engage in these actions. By contrast, only 5 to 20 percent have been involved in acts of *civil disobedience* (e.g., rent and tax strikes, wildcat strikes, painting signs on buildings, blocking traffic), which, of course, involve an escalated state of

Table 1. Actual and potential participation in specific protest actions

	United States	Italy	Great Britain	West Germany	Switzer-land	Finland	Nether-lands	Austria
Signing a petition								
Have done	63.4	19.7	23.5	32.0	50.8	22.4	21.2	22.4
Would do	20.3	45.8	33.2	40.6	30.8	30.5	57.4	30.5
Have done + would do	83.7	65.6	56.7	72.6	81.6	52.9	78.6	52.9
Joining in boycotts								
Have done	15.8	1.6	7.1	4.3	4.8	1.5	5.0	1.5
Would do	21.3	8.2	18.3	25.0	19.8	16.9	26.1	16.9
Have done + would do	37.1	9.8	25.4	29.3	24.5	18.4	31.1	18.4
Attending lawful demonstrations								
Have done	12.4	26.9	7.0	8.6	11.6	6.5	5.7	6.5
Would do	30.2	38.5	28.4	34.1	33.1	26.8	40.0	26.8
Have done + would do	42.6	65.4	35.3	42.8	44.7	33.3	45.7	33.3
Refusing to pay rent or taxes								
Have done	1.9	1.9	2.1	0.8	0.7	0.5	3.6	0.5
Would do	8.3	15.3	11.3	7.5	10.3	6.5	23.1	6.5
Have done + would do	10.2	17.2	13.4	8.3	11.0	7.0	26.7	7.0
Joining a wildcat strike								
Have done	1.9	2.2	6.4	1.1	0.1	6.2	1.7	6.2
Would do	5.9	5.4	8.7	4.7	4.9	6.9	13.9	6.9
Have done + would do	7.7	7.6	15.1	5.8	5.1	13.1	15.6	13.1
Painting signs on buildings								
Have done	0.7	3.5	0.2	0.2	0.7	0.0	1.6	0.0
Would do	0.4	2.4	0.5	3.5	3.4	1.8	5.1	1.8
Have done + would do	1.2	5.8	0.7	3.6	4.2	1.8	6.7	1.8

continued on next page

Table 1. (*continued*) Actual and potential participation in specific protest actions

	United States	Italy	Great Britain	West Germany	Switzerland	Finland	Netherlands	Austria
Occupying buildings or factories								
Have done	1.1	6.5	0.7	0.2	0.7	0.0	1.1	0.0
Would do	4.4	19.0	7.4	3.3	10.1	4.2	21.8	4.2
Have done + would do	5.4	25.4	8.1	3.5	10.8	4.2	22.9	4.2
Blocking traffic								
Have done	0.9	3.9	1.4	1.6	1.0	0.3	1.1	0.3
Would do	2.5	7.7	7.6	7.3	6.7	4.4	12.5	4.4
Have done + would do	3.4	11.7	9.0	8.9	7.7	4.7	13.6	4.7
Damaging things								
Have done	0.4	0.9	0.7	0.3	0.3	0.5	0.6	0.5
Would do	0.3	0.8	0.4	0.6	0.1	0.2	1.6	0.2
Have done + would do	0.6	1.7	1.1	0.9	0.4	0.7	2.2	0.7
Using personal violence								
Have done	1.0	0.6	0.2	0.4	0.3	0.5	0.6	0.5
Would do	0.4	0.3	1.3	0.7	0.4	0.2	2.5	0.2
Have done + would do	1.4	0.9	1.5	1.1	0.7	0.7	3.1	0.7

opposition and greater personal risk. There is nearly universal rejection of *violent protest* (physical damage to property or persons) in these countries; generally less than 3 percent claim they have done or would do such actions. Actual protest *participation* is largely centered in the more conventional types of action: over 60 percent participation in petitions (the United States), a quarter in demonstrations (Italy), and 15 percent in boycotts (the United States). By contrast, participation in acts of civil disobedience has drawn only 2 or 3 percent of the populace, the most frequently cited actions being sit-ins and wildcat strikes. Painting slogans, seen as a form of property damage, draws low responses. In line with Tarrow's (1993a) argument about modular forms of political contention, the petition, demonstration, and boycott are well known, amenable to mass participation, relatively flexible in terms of their targets, and indirect in the challenges that they present to those in power. They are therefore the most popular forms of protest action.

In rough terms, actual participation in legal unconventional protest and civil disobedience are twice as common in the pluralistic polities as in the other countries. There are also nationally popular forms of action. Two-thirds of Americans and half of the Swiss report actually signing a petition, while less than a quarter have done so in the other countries. In these two participatory democracies, petitions are so routine that they are virtually a conventional form of action. Reflecting the tactics of the labor movement, boycotts are especially prominent in the United States, Italy leads in sit-ins and public demonstrations, while Britain and Finland are the front-runners in wildcat strikes.

Violent protest is overwhelmingly condemned. Aside from the Netherlands, only about 1 percent have been engaged in violence or see themselves becoming involved. While these are small differences, it is striking that proportionately twice as many U.S. respondents have been involved in personal violence and a comparable margin in Italy and Britain in property damage. Aside from reflecting the almost universal condemnation of violence, these data also suggest that violence may be slightly more likely in the relatively open sphere of pluralistic polities.

Neocorporatism is even more dampening on political protest and industrial conflict. Table 2 shows the frequency of demonstrations, riots, political strikes, and political deaths per capita between 1963 and 1975 (Taylor and Jodice 1983) and the intensity of industrial disputes (ILO 1977). The three pluralistic polities are consistent front-runners with two or three times the levels of other countries for most of these indicators. The United States and Britain lead in demonstrations; West Germany, Italy, and Switzerland represent a middle level; and Finland, the Netherlands, and Austria fall at the bottom. Presumably this reflects the strength of the civil rights, student, and peace movements, which relied heavily on these tactics. Racial tensions in Britain and the United States, which have significant racial minorities, have led to rioting. The three pluralist countries lead by far in political strikes over the relatively quiescent corporatist states. But there are significant differences among the pluralists. The leader, Britain, nearly doubles the frequency of political strikes of runner-up Italy, which doubles again the third-place United States. These levels reflect a turbulent mix of protest movements in these countries ranging from highly contested conflicts over the restructuring of nationalized industries to student antiwar protests. The most telling measure is deaths resulting from political violence: Britain dwarfs the relatively high levels of deaths in the United States and Italy; the neocorporatist regimes are virtually violence-free according to this measure. Northern Ireland is largely responsible for the British violence, the urban riots in the late 1960s account for the U.S. violence, and the long "autumno caldo" of 1968 for the Italian violence. The pluralistic regimes are also more prone to industrial conflicts, with double the workdays lost per manufacturing worker (Table 2). Among the neocorporatist polities, Finland stands out in industrial disputes and wildcat strikes (Table 1), reflecting its high union density. While neocorporatism does not eliminate class conflict, it does alter its intensity.

Class Structure

Why these national differences? We begin by looking at class effects, then turn to the postindustrial trends, and finally examine the structure of political representation. Table 3 compares the class structure, class organization, and class awareness in our eight democracies. Panel A shows the class distribution using a modified version of Wright's (1979) neo-Marxian class scheme using the Political Action Project data. We exclude the unemployed, students, and economic dependents as well as those under twenty-one years of age. Wright's original class scheme uses three dimensions—control over the means of production, supervisory power, and occupational skill—to define class positions. This distinguishes capitalists from the petty bourgeoisie; upper managers who supervise ten or more workers from lower managers who supervise less than ten; semiautonomous workers who have an intermediary position in the administrative and skill hierarchies from the nonautonomous proletarians who rank low on all three dimensions. We modify Wright's original scheme by identifying the "new class" as professionals with a college degree or its labor market equivalent.[5] With the exception of Italy,

Table 2. Political and industrial protest events

	United States	Italy	Great Britain	West Germany	Switzer-land	Finland	Nether-lands	Austria
Panel A. Political protest, 1963–75[a]								
Protests per million	8.371	2.276	9.256	2.998	2.251	.638	.932	1.086
Riots per million	3.341	2.276	5.006	.903	.804	0	.311	.136
Political strikes per million	.664	1.260	2.215	.068	0	0	0	0
Political deaths per million	1.742	2.219	21.321	.715	0	0	.311	.678
Panel B. Industrial disputes, 1965–74								
Workdays lost per 1,000 workers	1,310	1,660	740	270	40	810	70	20

[a]Political protest data is calculated as total number of protest events in the 1963–75 period divided by 1969 population in millions.

Table 3. Class structure, class organization, and class awareness

	United States	Italy	Great Britain	West Germany	Switzer-land	Finland	Nether-lands	Austria
Panel A. Class structure								
New class	12.4	8.7	4.6	5.0	5.7	4.1	7.5	2.1
Capitalists	5.7	8.9	5.8	8.1	16.3	15.6	4.9	6.0
Petty bourgeoisie	3.5	12.4	3.7	3.6	3.3	1.2	5.7	12.9
Upper managers	7.3	–	9.5	6.2	8.5	7.6	6.0	6.4
Lower managers	9.5	25.0	13.5	15.3	13.8	8.2	18.8	17.4
Semiautonomous workers	10.0	13.1	17.5	21.7	21.1	29.4	16.9	12.5
Proletariat	51.6	31.7	45.5	40.1	31.2	33.9	40.2	42.7
Panel B. Class organization								
Union Density	16.4	42.5	37.0	33.5	20.0	80.0	29.0	55.1
Class Voting (Alford Index)	18	17	38	20	22	55	17	36
Left Party Governmental Influence Index (1965–80)	0	7	63	55	15	38	13	7
Panel C. Class awareness								
Upper-middle-class awareness	10.5	6.2	1.6	7.3	2.2	1.8	6.4	6.1
Middle-class awareness	18.0	21.6	9.4	40.9	15.8	24.8	21.7	28.8
Working-class awareness	7.3	38.0	25.7	23.5	11.0	40.8	15.7	31.3
No class awareness	62.4	32.5	61.0	28.1	61.0	30.5	54.1	33.2

which lacks the information to distinguish upper from lower managers, this scheme produces a comparable map of the class structure of these eight countries.

In general, these societies have similar class distributions. Reflecting a more hierarchical industrial structure, the United States and Britain are more proletarianized and exhibit a higher ratio of upper to lower managers, indicating greater centralization of economic control in terms of employing units and the scale of supervisory authority (see also Wallace and Jepperson 1986). If proletarianization alone is significant, these should be the most conducive settings for working-class protest. The new class is the most prominent in the United States, Italy, and the Netherlands, where knowledge workers make up 7 to 12 percent of the labor force. These three countries should offer the most fertile ground for the new class thesis and, in general, they do exhibit higher levels of actual protest—and, in the Netherlands, protest potential (Figure 1 and Table 1). Switzerland and Finland, by contrast, have the largest number of capitalists, which should moderate protest. Similarly, the decentralized economies of Italy and Austria generate a large petty bourgeoisie, which should also mute protest. Perhaps as a result of the higher representation of the petty bourgeoisie, Italy is slightly behind the other two pluralist countries, the United States and Britain, on most indicators of political unrest, although the Italian levels remain quite high (Table 2). Finland has the highest proportion of semiautonomous workers and a relatively small petty bourgeoisie. Fitting the picture of a middle-class society, Switzerland has large managerial, semiautonomous, and new class strata and a small proletariat. On balance, there seems to be a modest tendency for the pluralistic polities to be more proletarianized and, if the working class is a source of protest, to be more protest prone. Italy, however, with its highly decentralized, entrepreneurial economy, is a major deviation, suggesting the importance of other factors.

One such factor should be political organization, especially strong unions and class voting. The neocorporatism/political process argument, however, suggests a more complex relation by introducing a third factor: political power. Rising levels of class organization should mobilize protest up to the point at which working-class parties and labor unions secure political power. They should then achieve gains through conventional means, such as corporatist bargaining, and be less inclined to use protest. Our aggregate evidence provides some support for this view (Table 3, Panel B). First, union density, class voting, and left-party influence are roughly associated: highest in Finland, Britain, and West Germany; to a lesser degree in Austria; and lowest in the United States.[6] Italy is an interesting anomaly, with strong unions but low class voting and a weak left-party coalition. Second, left-party influence mediates between working-class organization and industrial conflict. Finland, Austria, and Britain display similarly high levels of class voting, union organization, and left-party influence. In Finland and Austria, industrial conflict and political protest are relatively low, but in Britain a decentralized labor movement has undercut the potential for corporatist bargaining, thus creating a splintered labor movement with high levels of industrial conflict. In the Netherlands, moderate organization is combined with a politically strong left party, creating low conflict. At the pluralist end, weak class voting and left parties in Italy and the United States have created high levels of industrial conflict.

In Panel C of Table 3, we look at class awareness and identification using the Political Action Project data of Barnes and Kaase (1979). Using a two-part question, we asked first whether respondents identified with a class and, if they answered yes, which class they identified with. We defined four groups: those who identified themselves as working class, as middle class, as upper middle class; and those who expressed no class identification. We derive four relevant hypotheses. First, a high level of working-class identification should produce greater industrial conflict, especially in the pluralistic polities. This should be exacerbated by a politically weak left-party coalition. Second, a high degree of working-class identification should curtail protest in neocorporatist countries where the working class is integrated into the political system. Third, following from the new class and postindustrialism theses, a high level of middle- and upper-middle-class identification should generate high levels of protest. Fourth, reversing these arguments, low levels of class awareness of any kind should generate low levels of protest.

Panel C provides inconsistent support for these theses. In general, working-class identification is positively associated with industrial conflict. The two anomalies—the United States and Austria—lie on opposite ends of the neocorporatism scale, indicating that neocorporatism mediates the relationship between class identification and working-class protest. In the United States, working-class identifications are low but, since pluralism is high, protest flourishes; in Austria, identification is high but neocorporatism is also high, hence little protest. As for the new class thesis, West Germany and the United States show the highest levels of middle- and upper-middle-class identifications. They were also fertile grounds for middle-class movements, especially environmentalism and feminism during the 1970s. Finally, four countries—the United States, Britain, Switzerland, and the Netherlands—exhibit extremely low levels of class identification. A strong majority of respondents in each of these countries indicated that they did not feel they belonged to an identifiable class. Two of these are pluralistic and two are more neocorporatist. They exhibit disparate degrees of protest, suggesting that class identification has little to do with protest or that protest is rooted in political identities other than class as it is traditionally conceived.

Postindustrialism

One variant of the postindustrialism thesis points to the clash between secularized protesters and supporters of traditional religious morality. In Table 4, we look at the distribution of religious affiliation and involvement using the Political Action Project data. In general, the greater the number of Protestant fundamentalists and Catholics, the larger the constituency for traditional cultural values. Conversely, the larger the pool of Jews, atheists, and "others" (which we take to be another category of nonbelievers), the larger should be the protest constituency. In support of this thesis, the United States has the largest group of evangelical and fundamentalist Protestants, lending a strong conservative individualism to its political culture. Similarly, Italy and Austria are overwhelmingly Catholic, creating a large constituency for conservative and confessional parties and antiprotest sentiments. West Germany is roughly evenly balanced between Catholics and mainstream Protestants, while Britain and the Netherlands have a significant minority of conservative Protestants. Reflecting the secularization of Dutch society, atheists and "others" represent over 40 percent of the respondents in the Netherlands, which may account for its high protest potential. Religiosity as gauged by church attendance is strongest in the United States and the Netherlands, while self-defined religious significance is strongest in the United States and Italy. The Netherlands stands out because it has a very high rate of church attendance but a very low rate of religiosity, reflecting the curious mix of forces contributing to the secularization of that society. We also combine these two measures to approximate the number of "secularists," those who never go to church and consider themselves to be not very religious. The Netherlands is clearly the most secularized society by this measure, followed by Britain and West Germany; the other five societies have between 8 and 9 percent secularists. Overall, these data suggest that the secular base of support for protest should be strongest in the Netherlands, Britain, and West Germany, and that the strongest base for conservative opposition should be in Catholic Italy and Austria and in the three countries with significant evangelical or fundamentalist Protestant populations: the United States, Great Britain, and the Netherlands.

Table 4. The Politics of Religion

	United States	Italy	Great Britain	West Germany	Switzer-land	Finland	Nether-lands	Austria
Panel A. Religious orientation								
Catholic	23.4	87.2	10.8	43.4	43.9	0.0	35.2	88.8
Mainstream Protestant	17.9	12.1	63.0	50.2	52.3	89.9	22.5	4.7
Evangelical or fundamentalist Protestant	53.5	0.0	15.3	0.0	0.0	0.0	9.1	0.0
Jewish	2.5	0.0	.3	0.0	.01	0.0	0.0	0.0
Other	2.0	.8	2.1	1.2	.9	2.9	12.7	1.0
Atheist	.7	0.0	8.4	5.2	2.9	7.0	28.6	5.5
N of respondents	1,625	1,733	1,458	2,303	1,286	1,223	1,193	1,583
Panel B. Religiosity								
Weekly church attendance	44.7	35.9	16.3	22.9	23.9	2.5	43.5	32.0
N of respondents	1,693	1,766	1,478	2,280	1,283	1,220	1,199	1,578
Consider oneself "very religious"	26.6	14.8	8.0	7.1	12.5	8.0	8.3	9.0
N of respondents	1,689	1,742	1,455	2,268	1,277	1,203	1,172	1,570
Secularists (not religious/ no church)	8.4	9.3	19.9	17.8	8.0	9.3	25.5	9.7
N of respondents	1,689	1,742	1,455	2,268	1,277	1,203	1,172	1,570
Panel C. Religious politics								
Confessional party presence	no	yes	no	yes	yes	no	yes	yes
Religious voting	20	40	13	36	64	0	36	49

The presence of a formal confessional party should also strengthen religious opposition to protest. To capture religious polarization we calculated a religious voting index as the percentage of Catholic voters who supported conservative or confessional parties minus non-Catholics who did so (derived from Powell 1982, pp. 90–91). In general, proportional voting systems have guaranteed the persistence of confessional parties. Of the proportional systems, only Finland lacks a confessional party. We count Catholic Austria among the countries with a confessional party because its Austrian People's Party, although nominally a conservative secular party, has confessional origins. The majoritarian systems in the United States and Britain lack religious parties, treating the religious right as any other interest group in the conservative coalition. Religious conservatism is amplified in Italy by the presence of the Christian Democrats and, in terms of religious voting, is strongest in Switzerland, Austria, and Italy. In these three states, traditional Catholicism should provide a strong counterweight to protest.

A related cultural theme pertains to the changing status of women. Increased education and labor force participation are significant contributors to women's support for feminist politics, while traditional religious morality is a significant factor discouraging a new social role for women (Plutzer 1988; Dauphinais, Barkan, and Cohn 1992). It would therefore seem that countries with larger female enrollments in higher education and greater female labor force participation would have a larger constituency for the new protest movements. Table 5 shows two indicators of women's status: the proportion of higher education enrollees who are women (UNESCO 1977; United Nations 1977) and women's labor force participation (ILO 1977). In general, women's enrollment is slightly higher in the pluralistic polities, and in West Germany and Finland should lead to protest. In terms of labor force participation, Italy and the Netherlands, which lie at opposite ends of the neocorporatist spectrum but share high levels of protest potential, are the most traditional. If the changing status of women has created a base for social protest, it should be greatest in the United States, West Germany, and Finland, where women's access to higher education and labor force participation are both greater, and lowest in the Netherlands, which has the lowest access.

Neocorporatism and Dealignment

The rise of neocorporatism is tied up with broad changes in political representation, especially the development of monopolistic bargaining between centralized peak associations and the decline of parties and parliamentary in-

Table 5. Women's status, 1970–75

	United States	Italy	Great Britain	West Germany	Switzerland	Finland	Nether-lands	Austria
Women as % of higher education enrollments								
	40.9	38.0	29.0	50.0	23.0	50.0	20.0	23.3
Women's labor force participation								
	29.5	19.6	32.9	30.0	32.1	37.5	19.0	30.3

stitutions. There are opposing interpretations of the impact on protest. Several researchers have argued that neocorporatism creates a stronger system of conflict regulation, reducing industrial conflict and political protest (Schmitter 1981; Katzenstein 1985; Nollert chapter 6 in this volume). Others have argued that neocorporatist policy making excludes groups other than capital and labor, thereby creating unrest among the new class and various outsiders (Offe 1981) and weakening the legitimacy of unions and left-party leaders, thus creating working-class unrest (Panitch 1986). Despite the apparent clash between these interpretations, there is evidence to support both. As we saw earlier, neocorporatism has discouraged industrial conflict and political protest (Table 2), especially the more unconventional forms of action. At the same time, it has not diminished the overall potential for protest, especially the more conventional forms of action (Figure 1 and Table 1). Its major impact seems to be in curbing actual expressions of protest, particularly acts of civil disobedience and violence.

A related set of arguments pertains to the nature of the party system, tendencies toward ideological thinking and political alienation, and the strength of the left parties. If the electoral system is a majoritarian or winner-take-all system, this should create two-party competition between broad "catch-all" parties. Some have argued that this blunts ideological differences, depoliticizing voters and discouraging a strong link between ideological self-placement and political action. By contrast, proportional systems create numerous parties, sharper ideological divisions, and greater protest. But Powell (1982) found that majoritarian systems were less responsive to citizen demands, thereby fueling greater alienation and protest. Finally, F. L. Wilson (1990) has argued that when the left parties were out of power, they promoted the new social movements and thus heightened the protest potential of the citizenry.

Table 6 supports Powell's system responsiveness argument. First, the two majoritarian systems have fewer parties and more protest events. The major left party is a broad coalitional party, and there is less ideological thinking. Respondents to the Political Action Project survey were less likely to locate

Table 6. The political representation system

	United States	Italy	Great Britain	West Germany	Switzerland	Finland	Netherlands	Austria
Panel A. Electoral system								
Type of electoral system*	Major	PR	Major	PR	PR	PR	PR	PR
Number of parties	3	12	6	5	9	12	15	5
Party base is class or religion?	Heterogeneous	Religion	Class	Religion	Religion	Class	Both	Both
Panel B. Political ideology								
"Can you place yourself?"								
Percent "no" or "no response"	32.4	26.1	18.3	7.8	21.2	7.5	9.7	24.9
Ideologues or near-ideologues	20.3	54.6	20.8	33.6	9.0	0.0	35.9	18.9
Meaning of leftism:								
socioeconomic order	9.6	15.7	6.6	9.9	7.6	–	15.9	7.2
ideological movements	39.5	16.3	28.1	50.7	27.3	–	21.5	46.6
mode of change	10.7	12.0	2.5	2.8	4.5	–	16.9	3.3
specific groups	2.5	13.3	3.5	1.8	9.0	–	9.8	6.8
political parties	1.3	30.4	41.3	29.9	34.1	–	22.9	25.3
error or "don't know"	35.4	12.3	18.0	4.9	17.8	–	11.9	10.9
N of respondents	3,206	1,740	2,140	3,042	2,228	–	2,316	2,649
Panel C. Left party identification								
Major left party**	Democratic	PCI	Labour	SPD	Parti Socialiste	SDP	PvdA	SPO
Left oppositional vote, 1965–76	0	37	3	3	8	25	13	1
Protest vote, 1965–76	0	6	0	2	0	2	0	0
Party loyalty	53	57	59	60	42	59	49	75

*Major = winner-take-all system; PR = proportional representation system.
**PCI = Communist Party; SPD, SDP, PvdA, and SPO = Social Democratic Party.

themselves in left-right terms and to provide a coherent interpretation of the meaning of left-right (Panel B). Italy, however, is a proportional system with a high level of ideological thinking and protest. Here, the relevant factor seems to be the oppositional stance of the Communist Party, which has been excluded from governmental power despite strong popular support. Following the political process argument about access, left-party governmental strength should be inversely related to protest. As the index of left-party influence shows (Table 3, Panel B), this is generally the case. Where the left parties were out of power, they promoted protest. Britain, however, has one of the strongest left parties but high levels of protest that stem from a fractious labor movement with decentralized and job-conscious unions. In the early 1970s, this decentralization blocked the Labour Party's attempts to institute a corporatist social contract, resulting in extensive industrial turmoil (Panitch 1986). A departure of a different type occurs in the case of Switzerland, where comparatively low levels of left-party strength are accompanied by low levels of protest. This probably results from the Swiss's coupling of a weaker version of neocorporatism with a degree of cultural pluralism that is unique in Europe (Lehmbruch 1984). Finally, the persistence of an oppositional left as reflected in oppositional and protest voting should strengthen protest. Drawing on Powell's (1982, pp. 95, 232) measures, which tap antisystem and alienated voting, these types of voting are associated with high levels of industrial conflict in Italy and Finland but inconsistently related to political protest.

Finally, partially tied to the neocorporatist thesis, there is the electoral dealignment argument that traditional class and religious divisions have withered away, creating less party loyalty and a more volatile electorate that is more susceptible to single-issue protest movements. While dealignment may not have fully developed by the early 1970s, the level of class voting and party loyalties do not support this thesis. Class voting is lowest in the United States and Italy, two of the most protest-prone countries, and higher in Finland, Austria, and Britain, which display varying levels of conflict (Table 3, Panel B). Party loyalty as gauged by the Political Action Project survey is strongest in Austria, lowest in Switzerland, and moderate in the other countries, following no consistent fit with aggregate protest levels.

These system-level comparisons provide support for several ideas. First, the new class does appear to be a source of protest, especially in the United States, Italy, and the Netherlands, where this class is relatively large. At the same time, working-class protest refuses to wither away, especially in countries where labor is organizationally strong but politically weak, the United States and Italy being the most notable cases. In Britain, a strong but decentralized labor movement undercut attempts at corporatist bargaining, creating an upsurge of industrial conflict. There is also some evidence of postindustrial protest. The secular bases of protest are the strongest in the Netherlands, the United States, and Italy, while conservative religious opposition remains strong in Italy, Austria, and the United States. Similarly, rising levels of women's education and labor force participation, especially in the United States, West Germany, and Finland, have created a new basis for feminist protest. The most important factor is the political representation system. Pluralistic regimes spawn more protest events, yet overall protest potential is roughly comparable in the neocorporatist countries. In other words, the integrative capacity of neocorporatist systems seems to defuse and mute some expressions of protest despite a latent potential for protest that rivals the pluralistic polities. Majoritarian electoral systems are less responsive to new groups and issues, thereby generating more protest, and out-of-power left parties promote protest. This macroanalysis, however, leaves unclear the impact of these structures on individual action. Moreover, several relevant factors, such as life cycle and generational changes, cannot be effectively examined through national patterns. We therefore turn to an analysis of protest participation in which countries are treated as contexts.

Individual Protest Participation: A Microanalysis

The aim of an individual analysis is to see if social characteristics are related to the likelihood of protest participation. Through comparative analyses of individual-level data, we can determine if particular national contexts are more or less conducive for launching protest. Drawing on the new class thesis, professionals with college degrees should be carriers of a "culture of critical discourse" and confront tensions between their work autonomy and the profit system, therefore turning to protest. If this new class has formed a coherent identity, those who identify as middle or upper middle class should be more protest prone. Following up the idea of traditional working-class protest, union members and those with working-class identifications should be more protest prone. As for the postindustrialism arguments, youth, the more educated, and those with weak religious commitments should also be protest prone while Catholics and evangelical and fundamentalist Protestants should be opposed. With regard to age, there are two interpretations: a life cycle hypothesis claims that protest is a function of psychological outlook and social commitments associated with aging; a generational hypothesis points to the unique political experiences of those who came of age during a particularly turbulent period (Braungart and Braungart 1986). Education is seen as a socializing experience that creates greater tolerance and willingness to engage in direct political action (Hall, Rodeghier, and Useem 1986). Similarly, women who are employed and unmarried should have narrowed the gender gap in protest (Plutzer 1988; Dauphinais, Barkan, and Cohn 1992).

Political identities are also a potential source of protest. The left has generally been defined as challenging inequality and traditional privileges, thereby using unconventional and disruptive tactics to bring about social change, while those on the right have relied on institutional inertia to thwart the left's agenda. Leftist identifications and left-party loyalties should therefore be sources of protest. This should hold especially in countries like Italy and Finland where the left party is historically a source of oppositional thinking and action. Alternatively, an "extremism" hypothesis argues that those who place themselves on either tail of the left-right spectrum should be more protest prone. They should have more passionate ideological commitments and therefore greater incentive to protest (see Opp et al., chapter 4 in this volume). We also look at the idea that the growth of "critical discourse" and cognitive mobilization has increased ideological sophistication and thereby protest (Huntington 1982; Inglehart 1990a). Changes in the political representation system should also alter protest participation. With neocorporatism, left parties are politically incorporated as central bargaining partners, muting the impact of leftist commitments. Similarly, electoral dealignment should weaken the link between ideological self-placement and protest. Finally, there is the idea of an expanded political repertoire with increased numbers of "political activists" (Barnes and Kaase 1979) or "dualists" (Herring 1989) who combine conventional and protest activism. We should therefore find a strong positive relationship between conventional activism and protest, especially the more conventional types of protest.

Method and Measures

To capture individual protest participation, we used the ten items shown in Table 1 to create four indicators of protest based on Kaase's (1990) classification. First, a *legal unconventional scale* taps milder forms of protest such as petitions, boycotts, and demonstrations. Second, a *civil disobedience scale* includes more confrontational strategies such as rent strikes, wildcat strikes, building occupations, painting slogans on walls, and blocking traffic. Third, a *violent protest scale* encompasses the tactics of damaging property or persons. Fourth, a *global protest scale* combines all ten items into a single scale of protest participation.[7] The ten items used in these scales reflect responses to a series of questions in which respondents expressed whether they "would never do" (= 1), "might do" (= 2), "would do" (= 3), or "have done" (= 4) these types of actions. While some have distinguished between *protest potential* and *protest participation* (see Budge's 1981 critique), supplementary analyses provided little basis for making such a distinction for these data, given the very similar origins of those who claim they have participated, or are likely to participate, in protest.[8]

We used regression analysis to estimate determinants of all four of these protest scales. However, we show results only for the global protest scale, because of its breadth, and the civil disobedience scale, because in many ways it represents the fulcrum of the new protest wave and, indeed, reveals most vividly the changing sociological roots of contemporary protest. We briefly discuss the results of the other two scales in terms of their key departures from the patterns revealed in the global protest scale and the civil disobedience scale.

Our regression analysis examines five clusters of variables: a set of demographics to capture the life cycle, generational, and women's status ideas as well as educational levels; class positions; class identities; religious orientations; and a set of political identities. Class structure is gauged by the modified Wright scheme discussed above (Table 3, Panel A), using the working class as a reference category. In other words, regression coefficients express the distance between a particular class category and the nonautonomous working class with regard to protest. Class identifications are scored with nonidentifiers as the reference category, distinguishing working-, middle-, and upper-middle-class identifiers. Union membership is a dummy variable based on the presence of a union member in the household (scored yes = 1; no = 0).[9]

To capture generational differences, we used a dummy variable to identify those thirty and under who came of age during the 1960s (scored yes = 1; no = 0). Life cycle position is based on respondents' age and should have a negative effect on protest. We experimented with including each term separately as well as treated additively in the same equations and found no significant differences or evidence of multicollinearity. We therefore show models with these two terms treated additively. To capture women's status, we began with a simple dummy, scored 1 for female and 0 for male. We went on to calculate a measure of "female independence," tapping women who are employed and unmarried to see if this measure will attenuate if not reverse the traditional male participation advantage. To capture the liberalizing impact of education, we included the years of formal schooling.

The idea of a clash between secular protesters and religious traditionalists is gauged in three ways. First, we examined religiosity based on a four-point Likert scale asking the significance of religion. Second, we measured church attendance on a five-point scale ranging from "never" (= 1) to "every week" (= 5). Finally, we included a dichotomous measure to indicate Catholic (= 1) versus non-Catholic (= 0) in all countries except Finland, where this distinction is not relevant. Religiosity and church attendance should generate opposition to protest. Catholicism should reduce protest where Catholics are a majority, but perhaps exacerbate protest in countries where Catholics are a minority.

In analyses not shown here, we also examined specialized expressions of both religious conservatism and secularized interests that reflect the concerns of postindustrial theorists. Our reasoning suggests that fundamentalist or evangelical Protestants should also form a conservative bloc against protest in countries where these groups are of significant size (the United States, Britain, and the Netherlands). We also created two measures of secularized populations to test the thesis that the secularization of society leads to a greater support for protest. Secular measure one taps persons who never attend church and do not consider themselves to be very religious (see Table 4, Panel B). Secular measure two identifies persons who identified as atheists, offered no response, or answered "other" to a question asking their religion.

We used a series of measures to tap ideological self-placement and sophistication. First, we constructed a simple leftism scale based on left-right self-placement on a conventional ten-point scale. We reverse-coded the original Barnes-Kaase scale so that extreme rightists were scored 1 and extreme leftists were scored 10. Because some failed to place themselves on this scale, we assigned them the mean score for their respective country and, to capture this failure, we created a nonideologue dummy variable scored 1 for those who expressed no ideological leaning and 0 for those who did. This controls for any bias introduced by the mean substitution and tests for the idea that nonideologues are apolitical and therefore less protest prone. Second, to capture ideological sophistication, we distinguished those who could offer a "correct" interpretation of the meanings of *left* and *right* as opposed to those who could not.[10] This permitted us to distinguish between a "naive" leftism scale for those who could give no intelligible reason for their political leanings and a "sophisticated" leftism scale for those who could.[11] In the regression analysis, we used a pair of dummy regression slopes to tap the effects of naive and sophisticated leftism, respectively (Hanushek and Jackson 1977, pp. 106–9). By including all three measures—sophisticated leftism, naive leftism, and nonideologues—we can distinguish three distinct levels of ideological thinking. (Also, to test the "extremism" hypothesis, we experimented with substituting a curvilinear derivation of the simple leftism scale.)

To capture party affiliations, we created a left-party dummy variable scored 1 for those who identified with any of the major left parties *or* voted for one of these parties in the most recent election, and 0 for those who did neither. We also created another dummy variable to capture nonaffiliated respondents who failed to reveal their party affiliation in both of these questions. While many who refused to reveal their political leanings might harbor intense political loyalties that they choose not to reveal for personal reasons, we contend that these nonaffiliated respondents should be apolitical and less likely to protest.

Finally, to capture the increased number of activists who combine protest and conventional activism, we included conventional participation based on a seven-item scale that asks about participation in such routine political activities as voting, reading political newsletters, engaging in political discussions, attempting to alter people's votes, working on community problems, attending political meetings, and contacting public officials. If changes in the political representation system indeed contribute to an expanded political repertoire, we would expect conventional activism to be strongly associated with protest activism, especially legal forms of protest.[12]

Findings

Table 7 shows the full regression models using these five clusters of variables to predict the global protest scale. The new class is a significant source of protest in five countries—the United States, Italy, Britain, Switzerland, and the Netherlands. Since these were generally the countries with the larger new class, this finding supports the idea that the growth of this body of knowledge workers has created a new basis for protest. A few of the other class variables are significant, but there is no consistent pattern. U.S. capitalists are antiprotest, reflecting their political strength in a heterogeneous electoral system. The petty bourgeoisie in Britain and Austria are protest prone, presumably reflecting their support for the dominant left party and sympathies for the working class, and in Austria the managerial strata are protest prone, perhaps reflecting their opposition to a strong neocorporatist system. In Finland, the working class is more protest prone, reflecting greater prole-

Table 7. Predicting protest participation: global protest scale[a]

	United States	Italy	Great Britain	West Germany	Switzer-land	Finland	Nether-lands	Austria
Demographics								
Gender (females = 1)	−.067**[b]	−.024	−.086**	−.047*	−.015	−.052	−.041	−.025
	(−.082)	(−.025)	(−.095)	(−.058)	(−.017)	(−.066)	(−.044)	(−.032)
Female independence (not								
married, employed women)	.022	.066	.033	.054	−.041	−.035	−.063	.013
	(.017)	(.040)	(.022)	(.033)	(−.030)	(−.029)	(−.039)	(.010)
Education	.013**	.001	.013	.029**	.003	.037**	.008	.018*
	(.094)	(.006)	(.064)	(.164)	(.022)	(.222)	(.045)	(.092)
Age	−.007**	−.004**	−.006**	−.005**	−.006**	−.004**	−.008*	−.004**
	(−.282)	(−.115)	(−.208)	(−.207)	(−.234)	(−.121)	(−.267)	(−.132)
Youth dummy (under 30 = 1)	.006	.034	.140**	.032	.053	.108*	−.036	.083*
	(.006)	(.035)	(.134)	(.030)	(.057)	(.122)	(−.036)	(.085)
Class structure								
New class	.064#	.128*	.167*	.015	.215**	−.117	.132*	.085
	(.052)	(.080)	(.080)	(.008)	(.126)	(−.059)	(.075)	(.031)
Capitalists	−.115**	−.080	.058	−.056	.052	−.053	−.088	.059
	(−.066)	(−.050)	(.031)	(−.037)	(.048)	(−.049)	(−.041)	(.036)
Petty bourgeoisie	−.000	−.068	.211**	−.002	−.099	−.132	−.024	.020
	(−.000)	(−.050)	(.092)	(−.001)	(−.045)	(−.037)	(−.012)	(.018)
Upper managers	.030	–	.030	−.006	−.002	.032	.017	.090#
	(.019)		(.020)	(−.003)	(−.002)	(.021)	(.008)	(.058)
Lower managers	−.003	.022	−.009	.027	.028	−.000	−.027	.107**
	(−.002)	(.021)	(−.007)	(.024)	(.025)	(−.000)	(−.022)	(.106)
Semiautonomous workers	−.030	−.000	.066#	.053*	.058	.024	.040	.022
	(−.022)	(−.000)	(.058)	(.054)	(.060)	(.026)	(.032)	(.019)

continued on next page

Table 7. (*continued*) Predicting protest participation: global protest scale[a]

	United States	Italy	Great Britain	West Germany	Switzerland	Finland	Netherlands	Austria
Class identities								
Upper middle class	.088**	–.015	–.288**	–.096**	.148#	.174	–.065	–.007
	(.067)	(–.008)	(–.082)	(–.061)	(.054)	(.059)	(–.034)	(–.004)
Middle class	.101**	–.023	.056	.001	–.017	.051	.039	–.001
	(.095)	(–.021)	(.037)	(.001)	(–.016)	(.056)	(.034)	(–.001)
Working class	.068#	.034	.031	.037	.043	.061#	.036	.065*
	(.043)	(.036)	(.031)	(.039)	(.034)	(.077)	(.028)	(.079)
Union member	.028	.025	.082**	–.025	.034	.024	.064*	–
	(.030)	(.028)	(.095)	(–.029)	(.037)	(.026)	(.067)	
Religious identities								
Religiosity	–.024*	–.068**	–.010	–.026#	–.020	–.028#	–.001	–.035*
	(–.057)	(–.130)	(–.023)	(–.053)	(–.044)	(–.067)	(–.003)	(–.074)
Church attendance	–.030**	–.005	–.022	–.017	–.023#	–.017	–.020#	–.006
	(–.113)	(–.015)	(–.060)	(–.047)	(–.071)	(–.024)	(–.070)	(–.017)
Catholic	.058*	–.130**	.062	.010	–.006	–	.025	–.102**
	(.059)	(–.107)	(.046)	(.012)	(–.007)		(.025)	(–.089)

continued on next page

Table 7. (*continued*) Predicting protest participation: global protest scale[a]

	United States	Italy	Great Britain	West Germany	Switzerland	Finland	Netherlands	Austria
Political identities								
Left party support	.046*	.140**	.067*	.072**	.066#	.096*	.077*	-.085**
	(.056)	(.154)	(.077)	(.087)	(.072)	(.123)	(.081)	(-.110)
Naive leftism	.014*	.020**	.005	.017**	.004	.024**	.032**	-.002
	(.091)	(.149)	(.032)	(.102)	(.029)	(.132)	(.210)	(-.014)
Sophisticated leftism	.034**	.031**	.018**	.023**	.026**	–	.048**	.013*
	(.209)	(.257)	(.135)	(.163)	(.199)		(.332)	(.105)
Conventional politics	.103**	.149**	.271**	.154**	.132**	.141**	.206**	.117**
	(.156)	(.252)	(.344)	(.244)	(.224)	(.212)	(.231)	(.193)
Constant	.698	.580	.345	.346	.686	.065	.566	.515
R^2	.317	.455	.365	.281	.302	.285	.306	.219
N	1,333	1,030	898	1,750	785	660	871	1,072

[a]Variables not shown: nonideologue dummy variable to index cases where mean value substitution was used for missing cases on the "naive leftism" variable; nonaligned dummy variable to index cases which were missing (and scored zero) on "left party support" variable.

[b]Unstandardized coefficients (standardized coefficients in parentheses).

** $P \le .01$, two-tailed test.
* $P \le .05$, two-tailed test.
# $P \le .10$, two-tailed test.

tarianization, stronger unions, and the persistence of an oppositional left party. Overall, however, class positions are not a powerful predictor of individual participation, explaining no more than 3 to 5 percent of the variance in the global protest scale.

Class identities exhibit only weak and irregular effects on global protest. Class identities have their strongest effect in the United States where working-, middle-, and upper-middle-class identifications all contribute to protest. Since the United States also has the highest level of nonclass identifiers, we think these results are more likely to reflect greater general awareness about social disadvantages than class consciousness per se. In Britain and West Germany, upper-middle-class identifiers are less inclined to protest, suggesting a conservative status consciousness. In Austria, working-class identifiers are protest prone, militating against the neocorporatist idea that the working class has been politically absorbed. Union membership is consistently positive but significant only in Britain and the Netherlands, attesting to the waning of the traditional working class as a vanguard of social protest. These are also countries in which wildcat strikes are popular and unions are organizationally strong, sustaining a basis for working-class militancy. Overall, these class factors are only modestly important, suggesting that other factors have been more central in creating contemporary protest participation.

The strongest factors are the postindustrialism-linked demographics. Men, the highly educated, and youth are more likely to protest. The simple gender coefficient was negative in all eight countries and significant in four, indicating that men are more protest prone (not shown). In Table 7, we show results after introducing a dummy variable for female independence; that is, for employed, unmarried women. Although this variable is not significant in any of the models for global protest, it is usually positive, as we would expect, and it tends to diminish the male protest advantage. In other words, the gender gap in protest participation is partly a result of women's traditional commitments and is narrowed when we look at the "new" women, supporting the postindustrialism thesis. More sophisticated measures of female independence might tend to diminish further, or even reverse, the gender gap in protest activism.

A higher level of education is consistently positive in all eight countries but significant in only four—the United States, West Germany, Finland, and Austria. By far the strongest demographic factor is age, which is consistently negative for all eight countries. The generational dummy variable is also positive but, net of the life cycle effect, significant only in Britain, Finland, and Austria. This does not discount the popular image of the rebellious under-thirty generation, but it does suggest that it was mainly rooted in life cycle changes that were perhaps exacerbated by generation-defining social tensions and up-heavals in the 1960s.

Religious identities play a significant role in the United States, Italy, and Austria and are modest elsewhere. In Italy and Austria, strong Catholic tradi-tions and church attendance work against protest. In the United States, reli-giosity and church attendance reduce protest; Catholics are more protest prone than non-Catholics. Supplementary analyses also revealed a strong negative effect of fundamentalist and evangelical Protestants in the United States, accounting in large part for the religiosity and church attendance ef-fects in that country. Church attendance is also negatively related to protest and significant in the United States, Switzerland, and the Netherlands. Fin-land is religiously homogenous, and the depillarization of the religious com-munities in Dutch society appears to have progressed sufficiently to weaken this basis of political contention, at least with regard to protest.

We found that religiosity consistently reduces protest participation, sig-nificantly in the United States, Italy, West Germany, Finland, and Austria. As expected, Catholic commitments produced mixed effects depending on the status of Catholics in the country. In the two countries where Catholics form a vast majority—Italy and Austria—Catholicism has significant negative ef-fects on protest. In the countries where Catholics form a minority, they are protest prone, but significantly so only in the United States, where ethnic Catholics have occupied an oppositional status in the labor movement, com-munity life, and electoral politics.

In additional analyses not shown here, we also tested the secularization ar-gument. Our first measure of secularism, which tapped persons who never at-tend church and do not consider themselves to be very religious (see Table 4, Panel B), showed a statistically significant positive effect on the global pro-test scale in six of the eight countries. The two exceptions, Britain and the Netherlands, can both be explained by special circumstances. In Britain, a high percentage of "secularists" are nominally Anglicans, the religious major-ity in that country. Their majoritarian status and their secularism crosscut each other, creating no net effect on protest. In the Netherlands, the depillar-ization of society has progressed so far that this group of secularists, by far the largest in our sample, does not differ substantially from the rest of the population on the protest question.

Our second measure of secularism, which taps the number of self-de-scribed atheists and adherents of "other" religions and those with no re-sponse, shows similar results. This second measure also yields significant positive effects on the global protest scale in six out of eight countries, this time excluding Italy and Austria, the two Catholic-dominated societies. Overall, one or both measures are strongly significant in each of the eight countries, yielding strong support for the argument that contemporary protest is rooted largely in the secularization of society.[13]

In additional analyses we also probed the impact of Protestant fundamentalists and evangelicals in the United States, Britain, and the Netherlands, where a significant number of these religious conservatives reside. Protestant fundamentalism negatively and significantly affected all forms of protest in the United States and Britain, the two majoritarian democracies, but showed no effects in secularized Netherlands, where, coincidentally, religious fundamentalists account for only about 9 percent of the population (see Table 4, Panel A). Combining these results with our findings for secularists, we find solid support for the contention that the cleavage between secularists and religious traditionalists is a potent source of contention in contemporary politics.

Several of the strongest protest factors stem from political identities. Leftist self-identification is a consistent source of protest; the strongest effects are in Italy, West Germany, and the Netherlands. Increasing ideological sophistication is also a source of protest: sophisticated leftists are consistently more protest prone than naive leftists. In five of these countries—the United States, Italy, West Germany, Finland, and the Netherlands—naive leftism is also a factor. Militating against the electoral dealignment thesis, leftism is consistently associated with left-party support, and both are sources of protest except in Austria, where only sophisticated leftists are protest prone. The left party is stronger in Italy and Finland, reflecting the strong oppositional traditions of the communist parties. In Austria, the Social Democratic Party has long been hegemonic, domesticating leftist protest and stirring up right-wing protest. To examine this phenomenon further, we looked at the "extremism" hypothesis that those on the ends of the political spectrum are the most protest prone. We derived a curvilinear version of the leftism scale to test the possibility that protest is higher at both extremes of the political spectrum (analyses not shown). Only in Austria was this pattern observed, supporting the contention that this is a contextual effect driven by the longstanding political strength of the Austrian Socialist Party (Table 3, Panel B). In this context, Austrian right-wing opposition has found expression in heightened protest levels that parallel their opponents on the left.

Finally, conventional activism is consistently one of the strongest protest predictors. The fact that routine political action is linked with the extraordinary and unconventional act of protest indicates that these two modes of political action are not mutually exclusive or even orthogonal. Rather, this strong and consistent finding points to an expansion of the political repertoire whereby social protest is regarded simply as "politics by other means," a strategy that complements, rather than supplants, conventional political action.

Several researchers have argued that contemporary protest movements are distinctive in their reliance on civil disobedience (Offe 1985b), so in Table 8 we analyze determinants for our civil disobedience scale. Some key results in Table 8 for religious identities and political identities virtually mirror those for the global protest scale in Table 7. Importantly, left-party support, leftism (both naive and sophisticated), and conventional politics remain as strong determinants of civil disobedience, as with the global protest scale. Since this is *not* true for the other two scales we analyzed, we conclude that the major variation in the global protest scale is attributable to its civil disobedience component. This is consistent with the claim that civil disobedience is a key dimension of the expanded political repertoires of citizens of the Western democracies.

There are, however, several important departures in the civil disobedience results compared to those of global protest shown in Table 7. First, West Germany joins Britain, Finland, and Austria as a country where the generational dummy variable (under thirty years old) has a positive effect on protest. West Germany's inclusion with this group probably reflects the emerging activism of youthful activists in a series of new protest movements—antinuclear, environmental, and women's movements—that practiced civil disobedience during the early seventies. Meanwhile, the life cycle effects of age remain negative and significant throughout all eight countries. The second key departure in the models for civil disobedience concerns the results for class structure. Confirming the new class thesis, we find that the new class is a carrier of the strategy of civil disobedience in six of the eight countries. Finland inexplicably departs from the other seven democracies in showing a negative effect of the new class on this scale; Austria's new class remains nonsignificant. The semiautonomous working class also is a statistically significant actor in three countries—Britain, West Germany, and Switzerland. The stronger results here for the new class and semiautonomous class support the contention that civil disobedience is linked to the conflict between autonomy and self-direction that citizens experience in their work roles and the encroachment of the forces of advanced capitalism on their quality of life. Third, working-class identifiers and union members are generally less likely to engage in civil disobedience, supporting the idea that it is a

Table 8. Predicting protest participation: civil disobedience scale[a]

	United States	Italy	Great Britain	West Germany	Switzer- land	Finland	Nether- lands	Austria
Demographics								
Gender (Females = 1)	-.056*[b]	.013	-.091**	-.029	.031	-.034	-.046	-.017
	(-.067)	(.012)	(-.096)	(-.033)	(.032)	(-.041)	(-.041)	(-.022)
Female independence								
(unmarried, employed women)	.030	.102*	.041	.070#	-.025	-.039	-.052	.007
	(.022)	(.052)	(.026)	(.040)	(-.017)	(-.031)	(-.027)	(.005)
Education	.004	-.010*	.006	.018**	.003	.019*	.005	.008
	(.029)	(.083)	(.026)	(.095)	(.021)	(.112)	(.024)	(.043)
Age	-.007**	-.005**	-.005**	-.005**	-.006**	-.005*	-.010**	-.004**
	(-.266)	(-.132)	(-.159)	(-.186)	(-.222)	(-.141)	(-.278)	(-.142)
Youth dummy (under 30 = 1)	.016	.062	.176**	.082*	.060	.177**	-.065	.110**
	(.017)	(.053)	(.162)	(.071)	(.060)	(.190)	(-.056)	(.114)
Class structure								
New class	.097*	.183**	.175*	.143*	.204**	-.181#	.171*	.039
	(.077)	(.094)	(.081)	(.071)	(.109)	(-.087)	(.081)	(.015)
Capitalists	-.078	-.042	.003	-.007	.134**	-.030	-.109	.050
	(-.043)	(-.023)	(.002)	(-.004)	(.114)	(-.027)	(-.043)	(.031)
Petty bourgeoisie	-.039	-.061	.190*	.002	-.030	-.011	-.029	-.023
	(-.018)	(-.040)	(.079)	(.001)	(-.012)	(-.003)	(-.012)	(-.021)
Upper managers	.013	–	-.004	.006	-.017	.043	-.003	.003
	(.008)		(-.002)	(.003)	(-.011)	(.028)	(-.001)	(.002)
Lower managers	-.042	-.013	-.062	.058#	.011	-.030	-.041	.113
	(-.030)	(-.011)	(-.046)	(.047)	(.009)	(-.020)	(-.029)	(.111)
Semiautonomous workers	-.015	-.034	.078*	.093**	.081*	.022	-.002	-.026
	(-.011)	(-.021)	(.065)	(.087)	(.076)	(.025)	(-.002)	(-.022)

continued on next page

Table 8. (*continued*) Predicting protest participation: civil disobedience scale[a]

	United States	Italy	Great Britain	West Germany	Switzerland	Finland	Netherlands	Austria
Class identities								
Upper middle class	.008	-.073	-.148	-.133**	.155	.165	-.134#	-.081
	(.006)	(-.032)	(-.042)	(-.079)	(.052)	(.053)	(-.060)	(-.051)
Middle class	.061*	-.058	.052	.016	-.045	.063	.029	-.050#
	(.057)	(-.044)	(.033)	(.018)	(-.037)	(.065)	(.021)	(-.059)
Working class	.049	.031	.023	.055*	.062	.027	.027	.024
	(.030)	(.029)	(.022)	(.053)	(.045)	(.032)	(.018)	(.029)
Union member	.018	-.007	.066*	-.050	.079*	.032	.056	–
	(.019)	(-.007)	(.073)	(.052)	(.079)	(.032)	(.049)	
Religious identities								
Religiosity	-.017*	-.094**	.023	-.024	-.000	-.019	-.001	-.021
	(-.039)	(-.152)	(.048)	(-.046)	(-.000)	(-.043)	(-.002)	(-.044)
Church attendance	-.037**	-.007	-.021	-.024*	-.019	-.016	-.026#	-.008
	(-.137)	(-.019)	(-.056)	(-.061)	(-.055)	(-.021)	(-.075)	(.026)
Catholic	.047#	-.120**	.041	.011	-.012	–	.019	-.093*
	(.048)	(-.083)	(.029)	(.012)	(-.013)		(.017)	(-.081)
Political identities								
Left party support	.054*	.129**	.125**	.084**	.074#	.099*	.078#	-.069*
	(.066)	(.120)	(.137)	(.095)	(.074)	(.120)	(.070)	(-.090)
Naive leftism	.020**	.038**	.009	.016*	.001	.026**	.043**	.001
	(.124)	(.241)	(.057)	(.092)	(.008)	(.140)	(.235)	(.006)
Sophisticated leftism	.035**	.048**	.015#	.019**	.018#	–	.057**	.011#
	(.209)	(.342)	(.102)	(.125)	(.128)		(.329)	(.085)
Conventional politics	.041*	.156*	.191**	.097**	.100**	.103**	.187**	.082**
	(.061)	(.223)	(.234)	(.143)	(.155)	(.148)	(.179)	(.136)

continued on next page

Table 8. (*continued*) Predicting protest participation: civil disobedience scale[a]

	United States	Italy	Great Britain	West Germany	Switzer-land	Finland	Nether-lands	Austria
Constant	.489	.522	.249	.221	.392	.035	.516	.392
R²	.212	.397	.270	.201	.199	.240	.250	.141
N	1,331	1,116	904	1,746	799	663	869	1,068

[a]Variables not shown: nonideologue dummy variable to index cases where mean value substitution was used for missing cases on the "naive left-ism" variable; nonaligned dummy variable to index cases which were missing (and scored zero) on "left party support" variable.
[b]Unstandardized coefficients (standardized coefficients in parentheses).
**P ≤ .01, two-tailed test.
*P ≤ .05, two-tailed test.
#P ≤ .10, two-tailed test.

"middle-class" protest tactic. Finally, in Italy and West Germany, "liberated" women who are employed and unmarried are significantly more likely than other women to participate in this type of protest.

One can best understand the results for global protest and civil disobedience by comparing them to our findings for legal unconventional actions on the one hand, and violent protest on the other (results available from the authors). We found, in general, that legal protests are viewed more favorably than other forms of protest within the working class. The new class, by contrast, is a much weaker supporter of unconventional legal strategies and is significant only in Switzerland. Similarly, the semiautonomous working class seems uninterested in legal actions, emerging as significant (at the .10 level) only in Finland. This reveals a sharp class differential in protest tactics: the working class favors legal measures like marches and boycotts and the new class endorses more confrontational strategies of civil disobedience that transcend legal boundaries.

Ideological orientations and party alignments were also weaker in predicting legal protest, meaning that these commitments have had a greater effect on support for the new civil disobedience tactics. Left-party allegiance is a strong predictor of legal actions only in Italy and the Netherlands. Sophisticated leftists remain strong in their endorsement of legal actions, but naive leftists show much weaker support for these tactics across the eight countries, indicating that, in several countries, the left is potentially divided over strategies as much as over protest objectives. Moreover, this division is not so much a result of ideology per se as it is of different levels of sophistication in ideological thinking. Conventional activism is also more strongly related to legal protest, suggesting that it is more in keeping with the routine of conventional politics. Education emerges as a strong determinant of legal actions, which indicates the powerful political socialization role of formal education.

As we noted earlier, violence is almost universally condemned. This is further reinforced by the much lower explained variances (between 3 and 8 percent) in our models of violent protest compared to other models as well as the largely indeterminant pattern of results for specific variables. Education fails to achieve significance in any of our eight countries, and the negative effect of age, one of the most consistent findings in all the other models, achieves minimal statistical significance (at the .10 level) in only three countries: the United States, Britain, and Switzerland. This finding qualifies our previous support for the life cycle hypothesis and suggests that the postindustrialist thesis of loosened social controls is not so elastic as to encompass violent tactics; the young typically join their elders in condemning more violent actions. On the other hand, the generational hypothesis is given qualified support; the political generation dummy is significant in the United States and Britain, indicating the militant state of the under-thirty youth culture in these two majoritarian countries during the early seventies.

Contrary to popular speculation, leftists generally failed to support violent tactics even during this turbulent period. Left-party ties are relevant only in the United States, suggesting greater support for violent tactics in the contentious politics of the post-McGovern-era Democratic Party, and only in West Germany did leftist identifications lead to violence. Conventional activism is not related to violence except in Italy and West Germany, where mainstream actors were willing to resort to militant tactics. In other words, there is a hierarchy of protest based on the departure from conventional activism; legal actions are the most continuous, civil disobedience is in between, and violence is the least related. Finally, class structure, class identities, and even religious identities are virtually unrelated to the degree of condemnation of violent tactics. Regarding the new class thesis, only the Italian new class endorses violent tactics, which is significant considering that this group failed to endorse unconventional legal actions.

Conclusions

Our analyses at both the macro and micro levels have revealed that none of the three images of social protest can be easily dismissed; rather, all three portraits are relevant to explaining the roots of contemporary protest in the Western democracies. The growth of the new class, the loosened social controls and new aspirations associated with postindustrialism, and neocorporatist influences on the changing system of political representation have all contributed to this upsurge of social protest. While working-class protest remains alive, there has been a general shift toward new types of action—civil disobedience—and to new groups of actors—the new class, youth, women, the better educated, and secularized supporters of modernism. The link between protest and social stratification may not be entirely inverted, but it has clearly undergone significant modification. Protest is no longer centered among those on the political margins or at the bottom of the class hierarchy but has become an accepted tool among groups that already have political standing. The standard interpretations of this protest wave are "overdetermined" in the sense that they typically posit a single dynamic or a structural change as its mainspring. We found instead that there is a broad set of loosely connected changes that has generated this political upsurge.

The new class is a significant source of protest, especially of civil disobedi-ence. This new class is not only better educated, more ideologically sophisti-cated, and less guided by traditional religious moralities, it is also more will-ing to experiment with new forms of political action. Its taste for civil disobedience sets it off from the working class, which favors older forms of legal protest like demonstrations and boycotts. Earlier portraits of this new class protest as indicating the making of an oppositional class that would be-come the vanguard of a major political transformation were seriously over-drawn (Touraine 1971; Gouldner 1979). Instead the new class appears to be a source of political experimentation driven more by an occupational culture that prizes self-direction and therefore political self-expression (Macy 1988; Jenkins and Wallace 1995). While this culture may create tensions between self-directed work and the requirements of the profit system, this tension does not appear to be a fundamental contradiction. Overall, these knowledge workers are but one of several groups that support the new protest move-ments (Kriesi 1989a).

The strongest structural sources of protest are associated with postindus-trialism, especially a new generation that is more open to political experimen-tation, major changes in the status of women, and the rise of secular outlooks. Earlier studies have emphasized the rise of a postmaterialist ethic, especially among youth, the better educated, and the more affluent (Inglehart 1990a). In line with these ideas, we found that the more educated, youth, and women who were employed and independent of traditional family responsibilities were more protest prone. Education increases political tolerance and boosts political efficacy, thus encouraging protest (Hall, Rodeghier, and Useem 1986). "Liberated" women were as prone to protest as men and sometimes more likely to experiment with civil disobedience, thus eliminating the tradi-tional gender gap in political participation. A life cycle argument about psy-chological changes and greater social investments over the life course ex-plains protest activism among youth better than a generational argument. Still, net of the overriding influence of age, the under-thirty generation re-mains resolute in its support for the tactics of civil disobedience in four coun-tries: Britain, West Germany, Finland, and Austria.

In an earlier age, religious differences were a central axis of political con-tention, giving rise to religious parties and social institutions to preserve reli-gious communities. In most of these countries, religion came to be as central as, if not more important than, class in defining the party system and the bases of political contention. Some have argued that the contemporary clash between religious traditionalists and proponents of secular morality defines a new axis of political division (Bell 1977). We found considerable evidence to support this view. Religious commitment as well as ties to conservative Catholic and Protestant traditions are sources of opposition to protest. Protest is greater in countries with more secularized institutions and among secular citizens. Yet it is not clear that this secularization process will create a new electoral alignment akin to the earlier clash between Protestant, Catholic, and secular populations. In the United States, for example, there are protest-prone Catholics, and in Britain religion is not a source of support for or opposition to protest.

The development of neocorporatism and associated changes in the political standing of labor have also altered the likelihood of protest. Neocorporatist bargaining strengthened the controls over labor relations and thus the likelihood of industrial conflict. The political incorporation of unions was a central part of this process, substituting bargaining and negotiation for open contention. In countries with a strong social democratic party and a centralized labor movement that was able to control plant-level bargaining, this process went further toward domesticating working-class protest. Pluralist countries where labor remained organized but politically weak or even excluded experienced greater protest. This did not, however, dramatically alter the overall potential for protest, which remained relatively high in several of the more neocorporatist countries. The Netherlands, for example, had a high level of protest potential despite less actual participation. In other words, neocorporatism had a greater impact on the actual expression of protest than on the underlying willingness to engage in it.

Several researchers have argued that electoral dealignment has weakened political controls and thus created a more volatile political system (Huntington 1982; Dalton, Beck, and Flanagan 1984). Although our data set predates the period in which the electoral dealignment thesis gained prominence, we found little evidence to support this contention. First, party loyalty remains fairly high in several of these countries, including in majoritarian systems, which have the greatest incentives for a blurring of ideological and party differences. While a considerable number of people are unable to locate themselves in left-right terms and lack party identification, it is not clear that their numbers represent a departure from an earlier period in which citizens held well-formulated ideological beliefs. In any event, these nonideologues appear to be no more or less inclined to endorse protest than more ideologically astute citizens. If we assume that educational levels and the growth of the new class are prevailing trends, the tendency toward ideological thinking may instead be on the increase. These are the groups that are the most likely to think abstractly about politics and, insofar as they are more prone to use general rubrics such as "left" and "right" to orient their political action, they may be becoming stronger sources of protest. Instead of an end to ideology, we may be witnessing a rebirth of ideological thinking with a new set of abstract themes and movement issues.

We used two complementary types of comparative analysis to capture these trends: a comparison of countries as *units* of analysis, and a comparison of countries as *contexts* for political action. The former highlighted the importance of neocorporatism and the changing position of organized labor, classes, and religious groups in these democracies. Several of these features are system-level properties that can be captured only with this method. This also paved the way for a microanalysis of the sources of individual protest that highlighted both uniformities and country differences in protest. The role of the new class, changes in women's status, generational changes, and shifts across the life cycle—much less ideological self-placement and party affiliations—could be identified only through an individual-level analysis. In this analysis, national characteristics define the political context in which these factors operate.

How durable are these trends? Judging by the second Political Action Project study, in 1980, protest participation has remained high in the United States, West Germany, and the Netherlands (Jennings and van Deth 1990). During the late 1970s and the 1980s, several of these countries experienced third-party challenges and further clashes between protesters and authorities. While they were not as tumultuous as those of the late 1960s and early 1970s, these events should have sustained the basic patterns that developed during the earlier wave of protest. Social protest has grown in the Western democracies, moving upward in the class hierarchy, building on a new generation, the growth in higher education, and the change in women's roles, and springing from the clash between religious traditionalists and secular modernists.

Notes

We benefited from the advice of Bert Klandermans, Susanne Schmeidl, and Elizabeth Cooksey; from the assistance of Omar Barriga and Kurt Schock in assembling the data; and from the financial support of the Research Foundation of Ohio State University.

1. The Political Action Project compared changing political participation and attitudes in Western democracies. The first-wave survey (conducted in 1973–76) dealt with eight countries; the second (conducted in 1979–81) was restricted to three countries (the United States, West Germany, and the Netherlands). We use as part of our data the first-wave sur-

vey because of its broader coverage. For a fuller discussion, see Barnes and Kaase (1979) and Kaase (1990b).

2. For an earlier treatment of these approaches, see Jenkins (1987).

3. We use as the measure of protest potential a battery of items that express willingness and past participation. This assumes that those who have participated in the past will continue to do so in the future. This is narrower than Barnes and Kaase (1979), who also include protest approval in their index. We think approval is too broad, indicating little about actual mobilization for action, and so focus on the measure that is premised on actual participation in protest.

4. Several analysts have created schemes for coding neocorporatism, and these schemes display remarkable agreement. Our approach is to combine these scores, creating the ordering of countries used in our figures and tables. This method represents a simple sum of the scores used by Schmitter (1981), Lehmbruch (1984, pp. 65–66), and Nollert (chapter 6 in this volume). For a fuller discussion, see chapter 6.

5. To create a comparable definition of the new class, we used higher education diplomas that produce similar labor market advantages and a curriculum that exposes students to the "critical discourse" of modern rationalism. This created the following definition of credentialed degree holding: bachelor's degree and above in the United States; upper middle and above, Italy; polytechnic, university, and postuniversity institute in Britain; Technikerschule, Ingenieurschule, and Universitaet in West Germany; University in Switzerland; semihigher and higher occupational study and graduate study in the Netherlands; and Fachschule, Handelsschule, Matura, and Abgeschlossene Hochschule in Austria.

6. Union density comes from the ILO (1977), class voting from Powell (1982, p. 90), and left-party governmental influence from Cameron (1984, pp. 159–60).

7. When we conducted reliability analyses on our four protest scales in the eight countries, we found that the Cronbach's alphas were in the acceptable range, all of them above .60. The alphas of each of the scales for each country are as follows: (1) *global protest scale*: United States .79, Italy .85, Britain .79, West Germany .81, Switzerland .79, Finland .79, Netherlands .82, Austria .79; (2) *legal unconventional protest scale*: United States .71, Italy .62, Britain .74, West Germany .74, Switzerland .69, Finland .73, Netherlands .69, Austria .66; (3) *civil disobedience protest scale*: United States .74, Italy .80, Britain .70, West Germany .81, Switzerland .74, Finland .72, Netherlands .74, Austria .78; (4) *violent protest scale*: United States .70, Italy .82, Britain .64, West Germany .73, Switzerland .60, Finland .64, Netherlands .66, Austria .80.

8. To evaluate the distinction between protest potential and actual participation, we also distinguished those who had actually participated from those who were simply willing, but found that these categories were virtually identical. The key difference was that younger people had greater protest potential but no greater actual experience. Since older respondents have had greater exposure to protest contexts, we interpret this as meaning that younger cohorts have greater protest potential while older cohorts have simply been more exposed to contexts that would convert potential into actual protest.

9. The union membership question is not available for the Austrian data since the question was not asked in the Austrian survey.

10. "Correct" images of leftism include those pertaining to the economic order (state control, worker participation), the social order (equality, elimination of hierarchy), reference to ideological movements (communism, socialism, radicalism), reference to social or political change, or mention of specific left parties. "Incorrect" images of leftism include idiosyncratic definitions like "good" or "bad," reversals in which the meaning is clearly in the wrong direction (e.g., "conservative"), or open admissions by respondents that they

don't know (see Table 6, Panel B). Similar criteria were used to discriminate between "correct" and "incorrect" definitions of rightism.

11. The questions about the meaning of *left* and *right* were not asked of Finnish respondents, so the distinction between "naive" and "sophisticated" leftists is not possible for the Finns. We collapse all respondents onto the "naive" leftism scale in the Finnish sample.

12. The Cronbach's alphas for the eight countries' conventional political activism scales are as follows: United States .81, Italy .87, Britain .75, West Germany .85, Switzerland .85, Finland .80, Netherlands .77, Austria .83.

13. Importantly, both measures of secularism showed their strongest effects in determining civil disobedience and were much weaker as a determinant of legal unconventional actions. This is consistent with the postindustrialist notion that secularization leads to a loosening of the social constraints that previously inhibited illegal actions such as civil disobedience. Further, our first measure of secularists also shows significant positive effects on violent protest in four countries—the United States, Italy, West Germany, and Austria—further underscoring this conclusion.

Chapter 6

Neocorporatism and Political Protest in the Western Democracies: A Cross-National Analysis

Michael Nollert

The idea that intermediate groups are a central factor in political stability has a venerable heritage. In the preface to the second edition of *De la division du travail social* (1986 [1893]), Emile Durkheim argued that strong intermediate groups were the most effective remedy for the increasing anomic tensions in modern society. Professional societies, unions, guilds, and community organizations would simultaneously regulate anomic tensions among individuals and restrain the increasingly powerful and centralized nation-state. In the 1950s proponents of mass society theory revitalized Durkheim's theory by arguing that pluralistic competition among strong interest groups mediated the relationship between individuals and the state, simultaneously reducing anomie and restraining elites. In the 1970s a new wave of political protest reinvigorated discussion of the relationship between interest groups and the state. Conservative proponents of an ungovernability thesis argued that interest groups had become too powerful, demanding too much from the state and thus making the Western democracies "ungovernable" (Crozier, Huntington, and Watanubi 1975). Excessive pluralism and societal demands were the source of the problem. In contrast, a leftist group of scholars blamed a legitimation crisis in which the liberal state was unable to simultaneously handle the increasing economic functions of late capitalism and address social demands (Habermas 1973; O'Connor 1973). Increasing state functions and weak state capacities were the source of the problem. Although they disagreed about the specific sources, these scholars agreed with the relative deprivation thesis (Gurr 1970) that there was an increasing imbalance between the population's political expectations and the capabilities of the state to address these expectations.

In response to this debate, Philippe Schmitter (1981) and others advanced a theory of *neocorporatism* emphasizing the social controls of a system of institutionalized bargaining between the state and encompassing associations of employers and workers. Noting that many Western democracies experienced little political protest while others were engulfed by political upheaval, Schmitter argued that the process by which the political expectations of the population were coordinated was a more important factor than the level of societal demands on public authorities or the lack of state capacities to satisfy these demands. Addressing the ungovernability thesis, he argued that the neocorporatist countries could contain political discontent more successfully than pluralist countries because they had devised a system of institutionalized bargaining between interest groups and the state. This system controlled the formulation of social demands, thus reducing political discontents. In contrast with the legitimation crisis thesis, it was not the new functions of the state but the ability to create and enforce a "social contract" between the various contending interests that reduced political discontent. In support, he presented cross-national evidence on the basis of fifteen Western democracies showing a strong negative correlation between the societal or "neo"corporatism and political unruliness.

In this study, I also argue that neocorporatism reduces the level of political protest. Yet, in contrast to Schmitter, I argue that it does so by reducing the gap between societal demands and state capacities. Specifically, neocorporatist countries have experienced better economic performance and reduced economic inequality, thus creating greater distributional equity and perceptions of reciprocity. To test this modified neocorporatism thesis, I extend Schmitter's original design, which relied on simple rank-order correlations, by using multiple regression. This also allows me to control for two possible sources of political conflict: world market integration and the governmental strength of the left party. Past work suggests that these two factors may simultaneously affect the mode of interest intermediation, macroeconomic performance, income inequality, and political conflict. But it is unclear precisely how these latter factors come to bear on political unrest. I therefore explore how they relate to neocorporatism as well as to political conflict.

While my main interest is the wave of protest that occurred in the Western democracies during the post-World War II period, we lack conflict data for the period after 1982. Evidence on income inequality prior to 1968 is also scanty. I therefore conduct two analyses: a descriptive trend analysis of the entire period 1948–82, and regression analysis of the 1968–82 period. It turns out that the post-1968 period displays greater differences between the pluralistic and neocorporatist countries. This suggests that the relationship between neocorporatism and political conflict is historically limited to periods of economic crisis, such as occurred in the post-1968 period.

First, I look at the conceptual discussions of the relationship between neocorporatist intermediation and political protest. I then turn to a cross-national analysis using the eighteen Organization for Economic Cooperation and Development (OECD) countries, looking first at a descriptive trend analysis of the entire post-World War II period and then at a regression analysis of the period after 1968. Finally, I use regression and scatterplots to evaluate the thesis that the effects of neocorporatism are mediated by better economic performance and lower levels of income inequality.

Interest Intermediation and Political Protest

In this section I elaborate my causal model, linking variations in political protest to the mode of interest intermediation via the mediation of macroeconomic performance and social inequality. First, I briefly review approaches to neocorporatism and then propose a classification of eighteen Western polities according to the major analytic dimensions of the concept. Next, I develop the argument that interest intermediation is indirectly linked to the level of political protest, because of the ability of neocorporatist polities to satisfy the population's claims for good macroeconomic performance and less social inequality.[1]

What Is Neocorporatism?

In recent years the concept of neocorporatism has had an impressive impact on comparative research on the Western democracies. Nevertheless, there is still no overall consensus on the defining traits of the concept. Hence, it seems appropriate to review the variety of different conceptual approaches to this "new" mode of interest intermediation. It is important to note that, although *neocorporatism* in general points out a reduction in importance of political parties in policy formation, the concept properly refers to a democratic mode of interest intermediation. Thus the prefix *neo* has often misled by linking the concept to a revival of medieval forms of authoritarian interest intermediation. To prevent this ambiguity, certainly it may have been better to label the democratic variant of corporatism "liberal" (Lehmbruch 1977), "societal" (Schmitter 1974), or "democratic" (Katzenstein 1985) corporatism and, vice versa, to label the authoritarian variant "authoritarian" (Lehmbruch 1977) or "state" (Schmitter 1974) corporatism.

Yet some of the major conceptual approaches neglect this trait of neocorporatism, for they refer the concept to the economic rather than to the political system. Thus, for instance, Panitch defined it as a "political structure within advanced capitalism which integrates organized socioeconomic producer groups through a system of representation and cooperative mutual interaction at the leadership level and of mobilization and social control at the mass level" (1979, p. 123). Starting from the assumption that the representation of economic interests is authoritatively condensed to "corporations" based on their members' economic functions, *neocorporatism* mainly refers to the integration of the labor movement into the process of economic policy formation. A similar formulation by Winkler (1976) refers to the function of the state in the economy. Impressed by the British conservative government's endeavor in the early 1970s to introduce income policies, he distinguishes corporatism from socialism, capitalism, and syndicalism on the basis of the two dichotomies, public versus private control and public versus private property. Thus Winkler defines corporatism as "an economic system in which the state directs and controls predominantly private-owned business toward four goals: unity, order, nationalism and success" (1976, p. 106).

The dominant approach, however, is Schmitter's (1974, 1981) conception of a monopolized and centralized system of interest organization within liberal democracies, of the state in policy in which the state formally designates and recognizes only a limited number of encompassing interest associations. This contrasts with pluralist polities where an unspecified number of "multiple, overlapping, spontaneously formed, voluntaristically supported, easily abandoned, and politically autonomous associations" (Schmitter 1981, p. 293) endeavor to influence public policy. Political parties and electoral polities have thus lost their dominant role as mediators of societal interests, but remain factors in the political system. Despite the fact that the process of incorporation of societal interests is mostly initiated by the state, neocorporatist interest intermediation is still democratic insofar as interest organizations represent societal rather than state demands.

A fourth approach treats neocorporatism as a tripartite decision-making structure, often labeled "concertation," that incorporates major associations representing interests of employers and workers (Lehmbruch 1977). In contrast to Schmitter's version, neocorporatism here differs from pluralism insofar as the function of parties as institutional mediators of interests and of noninstitutional pluralist lobbying is assumed to be undermined by the direct institutional incorporation of interest associations in policy formation and implementation. In sum, this approach suggests that in neocorporatist states,

Table 1. Classifications of countries according to different conceptual approaches

1a. Schmitter	1b. Lehmbruch	
1 Austria	Strong	Austria
2 Norway	corporatism	Sweden
3 Denmark		Norway
3 Sweden		Netherlands
3 Finland	Medium	Denmark
6 Netherlands	corporatism	Finland
7 Belgium		Belgium
8 Germany		Germany
9 Switzerland		Switzerland
10 Ireland		Ireland
10 Canada	Weak to no	United Kingdom
10 United States	corporatism	France
13 France		Canada
14 United Kingdom		United States
15 Italy		Italy

Sources: Schmitter 1981, p. 294; Lehmbruch 1985, p. 13.

the core of economic policy formation has shifted away from parliaments and their lobbies to exclusive places where a limited number of representatives of state and interest associations negotiate "political exchanges" (Pizzorno 1978) built on a consensus among the actors involved. Neocorporatist interest intermediation is also democratic, however, for the interest associations can exit and, after all, political parties in parliament often have to affirm the resulting policies.

This lack of consensus on the conceptualization of neocorporatism has given rise to various measures of the concept. My interest here is the political representation system. I therefore draw on Schmitter's fifteen-country rankings (1981) and Lehmbruch's three-category classification (1985) of policy formation and implementations. Table 1 shows how the major Western democracies are classified by these two schemes. To underline the disagreement, I have cross-tabulated fifteen polities according to both major conceptual dimensions. High degrees of centralization and monopolization of interest organization in Table 2 refer to those eight polities that cover in Schmitter's rankings (1981) rank 1 (Austria) to rank 8 (Germany). "Medium" refers to those three polities that rank 9 (Switzerland) to 10 (Ireland) plus Japan, whose system of interest organization is also medium centralized and monopolized (Pempel and Tsunekawa 1979). "Low" refers to those five polities covering rank 10 (Canada) to rank 15 (Italy) plus Australia and New

Table 2. A typology of polities according to the core dimensions of the concept of neocorporatism (n = 18)

Centralization and monopolization of interest organization						
high			3	Finland Belgium West Germany	1	Austria Sweden Norway Denmark Netherlands
medium			4	Ireland	2	Switzerland Japan
low	6	Italy United States Canada Australia New Zealand	5	France United Kingdom		
	low			medium		high
				Incorporation of interest associations in policy formation and implementation		

Zealand, whose systems of interest organization used to be classified as weakly monopolized and centralized (Czada 1983; Crouch 1985).

Turning to Lehmbruch's schemes, high involvement of interest organizations in policy formation and implementation refers to the four countries that are classified as strongly corporatist. In line with Katzenstein's (1985) classification, we also put Denmark, the "borderline case," Switzerland, and Japan ("concertation without labor") into this category. "Medium" then refers to four polities that Lehmbruch classifies as medium corporatist. In line with Czada (1983), we also put the United Kingdom and France into this category. Both polities distinctly show more corporatist elements than those polities in the remaining category "low," which are classified by Lehmbruch and, in the additional cases of Australia and New Zealand, by Czada (1983) as weak corporatist or pluralist.[2] As a result, Table 2 shows seven polities slightly deviating from the three diagonal cells containing those polities that are consistently classified. Thus, the polities of Japan and Switzerland, for example, are classified as highly corporatist if the concept of neocorporatism is restricted to institutional arrangements between the state and interest associations in policy formation and implementation. The associations incorporated in both polities, however, have neither a strong representational monopoly nor an impressive level of centralization. By contrast, interest organization in Finland, Belgium, and Germany is apparently more monopolized and more centralized than in Switzerland (see also Schmitter 1981, p. 294), whereas "concertation" in these three polities has been restricted to certain periods and singular policy sectors. Certainly, our classification does not end the debate on an adequate operationalization of neocorporatism. Nevertheless, Table 2 in general supports the consensus in the literature that Austria, Norway, and Sweden are the most highly corporatist of the eighteen polities, while the United States, Canada, Australia, New Zealand, and Italy are classified at the bottom of the rank order.

The Neocorporatist Control of Political Protest

According to Schmitter's (1981) arguments, polities classified as neocorporatist should have less protest than noncorporatist polities. Assuming political protest to be one general property of the concept of "ungovernability," he asserts that the "governability of contemporary, highly industrialized, advanced capitalist polities is less a function of aggregate overload, of 'imbalance' between the sum total of societal demands and state capabilities, than of discrete processes that identify, package, promote, and implement potential claims and commands" (p. 287).

This principal hypothesis contains at least two subhypotheses, which can be discussed separately. The first is that the shape of interest intermediation in general determines the level of protest that is discussed as a dimension of governability. The second is that the effect of interest intermediation is more important in explaining variations in protest than the gap between societal demands and state capabilities.

My aim here is not to contend with the first subhypothesis, for I generally agree with the view that interest intermediation is of major importance in explaining variations in political protest. My concern is why. Is it because of objective economic performance or the perceptions of various groups? I argue that the effect of interest intermediation on protest is indirect, passing through the gap between societal demands and state capabilities. Schmitter asserts that "the key of differing degrees of governability lies less in the 'objective' magnitudes of macroeconomic performance, social cleavages, and class relations than in the way differentiated interests are 'intermediated' between civil society and the state" (1981, p. 292).

This statement may now astonish, in the wake of the burgeoning literature of the 1980s on effects of neocorporatism on macroeconomic performance

(Crouch 1985; Katzenstein 1985; Schmidt 1986) and social inequality (Nollert 1990, 1992) on the one hand, and of the persistent debate on the linkage between social inequality and political protest on the other. Thus a plausible counterhypothesis is that neocorporatist interest intermediation contributes to a low level of protest exactly because it narrows the gap between societal claims for economic performance and social equity and the capacity of the state to satisfy these claims.

Two Paths from Neocorporatism to Lower Protest.   In fact, based on arguments derived from *rational choice* and *relative deprivation* approaches to the explanation of social conflict, we may suggest at least two causal paths indirectly linking neocorporatism with a low level of protest. Rational choice approaches (Pizzorno 1978; Przeworski and Wallerstein 1982; Lange 1984; Crouch 1985; Przeworski 1989) first lead us to expect that neocorporatist polities are more successful in satisfying societal demands for macroeconomic performance. According to this view, neocorporatism is a political exchange of power resources between trade unions, employers' federations, and state authorities. The unions' power is based on their ability to mobilize their members in support of or against business interests and state authorities, while the power of employers' federations is based on their members' ability to transfer capital across state borders. The power of the state derives from coercive resources and the ability to redistribute income and wealth. As to specific demands, unions are assumed to favor policies minimizing unemployment and maximizing wage increases, whereas employers' associations prefer low industrial and political protest, low inflation, low tax rates, and wage restraint. Finally, as Winkler suggests, the state is interested in the maintenance of social order, that is, political loyalty and sufficient monetary revenues.

In neocorporatism, these three major actors exchange their power resources to satisfy their interests. Thus protest restraint by unions, for example, is traded against employers' investments of capital and resulting increases in real wages. These aggregate political exchanges between the state, business, and labor should lead to low rates of inflation and unemployment, high growth rates, and a low level of industrial and political protest. During periods of economic crisis, neocorporatist polities should show higher economic performance, and this higher performance should lead to lower political protest. While many empirical studies support the neocorporatism-macroeconomic performance hypothesis on the basis of advanced Western capitalist countries (Crouch 1985; Katzenstein 1985; Schmidt 1986), the question of the effect of economic performance on political protest is controversial; in addition, it has been addressed mostly on the basis of world samples (Hibbs 1973; Parvin 1973; Sigelman and Simpson 1977; Jagodzinski 1983).

Although the rational choice perspective differs from Schmitter in claiming that trade unions gain real income increases and full employment for their members in exchange for their industrial and political protest restraint, it does not consider income distribution. It assumes that disadvantaged actors always prefer higher incomes and wealth to a more equal distribution of material resources. In consequence, one could argue that neocorporatism will perpetuate rather than reduce social inequality in the long run.

By contrast, considerable evidence suggests that protest also depends on economic distribution. Relative deprivation theory argues that disadvantaged actors will rebel against inequalities in the distribution of economic benefits. In contrast to the individualist concept of rationality in rational choice models, the sociological idea of "reciprocity," meaning that cooperation—however high its absolute value may be—is more probable the greater the balance between the receiving and giving of goods and services. Reciprocity is incompatible with grave social inequalities (Gouldner 1961; Mauss 1969; Moore 1978). Since corporatist polities should be characterized by lower levels of social inequality, they should thereby experience less protest.

My hypothesis that interest intermediation affects protest through the level of social inequality contradicts not only Schmitter's and the rational choice model, but also neo-Marxist ideas. Neo-Marxists argue that neocorporatism controls political protest coercively and is not compensated by material gains (Jessop 1979). My hypothesis is that the low level of protest reflects a satisfactory economic payoff to disadvantaged actors.

This hypothesis on the link between neocorporatism and social inequality has not been tested. At the same time, research on the inequality/protest hypothesis has not generated a consistent conclusion. Several studies (Russett 1964; Zwicky and Heintz 1982; Muller 1985; Muller and Seligson 1987) find evidence for the hypothesis. Others (Hibbs 1973; Parvin 1973; Zwicky 1989; Williams and Timberlake 1984) deny a direct link between income inequality and political protest. Some have argued that this means that individual discontent must be organized and mobilized to turn into collective protest (Tilly 1978). This is less likely the greater the inequality in political resources.

Moreover, there is the Thomas theorem that the subjective definition of the situation is independently important. Thus, bad economic performance and sharp social inequality must first be perceived before they turn into political discontent. Finally, the meaning of "social inequality" cannot be restricted simply to economic rewards. It refers also to mobility opportunities (Nollert

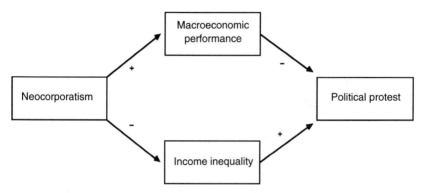

Figure 1. A causal model of neocorporatism, economic performance, income inequality, and political protest

1991) and to equal political rights according to the one (wo)man-one vote principle (Verba, Nie, and Kim 1978).[3]

A Causal Model.   Agreeing with Schmitter (1981), I argue that the key factor regulating protest is the political institutions through which demands are processed and that neocorporatist polities have lower levels of political protest because of their higher responsiveness to societal interests.

In conceptualizing neocorporatism as a political exchange resulting in a comparatively high economic benefit, however, and in assuming that, irrespective of the total benefit, actors accept a political exchange only if the benefits are reciprocally shared, I postulate two causal paths between neocorporatism and political protest. In contrast to both Schmitter's (1981) argument and F. L. Wilson's (1990) thesis that neocorporatism has directly fostered grassroots revolts, my model rejects a direct effect of neocorporatism on political protest, arguing instead for an indirect effect through economic performance and lessened inequality. My model differs insofar as it expects that the comparatively weak participants profit not only absolutely but also relatively from protest restraint. In contrast to rational choice theory, I argue that neocorporatism increases economic performance and thereby reduces protest. Contrary to neo-Marxism, I argue that neocorporatism reduces inequality and that greater inequality leads to protest. Finally, contrary to *resource mobilization theory*, I argue that neocorporatism reduces inequality and thereby lessens protest.

Because of problems in adequately measuring the degree of social inequality, I restrict my focus to income inequality. Furthermore, I ignore perceptions of social inequality, mobility, and political rights, assuming that these do not vary greatly among the Western democracies.

Finally, it is important to note that both causal paths linking interest intermediation and political protest in Figure 1 neglect the impact on protest of changes in levels of economic performance and income inequality. In other words, even a grave unequal distribution of the economic pie, for instance, may be tolerated as long as the slices of the pie grow and, vice versa, a reduction of the pie in absolute terms creates less unrest if the pie is equally distributed. Hirschman (1973) compares the impact of changes in economic growth and inequality on political protest to a traffic jam in a tunnel. If all drivers advance, he argues, there would be sufficient tolerance for increasing inequality. When economic improvement stops, however, the population will not tolerate significant inequality. Thus he expects the lowest level of protest at medium levels of inequality.

As to the historical range of my model, I argue that interest intermediation, macroeconomic performance, and social inequality matter more in periods of economic crisis. According to mainstream long-wave theories (Bornschier 1988), Western economies in general were prospering in the postwar era until 1968. Since then, most advanced liberal democracies have suffered increased unemployment, inflation, and declining growth. I therefore restrict my focus to the period after 1968, which long-wave theory sees as a period of economic stagnation.

A Cross-National Test of the Model

In this section, I test cross-nationally the causal paths between interest intermediation, macroeconomic performance, income inequality, and political protest among the eighteen OECD countries. Because of limited data on income inequality and the assumption that this model is more relevant during an economic downswing, the analyses are restricted to the 1968–82 period. First, I look descriptively at trends in protest to see if polities vary in levels of protest. Second, I use regression analysis to see if the hypothesized relations in Figure 1 are supported. Because data on income inequality are available for only thirteen polities, such an analysis is risky. Small samples tend to violate regression assumptions. Moreover, there were strong correlations between interest intermediation and both economic performance and income inequality, creating multicollinearity. Several outlying cases also biased the effect of income inequality on political protest. Thus, instead of testing the model on the thirteen countries for which complete data were available, I examined the effects of interest intermediation on economic performance and protest on the base of fifteen cases, and, second, through income inequality on the basis of thirteen cases. Since the correlation between levels of economic performance and income inequality is low (r = -.26; see Appendix), this seems like a valid procedure.

There are also arguments that the relationship between interest intermediation and political protest is spurious because of other factors. Cameron (1978) has argued that world market integration and strong left parties create contexts for both neocorporatism and economic growth. I therefore examine the simple correlations between interest intermediation and protest for the eighteen countries, and then control for world market integration and left-party strength in regression equations. A third section assesses whether the impact of interest intermediation on protest is direct or passes through cross-economic performance and income inequality. To avoid biased estimates resulting from small sample sizes, I use standard procedures to detect influential cases (Belsley, Kuh, and Welsch 1980; Cook and Weisberg 1982).

Political Protest across the Postwar Era: A Longitudinal Analysis

In this longitudinal analysis, I use the classification in Table 2. Since my arguments focus more on the interaction between the state and interest associations in policy formation and implementation, I rely on the columns.[4] Thus the polities in cells 1 and 2 of Table 2 are classified as neocorporatist, while the polities in cell 6 are classified as pluralist. Cells 3, 4, and 5 are treated as "medium."

To capture protest, I drew on Hibbs's (1973) typology to construct two indices: one representing *collective protest* is based on the number of antiregime demonstrations, political strikes, and riots; another representing *internal war* is based on the number of armed attacks, political assassinations, and political deaths. These data come from Taylor (1985) and are normed by the midinterval (1965) population in millions (Bornschier and Heintz 1979).

Figures 2 and 3 show trends in both protest indexes for the mean of the three types of polities (see Table 2) during the period between 1948 and 1982. Obviously, these findings support my hypothesis only for the period after 1968. Significantly, there is little variation in protest before 1960, and the medium corporatist states are often as unruly as the pluralist ones. In general, the empirical link between interest intermediation and protest varies across time. In terms of collective protest, the neocorporatist polities did not endure a wave of protest in the 1960s and 1970s. In fact, after 1960, protest de-

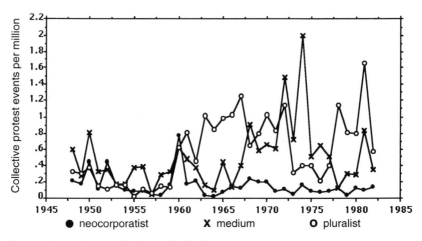

Figure 2. Interest intermediation and collective protest

clined slightly, while the pluralist polities experienced an increase. Between 1972 and 1977, however, the medium countries experienced the highest protest. A similar picture is reported by the internal war index. I report a natural logged function because of a skewed distribution. As expected, the neocorporatist polities have less internal war, especially after 1968. There are three noteworthy differences, however. First, internal war differences are stronger in the 1970s. Second, the neocorporatist polities experience a slight level of internal war in the 1960–82 period. Third, the medium polities have the highest levels of internal war. This is a result of including the United Kingdom and Ireland; their conflict does not stem from producer groups and therefore does not really deny the neocorporation hypothesis.

In general, this finding supports the contention that the neocorporatist polities have been immune to the governability and legitimation crises. Moreover, interest intermediation appears to have had a stronger effect during economic stagnation. Third, these trends suggest long cycles in interest intermediation and the level of protest.

This idea of long-wave-driven cycles of protest is also supported by earlier periods of economic crisis. In the late 1920s a world economic crisis paved the way for a variety of authoritarian and democratic modes of corporatist interest intermediation. In Germany, there was the authoritarian Volksgemeinschaft-Regime. In Sweden the Folkhem-Regime and in the United States the National Recovery Administration offered liberal variants of corporatism. Overall, it seems more appropriate to label the 1930s the decade of corpo-

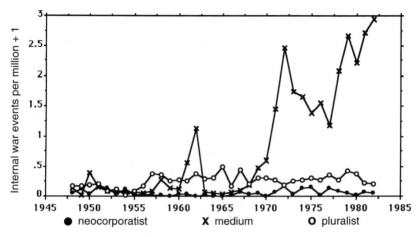

Figure 3. Interest intermediation and internal war

ratism than to affirm Schmitter's (1974) idea that we still live in the "century of corporatism."

Interest Intermediation and Political Protest, 1968–82

Next I turn to a regression analysis of protest during the 1968–82 period. First I have to consider changes in the mode of interest intermediation during this later period. There is only one case to reclassify. As Helander (1982) has noted, Finland shifted in the late 1960s from pluralism to neocorporatism after the electoral victory of the Social Democratic Party in 1966. I therefore put Finland in the neocorporatist category. I use two dummy variables—neocorporatism and pluralism—to capture the three types of interest intermediation (neocorporatism, medium, and pluralism). Neocorporatism is coded 1 for the seven polities previously classified as neocorporatist plus Finland and 0 otherwise, while pluralism is coded 1 for the five polities classified as pluralist.

Second, I use factor analyses to examine the dimensionality of the six conflict indicators. In contrast to the two-factor structure for the 1948–82 period, the 1968–82 period showed a three-factor structure, suggesting a separation of demonstrations from riots and political strikes.[5] Consequently, I used three indices: (1) *moderate protest*, based on political strikes plus riots, (2) antiregime *demonstrations*, and (3) *internal war* events. Each is summed for 1968–82 and divided by midinterval (1975) total population in millions (Bornschier and Heintz 1979). Because of their strong skewedness, all three indicators are expressed as natural logarithms (after adding an increment of one).

Table 3. Correlations between modes of interest intermediation and political protest dimensions (n = 18)

	Internal war	Moderate protest	Demonstrations
Neocorporatism	−.57	−.65	−.55
Pluralism	−.19	.10	.13

Table 3 shows that the bivariate correlations confirm the conclusion derived from Figures 2 and 3. Neocorporatism is linked to all three types of protest, while pluralist polities do not differ from neocorporatist and medium polities. While all coefficients for the neocorporatism dummy are significant at the .05 level (one-tailed test), there are no significant relations between the pluralism dummy and the three protest dimensions.

These could be spurious relations, however. From other work, we know of two possible factors that could affect both neocorporatism and protest: strong left parties and a high level of world market integration.

First, I turn back to the rational choice approach, according to which all participant actors in social systems principally try to minimize their individual cost-benefit ratio. Neocorporatism is conceptualized as a political exchange between the state and major interest associations. Since the reward for sacrifices may be a medium- to long-term process, however, private interest associations are assumed to cooperate with each other and with the state only if the state's coercive potential prevents them from refusing long-term returns. Hence trade unions distrust state authorities in general, especially if the government is dominated by business interests. In consequence, they more readily accept a long-term exchange if the government is controlled by parties of the left. Concretely speaking, unions are more likely to exercise wage restraint if left parties in the government reward their members by redistributive fiscal and social policies. A second argument is that employers' federations find it risky to pursue their objectives in the face of a strong labor movement simply on the base of parliamentary decision making. To prevent harsh protests against bourgeois policies, it is necessary to consider unions' interests in preparliamentary policy formation.

Second, there is the view that left-party strength is directly linked to political protest. Thus one can argue that strong left parties are linked to lower protest as a result of their redistributive efforts. On the other hand, one can argue that, where left parties are strong in public decision making, overt protest has lost its function as a strategy to influence policy formation on behalf of the lower classes. In sum, a strong left party should lead to both neocorporatism and a low level of protest. I therefore include the mean left party participation in the cabinet from 1946 to 1976, derived from Korpi and Shalev (1979), as a control variable.

A second argument, stemming from world system theory, says that inter-state relations explain both the emergence of neocorporatism and low levels of political protest as a result of world market constraints on nation-states (Bornschier 1988).

Cameron (1978) argues that a high level of economic openness promotes neocorporatist cooperation by increasing industrial centralization and help-ing to unify and strengthen the political representation of unions. Katzenstein (1985) argues that neocorporatism is a strategy to resist the constraints of world markets.

A similar argument that also leads to a direct linkage between world mar-ket constraints and political protest derives from Simmel as revitalized by Lewis Coser's *The Social Functions of Conflict* (1956). Coser's propositions 9 and 10 suggest that the structure and coherence of a social group, and the mode of regulating internal conflicts, are strongly determined by conflicts with outgroups. Translated in terms of theories conceptualizing the world economy as a competition between nation-states of different power capabili-ties, these propositions imply that economic dependence and military weak-ness are inversely correlated with social protest. As "dependence" principally points to a reduction in the number of options open to an actor, small states, which are highly integrated into world markets, should be less able to afford political protest than strong states. Thus, in contrast to the economically less vulnerable major powers, their moderate power capabilities prevent them from compensating an economic decline by military interference. To secure the willingness of the population to defend the country, small states have to attend to the population's demands for economic performance and equality.

The argument that a nation-state's international power capability deter-mines its range of policy options also draws on the view of John Hobson, a contemporary of Simmel, who hypothesized that world market competition would induce elites in small, weak countries to limit social inequality, hence reducing protest. In his study entitled *Imperialism* (1961 [1902]), he asserted that major powers would decline economically in the long run because of protest against their policies, while minor powers would adopt policies to boost economic growth. He wrote:

> A nation may either, following the example of Denmark or Switzerland, put brains into agriculture, develop a finely varied system of public education, gen-eral and technical, apply the ripest science to its special manufacturing indus-tries, and so support in progressive comfort and character a considerable popu-

lation upon a strictly limited area; or it may, like Great Britain, neglect its agriculture, allowing its lands to go out of cultivation and its population to grow up in
towns, fall behind other nations in its methods of education and in the capacity
of adapting to its uses the latest scientific knowledge, in order that it may squan-
der its pecuniary and military resources in forcing bad markets and finding
speculative fields of investment in distant corners of the earth, adding millions
of square miles and of inassimilable population to the era of the Empire. (p. 93)

To confront these hypotheses with the causal model, I include the participation of left parties in government and the level of economic openness, measured by the export of goods and nonfactor services as a percent of the gross
domestic product circa 1970 (Bornschier and Heintz 1979, pp. 88ff.), in the
multiple regression model.

Table 4 shows that the effect of neocorporatism on protest is not reduced
if the openness of the economy and the political orientation of the government are controlled. It also suggests that the effect of interest intermediation
is greater the more unruly the protest. In addition, the control variables have
no effects. Since both control variables are correlated with neocorporatism
(export ratio $r = -.44$ and left strength $r = .55$), it appears that the effects of
both economic openness and left-party strength pass through the mode of interest intermediation.

Indirect Effects of Neocorporatism

Next, I turn to the question of whether neocorporatism's effects on protest
pass through economic performance and income inequality. Unfortunately,
my indicator of income inequality covers only thirteen countries, while my
economic performance indicators cover eighteen countries. Since there is association between income inequality and economic performance ($r = -.26$, n =
13 ; see Appendix), I conduct two analyses with slightly different samples.

Effects through Macroeconomic Performance.   According to the causal model, I expect the bivariate associations between neocorporatism and political
protest reported in Table 3 to decline in a multivariate test design, controlling
for the effect of macroeconomic performance. Vice versa, I expect the bivariate relation both between neocorporatism and macroeconomic performance
and between the effect of macroeconomic performance and protest to be significant.

Since there may be trade-offs between major macroeconomic objectives
(Hibbs 1977), it is not appropriate to measure the overall level of macroeco-

Table 4. Regression of political protest dimensions on neocorporatism, controlling for world market integration and left party participation in government

	Internal war		Moderate protest		Demonstrations	
	3a	3b*	3c	3d**	3e	3f***
Intercept	1.71	1.66	1.032	.925	1.65	1.76
Neocorporatism	−1.954	−1.657	−.816	−.553	−.819	−.591
	(.01)	(.00)	(.00)	(.01)	(.02)	(.03)
	−.67	−.73	−.69	−.59	−.58	−.55
Export/GDP	.029	.033	.005	.007	.005	.12
	(.19)	(.07)	(.35)	(.23)	(.38)	(.18)
	.22	.33	.09	.17	.08	−.24
Strength of the left	.002	−.006	.0003	−.005	.0005	.004
	(.44)	(.30)	(.48)	(.16)	(.50)	(.24)
	.04	−.13	.01	−.25	.002	.19
Adjusted R²	.23	.47	.31	.40	.17	.22
N	18	16	18	17	18	17

Note: Probability of t-ratios is in parentheses, standardized coefficients in italics.
[a]Unstandardized coefficients.
[b]T-ratios.
[c]Standardized coefficients.
*United Kingdom and New Zealand excluded.
**United Kingdom excluded.
***Ireland excluded.

nomic performance by focusing on growth, on inflation, or on unemployment rates. Additive indexes like the misery index (Schmidt 1986) or simply adding absolute inflation and unemployment rates also do not adequately solve this problem because they neglect growth rates and do not distinguish between 5 percent inflation and 5 percent unemployment. Hence, I have constructed an index of macroeconomic performance using the economic growth rate as well as inflation and unemployment rates. I first z-standardize the average rates of inflation, unemployment, and economic growth rate per year during the 1968–82 period. Since a high growth rate indicates high macroeconomic performance, while high inflation and unemployment rates indicate a poor one, I use the negative of the z-standardized inflation and unemployment rates. Finally, the three values are summed up for each of the eighteen polities. According to the resulting values, Japan has shown the best macroeconomic performance (value of +3.9) between 1968 and 1982, whereas the United Kingdom shows the lowest (-2.7).[6]

Because of the low correlations between pluralism and each of the three

Table 5. Regression of political protest dimensions on macroeconomic performance 1968–82, controlling for neocorporatism

	Internal war 4a	Internal war 4b*	Moderate protest 4c	Moderate protest 4d*	Demonstrations 4e	Demonstrations 4f**
Intercept	2.26	2.07	1.004	.0945	1.557	1.468
Neocorporatism	-1.13^a	-1.353	$-.45$	$-.46$	$-.32$	$-.305$
	$(.05)^b$	$(.02)$	$(.05)$	$(.02)$	$(.17)$	$(.12)$
	$-.45^c$	$-.58$	$-.38$	$-.48$	$-.22$	$-.29$
Macroeconomic performance	$-.15$	.017	$-.145$	$-.09$	$-.21$	$-.15$
	$(.24)$	$(.46)$	$(.02)$	$(.07)$	$(.01)$	$(.03)$
	$-.19$	.03	$-.46$	$-.34$	$-.56$	$-.49$
Adjusted R^2	.26	.23	.50	.47	.44	.40
N	18	17	18	17	18	17

Note: Probability of t-ratios is in parentheses, standardized coefficients in italics.
*United Kingdom excluded; **Ireland excluded.
[a]Unstandardized coefficients.
[b]T-ratios.
[c]Standardized coefficients.
*United Kingdom and New Zealand excluded.
**United Kingdom.

protest indicators, reported in Table 3, I restrict my focus to the multiple regressions of the three logged protest dimensions (internal war, moderate protest, demonstrations) on neocorporatism and the level of macroeconomic performance. If the effect of neocorporatism on political protest passes through macroeconomic performance, this should indicate significant effects of macroeconomic performance but *no* significant effects of neocorporatism.

First, it is noteworthy that the bivariate correlation between neocorporatism and macroeconomic performance is, in fact, high (r = .61, n = 18; see Appendix). This finding supports the view that neocorporatist polities were economically more successful in the 1968–82 period. As Table 5 shows, the significant effects of neocorporatism on protest indicators do not consistently vanish if macroeconomic performance is controlled. Indeed, the effect of neocorporatism on demonstrations decreases, while the effect of macroeconomic performance is significant. By contrast, the effects of neocorporatism on internal war and on moderate protest are still significant at the .05 level (one-tailed test). In contrast to the internal war, the results on moderate protest also indicate a significant impact of macroeconomic performance.

In sum, the results in Table 5 only partially support our expectations. The effects of neocorporatism on demonstrations passes through macroeconomic performance, but those are direct effects on the more militant forms of action. For both moderate protest and internal war, neocorporatism affects both level of protest and level of macroeconomic performance.

Effects through Income Inequality.   The causal model predicts that the impact of neocorporatism on political protest also passes through reducing the degree of income inequality. Therefore, I consider in detail the linkages between these three variables. First, however, I look at a multivariate regression of income inequality on neocorporatism, controlled for the often mentioned forces of world market integration (Hobson 1961 [1902]; Cameron 1978; Katzenstein 1985; Bornschier 1988) and the strength of left-party participation in government (Parkin 1972, 1979; Jackman 1975; Hewitt 1977; Dryzek 1978; Stack 1979).[7]

Since my arguments focus on personal inequality in disposable income, this empirical test refers to data on income distribution after direct taxes and social transfers circa 1970 (Sawyer 1976). Although there is no consensus among economists regarding the question of how to measure adequately the overall size of income inequality (Allison 1978), I use the Gini coefficient of the "secondary" or post-tax and transfer payment of household incomes. Since my analysis refers to highly developed countries, it is not a problem that the Gini coefficient is more sensitive to inequality in the middle than at the top or bottom of the distribution.

Table 6 shows that there is no evidence that either the export ratio or the political orientation of the government directly affects income inequality. Nevertheless, since the export ratio and the strength of the left correlate with the neocorporatism dummy ($r = .43$ and $.55$; see Appendix), these results suggest that leftist claims for equality and the constraints of world markets pass through neocorporatist arrangements.

The strength of the effect of neocorporatism on the level of income inequality depends, however, on the inclusion of Australia, which has a low level of income inequality despite the absence of neocorporatism, a moderate export ratio, and bourgeois hegemony in the government after World War II. In consequence, it is no surprise that the parameter estimates from regression model 5b, which excludes Australia, indicate a stronger effect of neocorporatism than those in model 5a. From the discussion of the distribution data in Sawyer (1976), we know that variations in household size distort levels of income inequality. Because the unstandardized data for Australia probably underrepresent the number of one-person households, the degree of income inequality may be understated. By contrast, the data for the Netherlands and

Table 6. Regression of income inequality on neocorporatism, controlling for world market integration and left-party participation in government

| | Gini coefficient after direct taxes and social transfers | |
	5a	5b*
Intercept	.38	.39
Neocorporatism	−.045[a]	−.054
	(.04)[b]	(.01)
	−.55c	−.65
Export/GDP	−.0005	−.001
	(.32)	(.20)
	−.12	−.20
Strength of the left	−.0003	−.0002
	(.25)	(.18)
	−.20	−.14
Adjusted R^2	.41	.60
N	13	12

Note: Probability of t-ratios is in parentheses, standardized coefficients, in italics.
*Australia excluded.
[a]Unstandardized coefficients.
[b]T-ratios.
[c]Standardized coefficients.

Sweden overrepresent the number of one-person households. Thus, the results of equation 5b are less biased than the results of equation 5a.

According to my specification of the interest intermediation/protest hypothesis (Figure 1), a further analysis would ask whether income inequality mediates the effect of neocorporatism on political protest. Unfortunately, multicollinearity due to the strong link between neocorporatism and the income inequality ($r = .71$) prevents us from testing this hypothesis in multiple regression. Therefore, we have to rely on the correlations between neocorporatism, inequality, and the political protest indicators. Because of the sensitivity of correlation coefficients based on small sample sizes to outlying cases, and to test Hirschman's (1973) hypothesis of a U pattern between income inequality and protest, I use scatterplots (Figures 4 to 6). Although the protest indicators are expressed as natural logarithms, scatterplots on those thirteen countries for which reliable data on income inequality is available indicated that the United Kingdom and Ireland are influential outliers. Both polities show extraordinarily high levels of political protest between 1968 and 1982, reflecting the spillover from the Northern Ireland conflict (Figure 3). Therefore, the three scatterplots refer to only eleven countries, in which the neocorporatist polities are marked by squares.[8]

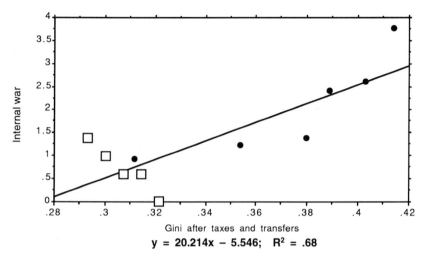

$$y = 20.214x - 5.546;\quad R^2 = .68$$

Figure 4. Income distribution and internal war

Figure 4 shows that there is strong empirical evidence (r = .82) that level of internal war is considerably lower the more equal the disposable income (r = .82). However, the Netherlands, with the lowest overall income inequality (Gini of .29), and Finland, with no internal war events, deviate from the pattern. Thus, an ex post facto interpretation of the scatterplot supports Hirschman's hypothesis predicting the lowest level of protest at medium level of inequality. As Figure 5 shows, income inequality is correlated less with demonstrations (r = .57). There are several outliers, indicating a moderate link between income inequality and demonstrations. As for moderate protest, there is a strong relation (r = .84), with less protest in more equal societies. Moderate protest in the form of political strikes and riots follows a pattern similar to that of internal war events.

Overall, these results support the relative deprivation theory that less inequality reduces protest. This is more true of internal war and moderate protest than of demonstrations. At the same time, neocorporatism is less strongly related to protest (internal war: r = -.65; moderate protest: r = -.74) but is strongly related to inequality (r = .79; n = 11), suggesting that part of the reason for lower protest in neocorporatist polities is their lesser inequality.

Conclusion

In this study, I have contended that neocorporatism reduces political protest primarily by increasing economic performance and reducing the degree of

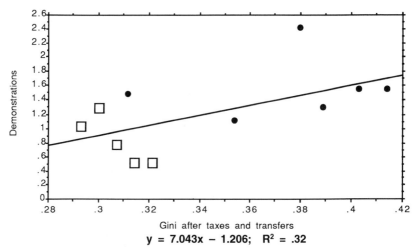

$$y = 7.043x - 1.206; \quad R^2 = .32$$

Figure 5. Income distribution and demonstrations

income inequality. In other words, I argue that the pluralistic states have experienced a wave of protest because they have failed to accommodate societal interests, creating a larger gap between societal expectations and these two dimensions of economic performance. At the same time, this gap is not symptomatic of late capitalism or a governability crisis in all Western democracies. States that have forged a strong social contract through the development of corporatist bargaining between encompassing national associations of capital and labor and top governmental officials have been relatively immune to outbreaks of protest and violence. This is especially the case for internal war and the more militant forms of protest. It is also especially relevant during the economic downturn of the 1970s. Prior to 1968, there was little difference between pluralistic and neocorporatist polities and, in general, there is little difference throughout this period between pluralistic states and the moderate neocorporatist regimes. Only fully developed neocorporatism appears to have a significant dampening effect on protest.

Yet the evidence for my modified version of Schmitter's neocorporatism thesis is not consistently supported. In using regression to examine the effects of neocorporatism on protest, I found that neocorporatism also directly suppresses the more militant forms of protest regardless of the degree of income inequality and economic performance. In other words, the neocorporatist effect is not strictly an indirect one, mediated by these intervening performance factors, but is also direct. Neocorporatism appears to give rise

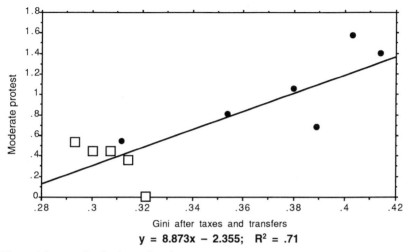

$$y = 8.873x - 2.355; R^2 = .71$$

Figure 6. Income distribution and moderate protest

simultaneously to both better economic performance and lower income inequality as well as directly reducing political protest.

These findings run counter to the rational choice thesis that protest is simply a response to short-term economic performance. Neocorporatism does improve economic performance, but it also sustains a commitment to reciprocity as a norm guiding economic distribution that cannot be reduced to the actual distribution of reward. In other words, there is a normative component above and beyond the factual distribution. The findings also militate against the neo-Marxist thesis that neocorporatism is simply a matter of stronger coercive suppression of interests. Neocorporatist polities do experience better performance as measured by economic growth and narrower income distribution.

I found some evidence to support the thesis that neocorporatism is a product of strong left parties and economies that are integrated into the world economy. As Cameron (1978) and Katzenstein (1985) have argued, these exogenous forces have helped to foster a willingness to forge a "social contract" and to abide by its terms, thereby boosting economic performance and reducing the degree of inequality.

It is important to keep in mind that these conclusions pertain to a specific phase of world history. During the immediate post-World War II period, there was no protest difference between pluralistic and neocorporatist polities. The link between interest intermediation and political protest may not exist during periods of prosperity. To use Hirschman's (1973) phrase, when "all dri-

Appendix

Correlation matrix of variables considered in the analyses
(n = 18 above the diagonal, n = 13 below the diagonal)

	Gini Income	Neocorporatism	Pluralism	Export/ GDP	Strength of the left	Macroeconomic performance	Internal war	Demonstrations	Moderate protest
Neocorporatism	-.71	1	-.56	.37	.53	.59	-.57	-.55	-.65
Pluralism	.30	-.53	1	-.51	-.42	-.43	-.19	.13	.10
Export/GDP	-.44	.43	-.48	1	.35	.12	-.01	-.13	-.16
Strength of the left	-.55	.55	-.45	.40	1	.11	-.24	-.28	-.32
Macroeconomic performance	-.26	.61	-.40	-.00	.14	1	-.46	-.69	-.68
Internal war	.43	-.64	-.17	-.01	-.17	-.60	1	.69	.90
Demonstrations	.35	-.66	.12	-.08	-.25	-.77	.74	1	.78
Moderate protest	.46	-.70	.09	-.13	-.27	-.72	.94	.80	1

vers advance," there is little impetus to protest. Neocorporatism also appears to be historically limited to countries that have strong left parties and face powerful international market competition, and possibly to those with specific political heritages (including small size) that have discouraged open class contention. Future research should address the barriers to corporatist bargaining and the reasons that some states have adopted neocorporatist arrangements while others have persisted in pluralistic arrangements despite the cost in lower economic performance and conflict.

Notes

1. In this paper, I ignore the debate on the link between income inequality and economic performance. Contrary to the common conviction that a more equal distribution of material goods is associated with economic inefficiency, I see no reason to focus the possible inefficiencies of redistributive policies. Although I do not deny, in principle, the possibility that the expansion of the public economy may lead to economic inefficiency, I find at least two reasons to reject the common conviction that an equalization of life chances would require an increase in state expenditures.

First, both theoretical plausibility and empirical evidence support the argument that state expenditures yield redistributive returns that favor upper as well as lower income groups (Olson 1982). Therefore, we would certainly need to examine whether social expenditures, which redistribute income in favor of lower income groups (Sawyer 1976), reduce economic performance, as opposed to other forms of state expenditures (Korpi 1985).

Second, there is no plausible reason to restrict the discussion of state activity to the monetary dimensions of revenues and expenditures, since the state can affect the distribution of material goods simply by redistributing income and opportunities for wealth (Parkin 1979). Taiwan and Japan, for example, have achieved by direct intervention a degree of inequality in disposable income approaching the postfiscal Western European distributions. In addition, we must recognize that Japanese plant unions have always been more interested in limiting primary income differentials than in measures to redistribute disposable incomes. In sum, it is plausible that neocorporatism has generated low political protest by equalizing the distribution of disposable income by welfare state measures and by limiting the inequality in primary incomes.

2. For further details on the measurement, see Nollert (1992, chapter 7).

3. The idea that social mobility and political protest are linked has a venerable history. Plato argued in *Politeia* that the stability of political order can be maintained only if the social status quo allows some social mobility. Some centuries later, this hypothesis was revitalized by Marx, Pareto, and Sorokin. Although their political values differed fundamentally, each claimed that societies heightened their legitimacy if the ruling class supported social exchanges between classes. Upwardly mobile people were assumed to internalize the political values of the class of destination (Lipset and Bendix 1959, pp. 70–71), and social mobility undermined solidarity among members of excluded social groups. In addition, democratic structures, indicating a high level of realization of the one man-one vote principle, generate less violence because each citizen has the opportunity to articulate discontent at the polls (Lipset 1960). While the social mobility thesis has never been tested at the macro level because of a lack of comparable data, most cross-national studies on political equality suggest that democratization is linked to lower levels of political violence, but higher levels

of collective protest (Flanigan and Fogelman 1970; Williams and Timberlake 1984; Muller and Seligson 1987).

4. For a critical assessment of other classifications, see Nollert (1992).

5. For the detailed findings, see Nollert (1992).

6. For further details on the operationalization and a listing of the values, see Nollert (1992).

7. The level of economic development, proposed as a determinant of income inequality by Kuznets (1955), is not included because of lack of empirical support in the sample of developed Western countries (Nollert 1990).

8. From left to right: Netherlands, Sweden, Norway, Australia, Japan, Finland, Canada, United States, West Germany, Italy, France.

Part III

The Structure of Political Opportunities: Protest and Electoral Politics

Chapter 7

The Political Opportunity Structure of New Social Movements: Its Impact on Their Mobilization

Hanspeter Kriesi

The crucial contention of the so-called political process approach to social movements is that social processes impinge indirectly, via a restructuring of existing power relations, on social protest (McAdam 1982). This contention has received considerable support from Skocpol's (1979) analysis of social revolutions. As she has shown, social revolutions are typically triggered by a political crisis that weakens the control exercised by the political system on the population. Similarly, the analysis of a century of collective violence in France, Germany, and Italy by Tilly et al. (1975) has indicated that the rhythm of collective violence did not so much depend on structural transformations of society, but was directly linked to shifts in the struggle for political power. More recently, the political context has also been shown to be of considerable importance for the mobilization and the impact of different types of new social movements. Thus, in what has probably been the first systematic study of the impact of the political context on the fate of a new social movement, Kitschelt (1986) has shown how the impact of the antinuclear movement varied according to specific characteristics of the political context of the countries he studied.

For the systematic analysis of the political context that mediates structural conflicts given as latent political potentials, the notion of "political opportunity structure" has become fashionable. First introduced by Eisinger (1973), it has been elaborated by Tarrow (1983, 1989b). As originally defined by Tarrow (1983, p. 28), the concept has three dimensions: the degree of openness or closure of formal political access, the degree of stability or instability of political alignments, and the availability and strategic posture of potential alliance partners. In his more recent conceptualization, Tarrow (1989b, p. 35) adds a fourth element: political conflicts within and among elites. While the first of these four definitional elements concerns the institutional structure of political systems, the others are concerned with the configuration of power among the relevant actors within such a system. Just how the latter three elements are related to each other remains, however, rather unclear in Tarrow's presentation.[1]

The concept of the political opportunity structure (POS) needs some clarification and specification in order to be useful for the analysis of the development of social movements. First, I propose to restrict the notion to those aspects of a political system that determine movement development independently of the purposive action of the actors involved.[2] This does not imply that the political opportunity structure is constant; it may shift over time as a result of factors that are not under the control of the actors involved or as a result of the cumulative consequences of their purposive actions. The point is that the actors cannot anticipate such shifts at the time when they engage in collective action, which means that they have to take the political opportunity structure as a given in their short-term strategic calculations.

Second, within the POS domain, I propose to distinguish three broad sets of properties of a political system: its formal institutional structure, its informal procedures and prevailing strategies with regard to challengers, and the configuration of power relevant for the confrontation with the challengers. The first two sets of properties provide the general setting for the mobilization of collective action, and they constrain the relevant configurations of power. Together with the general setting, the relevant configuration of power specifies the strategies of the "authorities" or the "members of the system" with regard to the mobilization of the "challengers."[3] In combination with the general setting, these strategies in turn define (a) the extent to which challenging collective actions will be facilitated or repressed by the "members of the system," (b) the chances of success such actions may have, and (c) the chances of success if no such actions take place, which may be either positive if the government is reform-oriented, or negative if the government in power is hostile to the movement (Koopmans 1990a). In other words, the country-specific mix of facilitation/repression and chances of success/chances of reform is, at least in part, the result of strategic calculations of the authorities. It is not exclusively determined by such strategic calculations, however, since the general setting also restricts this country-specific mix in a way that is independent of the concrete strategies devised by the authorities. Finally, this country-specific mix determines the set of strategic options available for the mobilization of the "challengers." It provides the crucial link between the POS and the challengers' decision to mobilize or not, their choice of the form of mobilization, the sequence of events to be organized, and the addressee of their campaign. Figure 1 presents a graphic summary of this argument. As Koopmans (1990a) points out, the way the country-specific conditions enter into the challengers' strategic calculations depends on the type of movement in question.

I am aware of the fact that both types of strategies—those of the authorities and those of the challengers—are to some extent mutually interdependent. This interdependence, however, does not enter into the present discussion because the focus is on aspects of the political context that have to be taken as given by the challenging actors. The mutually interdependent aspects of the political context belong to what I propose to call the interaction context of a specific challenge. The interaction context follows its own logic, which will not be treated here. Leaving mutual interdependence aside, the conceptualization of the political opportunity structure and its effects on the development of social movements in general is still a formidable task. In this essay, I shall not deal with the impact of political opportunity structure on social movements in general, but rather focus on its effects on a particular class of social movements in a particular region of the world society in a given period: the new social movements (NSMs) as they have manifested themselves in Western Europe and North America since the early seventies. Circumscribed in such a way, the task asks for concepts characterizing the variations in time and across countries of the relatively stable properties of the political context that have been relevant for the recent mobilization of new social movements in the West. I shall propose such concepts for the general institutional structure of the state, for the informal procedures and prevailing strategies to deal with challengers, and for the relevant configurations of power in the party system and the union system. The distinctions I introduce are simple and schematic ones, designed to capture the essence of what in reality are much more complex structures. I shall discuss the general concepts and present some hypotheses concerning the impact of the various aspects of the political opportunity structure on the mobilization of new social movements. The hypotheses are specified for four Western European countries—France, the Federal Republic of Germany, the Netherlands, and Switzerland.[4]

The Formal Institutional Structure of the State

In his attempt to conceptualize political opportunity structure, Kitschelt (1986) makes a useful distinction between "political input structures" and "political output structures." His distinction is less useful than it could have

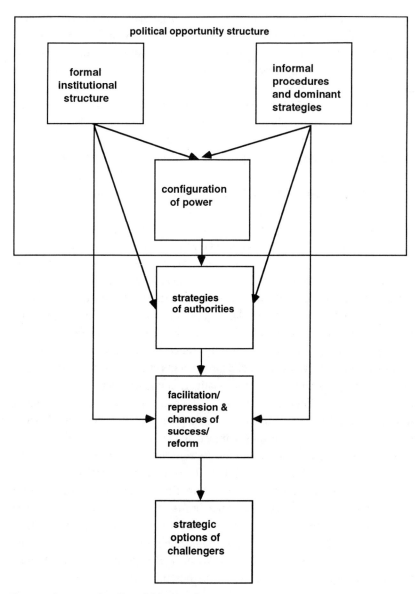

Figure 1. Conceptual outline of the general argument

been, however, because he uses it as a summary term applying to the institutional structure as well as to the actual configuration of power. In restricting the term to the formal institutional structure of the political system, I adopt the conceptual distinctions made by Kitschelt: with respect to the input side, a political system can be more or less open; with respect to the output side, it can be more or less strong. Openness implies formal access for outsiders; strength implies the capacity to get things done. At this point, I shall consider only access to the institutions of the state. Formal access to the party system will be treated in the context of the discussion of the configuration of power in that particular part of the overall system.

The degree of formal access to the state is, first, a function of the degree of its (territorial) centralization. The greater the degree of decentralization, the greater is the degree of formal access. Decentralization implies multiple points of access. In a federal system, such as those of Germany, Switzerland, and the United States, there are multiple points of relevant access on the national, regional, and local levels. In centralized systems, such as those of France, the Netherlands, and Sweden, there are virtually no access points on the regional level, and the local ones are insignificant. Second, the degree of formal access is a function of the degree of (functional) concentration of state power. The greater the degree of separation of power between the executive, the legislature, and the judiciary—that is, the more elaborate the checks and balances—the greater the degree of formal access. In political systems with a strong legislature and an equally strong judiciary, such as those of Germany and the United States, there are more points of access than in systems with an all-powerful executive, as in the case of France and, to some extent, the Netherlands. Third, formal access is a function of the coherence of the public administration. The greater the degree of coherence, internal coordination, and professionalization of the public administration, the more limited is the formal access. Fragmentation, lack of internal coordination, and lack of professionalization multiply the points of access. France again provides the prime example of a highly coherent administration, whereas the United States and Switzerland constitute the typical cases of lack of such coherence. The Netherlands and Germany probably are intermediary cases in this regard. Finally, formal access is a function of the degree to which direct democratic procedures are institutionalized. From the point of view of challengers, the most important direct democratic procedure is the popular initiative, which allows them to put an issue on the agenda of the political system and to ask for a vote of the whole electorate on the subject. Such procedures primarily exist in Switzerland, and in several states of the United States.[5] The procedures of compulsory and optional referenda give challengers an additional opportunity to intervene, but are of less importance because they allow intervention only after a decision has been taken by the political elite. Elaborate procedures of this type also exist in Switzerland, but not in the other three nations under study.[6]

On the basis of these four aspects of the institutional structure, we may roughly distinguish between open and closed states: Switzerland clearly seems to have the most open state among the four countries under study, France the one most closed. Because of its federalism and its strong judiciary, Germany also tends to be quite open, while the Netherlands tends to be rather closed formally because of its centralism and strong executive.

The same aspects that determine the formal openness of the state on the input side, in fact, also determine its strength on the output side. Federal, fragmented, and incoherent states with direct democratic institutions find it particularly difficult to arrive at decisions and to impose them on society. Centralized, concentrated, and coherent states with no direct democratic access, on the other hand, have a strong capacity to act. Strong states, then, are at the same time autonomous with respect to their environment and capable of getting things done, while weak states lack not only autonomy, but also the capacity to act.[7] This greatly simplifies our classification of states according to their institutional structure: we just retain the distinction between strong states and weak ones.

From the point of view of potential challengers, a weak state provides a more favorable setting for mobilization for collective action. In order to illustrate this, I shall introduce a distinction between three types of possible success. Following the lead of Gamson (1975, pp. 28ff.) and Kitschelt (1986, pp. 66ff.), we may distinguish between procedural and substantive success. Procedural success opens new channels of participation to challengers and involves their being recognized as legitimate representatives of demands. Substantive success involves changes of policy in response to the challenge. To assess the specific chances of success of a given movement in a weak state, it is important to make an additional distinction within the category of substantive success. This type of success can either be proactive (implying the introduction of "new advantages"), or it can be reactive (implying the prevention of "new disadvantages"). In the first case, the challenging movement acquires policy-making power, in the second case it is able to exert a veto. Characteristically, procedural success and reactive substantive success are more easily available in weak states than in strong ones. Proactive success is very difficult to get in any type of state: strong states may have the capacity to act on behalf of a movement's demands, but they also have the capacity to resist any temptation to do so. Weak states may be forced to give in to a movement's demands, but they are not likely to have the capacity to implement the re-

Table 1. Chances of success for challengers in weak and strong states

Type of state	Procedural success	Substantive success	
		Reactive	Proactive
Weak	formal facilitation of access	possibility of veto	no concessions
Strong	no formal facilitation of access	no possibility of veto	no concessions

quired policy changes. This is not to say that there are no proactive outcomes of mobilization processes, but short of massive and protracted mobilizations, such outcomes are expected to be quite rare in any type of state. Table 1 summarizes this argument.

Kitschelt (1986) also introduces an additional category of success—structural impact, which implies a transformation of the political opportunity structure itself. As I have argued, the opportunity structure refers to the aspects of the political system that are relatively stable over time. In the short run, structural impact is quite impossible in the type of countries we are considering here. In the medium or long run, however, such structural impact resulting from the cumulative impact of a large number of protest events may be possible. The most far-reaching structural impact results, of course, from a social revolution. Examples of less far-reaching structural impact include the durable establishment of Green parties in a given party system and the institutionalization of the social movement sector as discussed by Roth (1988) writing about Germany.

Informal Procedures and Prevailing Strategies to Deal with Challengers

The general approach of the authorities with respect to challengers is constrained not only by the formal institutional structure, but also by informal procedures and strategies typically employed by the authorities with regard to challengers. Organizational sociologists have long been insisting on the difference between the formal and the informal side of structure. Analogously, we should be aware of the distinction between the formal institutional structure and the informal ways it is typically applied. Scharpf (1984, p. 260) has used the concept of the "dominant strategy" to characterize the informal premises of procedure, the shared implicit or explicit understandings that emerge from the political process and guide the actions of the authorities. The informal procedures and prevailing strategies with respect to challengers are either exclusive (repressive, confrontative, polarizing) or integrative (facilitative, cooperative, assimilative). It is important to note that such procedures have a long tradition in a given country. According to Scharpf, they develop a powerful logic of their own. Efforts to change them are up against all the "sunk costs" of institutional commitments supporting them.

Given their long tradition, informal procedures and prevailing strategies have already had important consequences for the mobilization of the "old" labor movement. Thus, exclusive strategies that have typically been employed in Southern European countries but were also used in the Weimar Republic have led to an important split between the social democrats and the communists within the labor movement. As is argued by Gallie (1983), the split in the French labor movement after World War I has been the result of a particularly intransigent position of the French political elite at that time. While the British ruling elite chose to make important concessions to the radicalizing labor movement at the end of the war, the French ruling elite opted for a repressive strategy in similar circumstances. Gallie explains the difference in the reactions of the two ruling elites by earlier strategic decisions in an even more distant past. This illustrates the autodynamic of dominant strategies that makes for their reproduction across centuries.[8] The split between social democrats and communists has further radicalized the labor movement, which has again served to reinforce the dominant exclusive strategy of the authorities. In all the Southern European countries, a strong communist left has been excluded from power for decades. In Italy and France, the exclusion implied the delegitimation of the Communist Party; in Greece, Spain, and Portugal, the exclusion was the result of a long period of authoritarian repression (see Golden 1986). Finally, the radicalization of the labor movement has for a long time prevented the pacification of the class struggle in Southern Europe, which has had important consequences for the action space available to the new social movements in these countries, as we shall see in more detail.

Just as in the Southern European countries, the legacy in Germany is one of exclusion and repression. While the formal institutional structure of the Federal Republic has been completely rebuilt since World War II, the dominant strategy of its ruling elite with regard to challengers from below has continued to be marked by the experience of the past. In contrast to France, however, where the exclusive strategy is associated with a strong state, the exclusive strategy in the Federal Republic combines with a weak state, which will result in a different overall setting for social movements in general, and for new ones in particular.

Integrative strategies are typical for two types of countries. On the one hand, they are the hallmark of countries with a long history of coexistence of different religions, such as the Netherlands and Switzerland. On the other hand, they also prevail in Catholic countries that have experienced a split between religious and laic subcultures but have not experienced a prominent split between communists and social democrats; Austria and Belgium are the typical examples. Moreover, integrative strategies seem to be facilitated by the small size of a polity and its openness with regard to the world market; all the countries mentioned are among the small Western European nation-states (Katzenstein 1985). These countries have become known as consociational democracies, as typical examples of "neocorporatist" policy arrangements.

Like exclusive strategies, integrative strategies are compatible with rather different formal institutional structures. A comparison of the Netherlands and Switzerland illustrates the point: the Netherlands has a strong unitary state with a cabinet government comparable to that of the "Westminster model," and with a relatively coherent bureaucracy. The Swiss state, by contrast, is very weak because of its federalism, its fragmentation, and its direct democratic institutions. The crucial difference between the Netherlands and Switzerland with regard to the state's autonomy and its capacity to act probably has its origin in the different approaches to the solution of the religious conflicts of the two countries. Swiss federalism and Dutch pillarization can be regarded as functionally equivalent solutions to the same problem of integrating diverse cultural minorities within the same polity—with very different implications for the institutional structure of the state. While the territorial differentiation chosen by the Swiss implied decentralization and fragmentation of the state, the social differentiation in the Netherlands—achieved by the creation of Protestant, Catholic, socialist, and conservative pillars such that national consensus was negotiated among elites of different pillars and within each pillar between elites and constituencies—was compatible with a centralized and concentrated institutional structure (Kriesi 1990).

Combining the distinction between strong and weak states with that between exclusive and integrative dominant strategies, we thus arrive at four distinct general settings for dealing with challengers. As Table 2 shows, each of these general settings corresponds to one of our four countries. The combination of a strong state with an exclusive dominant strategy I call a situation of full exclusion. In such a situation, challengers can count on neither formal nor informal access to the political system. Instead they are typically confronted by strong repression. Moreover, since the state is a strong one, challengers are not likely to have any veto power nor to obtain any substantive concessions. This situation is represented by France. At the opposite end of full exclusion, we find full procedural integration, which is characterized by the combination of a weak state with an inclusive dominant strategy. In such a situation, repression is comparatively weak and the challenger's access to the system is formally as well as informally facilitated. Given the weakness of the system, challengers cannot count on important substantive concessions but may be able to block decisions by exercising a veto. This situation is represented by Switzerland. The direct democratic institutions as well as the federalist structure of Switzerland provide for a large number of formal access points for challengers. The traditionally integrative strategy enhances the general effect of the formal structure. Germany represents one of the two intermediate cases, formalistic inclusion. In this situation, challengers can count on formal but not informal facilitation of access. Moreover, they tend to be met with strong repression. There is a possibility of veto, but no concessions can be expected. The federal structure allows for multiple points of access. Moreover, the strong position of the German judiciary provides challengers with another set of independent access points. Compared to Switzerland, however, the number of formal regional and local access points is more limited because—apart from some exceptions—the Federal Republic does not have direct democratic institutions. Moreover, the repressive legacy of the system implies that those who speak outside of the formally available channels will be confronted with strong repression. The second intermediary case, informal cooptation, is represented by the Netherlands. In such a setting, challengers do not have a lot of formal access, but they can count on informal facilitation. Such informal measures may not go as far as the overt facilitation of action campaigns of social movements, but they may imply the facilitation of their organizational infrastructure, including public recognition, consultation, and even subsidization of social movement organizations. Since the Dutch state is also quite strong, it is able to make considerable substantive concessions, and it can prevent challengers from exerting a veto— that is, from blocking a decision-making process. Concessions have actually been forthcoming in the Netherlands because of the prevailing inclusive strategies, which serve to preempt challengers. A most striking example of preemption is the way the Dutch political system dealt with the challenge of the student movement of the late sixties: while the occupation of the administration building of the University of Amsterdam—the crucial action campaign of the movement—was met with direct repression, the national legislature quickly put forward a new university bill. It took only a brief and limited occupation to get the political system to produce a bill that included the most

Table 2. The general settings for the approach of members toward challengers

Dominant strategy	Formal institutional structure	
	Weak state	Strong state
Exclusive	formalistic inclusion –formal, but no informal, facilitation of access; strong repression –possibility of veto, but no substantive concessions (Germany)	full exclusion –neither formal nor informal facilitation of access; strong repression –possibility of neither veto nor substantive concessions (France)
Inclusive	full procedural integration –formal and informal facilitation of access; weak repression –possibility of veto, but no substantive concessions (Switzerland)	informal cooptation –no formal, but informal, facilitation of access; weak repression –no possibility of veto, but substantive concessions (Netherlands)

far-reaching democratization of the university system in the West (Zahn 1984).

These general settings can be expected to have a country-specific impact on all challenging mobilizations, not only on those of the new social movements, with respect to the general level of mobilization, the general form and strategy of the challenging mobilizations, and the system level at which mobilizations are typically oriented. Concerning the general level of mobilization, I propose that the far-reaching facilitation of mobilization by the Swiss system—especially resulting from its direct democratic institutions—implies a particularly high level of challenging actions. For the other three systems, it is difficult to make predictions regarding the general level of mobilization. On the one hand, as I have just argued, inclusive strategies have a tendency to preempt protest. However, it also seems plausible to argue that inclusive strategies imply elaborate decision-making processes that increase the chances for challengers to intervene and to exercise a veto. A telling example is provided by the series of nondecisions of the Dutch government with regard to the stationing of Cruise missiles in the early eighties, which has given the Dutch peace movement ample opportunities to continue its antimissiles campaign. On the other hand, one may argue that repressive strategies generally raise the costs of collective action, which serves to limit its scope in a general way. However, strong repression may also stimulate collective action. As Koopmans (1990a) points out, there are at least three ways this may happen: first, repression reinforces the identity of countercultural movements, which may stimulate offensive reactions of a rather radical type on the part of these movements. Second, repression may itself become a crucial issue for the challengers. Finally, and related to the second point, repression may focus media attention on the challengers, which may enlist the support of third parties that would otherwise not have supported the movement. Such supportive mobilization, in turn, may be expected to be of a rather moderate type. The urban autonomous movement of Zurich, for example, has profited from all three of these mechanisms (Kriesi 1984). Given these considerations, I abstain from any more specific predictions concerning the general level of mobilization in the other three countries.

With regard to the general forms and strategies of action typically used by challengers in the different countries, I can be more specific. I maintain that the French context of full exclusion invites disruptive strategies on the part of the challengers. As F. L. Wilson (1987, p. 283) observes, the strength of the French state gives rise to its greatest weakness: unable to allow challengers to articulate their concerns through formal or informal channels of access, it is periodically confronted by large-scale explosions of discontent. In such moments of great discontent, the French state may be forced to make substantive proactive concessions, or to abandon a project.[9] May 1968 illustrates the first point, the massive student protest in the fall of 1986, which forced the government to abandon its university reform bill, the second one. Even if, as I argued earlier, proactive success is difficult to attain anywhere, it is most likely to be forthcoming as a reaction to great social unrest in a strong state, which, in contrast to a weak state, is more likely not only to provoke a state of crisis, but also to have the capacity to end it by making proactive concessions.

By contrast, the highly accessible Swiss system invites moderate, conventional strategies on the part of its challengers. Such a system functions like a sponge: it absorbs all kinds of protest without granting much in the way of concessions to meet the demands of the challengers. In spite of a conspicuous lack of proactive concessions, challengers may continue to mobilize in moderate ways—because procedural success is to some extent a functional equivalent of substantive success (Epple 1988), and because occasional reactive success occurs frequently enough to provide an additional incentive for continued mobilization of this type. We may expect, however, considerable variation of this general theme within Switzerland, given that the informal procedures to deal with challengers vary substantially from one region to the other. A study of Swiss protest events (Kriesi et al. 1981) revealed that political protest events in the Swiss German-speaking part of the country have increasingly been met by repression since the late sixties, while a comparable tendency has not been observed in the French-speaking region. The general impression is that the authorities in the French-speaking area react to the challenges of the new social movements in a more subtle way, while the Swiss German authorities are increasingly adopting procedures reminiscent of German practices. Since the formal opportunities for access are so numerous in the Swiss political system, the authorities expect challengers to use these formal opportunities. The Swiss German authorities tend to react particularly repressively to those who do not use these opportunities.

In the general setting of informal cooptation in the Netherlands, we may also expect collective action to be moderate. The Dutch tradition of pillarized organizational structures will stimulate the growth of social movement organizations working through conventional channels that will be treated in much the same way as the religious minorities for which the system has been set up. This implies large-scale subsidization, integration in advisory bodies, and participation in the implementation of public policies. The Dutch system, however, is not as open as the Swiss one, given its lack of direct democratic channels of access and given the relative strength of the Dutch state. Therefore, the Dutch action repertoire may be expected to include a considerable amount of more radical forms of action as well. The low level of repression makes it likely that radicalization will stop short of violent action.[10]

Germany is most ambivalent with respect to the general forms and strategies of action. The relatively large number of formal access channels and the possibility of blocking political decisions through such channels invite moderate mobilization. The repressive legacy, however, may be expected to stimulate a significant number of disruptive events as well—at least more of such events than in the Netherlands or Switzerland.

With regard to the system level at which mobilization is typically oriented, I maintain that mobilization is predominantly oriented at the national level in centralized states, and at the regional or local level in decentralized states.

The Configuration of Power in the Party System

Regarding the third broad set of properties of the political opportunity structure—the configuration of power—I emphasize the configuration of power in the party system and take into account the corresponding configuration in the most relevant part of the system of interest intermediation: the union system. Compared to the party system, the union system is of only secondary importance for the mobilization of new social movements; at most it modifies the impact of the configuration in the party system.

General Concepts and Propositions

The configuration of power in the party system refers to the distribution of power among the various parties as well as to the relations that exist between them. As Figure 1 indicates, the configuration of power in a given political system can be thought of as an element of the political opportunity structure that intervenes between the formal institutional structure and the system's general strategic legacy, on the one hand, and the country-specific mix of strategies applied to challengers, on the other hand. Itself constrained by the general systemic context, the configuration of power in turn sets more specific limits to the strategies available to the authorities with regard to given challengers.[11] It modifies the openness of access channels and the system's capacity to act, and it modulates the general strategic legacy.

The main impact the formal institutional structure has on the configuration of power within the party system is that exerted by the electoral system. As is well known, proportional representation allows easier access for challengers than plurality or majority methods. Already established parties run a greater risk of competition from challengers in proportional electoral systems than in those with plurality or majority representation. New social movements are more likely to find allies within the party system in proportional representation systems. These allies may include challenging small parties as well as large established parties that adapt their positions in response to competition from the smaller challengers. Among the four countries of interest to us, the Netherlands has by far the most far-reaching proportional representation, given that the country forms a single constituency in national elections. The German system for all practical purposes is also proportional, with a 5 percent threshold designed to keep out minor (radical) challengers. The Swiss system is also proportional; the cantons form the constituencies in national elections. Since the cantons vary greatly in size, however, the proportionality of the Swiss system differs from one canton to the other. In smaller cantons it is considerably more restrictive than the German system, while in the largest cantons it allows for more accessibility to challengers than the German one. The French two-ballot system, reintroduced by Prime Minister Chirac in 1986 after a brief interlude of proportional representation, is of the majority variety that gives challengers little opportunity to establish themselves within the party system.

Not all the established parties have been of equal significance for the mobilization of new social movements in Western Europe. NSM supporters typically belong to the electoral potential of the left (see Muller-Rommel 1989; Kriesi and van Praag 1987), since the traditional challenges of the labor movement bear a close relationship to the challenges mounted by the new social movements. This is why we have to pay particular attention to the configuration of power on the left. As I have already indicated, the configuration of power on the left has been strongly determined by the heritage of prevailing procedures and strategies to deal with challengers. This is the main impact informal practices and procedures have on the configuration of power of NSMs. The heritage of exclusive strategies has resulted in a divided left, a split between a major communist current and a social democratic/socialist one.[12] In such a situation, social democratic parties have been relatively weak in electoral terms, and they have been engaged in a contest with the communists for hegemony on the left. This contest has above all been a contest for the working-class vote, which means that the traditional class conflict between labor and capital and the concomitant Marxist ideology have always played an important role in the strategy not only of the communists, but also of the social democrats. In such a context, the fundamental dilemma of social democratic parties put forward by Przeworski and Sprague (1986) has become particularly acute. According to their reasoning, the social democrats generally have to appeal to citizens other than workers in order to get a majority at the polls, since workers do not constitute (and never have constituted) a numerical majority in their respective societies. An effective appeal to a middle-class electorate, however, is likely to limit the social democrats' capacity to get the workers' vote. In a situation where the left is divided into a social democratic tendency and an equally important communist one, the risk of losing the workers' vote to the communists is obviously very serious. In such a context, one can expect the social democrats to subordinate their support of new social movements, which characteristically have a new middle-class core, to their struggle for hegemony on the left. Following Brand (1985, p. 322), I propose that where the left is split, there will be relatively little action space for the new movements in general, and that social democratic support of NSM mobilization will be strongly conditioned by the struggle for hegemony on the left. By contrast, in a setting with an inclusive heritage, where the left has not been divided and where class conflict has been pacified by the time NSMs emerge, there will be a larger action space for these movements and the social democrats can be expected to be much more likely to support the mobilization of these new challengers. The extent to which they will be prepared to do so depends, however, on a second set of factors.[13]

This second set of factors relates to whether the social democrats in particular participate in government or not and, if they do, what their position is. If the social democrats are in the opposition, they profit from NSM challenges directed at the government, which weaken their major opponents in the next elections. Moreover, since the NSM supporters also form an electoral potential for the left, the social democrats will appeal to them in the framework of a general strategy designed to build as broad an electoral coalition as possible. Being in the opposition, they will therefore tend to facilitate NSM mobilization. On the other hand, as the opposition, they have no way of making any material concessions to the new social movements.

If they are in the government, the social democrats not only face electoral constraints, they also operate under constraints of established policies and of pressures from dominant societal forces (industry, finance, technocracy). Given these constraints, they will have to make compromises with regard to their electoral promises. To maximize their chances for reelection, they will try to make compromises that favor the core of their electorate. In other words, they will tend to concentrate on working-class economic issues. They will, however, also try to make secondary concessions to more peripheral groups of their electorate, among them the NSM supporters, or at least they will promise reforms taking into account the NSM point of view. A social democratic government may profit from a cooperative movement that articulates limited demands in a generally acceptable way. Such a moderate movement can serve as a driving force for social democratic reform politics. In a generally integrative setting, it is possible that a social democratic government will support the organizational infrastructure of such a movement and will try to integrate it into established political channels. But even in this case, overt facilitation of NSM action campaigns by a social democratic government is unlikely because of the risk that such campaigns get out of hand (Kriesi 1989c).

The details of the strategy chosen by a social democratic governing party depend on its position in the government, too. If the social democrats govern alone, they will be more able to make concessions than if they depend on a coalition partner. If they are only a minority partner in a coalition government, they may not be able to make any concessions at all. A social democratic party in a minority position in a governing coalition, on the other hand, may feel more free to support the mobilization of new social movements.

These considerations imply decisive changes in the political opportunity structure of new social movements, when the left becomes part of the government and when it leaves government. If the left takes power, the necessity for mobilization decreases for NSMs because of anticipated chances of reform in their favor. At the same time, their mobilization is no longer facilitated by their most powerful ally. The net result predicted is a clear-cut decrease in the mobilization of NSMs, but not necessarily of other movements that are not dependent on the support of the left.[14] Conversely, if the left resigns from government, the necessity for NSM mobilization increases because the chance of reform becomes much more limited. Moreover, mobilization of NSMs is now facilitated by their most powerful ally. The net result to be expected in this case is a clear-cut increase in the mobilization of NSMs, but not necessarily of other movements that are not dependent on the support of the left. The impact of these changes in the political opportunity structure of NSMs may not exactly coincide with the change in government. We have to allow for some measure of anticipation or delay. For example, the deterioration of a government coalition in which the left participates may already improve NSM opportunities before the effective collapse of the coalition. Similarly, prolonged coalition formation and unstable prospects of a newly formed bourgeois coalition may delay the mobilization of the left against the new government.

The general outline of the configuration of power on the left given by the two crucial dimensions discussed so far—split or unified left, left in opposition or in government—is, finally, modified by the extent to which new forces on the left have constituted themselves as new actors within the party system, and by the extent to which the traditional major parties on the left—communists and social democrats—have been open with regard to these new forces. The first type of these new forces, the New Left, emerged in the sixties. Whether the New Left has crystallized into independent new parties and the extent to which these parties have become a relevant political force have mainly been determined by the degree of openness of the existing parties on the left and by the type of electoral system. The degree of openness of the existing parties, in turn, is likely to have been a function of the institutional framework and the prevailing strategy of the system, as well as of the extent to which the new forces themselves have chosen to work through the old parties. New Left parties have generally remained rather small in electoral terms, and they have not—with few exceptions—participated in governments. In spite of their limited scope, their presence may be expected to have played an important facilitating role for NSM action campaigns. On the one hand, New Left parties appeal to the same potential as the new social movements, and to a large extent they pursue the same goals. Moreover, they generally have a close affinity to the forms of political action preferred by new social movements. This is why they suggest themselves as the ideal ally of new social movements. On the other hand, their presence has probably also indirectly facilitated NSM mobilization by putting competitive pressure on the social democrats in particular. Competition from a New Left party puts the fundamental dilemma of the social democrats in a rather different light. Since New Left parties typically appeal to the new middle class, they do not pose a serious threat to the mobilization of the working-class vote. They may, however, drain away some middle-class support from the social democrats. Challenged by a New Left competitor, the social democrats will, therefore, be likely to take some facilitative steps in the direction of NSMs.

The second of these new forces is the Green parties that have emerged since the late seventies. While the New Left and its parties have been precursors of the new social movements, the emergence of Green parties can be viewed as one of their structural impacts. The timing of the emergence of Green parties and the weight they have been able to acquire have again been a function of the openness of the existing parties on the left (including by now parties of the New Left) and of the electoral system. It is obvious that the Greens play a facilitative role with regard to the mobilization of NSMs. Less obvious, however, is the fact that their presence is also likely to have an indirect impact on the major parties of the left, which is analogous to one of the parties of the New Left. As a consequence of the increasing competition for the new middle-class vote, the social democratic party is again pressed to take a more favorable stance with regard to the mobilization of NSMs. I will discuss briefly the strategies chosen by the social democrats in the four selected countries in light of the theoretical expectations. Table 3 indicates the situation of the social democrats in the four countries in the past twenty years.

Let us first take a look at the French social democrats. Among the four countries selected, they are the only ones who have been faced by a major communist party. In the early seventies, when the communists definitely were the dominant force on the left, President Pompidou predicted that, as a result of the bipolar dynamics of the presidential system, only two political forces would survive in French politics—the Gaullists and the Communists. He has, of course, been proved wrong. By the early eighties, the Socialist Party (PS) had become the dominant force on the left.[15] To gain predominance on the left, the PS opened itself to various leftist militants in the early seventies. It has attracted important groups of militants from the socialist labor union (CFDT), the leftist party (PSU), left-wing Catholics, and the new

Table 3. Situation of the social democratic parties in the countries under study

Social democrats in government	Left divided into major communist/ social democratic parties	
	No	Yes
Yes	Germany (1970s) Netherlands (until 1977, 1981–82), Switzerland	France (1980s)
No	Germany (1980s) Netherlands (1980s)	France (1970s)

social movements. The PS gave itself an internal structure that permitted the coexistence of very diverse tendencies—that is, it attempted to create a broad coalitional movement. Moreover, it concluded an alliance with the Communists (the *programme commun*), which reinforced its organizational and ideological base as well as its prestige among the militants from different quarters. The party acquired a young and, to a certain extent, feminine profile. At that time, the PS appeared to be the best of all possible choices for NSM supporters and activists (Ladrech 1989).

The renewed party rapidly booked success, which, as Lewis and Sferza (1987) point out, made it less accessible to new social movements and other outside forces. First, to the extent that most of the outside recruitment potential in the various parts of the left were incorporated into the PS, the PS tended to turn inward and become primarily involved in internal power games. Moreover, the party's important electoral gains in the municipal elections of 1973 and 1977 meant that the most capable party leaders had to give up reconstructing the party in order to take up administrative tasks—and also that a new class of notables was created within the party. Third, the reinforcement of the party intensified its competition with the Communists. The *programme commun* was called off in late 1977, and the alliance was reduced to a simple electoral one in 1978. To prevent the Communists from exploiting possible internal divisions, the PS felt compelled to close ranks. Party decision making was recentralized, and the party concentrated on attaining an electoral majority. Given intense Communist competition, the PS had to stick to a position close to the *programme commun*, with only limited openings for the concerns of the new social movements. Such openings were more likely if an issue raised by a movement became the focus of partisan conflict between left and right, as the issue of nuclear energy did.[16] Finally, the centralization of power within the PS was enhanced by the general centralization of the French political system, and by the two-ballot system in particular. The party's strategy in the course of the seventies has become less facilitative, although it has remained generally favorable to the new social movements.

Not soon after the PS came to power in 1981, its strategy changed again, in line with what we would have expected. The party abandoned the NSM concerns that would have imperiled its short-term management of the economy. Thus, it completely gave up its—admittedly always limited—antinuclear position (von Oppeln 1989). With respect to cultural issues, however, the PS in power has made some major concessions: it has, for example, substantially improved the status of homosexuals in France (Duyvendak 1990a). Depending on the type of NSM, the PS in power has, at its worst, followed a fully exclusive strategy, at its best one of repressive preemption. The governing PS could afford to follow such a course because it was not threatened by a Green party from the left—another result of the French electoral system. In her fine analysis of the PS strategy with regard to nuclear energy, von Oppeln (1989, p. 205) concludes that the party's strategy of early co-optation and later disappointment of the antinuclear movement contributed decisively to the weakening of the movement.[17]

The German Social Democratic Party (SPD) has traversed a trajectory exactly opposite to that of the French PS. All through the 1970s and up to 1982, the SPD was the dominant partner in a coalition with the liberal party (FDP). It has followed a strategy that comes close to full exclusion—like the French socialists in power. To understand why, we should first note that the SPD had to govern in coalition with the Liberals, which imposed a constraint on the concessions they could have made to the new social movements. Second, the generally repressive legacy prevented the governing SPD from taking a more integrative stance toward these movements. Third, the terrorist attacks during the seventies, while they were themselves in part a result of the generally repressive mood, reinforced the tendency of the governing SPD to resort to repression once again. Finally, although there was no communist competition in Germany, the SPD nevertheless was under pressure from the strong union movement to stick to the traditional goals of the labor movement.

Unlike the leadership of the French PS, however, that of the German SPD was not able to centralize the debate on the new issues and to keep internal discussions under control. Von Oppeln (1989) attributes this greater openness in part to the federal structure of the German political system. In a federal system, she argues, the number of independent leadership positions is larger than in a centralized system, which increases the opportunity of persons with new ideas to enter into leadership positions within parties. Second, she attributes the increasing openness of the SPD to NSM demands to the fact that many members of the party's youth organization—the JUSOs—have been particularly close to NSM concerns and have introduced a number of their demands into the party's internal debate.[18] A similar dialogue with the party youth organization did not take place in the French PS. Third, the SPD has been confronted by the challenge of the vigorous Green Party, founded in 1979, which has also contributed to its greater comprehension of NSM demands. Finally, the increasing openness of the German Social Democrats toward new social movements was reinforced by the programmatic disorientation of the SPD in the final stages of the left-liberal coalition, and by its eventual breakdown in 1982. When the SPD had to join the ranks of the opposition, it adopted a more facilitative strategy with regard to the new challengers.

In line with the integrative strategy of the Dutch political system, the Dutch social democrats (PvdA) have been open to new social movements since the early seventies. As a result of the impact of the depillarization of the Dutch political system in the late sixties, the PvdA radicalized and attracted many militants of the New Left, which eventually gained control over the party (Kriesi 1989b). Significant competition from two New Left parties (the PPR and the PSP)—a result of the open electoral system—probably contributed to the PvdA's opening up as well. Since 1971 the party executive has accepted extraparliamentary activities as part of its action repertoire, and since its 1973 congress the party has officially become an "action party" (*actie-partij*)—that is, a party oriented not only toward participation in government, but also toward provision of services and participation in movement activities. At the same time, the PvdA also became the dominant party in a coalition government that lasted from 1973 until 1977. At first sight, this configuration seems promising for the mobilization of new social movements and for their chances to obtain substantive concessions, but the action-party principles of the PvdA had little effect during this period, precisely because the party was in power. In line with the dominant Dutch practices, its strategy was more preemptive. Moreover, the number of concessions made was also quite limited because of the government's composition. On the one hand, the government included a new left party (PPR) and a party of the center left (D'66), which were open to the demands of the new social movements. On the other hand, the Christian parties still held a strong position in the coalition. As a result of depillarization, the Christian parties went through a reorientation phase during the seventies, which contributed to a slow, contradictory, and inflexible policy-making process of the Den Uyl government. In the area of economic policy, the result was political immobility, as Braun (1989) has shown. In the policy areas of more direct concern to NSMs, much the same may be concluded. With the move into the opposition in 1977, the PvdA came still closer to the NSMs than it already was. It joined the antinuclear power camp in 1979—after the Harrisburg accident (Cramer 1989, p. 66)—and, most importantly, it embraced the goals of the peace movement (Kriesi 1989b). Except during the PvdA's brief spell in government in 1981–82, one may describe its strategy with respect to NSMs during the eighties as one of strong facilitation. This situation changed radically after 1985. The new Christian Democratic Party has been able to unite the traditional Christian parties, to silence internal opposition, and to stabilize their electoral base. These developments seriously affected the Social Democrats' strategic position and the Social Democratic Party's chances to participate in government. The government's 1985 decision to deploy Cruise missiles signaled the final defeat of the alliance between the Social Democrats and the Dutch peace movement. When this decision did not result in the expected electoral gains for the Social Democrats in the subsequent elections in spring 1986, the Social Democrats changed strategy, almost completely dissolving their alliance with the new social movements and drawing nearer to the Christian Democrats to become acceptable as a government partner again. This example shows that there may be conditions under which even a social democratic party in the opposition may refrain from supporting new social movements.[19]

The Swiss social democrats (SP/PS) have had an ambiguous position with regard to NSMs. As part of the grand coalition that has governed Switzerland since 1959, they have shared the formal responsibility for the government policies against which the new social movements mobilize. Having always been in a clear minority position within the governing coalition, they have at the same time been opposed to the government on specific issues, including several issues of concern to NSMs. The ambiguity of the party's position is reflected by its internal division into a party left and a party right. The party left has consistently been in favor of NSM demands throughout the period under consideration; the party right, which is close to the unions and to the party's representatives in government, has consistently been skeptical of new social movements. Given the fragmented character of the Swiss party system, the specific configuration of power within the party has varied from one canton to the other. In the most developed cantons of Swiss German-speaking Switzerland, the SP has experienced a strong influx of New Left militants and has been confronted with vigorous competition from New Left parties since the early seventies. At the end of the seventies, the party left was able to take over power within the party in several cantons. As a consequence, in these

cantons—notably in Basel and Zurich—the SP became a major alliance partner of NSMs. This led to serious internal tensions with the party right, and
finally to splits in both Basel and Zurich in the early eighties.[20] In French-
speaking Switzerland, the PS has been challenged not as much by New Left
parties as by the traditional communist party (PdT/PdA), which may explain
why it has been less facilitative for NSMs in these parts of the country—and
why the Swiss Green Party first developed in the French-speaking cantons
(Ladner 1989).

   I maintain that the NSMs have generally played a less important role in
France than in the other three countries, given the situations described. The
split left in France has limited them to a greater extent than elsewhere. Moreover, in France a clear decline can be witnessed in the level of NSM mobilization from 1981 onward, that is, from the moment the left came to power. Mobilization of the labor movement did also decline, but not mobilization of all
the other movements. Conversely, for Germany an increase in the level of
NSM mobilization took place starting in the early eighties. The left lost power
in 1982, but the coalition had already started to get into difficulties before that
date, and the competition from the Greens set in after 1979. No corresponding increase took place for the other movements, with the possible exception
of the labor movement. In the Netherlands, the mobilization of NSMs, but not
necessarily of other movements, started to increase in 1978. For Switzerland,
predictions are more difficult since there has never been an explicit change in
government, as there has been in the other countries. Alternatively, one
might argue that the takeover of the Social Democratic Party organization by
its left wing in some cantons during the late seventies may have had a clear
mobilization effect on the NSMs in the regions concerned.

The Configuration of Power in the System of Interest Associations

The system of interest associations has several subsystems, each of which organizes a different category of interests. From the point of view of the political opportunity structure of new social movements, the unions constitute the
most relevant subsystem. Among the parties of the left, the unions form the
major organizations of the "old" labor movement. While unions are much
more class-specific organizations than parties, they may nevertheless be important possible allies of new social movements. Moreover, unions often have
a strong influence on the strategic position of the major parties on the left,
which means that their relevance for the new social movements may be
greater than appears at first sight. Other relevant parts of the system of inter-

est associations include churches and already established associations—such as various professional organizations—that operate in specific issue areas of immediate concern to NSMs. I shall limit this section to consideration of unions.

For the characterization of the structure and functioning of systems of interest intermediation, the distinction between corporatism and pluralism has assumed some prominence in political science. A corporatist union structure is highly comprehensive. It is both horizontally integrated (there is only one union system) and vertically integrated (the unions in this system are hierarchically ordered and directed from the top). In pluralist systems, by contrast, union structure is highly fragmented: there are multiple union subsystems, and they in turn are not hierarchically ordered and directed from the top. It has been suggested (Cameron 1984; Schmitter 1982; Visser 1987) that comprehensive organizational structures are a necessary precondition for the integration of unions (and business interest associations) into encompassing policy networks, as well as for the pacification of class struggle. In countries with a corporatist union structure—the Scandinavian countries, Austria, and Germany—the unions have indeed been integrated into elaborate policy arrangements, they have developed long-term policy perspectives, and they have to a large extent abandoned their strike activities. In other words, they have become responsible social partners. The obverse does not hold, however: not all countries with fragmented union structures have been unable to develop a stable social partnership. The reason is that there are different types of fragmented union systems. First, there are those in the Anglo-Saxon countries, where the union movement is split into a complex pattern of industrial, professional, and general unions—the pluralist paradigm. Second, there are the union movements of countries with a divided left, that is, a left with a major communist current next to the social democratic one. In such countries, the union movement is split along party lines, and the most important union federation has typically been under communist control. Finally, there are the union movements of countries with religious cleavages (including a cleavage between the secular and the Catholic subcultures in predominantly Catholic countries)—typical traditional consociationalism. In such countries, the union movement is split along religious lines. For our purposes, the difference between the latter two types of fragmentation is of particular interest. While a divided left prevents the unions from being integrated into stable policy networks and from abandoning traditional notions of class conflict (Golden 1986), the unions in the so-called consociational countries have been pacified and integrated in spite of their fragmentation.

A highly encompassing, corporatist union system is not very likely to facilitate the mobilization of new social movements, although it is no longer mobilizing for radical strike action. Such a union system still is a class organization "in the sense that it promotes and protects interests of workers as a class, their collective interests, and it enforces discipline on groups of workers that may be tempted by the advantages of pursuing particularistic interests" (Przeworski and Sprague 1987, p. 75). Moreover, the encompassing structure also implies a large amount of control over attempts of individual unions to support the mobilization of NSMs, which are generally of no direct interest for the preservation of the collective interests of workers as a class. In countries with such a union system, social democrats could pursue middle-class strategies at a tolerable or even negligible cost. But, as Przeworski and Sprague note, "that very same partner which took from the parties most of the burden of organizing workers as a class imposed constraints on the degree to which these parties could freely pursue their electoral opportunities" (1987, p. 119). Such union systems tend to exert pressure on the social democrats to give priority to the traditional labor class concerns, which means that the social democrats are less able to make concessions to, or to facilitate the mobilization of, NSMs than they otherwise could have been. Germany is an example of this.

Unions in systems that are fragmented along party lines and that are dominated by an ideology of traditional class struggle at first sight do not make likely candidates for facilitation of NSM mobilization. The major, communist-controlled union federation (CFT) cannot be expected to support NSMs. Under such conditions, however, there is considerable competition among unions. This may lead some minoritarian unions to appeal to segments of the new middle class that tend to be neglected by the dominant, communist-controlled union federation. The CFDT in France provides an example. Support from this union for NSMs may be forthcoming, as long as new social movements themselves do not directly compete with unions. Under conditions of strong class struggle, it is possible that NSMs will also couch their appeals in terms of the traditional conflict. If such is the case, the unions will be likely to opt for outright repressive strategies. The events of May 1968 in France were an early example.[21]

Countries with union systems that are fragmented along religious lines, but are nevertheless integrated into policy networks and pacified, present the most favorable case from the point of view of challenging new social movements. Not only has the class struggle been pacified in these countries, but the fragmentation of the union system makes for competition among unions.

The presence of confessional unions has traditionally diluted the class ideology, and the socialist unions have never been able to represent the whole working class. Under such circumstances, the competition is not couched in class terms. The socialist unions are free to adopt a new middle-class strategy in their competition for members, since they do not face a trade-off with a competitor that mobilizes as a class organization. This is the case in the Netherlands and Switzerland. In both countries, one would, therefore, expect the unions to have become major allies of the NSMs that facilitate their mobilization. In the Netherlands, this has in fact been true, at least with regard to the peace movement, which has received substantial support from the unions. In Switzerland, union support of new social movements has been much less forthcoming. Unions have never mobilized overtly against these movements. There have even been some unions, such as the unions of public employees, that have supported specific NSM action campaigns. There have also been several instances, however, where the unions have put pressure on the social democrats to keep their distance with regard to NSMs. This pressure combined with the intransigence of the right-wing minority of the party has, in some instances, led to a split in the cantonal Social Democratic Party, and to the creation of new democratic socialist parties.

Elaboration of the General Argument

The argument presented so far does not take into account differences between various new social movements with regard to their dependence on political opportunity structure. It is likely, however, that not all NSMs depend to the same extent on POS factors, and it is likely that they react differently to changes in the opportunity structure. I would like to make a distinction between "conjunctural" movements, which are heavily dependent on the POS and strongly react to changes in it, and "linear" movements, which are much less affected by such factors.[22]

The extent to which a movement's trajectory depends on the political opportunity structure is a function of its general orientation, of the level of development of its organizational infrastructure, and of the structure of the problem it is dealing with. First, I maintain that subcultural movements will be less influenced by POS factors than countercultural or instrumental movements.[23] Subcultural movements, such as that of homosexuals, aim at the (re)production of a collective identity that is primarily constituted in within-group interaction. Their predominantly internal orientation means that they are not very susceptible to changes in the political opportunity structure.

Countercultural movements, such as the urban autonomous movement, are also identity oriented, but they constitute their identity mainly in conflictual interactions with authorities or third parties. In other words, they react strongly to changes in the political opportunity structure. Similarly, instrumental movements that seek to obtain specific collective goods or to prevent specific collective "bads" are likely to be heavily dependent on the opportunity structure. Within the broad category of instrumental movements, however, dependence on the POS is expected to vary in accordance with the level of development of their organizational infrastructure. Instrumental movements, such as the ecology movement, that have developed a stable organizational infrastructure do not depend to the same extent on external support by allies as others with fragile and ad hoc organizational structures. Therefore, they will probably be less affected by changes in the configuration of power. Finally, instrumental movements dealing with a highly differentiated and complex problem structure, such as the ecology movement or the solidarity movement,[24] will be less dependent on aspects of the POS than movements with a highly focused problem structure, such as the peace movement or the antinuclear movement. Complex problem structures allow for substitution of goals, for shifts in the system level at which demands are addressed, and for long-term campaigning. By contrast, highly focused problems increase a movement's dependence on the POS, especially when the problem is itself linked to specific political decisions, such as was the case with the antinuclear missiles campaign. While I argue that certain movements react more strongly to changes in the POS than others, I am not able to specify which one of the conjunctural movements will react most. The type of movement that will mobilize most intensely depends on additional factors—some of them concerning the POS on levels of the political system other than the national one.

Except for Switzerland, where some regional aspects of the POS have been introduced, the general argument has been restricted to the national POS level. I start from the general idea that the national POS level still constitutes the major point of reference for the evolution of NSMs in a given country. But we have to allow for the fact that in some instances, the sub- or supranational opportunity structure is at least as relevant for the mobilization of a specific conjunctural movement as the national one. The subnational opportunity structure is particularly relevant for strictly local or regional movements, such as urban autonomous movements or—among the movements outside the scope of NSMs—regional movements. The international POS plays a crucial role for movements, such as the peace movement or the Solidarity movement, that react to aspects of international relations. I propose that the subnational POS is highly relevant in federalist countries, but not in centralized ones. In federalist states, a change in a subnational opportunity structure may trigger an action campaign, even if the national opportunity structure remains stable. I further propose that the international opportunity structure is of less relevance for neutral countries, and for countries with no colonial past. Countries that are part of international alliances or involved in international conflicts and countries that have a colonial past are more likely to react strongly with regard to events on the international level and to events in their former colonies. I suggest that, in such countries, changes in the international POS, when they coincide with changes in the national POS that contribute to the mobilization of new social movements in general, may give rise to action campaigns of conjunctural movements that react strongly to the international POS in particular. Finally, we should also allow for factors determining the kind of conjunctural movement likely to mobilize that do not directly depend on changes in the POS on any level. That is, we should also take into consideration processes of international diffusion with regard to the mobilization of NSMs. Successful mobilization of a given NSM in one country may trigger the mobilization of a corresponding movement in a neighboring country. I maintain, however, that, secondarily, the POS has an impact even in this case: processes of diffusion are supposed to occur in particular if the national POS in the country where the imitating movement starts to mobilize is undergoing an important change in favor of the NSMs. If there is no such change in a given neighboring country, we would not expect any diffusion effects. In addition, there are also the so-called suddenly imposed grievances, catastrophes such as the Three Mile Island and Chernobyl nuclear accidents or the war in the Middle East, that give rise to conjunctural mobilizations (Walsh 1981). Again, I would like to suggest that the extent to which such catastrophes give rise to mobilizations in a given country is also a function of the specific POS at the moment the catastrophe occurs.

To conclude this section, I should draw the reader's attention to the fact that I have not offered any hypotheses about the course of the events once the mobilization of NSMs has reacted with regard to a change in the POS as a result of a change in government. The basic idea is that the initial change in the level of mobilization caused by a crucial change in the POS will establish a specific interaction context that will follow its own autodynamic course. Karstedt-Henke (1980), Tarrow (1989a, 1989b), and Koopmans (1990b) have presented some theoretical arguments about how such interaction contexts may develop.

Conclusion

In this essay I have elaborated the notion that politics matter, even in the field of new social movements. In stressing the importance of conventional politics for movement politics, I have implicitly taken issue with the mainstream of NSM analyses in Western Europe; aspects of social and cultural change are central to understanding the evolution of their mobilization. In my view, social and cultural change become relevant for the mobilization of social movements only to the extent that they are mediated by politics. In focusing on politics I do not deny the relevance of other factors for the explanation of the origins and development of social movements in general, and of NSMs in particular. I maintain, however, that the visible series of collective action that constitutes the organized, sustained, self-conscious challenge to existing authorities is best understood, if it is related to formal political institutions, to informal political practices and procedures and to what happens in arenas of conventional party and interest group politics.

In addition to the literature cited at the outset, there is some new empirical evidence that supports this view. In a research project studying the development of five NSMs in the four countries I have discussed, we have started to test the ideas presented here. A first empirical analysis based on newspaper data about protest events is presented in Kriesi et al. (1992). The differences found with regard to the mobilization patterns of social movements in the four countries largely confirm the hypotheses elaborated here. The French pattern of mobilization, indeed, turns out to be the most centralized, the least formally organized, and the most radical. As a result of their overall radicalism and lack of formal organization, the French movements also mobilize a comparatively small number of people in moderate forms. Thus, the French pattern of mobilization mirrors the situation of full exclusion characterizing the political opportunity structure of social movements in France. The Swiss pattern, by contrast, is the most decentralized and the most moderate, mobilizing comparatively the largest number of people. Moreover, formalized social movement organizations operating through conventional channels are very strong in Switzerland, reflecting the characteristics of full procedural integration prevailing in this case. The Dutch and German patterns correspond to the contradictory situations social movements are confronted within these countries. Integrative strategies coupled with a strong state result in a centralized, but otherwise hybrid, mobilization pattern in the Netherlands. This pattern combines strong, formalized, and fully integrated social movement organizations mobilizing comparatively large numbers of people in rather conventional forms; there is a moderate, nonviolent radicalism among those protesting in the streets. Formalistic inclusion in Germany, finally, results in an equally hybrid but nevertheless distinct pattern that combines a largely decentralized mobilization of the majority of protesters by relatively moderate, but little formally organized, means with a far-reaching radicalization of a small violent minority. With respect to the evolution of the mobilization of new social movements in particular, we have tested the impact of the configuration of power in the party system and found some of the expected differences. Most significantly, the left's loss of power in Germany and its access to power in France indeed resulted in contrasting developments of the mobilization of new social movements in the two countries in the early eighties: the predicted decline in mobilization in France contrasts with the predicted increase in Germany. Case studies of the four countries using the framework presented here and studies comparing them in more detail will follow.

The invisible side of social movements, activities that do not become public and are not reported in the newspapers, is probably less related to POS factors. To stress the overt challenge of social movements is not to deny that movements have a less visible side as well. Since it does not treat the latent side of social movements at all, the theory presented here obviously is only a partial one. In my view, however, the crucial element of a social movement is its overt challenge to authorities—the series of action campaigns constituted in interaction with the authorities that defines a social movement in Tilly's (1984) terms.

My argument presumes that the most relevant level of the political opportunity structure is the national one. The other levels have entered into my discussion only in a subsidiary way. This raises the question of whether the theoretical argument is not only partial, but also no longer pertinent for the explanation of the evolution of contemporary movements mobilizing in a world that is increasingly determined by international politics. The international POS certainly is becoming more relevant for movement politics as well. Changes in the international POS now have important structural effects on the national POS. Thus, the breakdown of the formerly communist states in Eastern Europe and the end of the division between East and West introduce fundamental changes in the political opportunity structure of NSMs in the countries with a traditionally divided left: the end of the division between East and West implies the end of the divided left in these countries in the not too distant future. In this case, it is still the national POS that ultimately determines the mobilization of NSMs, although it is a national POS of an entirely different makeup. The relevance of the national POS may, however, decline in an even more fundamental way if the nation-state loses its prominence in conventional politics in a unified or regionalized Europe. There are strong indications of the decline of the nation-state, but they should not be exaggerated because they do not yet challenge the crucial importance of the national-level political opportunity structure for the mobilization of new social movements.

Notes

The author would like to thank the participants at the workshop Social Movements, Counterforces, and Public Bystanders, which took place at the Wissenschaftszentrum Berlin in summer 1990, for their helpful comments. Special thanks to Jan Willem Duyvendak, Ruud Koopmans, Friedhelm Neidhardt, Roland Roth, and Dieter Rucht, who have all given detailed comments on earlier versions of this essay.

1. Tarrow does not use the four elements consistently. After having introduced the fourth element in his revised version of "Struggling to Reform," he drops it again (1989b, p. 82), and in his book on Italy (1989a, pp. 22ff.), he drops the element of the "alliance structure" in favor of the "conflict between elites."

2. This definition has already been introduced by Duyvendak and Koopmans (1989, pp. 15–16). See also Rucht (1989).

3. I adopt here the simple distinction between "members" and "challengers" as it has been made by Tilly (1978). While it is not always possible to neatly separate members from challengers, I stick to this distinction to simplify the exposition. I shall frequently refer to the members in terms of "authorities"—that is, the two terms are used interchangeably.

4. These four countries are included in a comparative project on the development of new social movements in the eighties. The team that is currently working on this project includes Jan Willem Duyvendak and Ruud Koopmans from the University of Amsterdam as well as Marco G. Giugni, Florence Passy, and the author from the University of Geneva.

5. There are also direct democratic procedures ("Volksbegehren") in several member states of the Federal Republic (Jung 1990).

6. The French referenda are a prerogative of the president and give little latitude for the mobilization of challengers.

7. Zysman (1983, p. 298) also notes these two sides of the notion of the strength of the state.

8. A mechanism that is responsible for this autodynamic is political socialization. Thus, Gallie points out that Clemenceau, the French leader at the end of World War I, started his political career in 1871, that is, at the time of the repression of the Commune of Paris. Clemenceau was seventy-six years old when he became prime minister in 1917.

9. In other words, the French state may be forced to "learn" in such moments. As Fach and Simonis (1987) point out, the strength of the French state implies another major weakness: its very strength prevents it from learning from its own mistakes. Paradoxically, not having to learn turns out to be an important weakness: the French state is able to continue political programs that are highly ineffective or very dangerous—as in the case of the nuclear power program.

10. This characterization of the Dutch situation was suggested to me by Jan Willem Duyvendak and Ruud Koopmans.

11. The configuration of power is, of course, also a function of the cleavage structure of a given society (see Lipset and Rokkan 1967). I acknowledge this determinant factor, but I want to restrict attention here to the interrelationships among the elements of the political system.

12. The terms *social democratic* and *socialist* are used synonymously here.

13. The structure of the union system also plays a role in this context: a strong union system may exert pressure on the social democrats to give priority to traditional labor concerns, even if they do not face a serious trade-off in electoral terms.

14. The exception is the labor movement, which also has a greater incentive to mobilize under these circumstances.

15. On the right, the Gaullists soon had to contend with a second major conservative force, the UDF, not to mention the rise of the racist, right-wing party (Front National).

16. Up to 1981, the PS's critique of nuclear energy was integrated into the general attacks of the opposition party against the conservative government. However, the direct influence of radical opponents of nuclear energy was successfully blocked within intraparty discussions (von Oppeln 1989). The party demanded a rather moderate "two-year moratorium on nuclear development to reassess its problems" in both the 1978 and 1981 elections (Ladrech 1989).

17. Ladrech (1989, p. 275) reaches a similar conclusion. He points out that the attractiveness of the PS in the first half of the 1970s contributed to "an overall positive regard for institutional politics" within the NSMs—and, that is, implicitly to a weakening of the NSM sector as a whole.

18. One should add, however, that relations between the party and the JUSOs were rather strained during the seventies. In 1977, for example, the whole JUSO leadership was dismissed by the head of the SPD. The internal dialogue with the JUSOs became more open only in the eighties.

19. This point, too, was suggested to me by Jan Willem Duyvendak and Ruud Koopmans.

20. In both cases, it was the traditionalists who left the party or distanced themselves from the party's position, which was generally supportive of NSMs. The situation in Basel is described by Schmid (1986), that in Zurich by Kriesi (1984). In Zurich, the tensions within the party were greatly intensified by the mobilization of the urban autonomous movement at the beginning of the eighties. This is another instance of a structural impact of a NSM campaign.

21. In this case, the movement in question was the student movement, which is more a precursor than an example of the NSMs. See also Tarrow (1989a), who discusses Italy in the late sixties.

22. See Giugni and Kriesi (1990), who use this distinction for the description of the evolution of the various Swiss movements in particular. For a general discussion of the differential dependence of NSMs on aspects of the political opportunity structure, see also Duyvendak (1990b).

23. The distinction between these three types of movements has been introduced by Koopmans (1990a).

24. The solidarity movement as we define it encompasses all the mobilizations that are concerned with international solidarity. Included in this highly complex field are: humanitarian aid, support of political refugees in Western Europe, support of political prisoners elsewhere, antiracism and antiapartheid movements, and support of or opposition to regimes of particular Third World countries, such as Nicaragua or Chile.

Chapter 8

Opposition Movements and Oppositio′ Parties: Equal Partners or Dependent Relations in the Struggle for Power and Reform?

Diarmuid Maguire

Political Parties and Protest Movements

In capitalist democracies, political parties must work within both state institutions and civil society in order to maintain or increase their power. They have to operate within the institutional frameworks that shape state policy and through the social networks that help establish political consensus. Otherwise, they risk the possibility of political impotence and electoral defeat. Similarly, protest movements need to mobilize civil society and, at the same time, influence political institutions. Mass mobilization keeps a movement alive, while political influence gives it some relevance. In this way, political parties and protest movements operate on the same terrain; they often cross each other's paths, and they may form alliances that can affect their respective destinies. Political interactions between movements and parties are particularly prevalent when parties are in opposition and are building social coalitions for electoral purposes.

In a number of analyses of new social movements, it is claimed that there is an increasing disjuncture between the autonomous world of protest movements and the political institutions that they challenge. Alberto Melucci, for example, has argued that the "emerging forms of collective action differ from the conventional modes of organization and operate increasingly outside the established parameters of the political systems" (1989, p. 56). The new movements, according to Melucci, are formed in the dense undergrowth of "submerged networks" in which collective identities are negotiated and cultural symbols are produced. They surface to challenge authorities on specific issues, thereby acting "as 'revealers' by exposing that which is hidden or excluded by the decision-making process" (1989, p. 175). When the challenge is over, the movements return to the hidden social networks in which they usually operate, forming new organizations and constructing new collective identities.

This imagery of movement emergence and submergence is compelling because it captures vividly the role that movements can play in complex industrial societies. But the dichotomy drawn between the world of social movements and that of political institutions is too sharp. For example, protest movements tend to recruit the "already organized" (J. Q. Wilson 1973, p. 56) and thus attract members of political parties and related organizations. This means that party members can also be activists within protest organizations and influence not only the shape of the movements' organizational structure but also their strategic orientation. Also, the more movements put forward political demands, the more likely it is that they will encounter other political actors. These encounters usually have the cumulative effect of shifting movements from what Melucci calls a "nonpolitical terrain" to one that is political. That is, movements will seek to realize their goals by influencing political institutions such as parties.

It is also important not to overemphasize the institutional characteristics of political parties. At times, democratic parties may seem to be far removed from the members who sustain them and the masses they claim to represent. Yet they are not the predemocratic "parties of notables" described by Maurice Duverger (1967 [1954]). Melucci argues that "political parties and other political bodies mostly exercise power at the macro-levels of complex societies" (1989, p. 230). But they are active politically at the micro level as well.

For parties are organizations—Duverger uses the term *communities* (or "collections of communities")—that are made up of more than just elected representatives and functionaries in gray suits. They also have members who organize political meetings and carry out party work in communities. Party members, like movement activists, are involved in the "submerged networks" that sustain their organizations and "collections of communities." And they emerge every so often, not just at election time, to challenge state authorities and also their party leadership, of whom they may be critical.

Thus political parties are not just political institutions: they have one foot in the state and the other in civil society. As Giovanni Sartori has argued, "Parties are *the* central intermediate and intermediary structure between society and government" (1976, p. ix). It is this intermediary structure and role that creates tensions within political parties. Parties constantly confront the question of the extent to which they should adapt to the requirements of state management as opposed to the demands of their members and supporters.

For many members and sympathizers are involved not only in party life but also in other organizations and protest movements.

Studies of left-wing party members, for example, have shown that many of them are also active in protest movements. Some enter party life after a period of activity in protest movements (see Lange, Tarrow, and Irvin 1990 on the Italian Communist Party), while others pursue a life of "double militancy" (for the example of the Dutch peace movement, see Kriesi and van Praag 1987). This interaction between left-wing parties and progressive protest movements—such as the trade union, women's, and peace movements—has been characteristic of the history of the left since the late nineteenth century. It is not surprising, therefore, that scholars like Ronald Inglehart have found that, irrespective of social class, "affiliation with an institution of the Left is linked with a tendency to have Post-Material values" (1977, p. 92). Those values have been instilled through the political socialization created by active struggle and the collective traditions of parties of the left within civil society.

But even if a traditional left-wing party may not be involved in a movement's formation, it is likely to become a strategic target of the movement depending on its role within the political system. For example, if a party is a potential "party of government" (that is, it is electorally strong and integrated within the system) it could offer a successful movement an opportunity to realize its goals. While some movement activists might prefer to lay siege to the state in more direct arenas of interaction, others could find it difficult to ignore the strategic opportunities of changing a party's policy and possibly that of a future government.

On the other hand, a movement may seek to escape the strategic dilemma of dealing with existing parties by becoming a party itself. But if it manages to become a party with elected representatives, then it too will occupy an intermediate position between civil society and the state. There the new "party of movement" will face a series of strategic questions that are all too familiar to the parties it seeks to replace. What should be the relationship between party representatives and party members? Should the party try to realize some of the movement's goals by allying with institutional forces, or should it restrict itself to being the tribune of the movement in parliament? Should movement objectives be brought into line with electoral objectives or vice versa? Przeworski (1989), for example, has analyzed how these dilemmas have affected and shaped the labor movement. The recent history of new Green parties, in Germany and elsewhere, has shown how answering these questions can lead to the same sort of divisions and polemics that have traditionally scarred the Old Left (see, for example, Müller-Rommel and Poguntke 1989).

Therefore, the analysis presented here is in close agreement with the observations of Garner and Zald:

> Party structure is probably the single most important variable for understanding the pattern of social movements. Movements can be understood as one part of a range of options that also includes political parties. Parties spin off movements, either deliberately or in the process of factionalizing. Movements appear within parties. Both are organizational forms for pursuing political ends, so it is not surprising that they are so closely intertwined. (1987, p. 312)

We should also note that only one of these organizational forms—namely, the political party—operates both within state institutions and outside them in civil society. The party acts as a bridge between society and government, and it is a bridge that movement strategists cannot resist attempting to cross.

Opposition Parties and Opposition Movements

The political process of collective action (as expounded, for example, by McAdam 1982; Tarrow 1983, 1989a, 1989b; and Tilly et al. 1975) locates movements within a pattern of political as opposed to strictly social interactions. By analyzing the political process—which Tarrow (1989b, p. 28) defines as "people's actual behavior and the interactions among protesters, opponents, third parties, and the state"—one can examine not only policy outcomes but also the evolution of movement development over time. The question that will be explored here is: what is the likely pattern of interactions between opposition movements and opposition parties within this overall political process of collective action?

The relationship between a protest movement and a political party tends to be closer when the party is in opposition. Opposition parties lack the necessary power within state institutions to implement their policies, and they seek support from politically relevant constituencies in civil society in order to achieve it. To the extent that a protest movement can help serve that purpose, a political party will be interested in establishing contact. Similarly, an opposition movement facing a strong hostile government shares an interest with friendly opposition parties in putting the government on the defensive and possibly ejecting it from office. Put simply, most opposition parties want to come to power, and protest movements want to have their demands met. Thus opposition parties may promise to deliver movement policy goals in exchange for movement assistance in gaining power.

These sorts of deals, whether they are implicit or explicit, have given rise to the popular notion that parties will promise movements anything in order to get into power and fail to deliver once they get there. Certainly there are plenty of examples of such deals being made and broken, from the birth of party democracy to the present. In recent history, we can note how parties on the left in France, Spain, Australia, and New Zealand have followed largely neoliberal economic policies despite initial support from labor and new social movements. In the United States, the conservative Republican Party has been tardy at best in meeting the demands of the fundamentalist Christian movement on issues such as abortion and school prayer. But there are also examples of movement success—for example, the New Zealand peace campaign—whereby parties have managed to carry out their election promises.

Yet we should not confine our analysis of the relationship between opposition movements and parties merely to the question of policy outcomes. The fact that opposition parties have the potential to form or influence a government is clearly a crucial feature in their relationship with mass movements seeking allies. The role of perception in this regard is also very important. As Tarrow notes, "Here the issue is less whether the influential ally exists, [than] whether it is *seen* to exist by a potentially insurgent group" (1989b, p. 36). In this way a movement may emerge and target not only hostile authorities but also what it perceives as friendly elements of the elite. Therefore, an opposition party can find itself subject to the attentions of a movement whether the party initially is favorably disposed or not.

But the relationship between an opposition party and a movement can also affect their respective strategies, tactics, and activities in the everyday struggle for political power and reform. What each can offer the other depends, to a large extent, on their relative balance of resources. These might usefully be divided into four areas: organizational, cultural, constituency, and policy resources.

Organizational resources such as money, infrastructure, expertise, and activists are essential for the mobilization of movements and parties. Central questions in examining movement-party relations are whether these actors have much to offer each other organizationally and the extent to which they generate and control their own resources. Obviously, an organizationally strong and autonomous movement is better able to influence a weak opposition party. Similarly, a weak and dependent movement can end up being subject to a strong party's political dictates. An example of the former would be the early British trade union movement, which exerted a powerful hold on the Labour Party. Examples of the latter would be the communist-dominated workers' peace and unemployment movements of the 1930s.

Cultural resources are more difficult to define and measure but involve the capacity and autonomy of each actor in representing the value orientations and forms of behavior of particular social constituencies. Does the movement or party have cultural access to elements within civil society that the other would be unable to reach on its own? If so, what is the pattern of cultural interactions and exchanges that emerges and how does it affect political behavior? For example, a cloth-capped Labour Party or a gray-suited social democratic party may find it politically necessary to establish cultural contact with a more colorful and youthful constituency. Similarly, a minority new social movement may need to forge links with a culturally suspicious working class. Movements and parties can act as cultural conduits for each other, and their relative cultural strengths can determine this aspect of their relationship.

Constituency resources are the social coalitions that have been forged by movements and parties. Both use organizational and cultural resources to establish their social bases, and their interactions at these levels may be shaped by the goal of broadening their respective areas of support. The constituency objective is particularly important for an opposition party seeking to gather potential votes. The key question in analyzing this constituency relationship is whether the movement or party has constituents that the other lacks and wants. It is at this stage, for example, that an opposition party may choose or be forced (again depending on relative strengths) to enter an implicit or explicit arrangement to exchange election promises for electoral support. A party, therefore, may choose to embrace a movement constituency, but only if this does not result in the loss of core support (see Kriesi, chapter 7 in this volume).

Policy resources are the capacities of political actors to influence and determine policy on certain issues at the state level. Clearly, a party in government will be stronger on this dimension than a party in opposition, but this does not mean that the opposition party is completely powerless. As Rochon argues in his analysis of the West European peace movement:

> Not only does a majority party or coalition determine government policy, but even opposition parties can focus attention on nuclear weapons by questioning government ministers, proposing amendments to legislative proposals, and other parliamentary devices. (1990b, p. 112)

And movements may possess policy resources depending on, among other factors, their level of formal access to state institutions. A party that is excluded from the political system (see Kriesi, chapter 7 in this volume)—a radical leftist party, for example—may seek to use such a protest movement in order to increase its political opportunities and gain access to the system.

It is possible that a movement that has strong organizational, cultural, con-stituency, and policy resources—typically in an electoral system with low bar-riers to entry—may decide to form a new party. This strengthens the move-ment's relationship with other opposition parties, since it is able to compete directly on their terrain. Playing the electoral game, however, gives rise to the problems of co-optation and goal displacement mentioned earlier.

But what happens to protest movements that are strong but choose not to become a party, or to movements that are weak and are unable to do so? For most new social movements in capitalist democracies do not have strong New Left or Green parties in parliament and local government on which they can rely exclusively for representation. Therefore, they have to establish a re-lationship with parties that are relevant to their movement, and there devel-ops the pattern of organizational, cultural, constituency, and policy interac-tions and exchanges I have outlined.

The relationship between a movement and an opposition party is deter-mined not only by their relative strengths and weaknesses at a given moment but also by an evolving political opportunity structure that can affect them both. A favorable structure of political opportunities can infuse a movement or party with resources; an unfavorable structure can act as a drain (Klander-mans 1990). It should also be noted that the political opportunity structure of a movement and that of a party, while overlapping, may not necessarily be identical.

For example, if we adapt Tarrow's (1989b, pp. 34–35) four dimensions of the political opportunity structure to analyze the position of opposition par-ties, we can ask (1) the degree to which such parties have formal access to the state; (2) the party's position in an evolving pattern of political align-ments; (3) the party's potential alliance partners at the social and political level; and (4) whether the party is combating a united or divided governing elite. The opposition party's political opportunity structure may be an impor-tant part of a movement's political opportunity structure and vice versa. But they are engaged in different pursuits, and this can lead to divergent political contexts and strategies. As Kitschelt notes:

> Unlike the social movements, parties not only express substantive political de-mands, but also strive to accumulate a generalized power resource—votes. In order to accomplish this, they immerse themselves in a unique competitive set-ting with other players pursuing the same objective. (1980, p. 181)

An unfavorable political opportunity structure for one opposition party might actually strengthen the position of a social movement so that, for example, it can have greater influence over that party's policies or win over other opposition parties to its cause. Similarly, a favorable opportunity structure for an opposition party might give it the upper hand in relation to a movement and possibly dispense with it altogether. The point is that changes in the political opportunity structures of movements and parties affects their potential hold on organizational, cultural, constituency, and policy resources. This in turn affects their relationship with each other.

One final theoretical consideration is necessary. Movements and opposition parties operate along similar though distinctive patterns of accumulating resources within evolving structures of political opportunities. We know that movements emerge, peak, and decline because of their internal characteristics and the political contexts in which they operate (Tarrow 1989a, 1989b). On the other hand, opposition parties, like all political parties, have more staying power than social movements. Citizens in capitalist democracies are asked to vote every four or five years, whereas there is no such obligation to engage in regular protest.

Yet opposition parties might also be described as being in certain political phases or positions depending on their internal party politics and external political environment. For example, an opposition party might be going through a phase of internal party conflict and reorganization in the wake of electoral defeat or as the result of the emergence of new factions and new parties. An opposition party in such a position might be vulnerable to social movements that work to change its leadership or policy framework. In some ways this characterizes the relationship between the West German peace movement and the Social Democrats (SPD) in 1983. The SPD reversed its policies on the issue of Cruise and Pershing II missile deployment after being ejected from office (see Rochon 1988, pp. 160–61, 165).

Alternatively, an opposition party might be in a position to oppose the government effectively and put it on the defensive. Its political opportunities may have improved, for example, as a result of internal government divisions. A party in this position would be better able to channel movement demands in parliament and help expand the movement's political opportunity structure.

Finally, an opposition party could demonstrate the clear potential of winning an election or joining a government coalition in the short term. Being on the potential threshold of government could mean that the party is internally united (the phase of internal party conflict is over); it has been a successful opponent of the government (the position just described); and the government itself is in trouble (as manifested by, for example, low public approval, back bench revolts, cabinet splits, and visible societal opposition from protest movements). An opposition party in this situation obviously would be very strong and would have the potential to deliver movement demands should it cross the threshold into government.

But the central question that emerges in such a political context is whether the opposition party can afford to carry movement demands into an electoral campaign or coalition negotiations. Electoral and coalitional calculations would certainly be paramount for the party at this stage, and it would have to decide if the movement's policies served its own central objective of gaining governmental power. If movement demands did not fit into a party's calculations, then the movement might be jettisoned, depending on its strength relative to the party.

In the rest of this chapter I analyze the relationship between two opposition movements and opposition parties—the British peace movement and the British Labour Party and the Italian peace movement and the Italian Communist Party (PCI)—between 1979 and 1989. The comparison is organized by the organizational, cultural, constituency, and policy resources of these movements and opposition parties. I compare their evolving political opportunity structures to identify points of convergence and divergence. Relatedly, I compare the positions of the opposition parties—(1) internally oriented, (2) effective opponents of the government, or (3) potentially on the threshold of governmental power—in both cases with the stage of movement development (ascendence, peak, decline). The argument throughout is that the relationship between these peace movements and opposition parties on the left largely determined the tactics, strategies, and political outcomes of the movements themselves.

Comparing the British and Italian Peace Movements

One of the great methodological legacies of NATO's 1979 decision to deploy Cruise and Pershing II missiles in Western Europe is that it allows us to compare different national protest movements reacting to the same grievance in the same period. We do not need to use conceptual abstractions like "modernization" or "patriarchy" to structure the grievances of different national movements. Nor is it necessary to ignore chronology in order to compare the evolution of different protest campaigns. NATO's decision affected a number of domestic polities simultaneously and had the character of an external "suddenly imposed grievance" (Walsh 1981).

But it should also be noted that it was the decision rather than the deployment that was "suddenly imposed"—the missiles were not to be deployed until four years after the decision. As far as peace activists and sympathizers were concerned, this was rather like the managers of Three Mile Island announcing that they were planning to stage an accident on a particular date. As James Hinton put it, "By announcing the planned deployment date as 1983, NATO gave the peace movement a timetable as well as a target" (1989, p. 182). Before the arrival of the missiles, movement organizations worked to create and take advantage of domestic political opportunities.

The timetable and the target of peace movement campaigns affected all the deployment countries equally, and preexisting peace movement organizations had to orient themselves to the logic of time frame and target. They had to drop whatever they were doing, confront political opportunity structures that were more or less unfavorable, and try to make effective use of a new flood of recruits. Examining how each of the national movements responded to these tasks allows us to capture part of the relationship between protest movements and political parties comparatively. Why did some movements emerge before others? Why were certain strategies and tactics pursued in particular nations? Why did some movements have more political impact than others?

Here the comparative focus will be restricted to the British and Italian peace movements, chosen because of the very different character of the mass parties of the left in these countries. The British Labour Party has the potential for direct policy access to the state. It has been in government on three occasions since 1945 and is the second-largest party in the polity. Despite its institutional links with the trade union movement, the Labour Party is largely electoralist and parliamentarian in origin (Coates 1975; Miliband 1961)—that is, it puts great emphasis on the goal of forming a government, often at the expense of developing strong organizational and cultural resources within civil society. The main constituencies of the Labour Party traditionally have been the working class and the public sector middle class, but during the 1980s the party lost significant support from the skilled working class (Krieger 1986, pp. 84–85). The major challenge to the Labour Party in the 1980s came from a new centrist alliance of Social Democrats and Liberals rather than from the New Left or the Greens.

The Italian Communist Party (PCI)—now called the Party of the Democratic Left (PDS)—by contrast is a movement-oriented party. As a result of its repeated unsuccessful attempts to enter government, it has been forced to maintain itself organizationally and politically by establishing deep roots in civil society (Blackmer 1975). The PCI is a mass party with strong organizational and cultural resources, but weak policy resources because of its history of political exclusion from the polity. The PCI has a heterogeneous class constituency, and its major political problems in the 1980s were less a result of electoral dealignment than of the lack of a successful strategy for entering government. The PCI confronted a strong government coalition that excluded it from power, and the party mobilized movements on the left in an attempt to get around this political embargo. The PCI faced no strong electoral challenges from a New Left or Green party, but it was concerned about the political potential of independent new movements.

The main question I ask here is this: to what extent did the structures, roles, and circumstances of these very different political parties on the left affect the evolution of their nations' peace movements in the 1980s? I argue that in both cases, in many instances, the political impact of these parties on the movements was determinant.

The British Labour Party and the British Peace Movement

The Political Context

The British peace movement was reborn in a period when state, party, and economic structures were undergoing fairly severe structural and conjunctural crises. The structure of Britain's Keynesian welfare state had been under pressure since the early 1970s (Gamble 1986). The Labour Party was most affected by this crisis, and it was ousted from government in 1979 after a massive wave of strikes by public-sector unions. Labour was replaced by a Conservative administration that was determined to return to the ante-Keynes status quo (Kesselman et al. 1987; Krieger 1986).

Britain's party structure creaked and groaned under the weight of a crisis that was more than a decade old. The Liberals had made significant inroads in the 1974 elections, and there were other challenges to the two-party system—not to mention the integrity of the United Kingdom—from the Scottish and Welsh nationalist parties. The birth of the Alliance (an alliance between the newly formed Social Democratic Party [SDP] and the Liberals in 1981), was seen by many as the beginning of genuine multiparty politics in Britain.

But the creation of multiparty politics emerged from the conjunctural crisis of one party in particular—the Labour Party. After the trauma of electoral defeat in 1979, the party had become internally divided; open warfare was declared between hostile factions. Members argued over whether the party should attempt to reconstruct a coalition around the Keynesian welfare state or pursue an alternative left strategy. Some proponents of the former strategy abandoned the party and formed the SDP, while others stayed on to fight an increasingly dominant left (Seyd 1987).

This conflict between Labour's left- and right-wing factions initially revolved around the issue of the parliamentary Labour Party's accountability to the party membership. Labour had been in office on two occasions since 1964, and in both periods the parliamentary leadership reneged on conference and manifesto commitments. From 1979 onward, the Labour left was successful in passing a series of reforms that were designed to change the party's structure and thus, from its perspective, tackle this problem at its roots. This struggle for Labour's "soul"—or less exaltedly, its decision-making apparatus—created deep divisions within the party, but it was a struggle that the left initially won.

Thus when NATO announced in December 1979 that Cruise missiles were to be deployed in Britain, the political system was in flux. The main features of postwar politics—Keynesianism, a two-party system, and a moderate Labour Party—looked as if they were about to disappear. Many who became attracted to peace movement activity in this period saw new opportunities offered by this political context. With a massive peace movement and the election of a left-wing Labour government lay the possibility of movement success. But for a Labour government to be elected it had to move from internal conflict to mounting an effective opposition and increasing its electoral potential.

A second possibility for movement success was the election of the moderate alliance parties—or an Alliance coalition—favorably disposed to some of the peace movement's demands. While the peace movement's political opportunities would have expanded with this second option, those of the Labour Party, in the short term and possibly the long term, would have diminished. The election of an Alliance government within a two-party system would have threatened Labour's position within British politics as the second party.

The Emergence of the Peace Movement

The electoralist orientation of the British Labour Party and its organizational and cultural weaknesses have allowed development of a social movement sector on the left that has been relatively autonomous from the party. In fact, the birth of the Labour Party itself was largely a result of the needs of the leading social movement actor in the late nineteenth and early twentieth centuries—the trade union movement—on which it still relies for funds and mass membership. Historically, the Labour Party has an ideologically heterogeneous

membership and pays little attention, organizationally, to the activities of social movements in civil society. This is part of the reason why Britain has produced organizations like the Anti-Apartheid Movement and Amnesty International, which are autonomous from political parties. This stands in contrast
to many countries on the European continent, where parties historically have
exercised greater control and influence over mass movement organizations.

The Labour Party's lack of organizational presence in the social movement
sector allowed the British peace movement to reemerge in the 1980s without
being dominated by the party. In fact, the movement's political autonomy was
demonstrated by the way in which it first emerged at the local level before
finding national forms of direction and organization. Many local groups
began their lives after organizing a public showing of the film *The War Game*
—made in the 1960s and banned by the British Broadcasting Corporation—
which dramatized the likely effects of a nuclear attack on Britain. After the
showing of the film the organizers and the audience would constitute themselves as a local peace group. The names of most groups stressed their local
orientation (e.g., Peace Action Durham) and many were content initially to
work purely on the local level.

It is important to note that although the Labour Party was not present as
an organized political entity at this stage of the movement's development,
many of its individual members were. Local Labour Party members worked
with religious leaders, former peace activists from the 1960s, and organizers
of other movements to get the peace campaign of the 1980s off the ground.
Local communities and networks of the "already organized" were the central
coordinators of the new peace movement at the local level.

Soon the local peace groups came under the umbrella of what had been
the leading peace movement organization of the 1960s, the Campaign for Nuclear Disarmament (CND). CND had a membership of 4,000 in 1979; according to its then general secretary, Bruce Kent, their names and addresses
were recorded on index cards and kept in shoe boxes (interview, July 11,
1987). The campaign found its membership more than doubling each year
until in 1984 it had more than 100,000 paid-up members whose names and addresses were stored in the organization's computers.

CND guarded its autonomy from political parties and the Labour Party in
particular. This helped the campaign win broad support and allowed it to
dominate peace movement politics in Britain throughout the 1980s. At its
peak in 1984 the organization had 100,000 national members and an estimated 250,000 in affiliated local groups. It had more individual members than
any of the political parties, with the exception of the Conservatives. Further-

more, CND's capacity for independent mass mobilization was unsurpassed by any other movement or party on the left, let alone any other peace movement organization. It has been estimated, for example, that CND's national demonstration on October 22, 1983, "was probably the largest in British history, with the possible exception of the women's suffrage rally of 1909" (Hinton 1989, p. 183). Also, the campaign had independent sources of finance and an annual budget that sometimes approached a million pounds.

The Internal Evolution of the Peace Movement

Yet despite the emergence of an independent peace movement organization, it was not free from party political conflicts. The individual Labour Party members who flooded the ranks of the movement at its inception brought their political orientations with them. Labour Party peace activists had their own views about how a movement should be organized and how it could realize its goals. They were also fighting what they saw as a life and death factional struggle within their party, and some could not resist using the peace movement as either a battlefield or a weapon.

Paul Byrne has noted how CND "adopted an organizational structure which, in outline, resembles the formal representative structure of the Labour Party but which in its day-to-day operation has the same kind of emphasis upon personal contact and informality which is found among the more unconventional peace activists" (1988, p. 82). This organizational structure is largely the product of a compromise between Labour Party activists who favor formal structures and new movement leftists who do not. Always wary of a split between different movement constituencies—like the one that occurred between conventional and direct-action wings in the 1960s—CND has sought to accommodate both. In this way, the British peace movement does not entirely fit the model of a new movement organization. This is because the movement has attracted representatives from what Offe (1985b) has called the "Old Paradigm"—in this case Labour Party activists—and this has affected its organizational structure.

But the influence of Labour Party peace activists was not restricted to the organizational level. They also sought to influence the political strategy of the peace campaign. They argued that mass protests, linked to concerted pressure in the trade unions and the Labour Party, would allow CND to realize its goals. Only the election of a left-wing Labour government, they claimed, would result in policy success for the movement. Naturally, this did not sit well with the new movement left, which took a less institutional approach to movement politics.

Labour Party activists also created internal problems when they carried their factional disputes into the CND. On one occasion Scottish CND organizer Ian Davison publicly accused certain Labour leftists of using the policy of unilateral disarmament as "a stick with which to beat their political rivals: especially 'SDP renegades,' Labour right-wingers and even 'leaders' of the Labour and peace movements" (*Sanity*, December 1983). In fact, divisions within the party's specialist group, Labour CND, became so bad that in June 1983 CND's National Council decided to put four of its members on the Labour CND executive with collective power of veto (*London Times*, August 20, 1983). Apparently some Trotskyites had been attempting to use Labour CND as a springboard to further influence in the Labour Party.

Thus CND's national organizers had to manage a campaign with diverse and often opposing constituencies. The new movement left opposed the Labour left's formalistic approach to organization and political strategy. At the same time, many Labour Party activists had little time for those who sat in circles, snipped at fences, and slept under tarpaulin at peace camps. Between these two groups sat a third that I call "mainstream centrist," which encouraged the movement to court public opinion through conventional activities that were not party oriented. Maintaining the unity of all three groups was a constant headache for CND's full-time staff, but they managed to do it successfully because of their independent organizational resources and their capacity to combine different forms of organization and protest.

The Political Impact of the Peace Movement

The Labour Party affected the peace movement not just through the presence of party members within the movement's leading organizations. The Labour Party's role as a political institution and, more specifically, as a potential party of government, had a direct bearing on the movement's strategic orientation. Even those on the new movement left or at the mainstream center recognized that the election of a Labour government provided the peace movement with its best opportunity for success. But they also wanted to keep open other options, such as influencing a future Alliance government or, in the case of the new movement left, confronting the state directly.

British peace campaigners used their considerable resources to pressure the authorities throughout the 1980s. Protesters lobbied Parliament, marched on the streets, and surrounded military bases. With the left dominant in the

Labour Party, they helped change and maintain party policy in favor of unilateral nuclear disarmament. The Labour Party fought two general elections, in 1983 and 1987, with this radical defense policy on its official manifesto. The Scottish and Welsh nationalist parties also adopted unilateralist policies, and the Liberal Party advocated prodisarmament positions—much to the chagrin of its Alliance partner, the Social Democratic Party—by the middle of the decade.

The general election of June 1983 was the first in which a major political party put the policy of unilateral nuclear disarmament before the electorate. This fact alone must count as a significant success for CND and the peace movement. But once the election campaign began, CND learned the cost of depending too heavily on an external ally. The Labour Party was still faction ridden, and its leaders squabbled publicly over their own defense policies. That is, the party was still internally oriented despite the fact that it was supposed to be fighting a general election. Even the genuine advocates of unilateralism within the party did not do a good job of presenting the case to the public. CND found it almost impossible to get "air time" during the election because the media regarded the political parties as the only legitimate actors in the contest. In June 1983 it was clear, whether CND liked it or not, that the future of the campaign was hitched to the electoral fortunes of a party that had adopted nearly all of its policies. The dramatic Labour loss of the election was also a bitter blow to CND.

The 1983 general election was the first major defeat for CND in this period. The Falklands War of 1982 had stabilized political alignments within the electorate, and the Conservative administration held a commanding lead in the opinion polls in the final year of Margaret Thatcher's first administration. The Labour Party was unable to emerge from its internal conflicts and present an effective challenge to the government. The Alliance parties only served to divide the opposition to the Conservatives. All the hopes of a first-choice Labour and a second-choice coalition government were dashed by the crushing defeats of Labour and the Alliance in the 1983 election. A second blow to the movement was the deployment of Cruise missiles at Greenham Common later the same year.

After 1983 the peace campaign began to drift as it tried to operate with diminishing resources and political opportunities. CND's membership began to decline and fewer people participated in peace protests. But a number of political ifs kept up supporters' morale and maintained the movement as a going concern. The Labour Party was now led by Neil Kinnock, who had been a CND member as a student and who, unlike his predecessor, seemed capable of leading an effective electoral campaign. Also, according to the opinion polls, the Alliance was still a viable electoral option. A mistake, or a series of mistakes, on the part of the government might lead to its eventual downfall.

In April 1986, the unpopular U.S. raid on Libya and the effects of the Chernobyl disaster breathed new life into the peace movement. The U.S. Air Force had used British bases to launch their bombers against Tripoli, and this highlighted for the peace campaign the issue of America's military presence. CND also argued that the fallout from Chernobyl illustrated the potential environmental impact of even a small nuclear weapon. Money flowed into CND's coffers, and there were mass protests over these two issues.

But the mood did not last and the peace movement faced its real challenge in the June 1987 election. CND tried to make a bigger impact this time by targeting marginal constituencies for its campaigning activities. The Labour Party had begun to emerge from its internal bickering but was still part of a divided opposition within a two-party system. Thatcher's government was returned for a record third term in office with an unassailable majority. Despite the peace movement's success in mobilizing significant resources within civil society and presenting an independent challenge to the authorities, it still depended on the Labour Party to deliver its policy demands. Once again, the electoral failure of Labour meant political failure for the campaign.

On December 8, 1987, President Reagan and General Secretary Gorbachev signed the Intermediate Range Nuclear Forces (INF) Treaty in Washington, D.C. Now the Cruise missiles were to be removed from Britain but, apparently, not as a result of CND's efforts. As veteran CND activist John Cox noted prophetically at the time, "Whilst the removal of Cruise missiles is a cause of celebration, the INF Agreement may prove more effective in disarming the peace movement than in ending the arms race" (*Sanity*, January 1988).

The Labour Party Ends the Peace Movement's Campaign

After December 1987 the Labour Party leadership had the opportunity to break with CND and took it. The leadership had never been happy with their party's commitment to unilateral nuclear disarmament. They also argued and may have believed that this policy was largely responsible for successive defeats in two general elections. With the changed international situation after the INF treaty and the rapid decline of CND, the Labour leadership made its first moves to reverse party policy. This coincided with a period in which the

Labour Party was much more united internally; it was a more effective opposition to the Conservatives on issues such as the poll tax and Europe; and its fortunes were beginning to improve in the opinion polls.

There was no attempt to drop unilateralism at Labour's annual conference in 1988. It was too soon and the ground had not been properly prepared. But in the autumn of that year the leadership's campaign began in earnest. On October 24, 1988, Kinnock sacked Ann Clwyd as junior spokeswoman on women's affairs because she opposed the Conservative government's spending plans on defense—plans that the parliamentary Labour Party did not oppose. She and twenty-eight other Labour rebels had voted against the budget rather than abstain, as the parliamentary leadership had decided. The sacking of Clwyd was a clear warning to aspiring Labour parliamentarians that dissent on defense meant no position in the shadow cabinet.

Then the Labour Party leadership made a move that was without doubt one of the most remarkable episodes of the peace campaign of the 1980s. They sent a delegation made up of two party leaders and two trade unionists to Moscow. When the delegates returned they announced that the Soviets were not interested in Britain's promoting unilateral initiatives and were more open to bilateral deals. (This claim was later denied by the Soviet embassy in London.) This attempt to enlist Soviet assistance in changing internal party policy was certainly a novel feature in British politics.

Then, in the first half of 1989, the Labour Party published a policy review and, not surprisingly, it contained a proposal to abandon the party's commitment to unilateralism. The CND reaction was a mixture of anger and resignation. E. P. Thompson described the entire process as "a farcical re-run of 1960/1" (*Sanity*, April 1989), when Labour had adopted and then dropped unilateralism for the first time.

In fact, the peace movement's political opportunity structure had just closed, as there was now little to separate the defense policies of Britain's political elite. In October 1989 the Labour Party officially endorsed the policy review's recommendations and thus effectively severed its relationship with the campaign.

And so history repeated itself: Labour abandoned CND after an orchestrated campaign by the party leadership. This change in Labour's stance was a sure sign that what had been a "party of movement" under left leadership in the 1980s was now preparing to become a "party of government" under centrist and right-wing control in the 1990s. The party believed that it was on the threshold of forming a government and did not want to carry what it saw as unnecessary baggage into an electoral campaign. The party leadership at this time was more interested in recapturing its core working-class constituency, particularly skilled workers, than in continuing its alliance with middle-class radicals. The episode represented the playing out of an old story in Labour politics—which will certainly be "told" again—and CND veterans of the 1960s experienced an awful feeling of political déjà vu.

Conclusions on the British Case

Although Britain's peace movement organization, the Campaign for Nuclear Disarmament, had strong organizational, cultural, and constituency resources, its emergence, evolution, and impact was shaped by its relationship with the Labour Party. The presence of individual Labour Party activists in the campaign provided an internal constituency that movement leaders had to accommodate organizationally, tactically, and strategically. Although there were internal problems because of differences between Labour and other groupings, CND was able to manage them through organizational compromise and flexibility with respect to protest tactics.

It was the external strategic logic of the movement's relationship with Labour that determined the political outcome. The structure of political opportunities in Britain meant that CND and the peace movement had to rely heavily on an external ally—that is, the Labour Party as a political institution. The Conservative government and state authorities were united on the issue of nuclear defense. Electoral alignments were unstable, but despite perceptions to the contrary this instability ultimately benefited the Tories. The movement's only potentially influential allies—the Labour Party and, to a certain extent, the Alliance—were unable, therefore, to deliver policy success. Thus Labour's electoral failures in 1983 and 1987 were also political setbacks for the movement. Movement activity and CND membership dropped precipitously after these two elections.

The Labour Party's political opportunities improved after 1987 because of greater internal party unity, the electoral decline of the alliance, and divisions within the government over the poll tax and Europe. The newly strengthened leadership judged the peace movement to be an electoral liability and now that the CND was in decline there was little the peace movement could do in response. Labour's official decision in October 1989 to drop unilateralist policies meant that the peace movement no longer had any political influence. Its campaign effectively had been declared over by its major ally in the political system.

The Italian Communist Party and the Italian Peace Movement

The Political Context

We have seen how the electoralist and parliamentary orientation of the British Labour Party allowed for the development of an independent peace movement organization, the Campaign for Nuclear Disarmament. This is characteristic of a social movement sector that, historically, has had considerable autonomy from the mass party of the left.

In Italy, the situation was reversed. The Italian Communist Party (PCI) has always been a "party of movement," and it keeps a close eye on potential competitors in civil society. Unlike British Labour, it plays a strong role in educating its members and establishes its political and cultural tentacles at every level of society. The contrast between these two parties is best illustrated by the fact that the Labour Party grew out of the British trade union movement, while the Italian trade union movement was largely a product of the PCI.

As we saw, the Labour Party had the potential to deliver the peace movement's goals in the 1980s. The Labour Party had been "domesticated" (made national and reformist) in the 1920s and thereafter became both a "party of government" and "Her Majesty's Loyal Opposition." The PCI, by contrast, cast off its internationalist and revolutionary clothes quite slowly between 1945 and the mid-1970s. Despite this change, it was still denied access to government, and thus it was unlikely that it could directly help a national peace movement realize its policy objectives.

The Italian peace movement emerged slowly at a time when the term *crisi* was automatically applied to any discussion of the country's state institutions, political parties, and economic system. The Italian state had faced severe challenges from left- and right-wing terrorists in the 1970s, and profound public discontent over its corruption and inefficiency. The two major parties—the Christian Democrats (DC) and the PCI—had to deal with the related problems of electoral decline and strategic stalemate. The economy was racked by high inflation, unemployment, and a trade deficit.

In the early 1980s, the PCI was attempting to reorient itself strategically after the end of the "historic compromise." The party had sought to implement this strategy in the late 1970s by supporting Christian Democrat-led "national unity" governments in Parliament. The Communists received very little in return and were never able to gain access to executive power (Allum 1979; Amyot 1981). As a result, the party lost considerable space on its left to a host of alternative parties and movement organizations: the Radical Party (PR), the Party of Proletarian Unity (PdUP), Proletarian Democracy (DP), and Continuous Struggle (Lotta Continua). None of these organizations had the capacity to challenge the PCI's domination of the left effectively, particularly at the electoral level, but together they had nibbled away at its influence in the social movement sector.

With the end of the national unity experiment in 1980, the PCI had failed in its mission to become a "party of government." A strong five-party coalition was formed after the end of the historic compromise; it was led by the Christian Democrats, included the Socialists, and excluded the PCI. In this unfavorable political situation, the PCI was determined to recapture the political space it had lost in civil society and return to its roots as a "party of movement."

At the onset, the PCI was adopting the same strategy that it had followed during the cold war: it was developing "its organizational skills in order to acquire power at the roots of Italian society" as a way of "compensat[ing] for its weakness at the summit" (Blackmer 1975, p. 51). Accordingly, the PCI also shifted its political strategy from the historic compromise to the "left alternative": that is, the party called for the establishment of a left coalition government that would exclude the Christian Democrats. PCI leaders realized that if this strategy were to work, the party had to reassert its dominance over the left in general.

We have seen how, in the political conjuncture of the early 1980s, the British Labour Party was deeply divided and came under the effective control of an increasingly dominant left. It was also open to challenge and capture by strong movement organizations like CND. The Italian PCI, on the other hand, was experiencing a period of internal reunification after years of intense division (Barbagli, Corbetta, and Sechi 1979). It wanted to recapture lost ground in civil society, and it surveyed a social movement sector that was filled with rival groups and organizations. It also wanted to establish contact with a youth culture that had become disillusioned with the PCI during the period of the historic compromise.

The Emergence of the Peace Movement

The first fact that should be noted about the Italian peace movement in the 1980s is that it was the last to emerge among the five countries scheduled for the deployment of Cruise missiles. While demonstrators first voiced their opposition on the streets of London, Brussels, Amsterdam, and Bonn in 1980, the streets of Rome were silent. What explains the tardiness of Italian peace protesters, who took another year to organize their first demonstration?

Senator Renzo Gianotti, who was made head of the PCI's newly created Office of Peace and Disarmament in September 1983, stated that there were four reasons for the late development of the Italian peace movement: (1) Italy is on the periphery of European defense and, therefore, the issue is regarded as less relevant by the Italian public. (2) The crisis of social democracy in Northern Europe facilitated the rise of peace movements there. No such crisis was prevalent in Italian politics in the early 1980s. (3) The lack of a coherent and established national identity in Italy did not allow the peace movement to tap nationalist resentment against American missiles early on. (4) The weight of political parties in Italian society makes it difficult for new movements to emerge (interview, June 5, 1985).

While there is considerable validity to all these arguments, it was the last factor—the weight of political parties and the PCI in particular—that prevented the initial emergence of the peace movement. Senator Gianotti denied the suggestion that the PCI's decision to abandon the historic compromise and its return to opposition played a significant role in allowing a peace movement to develop. Yet prior to the party's adoption of the "left alternative" strategy, it was decidedly lukewarm in its opposition to the Cruise missiles and its support for any peace campaign. When the party eventually decided to adopt and sponsor the movement, it played a key role in mobilizing 500,000 demonstrators onto the streets of Rome in October 1981.

When the PCI gave the green light to peace movement activity, militants from the party and its Youth Federation (the FGCI) entered the ranks of local peace groups. Where none existed, they set them up. In fact, many of these peace committees obtained their offices and other resources from local PCI headquarters. Thus from the very start the peace movement had little financial or organizational independence. Subsequent attempts to gain autonomy quickly turned into a political campaign to wrestle the movement from the grips of the PCI.

The Internal Evolution of the Peace Movement

One group of peace activists, in an open letter to the movement in 1983, argued that the national coordinating committee was little more than "a negotiating forum for the political parties." They argued that the only way to form a genuinely independent peace movement organization was to establish "the financial autonomy of the movement." One document put out by the movement's secretariat in 1984 complained that "the only way we know how to raise funds is to knock on the doors of groups of parliamentary representatives."

The only financial accounts of the Italian peace movement's national coordinating committee that are publicly available date from November 2, 1984. They demonstrate the disorganization, poverty, and dependent status of the movement's central coordinating body. Apparently, nobody was responsible for controlling the accounts; certain budgets were used to finance projects for which they were not allocated; and it had proven extremely difficult to keep track of the contributions of political parties. The national office was in debt and was behind in its payments for rent, telephone bills, and the salaries of its two full-time workers. The dependent status of the peace movement was revealed by the entries for its expenses on a referendum campaign: the Independent Left group in Parliament, which is elected on the electoral lists of the PCI, was responsible for three-quarters of the money spent on the referendum campaign.

Organizationally, the non-PCI left was unable to establish an independent structure for a movement that was a Communist-led coalition of political parties, their flanking organizations, and religious groups. This meant that the PCI was better able to recruit young peace movement leaders into the party's Office of Peace and Disarmament and its Youth Federation's Center for Projects on Peace. When the peace movement's fortunes began to wane after the installation of Cruise missiles in 1984, the movement lacked solid organizational foundations to hold onto its activists. Many of those without a political home then sought shelter in the lavish dwellings of the PCI and the FGCI.

The question of founding a national movement organization with individual membership modeled on Britain's CND was constantly debated in the movement but never implemented. In fact, a proposal to require peace committees to accept individual members rather than just political party representatives was passed by a vote of 192 to 176 at a national peace assembly in 1984. It was also decided that elected delegates from the peace committees had to occupy eighty out of one hundred positions on the national coordinating committee of the national peace movement organization.

Yet all this came to nothing on the late afternoon of the last day of the conference. As delegates began to drift away to catch their trains home, someone called for a new vote on all these issues. An angry delegate, sensing a party maneuver, grabbed a microphone and suggested that those peace committees that did not permit individual membership should leave the assembly immediately. Some people, in fact, did leave—because of the late hour—as a hubbub arose on the conference floor. The issue of individual membership was voted on five times before someone suggested that all unresolved questions be discussed at a future conference. The question of organizational autonomy was supposed to have been settled at a special national assembly in Catanzaro three years later (*La Repubblica*, March 28, 1987), but once again the political parties prevented this from happening.

It would be tempting to argue that all these problems of the Italian peace movement were a result of what one PCI peace activist satirized as "the astute maneuvers of a secret lobby or perhaps a midnight telephone [call] from Natta [then general secretary of the PCI]." The fact is that the peace movement, like all other movements in Italy, had to work within a civil society that is overwhelmingly dominated by political parties. As Tarrow (1990) argues, one of the causes of this is that Italy has weak state institutions surrounded by strong political parties. A consequence of this political and cultural framework is that it is extremely difficult for party activists to imagine working within movements outside of "party logic." This was evidenced in the behavior within the peace movement not only of the PCI but also of its competitors such as the far leftist Proletarian Democracy.

A couple of political groups might have played the role of providing an organizational counterweight to the PCI without dominating the movement themselves. The Radical Party had led peace campaigns long before the INF decision and had the resources to assist an independent organization. But Radical organizers refused to participate in the new peace movement because they argued it was PCI dominated and had "misframed" its demands. Radical activists were also concerned about losing their own political turf on the peace issue.

The Proletarian Unity Party did play this role in the early days of the movement and helped set up an independent peace magazine, *Pace e Guerra*. But the PCI had strategic designs on Proletarian Unity and was determined to incorporate this splinter party as part of the process of constructing the "left alternative." In June 1983 the Proletarian Unity Party stood in national elections on the electoral lists of the PCI. Later the two parties merged and Proletarian Unity leaders and cadres were given jobs in the upper echelons of the PCI. According to one peace activist, this "disappearance" of Proletarian Unity was "a severe blow to the autonomy of the peace movement" (interview, June 1987).

Religious organizations such as Pax Christi, the International Movement of Reconciliation, and the evangelical churches were involved in the nonparty wing of the movement. Like the mainstream centrists in Britain, they preferred conventional forms of protest free from party control. They marched, held candlelight vigils, and framed their demands in abstract terms. Some groups, particularly in the Catholic Church, had to look over their shoulders at competing organizations from the right (such as Comunione e Liberazione), and this limited how far they could go. Their religious orientation and political moderation made them weak candidates for providing an alternative leadership to the PCI.

The final alternative to the PCI in the peace movement was the new movement left, which was made up of radical pacifists, feminists, and environmentalists. This tendency rejected the political maneuvers of the Proletarian Democracy and Proletarian Unity parties, the petulance of the Radicals, the tepidity of religious groups, and the dominance of the PCI. Pacifist groups such as the League of Conscientious Objectors, the League for Unilateral Disarmament, and the Non-Violent Movement cooperated to organize nonviolent direct actions and pressure the movement to adopt a unilateralist platform. But the new movement left was no match for the PCI and had to play a secondary role at best. For one thing, their ideological opposition to organization in principle weakened any internal challenge that they made.

The Political Impact of the Peace Movement

The political impact of the Italian peace movement was weakened by the character of its internal development. PCI activists were not just one constituency among many, the way individual Labour members were in Britain. They were part of an institution that was determined to control the movement itself. This meant that the Italian movement lacked a strong and independent central organization to unite its diverse factions around unified protests and demands. The main political consequence of the movement's lack of financial, organizational, and political autonomy was that it was easier for the Italian government to ignore this challenge from below. It could simply argue that the peace movement was yet another political weapon in the hands of the PCI. In this way, the movement was unable to have its policy demands met through direct contacts with the authorities. Given that the PCI was excluded from government, it too was unable to deliver.

The movement was crippled by disunity from the moment it launched its first protests. For example, the Italian Socialist Party (PSI) refused to participate in the first mass demonstration in Rome on October 24, 1981. When all the trade union confederations and the PCI, Socialists, and Christian Democrats supported a peace demonstration in Florence on November 26 that year, the Proletarian Democracy, Proletarian Unity, and Radical parties and a rebellious Communist Party Youth Federation refused to take part (Lodi 1984, p. 37). Three days later the Proletarian Democracy and Proletarian Unity parties organized a march separate from that led by the trade unions in Palermo. On June 5, 1982, an anti-Reagan march was organized in Rome and although it attracted 100,000 participants, it created enormous internal conflict over its tactics and demands (Lodi 1984, p. 51).

The emergence of nonviolent direct action protests only added to the internal bickering. The PCI regarded nonviolent direct action as a potentially dangerous form of protest because it could attract supporters who might adopt the direct action and forget the nonviolence. As a safeguard, the PCI insisted that nonviolent direct action had to involve mass participation before it would lend its support (Marasa 1986, p. 59).

But the PCI also recognized that the organization of nonviolent direct action, informal networks, and affinity groups was an attempt by the new movement left to counter its power. Peace camps were set up outside the Cruise missile base at Comiso. Women knotted their bodies together, Greenham style, to block its entrance. Some pacifist and environmental groups bought land nearby and set up a camp in which they grew produce. Peace activists from elsewhere in Europe descended on Comiso—usually during the summer—and helped establish an International Peace Camp and an International Meeting against Cruise. The local disarmament committee (CUDIP)—which was dominated by the PCI—viewed these developments with some concern.

Thus the Italian peace movement never succeeded in mounting an effective challenge against the state. Its actions were anything but collective, and it was more contentious internally than against the authorities it sought to pressure. There were also angry internal debates about unilateral disarmament and Italy's withdrawal from NATO. The PCI was opposed to both and was able to prevent them from becoming central movement demands.

The Italian Peace Movement's Impact on the PCI

One surprising aspect of the Italian case, however, was the way in which even such a weak movement affected the party that dominated it. The regional secretary of the Sicilian PCI, Pio La Torre, adopted some radical positions on disarmament that led to concerned telephone calls from Rome. The former PCI mayor of Comiso, Giacomo Cagnes, engaged in some nonviolent direct actions and went on hunger strike in protest against Cruise deployment. When the missiles were deployed and the national PCI called on its members to accept the situation and await the outcome of superpower talks in Geneva, party activists like Cagnes refused to compromise. In fact, the PCI in Comiso was so divided on this issue that many of its members refused to speak to each other in public (interview, March 28, 1987).

On a national level, the PCI's return to movement activity led to changes in party policy and structure. The party's Youth Federation (the FGCI) and its cultural and sporting organization (ARCI) both opposed the PCI's pro-nuclear-energy policies. It was partly as a result of their efforts that the party reversed its position on this issue in 1987. Also, the Youth Federation was the first party organization to abandon democratic centralism as it sought to adapt its structures to various aspects of its movement activities.

Any sober analysis of the Italian peace movement must conclude that the PCI had more of an impact on this new movement in the 1980s than vice versa, but it is interesting to note that the party was also changed by the relationship. This highlights the fact that there are some costs involved for a political party that attempts to dominate a protest movement: its activists may be transformed by the experience and work to change their party of origin.

Conclusions on the Italian Peace Movement

The emergence, evolution, and political impact of the Italian peace movement was shaped by the movement's relationship with the PCI. It could emerge only with PCI support, and it was organizationally and financially dependent on the party. Without an independent movement organization, it was unable to launch unified protests, develop its own protest repertoire, and put forward a set of autonomous political demands. Obviously, this blunted the movement's challenge to the state. Perhaps if the campaign had been led by religious groups—like the Netherlands' IKV—it might have caused some headaches for the ruling Christian Democrats, but the government was able to dismiss a movement dominated by the PCI. The PCI, in turn, lacked the policy resources to grant the movement success because of its continued exclusion from governmental power. The political opportunity structures of the PCI and the peace movement, therefore, were identical and bleak. Thus, although there was massive public sentiment against Cruise deployment, party-movement relations in Italy prevented effective mobilization of it.

The lasting legacy of the movement of the 1980s was to develop some independent organizations and create divisions on nuclear energy and defense within the PCI. The PCI now calls itself the Party of the Democratic Left. The continuing crisis of this factionalized party may give new social movements more political space and allow a very different pattern of party-movement relations to emerge in the future.

Conclusions: Opposition Parties and Protest Movements

Even though the INF decision imposed the same grievance on national movements in Britain and Italy, they emerged and developed in radically different ways. While important international links were established among European peace movements in the 1980s, the British and Italian movements demonstrate how their tactics and strategies—even their internal organizational structures—were shaped by their relationship with domestic political parties. In Italy, the importation of nonviolent direct action tactics and unilateralist policies failed to take off in the face of PCI opposition. Attempts to construct an Italian social movement organization modeled on Britain's CND floundered for the same reason.

These findings of national distinctions emerge from an international process that is remarkably kind to practitioners of the comparative method. This comparison has shown the importance of "national political traditions and alignments" in conditioning "the formation, the strategies, and outcomes of the new movements" (Klandermans and Tarrow 1988, p. 23). National movements may cooperate and learn from each other, but domestic political contexts can determine their organization, strategies, and fate.

The British and Italian comparison also illustrates why it is crucial to understand how political parties affect protest movements in general. First of all, the organizational and cultural weight of political parties in civil society is an important variable for understanding movements' capacity for political autonomy. Here it is important to identify the orientation of ideologically relevant parties—that is, relevant to the issues raised by protesters—toward the social movement sector in general. Do they regard it as a central arena for party activity or one that they can occasionally afford to ignore? Parties that lack policy resources, like the PCI, will tend to place great emphasis on the world of social movements. Parties that are strong in policy resources or have immediate potential in this regard will not.

Second, one must understand the character of party activists and the political baggage they bring into movements. What are their attitudes toward organization, tactics, and strategy, and what is their political relationship with their own party? This can shape the internal organization, protest repertoire, and political direction of the movements themselves. We saw even in the case of a party that was weak organizationally and culturally (the Labour Party) that it had members who as peace activists affected the internal politics of the movement. In a party that has great organizational and cultural strengths (such as the PCI), party involvement in the base of a movement can deprive it of organizational and political autonomy.

Third, what can a party offer a movement in terms of resources and granting its policy demands? For example, if a party is a potential "party of government," it must enter a movement's strategic calculations for achieving policy success. Even a movement that has an autonomous social base, like Britain's CND, has to establish a relationship with such a party if it wants to achieve political success.

Finally, the political circumstances of a party in a particular context clearly determine its strategic orientation toward an emerging protest movement. For example, a party that faces an unfavorable political opportunity structure and has been weakened by internal conflict is vulnerable to external protest movements. A party that is united and combative and has the opportunity to come to power is better able to cast off unwelcome outside influence.

Britain and Italy provide important lessons about party-movement relations. The British peace movement captured the Labour Party with the cooperation of the Labour left. The cost of this success was that the movement came to rely excessively on an external ally that was unable to deliver the goods. The Italian peace movement, by contrast, was swallowed by the PCI and was unable to launch genuinely independent initiatives. Yet the PCI had to bear the costs of some of its militants and flanking organizations being influenced by the new movement left. The British experience teaches us that if a protest movement wins over a political party, the movement can become hostage to the party's electoral fortunes. Also, if the internal politics and electoral position of a party improve and a movement's mobilization potential weakens, the movement can be jettisoned by its erstwhile ally. The lesson from Italy is that if a political party dominates a protest movement organizationally, the movement is subject to the political opportunity structure of the party. If the political outlook for such a party is gloomy, then this will also be true for the movement.

The British and Italian experiences also add an interesting twist to the debate about whether movements should rely on their capacity for disruption or for organization. The British peace movement had a strong central organization that promoted disruptive activities throughout the 1980s and presented a concerted challenge to the state. With CND as an organizational resource, the British peace movement prevented any one faction from becoming dominant. Without a central organization, however, the Italian peace movement was unable to coordinate unified collective action. It may well be that organizations promote hierarchy and discourage militancy, but they also ward off outside predators, nurture new recruits, and allow for a genuine "double militancy" from those who have arrived from elsewhere.

It seems that protest movements need to get close enough to political parties to exploit their position in the structure of capitalist democracy. But if they get too close, they may be swallowed up or come to rely on an institution whose fortunes they cannot determine. Party activists march on the streets with protesters, and party representatives can often meet movement demands. These dual features of political parties offer great opportunities that movement organizers would be foolish to ignore, but they should also not forget that the ultimate goal of most political parties is to walk in the corridors of power. Protest movements will gain party support only to the extent that they can help them get there.

Chapter 9

Left-Libertarian Movements in Context: A Comparison of Italy and West Germany, 1965–1990

Donatella della Porta and Dieter Rucht

Several attempts have been made to analyze social movements from a di-achronic or a synchronic perspective or both. Inspired by Eisinger, who demonstrated a curvilinear relationship between the incidence of protest in U.S. cities and the challengers' access to local political decision making (Eisinger 1973, p. 28), increasingly complex models have been elaborated to explain a growing number of dependent variables. Most of this work has referred to a "political opportunity structure" as a set of independent variables (Tarrow 1983; Tarrow 1989b; Brand 1985; Kitschelt 1986; Kriesi 1989b, 1991). The use of this concept in cross-national comparison, however, involves three problems. First, the limited number of investigated cases does not allow for fruitful generalization. Second, the multiplicity of factors makes it virtually impossible to assess accurately the causal relationship between independent and dependent variables. Third, there has been a tendency toward static analyses, insofar as several explanatory models attributed general movement characteristics to more or less inert structural conditions, and therefore were unable to explain the relevant conjunctural shifts. In this introduction, we will discuss in some detail the choices we made in order to deal with these three problems.

In response to the first problem, our strategy was not to increase the number of countries and in turn broaden the scope of analysis, but rather to treat a multitude of movements in each country. In research on social movements, the unit of analysis usually has been an individual movement or, more specifically, a particular campaign or conflict involving parts of a social movement. Although it has been emphasized that a social movement should not be seen as isolated from the plethora of coexisting movements, few attempts have been made to refer to a set of movements as the unit of analysis (but see Garner and Zald 1985; Brand 1985; Kriesi 1989b, 1990; Rucht 1991). There may be good reasons for that omission. First, the categories created to deal with such sets of movements are not well elaborated conceptually. Second, it is difficult to delineate a set of movements empirically. Third, given the fact that single movements in themselves are complex phenomena that are hard to grasp, it is even more difficult to reconstruct a configuration of several movements. These problems notwithstanding, we think that focusing on a specific set of movements—what we would call a social movement family, analogous to "party family," "famille de politique," and "famille spirituelle" in the literature on political parties—offers some advantages. A broader view on social movements may reveal in a given historical context general characteristics that otherwise would be ignored. Moreover, such an encompassing view can provide us with information on both the impact of national political contexts on social movements in general and, vice versa, on the role of social movements in the context of broader social change. Choosing such a broad object of analysis, we can hope to make some generalizations on the interplay between unconventional politics and conventional political parties and the society as a whole.

As for the second problem, we chose to concentrate on only one dependent variable, namely the behavior of a social movement family, and to relate it to a narrow set of independent variables. Social movements have many facets and can be viewed from different perspectives. Ideologies, organizational characteristics, mobilization potentials, and impacts of social movements are beyond our immediate interest. Our focus lies instead in the changes in the overall behaviors of a social movement family, as measured on a limited set of dimensions. As for the explanation of this dependent variable, we will concentrate mainly on two intervening variables—the influence of the conflict system and the alliance system. Our central aims are elaborating an explanatory approach, developing a number of hypotheses, and discussing these hypotheses in the light of our empirical material.

As for the third problem, we decided to pinpoint changes over time by looking at the effects of conjunctural opportunities. We see several advantages in focusing on changing opportunities. First, we think that such a perspective comes closer to the complex reality. Unlike other authors (Brand 1985; Kitschelt 1986), we assume that social movements in a given country undergo considerable changes in their ideologies, strategies, forms of organization, and levels of activities. It is therefore difficult to characterize these movements without a specific time reference. Moreover, inert societal and political characteristics, as they have been emphasized by these authors, can hardly explain changes on the part of the movements.[1] As a consequence, we also needed to take a close look at varying structures and power constellations. Second, our emphasis on changing conditions and effects allowed us to distinguish between various developmental phases and therefore to compensate, at least to some extent, for the disadvantage of comparing only two countries. Making use of this strategy, we multiplied our cases, because each phase in each country could be perceived as a separate case.

For pragmatic reasons, we chose to limit our analysis to two countries and a specific family of movements. We chose Italy and Germany for several reasons. These are our respective native countries, and we have devoted much scholarship to their contemporary protest movements. This provides us with a solid background. Moreover, we believe that these two countries are an adequate starting point for cross-national comparison. Broadly speaking, both countries have similar size, degree of modernization, and political institutions, and thus could be expected to produce some similar social movement characteristics. At the same time, however, the countries also exhibit some differences with regard to their party systems, governmental constellations, relevance of the left-right cleavage, and aspects of political culture—characteristics that, among other things, are related to the intervening variables mentioned earlier. These dissimilarities can thus be expected to have a differential impact on our dependent variable.

We also decided to restrict our analysis to one social movement family, the left-libertarian social movements. We adopt this term from Kitschelt, who used it for a specific type of party:

> They are 'Left' because they share with traditional socialism a mistrust of the marketplace, of private investment, and of the achievement of ethic, and a commitment to egalitarian redistribution. They are 'libertarian' because they reject the authority of the private or public bureaucracies to regulate individual and collective conduct. They instead favor participatory democracy and the autonomy of groups and individuals to define their economic, political, and cultural institutions unencumbered by market or bureaucratic dictates. (1990, p. 180)

We think that this social movement family is highly relevant in contemporary Western societies insofar as it includes the New Left movements, which tended to be dominant at an early stage, and the so-called new social movements, which predominated later on.

An Explanatory Model for Social Movement Family Behavior

In our understanding, the dominant behavior of a social movement family is influenced by internal and external factors. We expect that some of these fac-

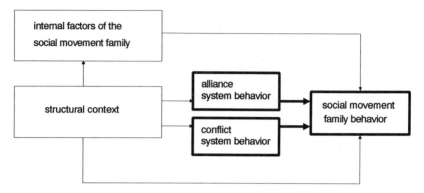

Figure 1. Explanatory scheme for the behavior of a social movement family

tors are mediated through two clusters of intervening variables, which we define as the behavior of the alliance system and the behavior of the conflict system. Together, these assumptions can be integrated into the explanatory model illustrated in Figure 1.[2] In the following, we will specify our definitions of these variables and indicate the main focus of our analysis.

The Dependent Variable:
The Dominant Behavior of a Social Movement Family

A social movement family can be conceived of in a preliminary manner as a set of coexisting movements that, regardless of their specific goals, have similar basic values and organizational overlaps, and sometimes may even enjoin for common campaigns. This definition comes close to what McCarthy and Zald (1977, p. 1219) have called a social movement industry, defined as the set of all movement organizations oriented toward a similar social change goal. We have not adopted this category for two reasons. First, it is not clear if a social movement industry refers to one or several social movements. Second, the authors' concept implies a strong organizational bias, as they define social movement industries only on the basis of social movement organizations. By contrast, our definition of a social movement, and consequently of social movement families, goes beyond social movement organizations, including also occasional contributors and nonorganized, spontaneous activities. Our category is clearly narrower than Garner and Zald's social movement sector, which is defined as

> the configuration of social movements, the structure of antagonistic, competing and/or cooperating movements which in turn is part of a larger structure of action (political action, in a very broad sense) that may include parties, state bu-

reaucracies, the media, pressure groups, churches, and a variety of other organizational actors in a society. (1985, p. 120; see also McCarthy and Zald 1977, p. 1220)

According to our more restrictive category, more than one social movement family can be present in a given society. There may be a movement family composed of countermovements that oppose one or several movements of the initial movement family; there may be even a further social movement family that is more indifferent to both the initial movement family and to its challenging movements. We think that there are good reasons to focus on the narrower and more coherent phenomenon we call a social movement family. Although we agree with Garner and Zald that social movements should not be seen as isolated phenomena, we do not necessarily share the authors' conclusion that one must examine the "the totality of social movements in a society" (1985, p. 119) in order to understand the course of a specific set of movements, or a single movement. Social movements may be indifferent to each other or have distinct determining environments. In this case, it would be more promising to study specific kinds or sets of movements within their specific environments.[3]

Moving a step further, we think that a social movement family should be defined with regard to spatial and temporal limits. For our purposes, the spatial reference of a social movement family is its national territory. As for the time dimension, we think that the concept of a social movement family implies a cyclical development lasting several years or even some decades.[4] During such a cycle, a specific historical configuration, based on both structural and ideological convergences of a set of social movements, emerges, stabilizes, and finally fades away. Though it may be hard to draw a clear boundary between the end of an "old" and the beginnings of a "new" cycle, we think that such an effort should be made. Otherwise, we would have to assume the virtually permanent existence of the same social movement family. We therefore define a social movement family as a nationally based, historical configuration of movements that—though they have different specific goals, immediate fields of struggle, and strategic preferences—share a common worldview, have organizational overlaps, and occasionally ally for joint campaigns. Regarding the second categorical element of our dependent variable, we refer to behavior as a broad category including both strategic action[5] and forms of spontaneous, uncoordinated, and probably un- or semiconscious action.[6] Although the term *behavior* usually is related to a distinct individual or collective actor, we think that this term can also be used with regard to more complex and internally differentiated actors such as social movements, or even social movement families. In this case, behavior is an emergent phenomenon that results from the overall effect of the activities of many actors, who do not necessarily all have the same motives, situational definition, and direct coordination. Nevertheless, in speaking of the behavior of a social movement family we still assume the existence of general, identifiable features of its activities. We would not, however, apply the term *behavior* to the interaction of totally diverging actors or to a system of antagonistic actors.

Analytically, we can contrast more cultural and more political orientations of the collective actors in whom we are interested. Focusing on political orientations, we will distinguish between different degrees of "radicality" in the dominant behavior in the social movement family (see "The Intervening Variables").

The Independent Variables:
Structural Context and Internal Factors

Because we are uncertain about the weight of specific factors in influencing the behaviors of a social movement family, we first broaden our view of the range of potentially relevant independent variables. First, we identify the *structural context* as the setting for both the social movement family and the alliance and conflict systems. This context represents relatively stable conditions that favor or restrict the activities of the major actors, such as governments, parties, interest groups, and social movements. These conditions can hardly be changed by one single actor within a short time period (if at all) and therefore tend to be perceived as given. This applies in particular to internationally determined factors such as developments in the world economy; international power constellations; and the cross-national diffusion of themes, knowledge, and action repertoires. We assume that the structural context, in part, has a direct impact on social movements' internal properties and behaviors, but to some extent also influences social movements through the mediation of conflict and alliance systems.

Second, we identify *internal factors* as encompassing organizational and cultural resources. Organizational resources, which provide the "material" basis for communication and action, include the movements' networks, infrastructure, and organizations. We define cultural resources as worldviews, values, frames, symbols, skills, experiences, and motivations. We expect these internal factors to have direct, unmediated impacts on the behavior of social movement.

The Intervening Variables:
The Behaviors of Allies and Opponents

First, our approach features what we consider to be an instructive shift in emphasis from a conception of a movement's external context as relatively inert to one concentrating on the interplay of social movements, or movement families, and other actors. We identify such intervening variables as the behaviors of the *alliance system* and the *conflict system*, which, among other things, shape the behavior of a social movement family through interactive processes. We assume that, as a rule, the external context variables are at least partly mediated through these intervening variables, and that the latter exert a direct influence on several characteristics of a social movement family. Consequently, we focus our empirical analysis on the behaviors of allies and opponents of social movements in the two countries. Drawing on recent approaches emphasizing fields of interaction (Kriesi 1989b, 1991; Klandermans 1989b, 1990), we define an alliance system as being composed of the political actors supporting a social movement family, and the conflict system as being composed of those opposing it. While the alliance system provides resources and creates political opportunities for social movements, the conflict system attempts to worsen these conditions to the detriment of social movements.[7] It should be emphasized that according to this definition, conflict and alliance systems are not considered a stable set of actors. A collective actor may change its positions vis-à-vis a social movement family, and thus shift from the alliance to the conflict system or vice versa.

Second, and more specifically, we assume that in order to explain such political variables as the behaviors of a social movement family we have to take into account, above all, the *political behavior* of both the alliance system and the conflict system. Both systems can be more or less "open" to the social movement family. In order to simplify our analysis, we conceived the attitudes of each of the allies and opponents as dichotomous variables. As for the allies, their interactions with social movements vary from a friendly attitude of cooperation to a more unfriendly attitude of competition. As for the opponents, their interactions with social movements vary between the more moderate attitude of bargaining and the more radical, and even repressive, attitude of confrontation. Both types of behaviors describe reciprocal patterns of interaction, so that a movement family can have four different kinds of behavior: cooperation, competition, bargaining, and confrontation.[8] Cooperation and confrontation are the attitudes of the movement family toward its allies; bargaining and confrontation its attitudes toward opponents.

Table 1. Behavioral patterns of social movement families and alliance and conflict systems

Cooperation Bargaining	Competition Confrontation
Social movement family and alliance system	Social movement family and conflict system

Third, it is necessary to take a closer look at the composition of alliance and conflict systems as well as the behavior of actors within them. According to Kriesi (1989b, p. 296), the most important actors within these systems are (major) political parties and interest groups such as the unions. In addition, we think that cooperative movements and countermovements also may come into play. Regarding the relative weight of allies and opponents, it is agreed that an actor's behavior is strongly influenced by the behavior of its opponents. Because this is probably less evident for the behavior of the allies, we pay much attention to their role. So far, only Kriesi has focused on this aspect. In his analysis of the political opportunity structure of the Dutch peace movements, he has demonstrated the impact of the "configuration of the relevant actors of the left" (1989b, p. 296). According to Kriesi, the high degree of integration of the Dutch peace movement is mainly caused by the "strategic posture of the dominant party on the left" (1989, p. 306). As will be shown in our analysis, this is also a crucial factor for social movement behaviors in Italy and West Germany.

The Development of Left-Libertarian Movements and the Reactions of the Alliance and Conflict Systems

In the following we will describe left-libertarian movements and their political context in Italy and West Germany in the past three decades. Both countries have seen the rise of four movements we analyze here: the student movement, the (new) women's movement, the ecological movement, and the (new) peace movement. For most periods in our study, the alliance system coincided with the main left-wing party and the trade unions. The conflict system included conservative parties, state institutions (in particular policy makers and control agencies), and countermovements.

In our brief overview, we will concentrate mainly on behavioral shifts of the left-libertarian movements, and on the conflict and alliance systems, in Italy and West Germany for each of the phases we have distinguished on the basis of the dominant behaviors of the movements. We sometimes also provide additional information on organizational or ideological changes of the social movement sectors.

The Development of Left-Libertarian Movements in Italy

Commencing generally with the emergence of the New Left in the mid-1960s and early 1970s, Italy experienced a cyclical development of the left-libertarian movement family. This period was characterized by a very high level of mobilization in different sectors of the society—what Tarrow (1989a) described as part of a "cycle of protest." The protest declined in the 1970s, leaving behind small and radicalized left-libertarian movements. Lacking the protest peaks of disruptiveness and visibility of the previous decades, the 1980s testify to the growth and "institutionalization" of new social movements.

The Protest Incubation Phase: 1960–66.   The high mobilization of the late 1960s was preceded by a first offensive wave of strikes in the big factories in the beginning of the decade. The economic boom and the (almost) full employment of the labor force had strengthened the structural position of the working class. While the trade unions and the Communist Party (PCI) gained some access to institutional power after the repressive politics of the 1950s, criticisms emerged from their left. Dissidents from the PCI and the Socialist Party (PSI) created a number of "study groups" and "theoretical magazines" that attacked the "revisionism" of the Old Left. Calling themselves *operaisti* (laborist), these groups stressed the "centrality" of class conflict and the need for an "autonomous" organization of the working class. Members of these small groupings were active in some big factories in the industrial zones of northern Italy and formed intellectual circles at the universities. Although some aspects of the emerging youth cultures were "imported" from the Anglo-Saxon culture in this period, these cultures did not play a significant role within the social movement sector.

Phase 1. The Revolutionary Years: 1967–76.   This phase was characterized by a clear dominance of the New Left, while the cultural wing always remained weak. Hopes for radical social changes were couched in a traditional "class language."

This was true, first of all, for the student movement, which—in Italy as well as elsewhere—had been the first "new" social movement to appear on the stage. The ties between the students and the workers were tight and numerous. Since the very beginning of the student protest, political skills were formed in the student unions, but also in the *operaisti* groups. Accordingly, the students aimed at linking their antiauthoritarian sentiments with working-class revolution and looked for allies in the large factories. The

image of the student movement as an ally of the working class became dominant when the university nuclei strengthened their ties with one or the other
of the *gruppi operaisti* in order to organize common activities outside the university. These now represented the main organizations of the New Left.[9]
More than elsewhere in Europe, the New Left in Italy used symbols and
frames of reference that were known and accepted by the Old Left, and was
able to extend its influence on groups of workers who opposed the trade
unions' strategy. So although the Old Left and the New Left competed for the
support of leftist activists, their goals and strategies coincided to a large extent. At least until 1974, the left-libertarian movements perceived the Old
Left, and in particular the PCI, as their main ally and source of support.

The women's movement also had a prevailing New Left orientation. In its
initial phase, at the end of the 1960s, the women's movement was composed
of small "study groups" and other informal groupings. Based on the model of
American and European women's movements, these groups had developed
forms of civil disobedience and self-help groups on problems of contraception
(still illegal) and women's health. After 1972, however, women's collectives
had also been formed inside the New Left, taking up more "political" issues.
Triggered by the Catholic Church-sponsored campaign for the repeal of the
law governing divorce, mass mobilization developed in favor of the legaliza-
tion of abortion, lasting until 1976. The campaign to liberalize abortion broad-
ened the scope of the women's movement, bringing about important cooperation with women's groups inside the PCI and the trade unions. Because of
the presence of a strong (old and new) left, widespread analyses of the role of
women in society used some traditional "class conflict" categories: "exploitation" of women as sex objects and housewives, "imperialism" via macho values, the "structural nature" of the "contradiction" between sexes (Ergas
1986, p. 64). Here too, the Old Left was seen as a main ally for a number of
issue-oriented protest campaigns.

As for their repertoires of action, both movements "imported" forms of
protest developed by the U.S. civil rights movement, but also borrowed to a
large extent from the Old Left. The students occupied their schools and universities and the workers their factories, as strikes were called and pickets organized. Students and workers joined in several protest campaigns (urban
protests, among others) and together they faced clashes with neofascists and
police. Although the trade union leaders often criticized the students for their
excessively radical forms of action, the more disruptive protest events happened when workers and students acted together (Tarrow 1989a, p. 186). In
the women's movement, too, the presence of the Old and New Left widened

the range of actions implemented in the various campaigns: more conventional tactics (such as petitions) were combined with new forms of civil disobedience (such as "visible" illegal abortions). Although the hope for radical political changes fueled the cooperation between the left-libertarian movements and the Old Left, the position of both allies vis-à-vis the elites was characterized by a quite radical confrontation. More than anywhere else in Western Europe, violence escalated during the period: it occurred in unplanned and mass forms in the beginning; the organized, small-group-based forms of violence predominated at the end of the period (della Porta and Tarrow 1986, p. 619). The period ended with the first premeditated murder carried out by the Red Brigades.

In the alliance system, the PCI attempted to integrate protest in a reformist and oppositional strategy. Harsh internal criticisms and ideological controversies notwithstanding, the Old Left had a cooperative attitude toward the New Left. The trade unions tried to "ride the tiger of the workers' rage," as it was said—that is, to use the spontaneous, and often violent, protest actions in the factories as a resource for strengthening their bargaining position vis-à-vis the employers. Only a handful of the activists of the student movement joined the Federazione Giovanile Comunista Italiana (FGCI), the youth organization of the PCI (Barbagli and Corbetta 1978). But at least until the end of 1973, the PCI welcomed the more varied forms of protest and considered the social movements as part of the united left front that had to fight for structural reforms. Although the PCI was weak and isolated in the Italian party system, its growing electoral strength kept alive hopes for radical political change. The change in government they desired was not to be fulfilled, however. In the 1976 national elections the PCI gains were not sufficient to surpass the Christian Democrats, and the first attempt of the main New Left groups to run under a single banner failed.

The conflict system reciprocated the radical orientation of the left-libertarian movements in this phase, as they attempted to resist changes demanded by the various social and political actors through confrontational behaviors (for a political history of Italy, see Ginsborg 1989). The new center-right coalition tried to block the reforms put on the agenda by the center-left governments of the 1960s. Although some elements of a modern system of industrial relations were introduced, very little reform was implemented in other policy areas. After 1973 deflation policies were chosen to confront the economic crisis. Control of political protest was characterized by extremely violent repression. Following a deep-rooted tradition that had produced several fatalities during workers' protests in the postwar period, police often used

brutal violence to break up public marches (see Canosa 1976). The peculiar-
ity of the Italian case lies especially in the presence of neofascist (counter)
movements supported by a portion of the political and economic elites. Neofascist "squads" violently clashed with movement "marshal bodies" all
through the 1970s, with several victims and acts of revenge on both sides
(della Porta 1990, 1991). Right-wing terrorists committed massacres, apparently with the help of secret service agents. During the whole period, there
were rumors of plotted coups d'état involving army generals and politicians of
parties in government.

Phase 2. The Years of Despair: 1977–83.   These years were characterized by
the latency of mass movements, interrupted only during a wave of youth
protest in 1977, the antinuclear campaign, and the anti-Cruise missile campaign.[10] Terrorism gradually undermined most chances for collective action
and protest.

The year 1976 represented a turning point for the women's movement,
which during the parliamentarian debate on the abortion law did not engage
in the more political forms of action (Ergas 1982, pp. 268ff., 1986, p. 78).
While a few groups took advantage of new institutional opportunities and
started to act as interest groups, the majority of the participants in the movement shared a pessimistic mood generated by the loss of mobilization capacity. The movement was split into a number of small, informal collectives—several conscious-raising groups—with self-oriented aims ("search for the self")
and no interest in advertising their existence or recruiting new members.[11]
Also, the students could rarely be mobilized. The student activists preferred
to intervene outside the school and university, organizing protests against
heroin and the transformation of "squatted" (occupied) public buildings into
"youth centers" (Sorlini 1978). A wave of antinuclear protests characterized
the incubation of the ecological movement. Some political protest—activities
mobilizing a maximum of 50,000 protesters (Rome in 1979)—followed the approval of the National Plan for Energy (including the construction of twenty
nuclear plants) and the building of the first nuclear plant, in Montalto di Castro. However, a mainly cultural approach also prevailed on the environmental
issue, which mobilized groups on animal rights and environmental protection
under the auspices of the Radical Party and small circles of intellectuals and
scientists. The activists of the New Left were slow to become interested in
ecological issues ("One has to be red before being green").

The component of the left-libertarian movements that had kept its genuine
political orientation was confronted with a hyperradicalized atmosphere. Still

influenced by the New Left organizations, many small groups—active especially in youth issues—had radicalized their tactics and assumed the so-called autonomy ideology, precariously combining old Leninist frames with pessimistic images of the "totalitarian" society. The working class was less and less a point of reference, and the Old Left started to be seen as an enemy. Autonomous groups that had tried to promote youth protest failed to articulate political campaigns. The daily fights with neofascists, drug dealers, and police led to a rapid radicalization with dramatic forms of violence. These youth groups provided new recruits for the terrorist organizations, which grew stronger in these years. Protest demobilized after the Red Brigades kidnapped and killed the president of the Christian Democratic Party, Aldo Moro, and an antiterrorist emergency policy was implemented. Only terrorist organizations seemed to be on the rise, at least until 1980, when a few of their members started to collaborate with the police, producing serious setbacks for the main underground groups. As for the women's movement, some of the small collectives tried to keep the political fight alive by resorting to violent, sometimes terrorist actions (such as the bombings of pornographic movie houses). Some violence occurred in confrontations with the police during the antinuclear marches at Montalto di Castro. In short, confrontational behavior characterized their relationships with both the conflict and the alliance systems.

The situation started to change between 1981 and 1983 with the protest campaign against the deployment of Cruise missiles. Until then the peace issue had attracted only religious groups and a "libertarian" spectrum, close to the Radical Party. These groups combined cultural actions (conferences, for example) with more conventional forms of pressure, including the Radical Party's proposing new legislation and laws. The Old and New Left were virtually absent until the campaign against the Cruise missiles.[12] With its 600 or so peace committees and a few coordinating meetings, the peace movement (re)mobilized in a political campaign the collective actors of the previous years, such as the new student activists, the feminist groups, some residual youth centers, and the ecological groups. The peace issue was phrased in the various frameworks familiar to the different actors: "peace and economic welfare" for the PCI and trade unions, "peace and aid for the Third World" for the Radical Party (PR), "peace and individual consciousness" for the religious groups, "peace and motherhood" for the women's groups, "peace and critique of the adult world" for the student groups, "peace and natural equilibrium" for the ecologists, "peace and anti-imperialism" for the more radical fringes (Lodi 1984, pp. 138–50). The definition of an action platform was, however, still reactive and pessimistic: shared belief in a possible catastrophe (Melucci 1984b, p. 7) and disillusionment with the chances for progressive changes. For the first time after the radicalization of the political conflicts in the 1970s, however, the Old Left, the New Left, and the emerging new social movements cooperated in a political campaign. As opposed to what took place in the previous decade, conventional forms of pressure (petitions, parliamentary initiatives, conferences, courses, tax boycotts) were used together with the first nonviolent direct actions (the march from Catania to Comiso and occupation of the military base at Magliocco in January 1982), and violence only rarely occurred.

As for the alliance system, in the years in which terrorist activities peaked, the relationship between the PCI (together with the trade unions) and the New Left was marked by reciprocal competition. The economic crisis and the so-called austerity policy had pushed the trade unions into a defensive position. From 1974 on, and especially after the 1976 election, the PCI had tried to gain legitimation with the strategy of the "historic compromise," that is, with the proposal of a cooperation between "Catholic and Communist masses." Between 1977 and 1979 the PCI offered support to the national governments led by the Christian Democrats. This defensive strategy was also characterized by mistrust of the social movement organizations, which was expressed not only in the refusal of common protest campaigns but also in physical confrontations between the guardsmen of the PCI and those of the New Left and "autonomous" groups. Even the movement's issues found a difficult path inside the Old Left, even in the mass organizations affiliated with the party but open to external sympathizers.[13] Within this defensive strategy, the governmental positions won at the local level in the 1975 elections were rarely used in an offensive program of reform, and even more rarely did they lead to the integration of movement activists into the local political system (Seidelmen 1984). The fact that the number of PCI members with previous "movement" experience increased in this period notwithstanding (Lange, Tarrow, and Irvin 1990), strong left-wing terrorism pushed the PCI even further away from a reformist or oppositional program. Only at the end of the period did the party's attitude change, and this was in respect to the peace movement.

Also in this phase, the behavior of the left-libertarian movements evolved parallel with that of the conflict system, both characterized by confrontational attitudes. All through the 1970s, the conflict system was still hostile to reform and maintained its repressive course, although abandoning the more right-wing stances of the early seventies. Some new channels for protesters were available—namely, elective bodies—but with merely a consultative role in schools, universities, and neighborhoods. Although the bill allowing abortion was eventually passed in 1978, economic crisis eroded the advantages won in the previous period. Conflicts among the governmental parties and the related governmental and parliamentary instability reached their peak and reduced the capacity for policy implementation. Although the more repressive strategies—including protection of the neofascists—had been abandoned in the second half of the 1970s, the development of terrorism, together with a wave of organized and petty crime, offered a justification for the implementation of new laws on public order that increased police power (della Porta 1989). Public marches were often prohibited, and in some cases activists and bystanders lost their lives during street fights and police actions.

Phase 3. The Pragmatic Years: 1984 to the Present. This period is characterized by a deep change in the left-libertarian movements. After the lull of low mobilization in the previous years, collective action in the 1980s assumed very different characteristics: the impact of socialist ideology waned with the decline of the New Left groups, and many of the organizational and cultural characteristics that are often described as peculiar to the new social movements emerged.

The most important event in this phase was the rise of the ecological movement with a pragmatic political orientation.[14] The movement gained an autonomous identity, campaigning for the protection of nature without stopping progress. The capacity for mass mobilization reached its pinnacle when 150,000 people participated in a march in Rome after the Chernobyl disaster in 1986. In general, however, the ecological movement did not seem to be interested in organizing national campaigns. The scope of action was usually limited to a neighborhood or a small area, with some attempts at coordinating campaigns at the city level. The campaigns were often defensive (against laws that would endanger the natural or artistic heritage) but occasionally offensive as well (such as the campaigns for establishing and expanding pedestrian areas in city centers). The forms of action were mostly conventional (petitions and debates), but there were also innovative forms of symbolic action, such as constructive exemplary actions (working as volunteers to manage a park, organizing "work camps" in impoverished areas) and direct action (such as harassing hunters by making noise to warn the birds). Violence never occurred.

A pragmatic attitude dominated the relations of the left-libertarian movements with their allies, with frequent cooperation on single issues. The decentralized structure of the ecological movement—about 2,000 groups in

1987—increased the opportunities for collaboration with the Old and the New Left. New political cleavages emerged, evident in the appearance of several Green electoral coalitions, but they did not seem to affect the groups at the local level, since they were considered to be initiatives by individual militants not committed to formal organizations. A meticulous study on the organizational networks in the ecological movement has shown that the ideological cleavages had very little effect on the coalition-building strategies of the single-movement organizations (Diani 1990).

The attitude toward opponents was moderate and open to bargaining on single issues. In order to obtain concrete results, candidates elected on various Green lists did not hesitate to enter local governments with different political coalitions, occupying newly created *assessorati all'ambiente* (local ministries for environmental issues). Virtually all groups welcomed collaboration with institutional actors and accepted financial support from the state. Relations with the administration were defined as "constructive." In addition to direct participation in governments and parliaments, there were alliances with politicians from a broad spectrum of political parties to carry out single-issue campaigns (animal protection, phosphate-free detergents, unleaded gasoline) (Diani 1990). During election campaigns the movement press published lists of the candidates from various political parties that they supported.[15] The movement seemed satisfied with its policy success and the support it gained on some issues, attested to by votes of 70 to 80 percent against nuclear energy in a national referendum in 1989. The countercultural dimension was weak, limited to sensitizing the public to practical issues and developing alternative technical and scientific knowledge. Together with the ecologists, the other movements—especially the students' movement and the women's movement (on the latter, see *Memoria* 1986)—also participated in several campaigns, as for instance in the anti-Mafia campaign of the late 1980s. The forms of action were both conventional and unconventional, but nonviolent.

The behavior of the alliance system changed, too, moving toward increasing cooperation with the left-libertarian movements. The PCI, once again in the opposition, became more receptive to protest activities. In order to stop a steady electoral decline, the party shed the image of the working-class party and tried to diffuse a wider image as a point of reference for progressive forces. The party's attitude toward the social movements came to include cooperation on various issues. Organizational "mass structures," once dependent on the centralized structure of the party, gained increasing, and sometimes total, autonomy and joined the left-libertarian social movement sector.

In 1990 the Communist leadership stressed the need to build a new political identity, even proposing to change the name of the party. The twentieth congress of the PCI in February 1991 thus became the first congress of the Democratic Party of the Left; the party declared itself open to "all the leftist, progressive, alternative, environmentalist forces." As for the trade unions, common campaigns have been occasional, but there has been little acrimony between unions and new social movement organizations.

The moderate attitude of the left-libertarian movements was reflected in the conflict system, which became more open to bargaining. In the early 1980s, the first governments with non-Christian Democratic prime ministers in the history of the republic signaled willingness for change, and the governmental parties insisted on a new image of efficacy. The steady decline of terrorism allowed for the so-called strategy of reconciliation, and violent repression virtually disappeared. The left-libertarian movements also won some battles in the national parliament and were represented (through the Green lists) in several local governments. Table 2 gives a schematic overview of the reciprocal behaviors of the Italian left-libertarian movements and their conflict and alliance systems.

The Development of Left-Libertarian Movements in West Germany

Like Italy, West Germany experienced a period of intense social and political conflicts in which social movements were involved (Brand, Büsser, and Rucht 1983; Roth 1985; Rolke 1987). These conflicts started around the mid-1960s, peaked in terms of mass mobilization during the first half of the 1980s, and then lost some of their significance, though protest activities continued on a relatively high level well past the mid-1980s.

The Protest Incubation Phase: 1960–65.   In the years preceding the outbreak of the student revolt, there were two major currents of growing discontent: one countercultural and the other political. The countercultural current was driven by dissatisfaction with the authoritarian culture of postwar Germany. It was a protest against bourgeois values and lifestyles that peaked in certain strata of young people in both a more intellectual and a more proletarian version. These young people broke the rules of conventional behavior; they tried to shock the older generation and the establishment through their music, idols, literature, dress, and language. The small intellectual counterculture found expression in the Situationistische Internationale and the Subversive Aktion.

Table 2. Behaviors of the left-libertarian movements (LM), the alliance system (AS), and the conflict system (CS) in Italy

	AS toward LM	LM toward AS	LM toward CS	CS toward LM
1967 to 1976	Cooperation		Confrontation	
	strategy of "structural reform"	"frontist" strategy	disruptive protest for radical changes	"strategy of tensions"
	increasing competition since 1973 ("historical compromise")	increasing ideological disputes	frequent violence	some reform on labor issues
1977 to 1983	Competition		Confrontation	
	rare openness in the decentralized structures	sense of a "betrayal" from the PCI	high levels of violence and terrorism	authoritarian "emergency policy" of the National Unity Government
	new cooperation within the peace movement in 1981	alliance in the peace campaign	countercultural retrieval	
1984 to 1990	Cooperation		Bargaining	
	attempt to build a "Democratic Party of the Left"	pragmatic openness to alliance with some disagreements	political bargaining, especially at the local level	policy of "exit from the emergency" openness to bargaining

The political current was attracted by some ideas of the Old Left, by Marxist psychoanalytic theory, and by the cultural critique of the Frankfurt school. This strand rediscovered theoretical writings that had long been at the fringe of intellectual interest. As a result of the marginalization and criminalization of the communists during the cold war period, the programmatic shift of the Social Democratic Party (SPD) toward acceptance of the capitalist welfare state in the late 1950s, and the tendency of the labor unions and the SPD to compromise in all substantial matters of conflict put on the political agenda by the extraparliamentary opposition, the radical groups had no strong organizational anchor. They were thus obliged to form their own networks. One was the network of peace movement organizations, in particular those involved in the "Easter marches." A second was the Kampagne für Abrüstung und Demokratie (Campaign for Disarmament and Democracy), which was primarily concerned with approval of the legislation on the state of emergency. A third was the SDS (Socialist German Student Alliance), which, after its expulsion from the SPD, quickly radicalized and became the center of theoretical and strategic debates. After the mid-1960s, these three currents gradually merged and formed a strong extraparliamentary opposition (Otto 1977).

Phase 1. The Revolutionary Years: 1967–69.   After the period of the unspectacular incubation of New Left protest, dissenting groups, mainly located in the universities and other branches of the educational system, disruptively challenged the postwar consensus based on economic welfare, formal democracy, and anticommunism. With the establishment of the Grand Coalition formed by the SPD and the Christian democratic parties (CDU/CSU), and the entrance of the NPD (a nationalist right-wing party) into various state parliaments, political dissent shifted definitely to the extraparliamentary arena. The desire for a fundamental change also covered cultural life. Bourgeois values were attacked heavily. Much emphasis was put on expressive forms of action, including amusing political "happenings." Revolutionary hopes and utopian thoughts flourished for a short time, giving rise to a radicalization of left-libertarian views and action repertoires. Congresses were held and thousands of demonstrators marched in the streets, where they occasionally clashed violently with the police. The opposition groups relied mainly on unconventional forms of expressing political dissent, including civil disobedience and disruptive actions. The revolutionary impetus, however, never reached the masses and soon diminished. The student movement became fragmented and quickly lost momentum. As a consequence, the SDS deliberately dissolved. On the level of ideology, there was probably still an increase of revolutionary thinking among the Marxist and Maoist splinter groups (Langguth 1983). On the level of concrete action, however, these groups were irrelevant for the broader public and unable to form alliances among themselves. Though the student movement experienced a rapid decay, it inspired not only established politics but also a multitude of newly emerging protest actors. The forms of actions, however, radicalized into confrontational behavior toward the conflict system. As for the alliance system, the relationships with the Old Left and the trade unions were never free from tension: competition prevailed over cooperation.

The alliance system was scattered and weak in this phase. The Old Left trade unions did not trust the students as allies and condemned the more radical forms of action. Though the trade unions and other traditional leftist interest groups sympathized somewhat with the New Left movements, the latter were by and large isolated both socially and politically. Only minorities within the SPD, among them some intellectuals and the party's youth organization, had a more open attitude toward the social movement sector. The liberal FDP was alone in parliamentary opposition and was far too small a party to challenge the parties in government. In addition, the movements were far too radical to form an alliance with this party. Therefore, the gap between extraparliamentary and parliamentary politics could not be bridged.

In contrast, the conflict system was powerful and relatively coherent. The conservative parties and the Social Democratic Party moved closer together in their perceptions of problems and search for solutions, thus providing the basis for the formation of the Grand Coalition. By this time, the SPD had managed to win a voice in the national government for the first time in the Federal Republic. Not surprisingly, the SPD defended this new legitimation by taking a harsh stance toward the student protest. Altogether, in this period of radical thinking and radical action, even with the wide social and ideological gap between the active minority of students and the broader population, the political elites in power felt seriously challenged and reacted in a confrontational fashion.

Phase 2. Reformist Hopes: 1970–74. The new actors, which later were called new social movements, converged in their demand for more political participation. The first movements that took shape were the new women's movement and the loose network of citizen initiatives (which, according to some observers, represented a genuine social movement). These groupings experienced considerable growth and succeeded in putting their issues on the political agenda—without, however, creating a coherent political ideology. The partly successful integration (or co-optation) of the 1968 activists furthered the radicalization of some groups within the movements. First, many relatively small Marxist, Maoist, and Trotskyite groupings were formed. Second, a spectrum of unorthodox autonomous groups emerged; in part they became the basis of the later Spontis, a kind of libertarian, antiinstitutional socialists. Finally, on the extreme fringe, some leftist activists formed terrorist groups that, although they were insignificant in size, had a high symbolic impact on the political culture of the 1970s. The basic concerns of the mainstream protest groups were problems of marginalized and underprivileged people (clients in psychiatric clinics, homeless people, etc.), women's issues (liberalization of abortion, violence against women, discrimination at work, etc.), and environmental and urban issues (housing, public transport, etc.). The focus of action was on both conventional and unconventional political participation. Apart from some terrorist acts and conflicts about house squatting, political violence was largely absent. Cooperative attitudes toward the alliance system prevailed, and a bargaining attitude toward the conflict system also developed.

Compared to the former period, major chances now became available in the alliance system. The conservatives and the Social Democrats diverged considerably in terms of attitudes and behaviors, whereas the liberal party shifted more to the left and entered into a governmental coalition with the Social Democrats in 1969. The social-liberal forces, as a result of their vehemence to "dare more democracy" (Willy Brandt), their ambitious reform program, and their open-mindedness toward the left-libertarian social movements, were largely seen as allies of the movements, though they followed a different logic of action. The reform program deradicalized the movement sector but did not hinder its quantitative growth. In contrast, the reform course raised many far-reaching expectations that motivated not only party members but also social movement activists. In part, these favored a dual strategy of political activities inside and outside the established parties—a strategy explicitly promoted by the Jungsozialisten (Young Socialists). The Young Socialists' membership grew considerably in the first half of the 1970s and peaked at 350,000 in 1975. Parts of the liberal party, and in particular its youth organization, sympathized with the moderate groups of the social movement sector, whereas its radical wing, as represented by a plethora of political sects, became more and more isolated from the established actors as well as from the mainstream of the movements.

In relative terms, the conflict system was not very influential in that period. The core group of this system, the conservative party, was in parliamentary opposition and did not play a dominant role in established politics, at least on the federal level. The more radical conservatives pushed for a rollback, but were not very successful. It has to be mentioned, though, that the SPD was not in total agreement with the movements. On the one hand, the party embraced the movements and also provided substantial support, but, on the other hand, it tried to marginalize the more radical wing of the movements. Ironically, it was Chancellor Willy Brandt, usually associated with his cry for "more democracy," who in 1972 put forward the so-called Berufsverbote, the regulations to keep radical activists out of civil service. Also at the local level, parts of the SPD were more inclined to repress than to support the left-libertarian movements.

Phase 3. Challenging the Established System: 1975–82.   The years 1974–75 were a turning point. The hopes of attaining fundamental changes through a dual strategy of reform within the institutions and extraparliamentary pressure were disappointed. Once it became clear that institutional reform would be largely unsuccessful, many people turned completely to extraparliamentary politics and, in particular, to social movement politics. The behavior of the movements radicalized, with increasingly confrontational attitudes toward the conflict system and increasing competition with most of the potential allies.

Strong movements, among them the new women's movement, the antinuclear movement, the environmental movement, and the so-called alternative movement, developed and formed their own networks and infrastructures. These highly decentralized networks ranged from local grassroots groups to alliances at the national level. Moreover, these movements tended to overlap and consequently develop an overarching infrastructure and a particular social milieu with its own lifestyles and means of communication (Roth 1987). For a second time, established politics in West Germany were seriously challenged in the field of extraparliamentary politics and later—with the rise of the alternative lists and the Green Party—in parliamentary politics. Radical demands and actions peaked between 1977 and 1981, accompanied by an increase in terrorist activities. In particular, the antinuclear movement and the movements centered around other environmental issues succeeded in mobilizing masses of people. Parts of these movements also used acts of civil disobedience, such as the occupation of reactor sites. Moreover, demonstrators and police clashed several times, thus leading to a paramilitary orientation of the police forces. Left-wing terrorism in particular provoked hard reactions and fueled law-and-order sentiments.

Trust, not only in the established political system but also in the benefits of economic growth and technological progress, eroded during this period. Many dissenting groups reacted to the negative consequences of modernization. The groups' engagement in many specific issues was fueled by strong anticentralist, antimodernist, and, in part, antirationalist attitudes. Not accidentally, youth religions boomed in this period. Groupings within the women's movement and the so-called alternative movements became interested in holistic worldviews, spiritualism, and therapeutic techniques. In 1978 a call for a symbolic exit from the "Modell Deutschland" unified some 20,000 people in Berlin. In reaction to this event and its underlying general cultural and political critique, some observers proclaimed the emergence of a "second culture." Between 1979 and 1981 there was a wave of aggressive youth protests focused on such issues as squatting in empty houses and the formation of autonomous youth centers. These protests were centered more in cultural areas, with the adherents adopting provocative lifestyles and other expressive behaviors. Many young people felt that there was no future for them in society. Other protest was more directly oriented toward the realm of politics, focusing on environmental policy, the exploitation of Third World countries, human rights, and so on. Antinuclear campaigns continued and attracted more people to mass demonstrations than before. Some 100,000 people attended antinuclear demonstrations in 1979 (Hannover) and 1981 (Brokdorf) respectively. Even the struggle over extension of the Frankfurt airport lead to a similar mass mobilization and a high degree of militancy, though the protesters lost this battle. According to official statistics of the Ministry of the Interior, the number of nonpeaceful demonstrations in 1981 was the highest since 1970. The greatest mobilization capacity, however, was attained by the newly emerged peace movement, whose immediate goal was to prevent the deployment of Cruise missiles. Because of its strong backing by already existing movements, the peace movement succeeded in mobilizing 300,000 people in fall 1981 in Bonn, roughly 500,000 people during various activities surrounding the Easter marches in 1982, and in collecting 5 million signatures in 1983–84 against deployment of the missiles.

In this third phase, the conflict system was again relatively broad and powerful. The governmental coalition, though it remained in power, pulled back sharply from its ambitious reform course. For many reasons it now moved more toward the right. At the same time, the left-libertarian movements developed a strong anti-institutional attitude. The mainstream of the Social Democrats reacted offensively to the challenge of the extraparliamentary opposition and the emergence of Green and alternative "lists" at the end of the 1970s. A minor faction inside the party, however, sympathized with these groupings and thus provoked a strong internal tension within the party. In many issues, the majority of the SPD and FDP together with trade unions and other powerful interest groups took a confrontational stance toward the movements. It was no accident that the movements perceived themselves as struggling against an "all-party coalition"—a situation that fostered the tensions between established and nonestablished political actors. Given the high degree of mobilization of the new social movements on the one hand and the increasing relevance of the neoconservatives on the other hand, the Social Democrats came under strong cross fire. As a result of this situation and of growing internal factionalism, the party lost its political hegemony in national politics.

Only from a superficial point of view could one think of a completely isolated social movement sector and thus a virtually nonexistent alliance system. Though the major parties were predominantly critical or even hostile toward most of the movements, there were always minorities within the established forces that were more sympathetic to the movements. This is particularly true for strands within SPD, which cooperated (although with some competition) with movement organizations on issues of nuclear energy, ecology, women's issues, and disarmament. Some of the trade unions became more open-minded toward the movements, though direct cooperation rarely occurred. Finally, at a later stage of this phase, Green and alternative "lists," first at the local and state level, were formed and became surprisingly successful. For the first time, the social movement system had a chance to be directly represented by parliamentary groups.

Phase 4. The Pragmatic Years: 1983 to the Present.   In 1983 and 1984, mass mobilization and acts of civil disobedience carried out by the new peace movement (Schmitt 1991) overshadowed all other movement activities. In 1983, official statistics registered the highest number of demonstrations in West German history. In terms of participants, West Germany's largest protest demonstrations occurred in these years. Unlike the other movements, the peace movement had a strategically oriented national coordination committee composed of representatives from virtually all relevant organizations and groupings (Leif 1990). Although it was the largest protest movement in West German history and was strongly backed in the wider public, the movement soon lost momentum when at first the government maintained its support for the NATO decision to deploy Cruise missiles, and later, with the declining confrontation between the military blocks, the government became more flexible in matters of disarmament. Although in terms of their mobilization capacity and infrastructural basis the new social movements were probably stronger than ever before, their capacity to challenge the system clearly decreased after 1984. The movements tended to become a part of politics as usual, and their radical emphasis gradually faded away. The established political system reacted to the movements' demands both on a substantive and a symbolic level, offering limited participation and even financial support. Both sides became more pragmatic and began to bargain and cooperate. A clear indicator of this more pragmatic attitude was the discussion about *Staatsknete* (state bucks). Whereas in the early 1980s many activists in feminist and alternative groups refused to take public subsidies and attacked those who were inclined to do so, a few years later this was no longer an issue. Another factor bringing about more pragmatism was the increasing professionalization and specialization within the movements.

Far-reaching expectations for social change gradually vanished, although the activities of the various movements continued on a high level and sometimes even increased, and the movements' infrastructure consolidated. Many young people shifted from countercultural challenge to subcultural retreat. The movements maintained their activities in regard to virtually all issues. The dominant aim, however, was no longer to attack the system but to solve concrete problems. Not surprisingly, the first half of the 1980s saw the rise of many self-help groups in the social and health sectors, and the establishment of pragmatic, and sometimes highly professional, co-operatives. The Greens —in the meantime represented in the national parliament (with 5.3 percent of the vote in 1983 and 8.3 percent in 1987) and in most state parliaments—also gradually lost their image as an "anti-party party," adopting a number of structural features of the established parties.

The deradicalization of the social movement sector as a whole notwithstanding, there were still salient violent conflicts—for example, the struggle against the nuclear reprocessing plant in Wackersdorf and other nuclear facilities. In 1986 demonstrations in Wackersdorf and Brokdorf each attracted roughly 50,000 people. Moreover, some 880,000 people signed a petition against the Wackersdorf project during a formal licensing procedure. In general, however, most of the groups turned to unspectacular political engagement.

It was probably this normalization of protest politics that fostered radical tendencies at the fringe of the social movement sector, namely, the formation of the so-called Autonomen, who maintained a diffuse anarchistic, anti-imperialistic ideology. In all, the groups that form the so-called black block were able to mobilize several thousand supporters prepared for militant action. Given the much larger potential of free-floating protest, radical dissent could arise quickly on highly symbolic issues such as the national census, Ronald Reagan's visit to West Germany, and the conference of the International Monetary Fund and the World Bank in Berlin (Gerhards 1991; Gerhards and Rucht 1991). Apart from the very radical groups that tended to become more isolated from the major movements, the movement family as a whole had lost the disruptive capacity of its third developmental phase.

The electoral success of the conservative party in 1983 does not necessarily point up an increasing confrontational attitude of the conflict system. The movements, because of their quantitative growth and backing in broader social strata (Fuchs 1990; Pappi 1989), could no longer be frontally attacked.

The general behavior of the conservative party toward the movements was marked rather by bargaining than by open confrontation. This changing attitude was certainly facilitated by the deradicalization of the mainstream of the movements. Only the radical wing of the movements continued to be an object of open repression.

By and large, the alliance system experienced a considerable change in this fourth period. Being squeezed between the neoconservatives on one side and the Green Party (since 1983 in the national parliament) on the other, the Social Democrats were split over the question of whether they should make more concessions to the right or to the left. Now seated in the parliamentary opposition, the majority of the Social Democrats had no more difficulties perceiving themselves as (potential) allies of the movements. As in the case of the conservatives, this increasing tolerance was facilitated by the deradicalization of the core of the social movement sector. Supposedly, the presence of the Green Party in the national and in most state parliaments also contributed to the deradicalization of the movements and a shift of emphasis from far-reaching demands toward a more incrementalistic attitude. Overall, the movements tended to become a part of normal politics (Roth and Rucht 1991). As a consequence, the dividing lines between the social movement sector and both the conflict and the alliance systems gradually blurred.

Table 3 schematically summarizes the major behaviors of the relevant actors in West Germany according to the four phases described here.

Explaining the Behaviors of Left-Libertarian Movements

Our descriptions provide a basis on which the Italian and German left-libertarian movements and their allies and opponents can be compared. We will first summarize the relevant similarities and differences with special emphasis on the social movements' behaviors. Second, we aim at developing empirically grounded hypotheses about the impact of the conflict and alliance systems on the behaviors of these movements. Finally, we will look, though in a less systematic way, at internal factors and structural context in order to suggest some complementary hypotheses for explaining behavioral shifts of the social movements.

A Cross-National Comparison of Left-Libertarian Movements

Starting with the comparison of the four social movements we focused on in each country, a striking result is the high degree of convergence in their overall development. Not only were the four movements present and relevant

Table 3. Behaviors of the left-libertarian movements (LM), the alliance system (AS), and the conflict system (CS) in West Germany

	AS toward LM	LM toward AS	LM toward CS	CS toward LM
1967 to 1969	**Competition**		**Confrontation**	
	political isolation of students, but sympathy from intellectuals	few and unsuccessful attempts to build a coalition with the Old Left	disruptive challenges to the political elite	Grand Coalition represses protest
1970 to 1974	**Cooperation**		**Bargaining**	
	integrative strategies of the Brandt government	hopes for more democracy and far-reaching reform; division of labor between parliamentary and extraparliamentary activities	strategy of a "long march through the institutions"	occasional pressure for "law and order" policy
1975 to 1983	**Competition**		**Confrontation**	
	some openness in the decentralized structures	feeling of estrangement from the Old Left; rise of Greens	feelings of fighting an all-parties coalition occasional acts of terrorism	"law and order" attitudes within a neoconservative strategy
1983 to 1990	**Cooperation**		**Bargaining**	
	SPD self-definition as ally of the movements	openness to parliamentary allies such as SPD	cooperative and pragmatic attitudes militancy of marginal "autonomous" groups	offers of financial and other support; tolerance and occasional repression of the radical groups

in both countries—with the noticeable exception of the ecology movement—their timing was very similar, as Figure 2 shows.

The first new movement to appear on the stage was the student movement, which in both countries peaked in 1968, lasting longer in Italy and rapidly declining in West Germany. In a similar manner, the two student

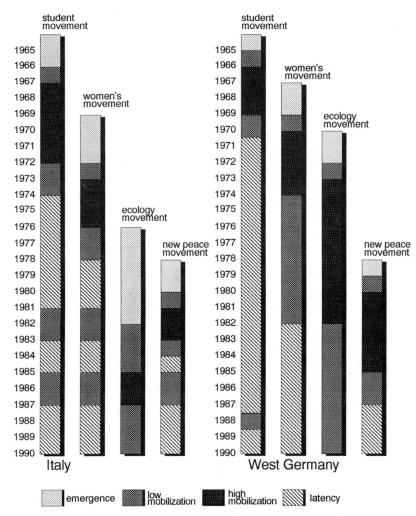

Figure 2. The development of social movements in Italy and West Germany, 1965–90

movements imported protest techniques developed by the civil rights and the anti-Vietnam War movements in the United States. The women's movements followed in both countries, reaching their highest political visibility around the mid-1970s through a campaign for liberalization of abortion laws. The evolution of the repertoire of the two women's movements was parallel, from the use of civil disobedience in the first half of the 1970s to the creation of conscious-raising groups in the phase of the "return to the private" in the second half of the decade. Antinuclear protests spread in both countries in the mid-1970s, although with much greater intensity in West Germany, providing the emerging ecological organizations with their first occasions for mobilization. Between 1981 and 1983 the new peace movement—in Italy as well as in West Germany—organized massive and mainly nonviolent actions against the deployment of Cruise missiles. The Italian ecological movement flourished for the first time in the second half of the 1980s, while its West German counterpart continued the activities already begun in the mid-1970s. The ecological movements in both countries were characterized by a large number of local protest actions aimed at getting media coverage and public attention through creative actions rather than disruptiveness. Although we had expected many parallels, this almost complete year-by-year coincidence in the evolution of the four social movements appears to be an intriguing new finding.

Several similarities, along with some relevant differences, can be observed in the evolution of the prevailing behavior of the left-libertarian movements, which is our dependent variable. In both countries, the student movement was characterized by confrontational behavior and disruptive actions with some episodes of mass violence mixed in. Conflicts were framed in a revolutionary perspective, with an optimistic image of the future and hopes for fundamental political changes. After the decline of the student movement and its revolutionary discourse in West Germany, hopes for reforms seemed to materialize between 1970 and 1974 (during the Brandt administration). The social movements were thus predominantly oriented toward cooperation or bargaining with the leftist party in government. The forms of action were quite moderate, although (as in Italy during the same period) violence sporadically appeared in conflicts related to, for example, house squatting. In Italy, on the other hand, confrontational behavior characterized the whole period. Although an offensive emancipatory perspective still prevailed, some forms of action gradually escalated into violence. While the New Left still exerted a kind of hegemonic control over left-libertarian protests in Italy, new social movements emerged in West Germany and soon gained relevance in terms of ideological discourse and protest activities.

In the second half of the 1970s, radical confrontations prevailed in both countries and violence spread, together with a growing defensive and pessimistic attitude. In both countries, the peace movements formed a bridge between this phase and the next, insofar as these movements greatly overlapped with the other movements. Because of their very concerns, they were not, however, prone to use violent actions. Although still in a defensive ideological frame, the forms of action slowly deradicalized. In Italy, the New Left organizations lost control over the protest movements, and no substitute for them emerged. In West Germany, the foundation of the nationwide Green Party in 1980 further diminished the significance New Left groups.

Striking similarities in terms of behavior were found in the last phase, which began around 1984, that is, after the decline of the antimissile campaign. In both countries, moderate behaviors prevailed in the left-libertarian movements. Conflicts now concentrated on urban problems, health, ecology, consumer behavior, and so on. Bargaining-oriented forms of action dominated, despite some more violent fringe tendencies, especially in West Germany. In Italy, the new social movements tended to gain the relevance they had already enjoyed for many years in Germany.

Summarizing, we can point out some particularly striking similarities, especially regarding the rise and climax of the student movement and the prevalent behaviors of other movements in the second half of the 1970s and thereafter. A significant difference is the more pervasive and longer-lasting impact of an *operaista* New Left with its class struggle orientation in Italy; in Germany, class struggle frames soon lost relevance, and workers could not be reached. Another major divergence was the existence of a phase of deradicalization in West Germany during the first half of the 1970s. The change in national government encouraged movement activists to proclaim the "long march through the institutions." In contrast, the Italian left-libertarian movements at that time were still dominated by hopes for a revolution as well as confrontational behavior. In addition, the somewhat more radical behavior of the West German movements during the 1980s is worthy of mention.

As for our intervening variables, the behaviors of allies and opponents evolved in a similar way in the second half of the 1970s and in the following decade: from harsh conflicts to a more moderate position. Again, the main differences are to be found in the beginning of the 1970s. The New Left in Italy, its strong ties with the PCI and the trade unions notwithstanding, had to face harsh governmental repression. In West Germany, conversely, the SPD (in a governmental coalition with the liberal party) was more distant from the social movements than the PCI was, but its assimilative attitude had a moderating effect on the behavior of the left-libertarian movements.

The Impact of Alliance and Conflict Systems

Our model assumes that the intervening variables play an important role in explaining behavioral shifts of the social movement families. This assumption is not new in the literature. Several models have related repertoires and evo-

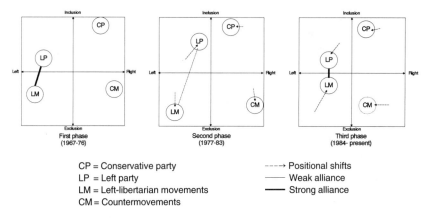

CP = Conservative party
LP = Left party
LM = Left-libertarian movements
CM = Countermovements

----→ Positional shifts
——— Weak alliance
▬▬ Strong alliance

Figure 3. Alliance and conflict system in Italy

lutions of unconventional political behaviors to the repressive strategies of their opponents (for instance, Tilly 1978, pp. 98–115). The availability and strategic posture of potential allies are already included in early definitions of the political opportunity structure (Tarrow 1983, p. 28). Among others, two variables are mentioned to explain the relationships between protest actors and their allies and opponents: positions on a right-left axis and access of the challenger to political power. In order to discuss these factors, we tried first of all to locate our main actors—left-libertarian social movements (LM), the main leftist party (LP), the main conservative party (CP), and the counter-movements (CM)—according to the left-right dimension and inclusion-exclusion dimension. The resulting constellations for each country and each of the mentioned phases are shown in Figures 3 and 4.

The Role of the Movements' Opponents.   It is widely held that social movements are strongly influenced by the behavior of their opponents. A higher degree of repression is usually associated with radical behavior on the side of the challengers. Goldstein concluded in his comparative analysis of European countries in the last century that "those countries that were consistently the most repressive, brutal, and obstinate in dealing with the consequences of modernization and developing working-class dissidence reaped the harvest by producing opposition that was just as rigid, brutal and obstinate" (1983, p. 340). In a review of studies on the American protest movement in the 1960s and 1970s, John Wilson (1977) observed that the empirical results are somewhat contradictory, sometimes indicating a radicalization of groups exposed to police violence and sometimes a withdrawal from unconventional actions.

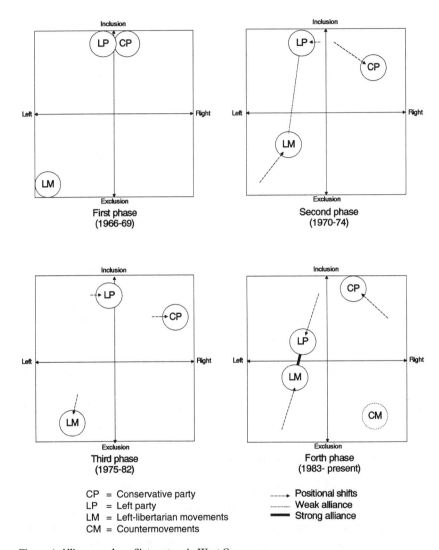

Figure 4. Alliance and conflict system in West Germany

In order to explain such different results, he suggested taking into account variables such as the level of repression, the degree of commitment to the protest issue, and the popular support for elites and challengers respectively. Seemingly contradictory findings could be integrated into a more coherent explanation if one assumes a curvilinear relationship for the interplay between the challenger's violence and the repression of authorities (as did Neidhardt 1989).

As can be seen in Figures 3 and 4, we have evidence to hypothesize that *the more the conservative party moves to the right, and therefore the more repressive its behavior toward the left-libertarian movements, the more radical the reactions of the latter.* In Italy during the 1970s, the elites in power were fully engaged in blocking demands for radical reform. Confronted with a cycle of protest that spread from the big factories to heterogeneous social groups, the conflict system used a confrontational and even repressive strategy that, in turn, contributed to the higher degree of radicalism in the Italian left-libertarian movements. In West Germany in the early 1970s we saw in contrast that the counterstrategies directed against social movements never reached the illegal and violent repressive forms used by the Italian conservative party and neofascist countermovements, though to a lesser extent repressive behavior of the conflict system also fostered radical behavior in the West German social movements in the late 1970s and early 1980s. We could observe that the highest level of repression coincided with a shrinking of the more politically oriented part of the social movement sector, which indirectly helped the more radical behavior to prevail.

Taking a closer look at Figures 3 and 4, we can narrow our initial hypothesis. First, regarding Germany in the second phase, we can observe that a move by the conservative party to the right is not always paralleled in the movements' behaviors when this party finds itself in the opposition. Second, Italy in the second phase demonstrates that a move of the conservative party to the center does not automatically warrant a moderation of the social movements' behavior. An additional explanation for the further radicalization of the movements in this case seems to be the presence of organized and violent countermovements. We can therefore conclude that *the presence of countermovements tends to increase the radicalization of the movements' behavior.*

The Role of the Movements' Allies.   Another variable that can contribute to explaining the high degree of violence in the 1970s is the position of the social movements' (potential) allies. Among the few scholars who have paid attention to the relationship between left-wing parties and protest, Kriesi has attributed a high explanatory power to the position of the main left-wing party:[16]

If the Social Democrats are *in the opposition*, they profit from the challenges NSMs [New Social Movements] direct at the government. . . . If *in government*, the Social Democrats not only face electoral constraints, but they also operate under constraints of established policies and of pressures from dominant societal forces. . . . To maximize their chances for reelection, they will try to make compromises which favor the core of their electorate. (1991, p. 19)

262 DONATELLA DELLA PORTA AND DIETER RUCHT

Our results indicate that a left-wing party in the opposition will not always co-operate with the left-libertarian movements, and, conversely, a left-wing party in government does not always compete with these movements. For instance, in the second phase in Italy, the PCI was in bitter competition with the left-libertarian movements, although the party was not in the national govern-ment (see Figure 3). In the second phase in West Germany, the SPD cooper-ated with the movements (see Figure 4).

We conclude that it is not necessarily the position of the left-wing party in-side or outside the government but the general orientation of the left-wing party toward far-reaching reform that determines the attitude of the left-wing party vis-à-vis the left-libertarian movements. *When the left-wing party shifts to the center, the left-libertarian movements find themselves with fewer channels of access to the decision-making system, and the movements tend to radicalize.* We argue that the position and behavior of the major left-wing party is the most relevant factor in determining the social movements' behavior. Figures 3 and 4 illustrate that the phases of moderation of the movements' behavior coin-cided with a shift of their main ally to the left, while the shifts toward more a moderate position of the left-wing party produced a radicalization on the side of the movements.

The most striking cross-national difference in the behavior of the social movements—that is, the relative absence of radical strategies in West Ger-many during the first half of the 1970s—is clearly an effect of the reformist at-titude of the social-liberal government and the openness of the social democ-ratic and liberal parties to movement concerns. Extraparliamentary and parliamentary groups coexisted and, based on an implicit division of labor, oc-casionally worked together for far-reaching reforms.

In the second half of the 1970s, both the PCI and the SPD moved toward the center, and their shifts coincided with a radicalization of the movements. The PCI, aiming at a "historic compromise," kept alive an antagonistic atti-tude toward the left-libertarian movements and contributed to the New Left's maintaining its confrontational behavior toward the conflict system. In Ger-many, the SPD, keeping its position in government but abandoning its reform orientation, assumed a more competitive and even confrontational stance to-ward the movements and thus provoked a more confrontational behavior on the part of the movements. In both Italy and Germany distrust of leftist par-ties, and parties in general, grew among social movement activists along with the recognition of the need for autonomous organization and action. Also, the striking similarities after 1983–84 in both left-libertarian movement families can be explained to a large extent by the similar shift in the major leftist parties, which both presented themselves as "natural" allies of the movements. Finally, "left-libertarian parties" (Kitschelt 1988), which can be considered an offspring of movement politics, became significant in the electoral arena and contributed to the deradicalization of the movements. Summarizing these observations, we believe that the major leftist parties played a crucial role in influencing the behavior of the left-libertarian movements.

The Role of the Overall Ideology of Left-Wing Parties. So far we have focused on the position of the major left-wing party in the power constellation and its shifts on the right-left axis. Several authors have emphasized the impact of ideological cleavages in the party system for the development of social movements, although there is little agreement about the quality and the decisive factors of this relationship. Brand (1985, p. 319) hypothesizes that a sharp left-right cleavage hinders the evolution of new social movements, and vice versa. According to Kriesi, a divided left hampered the development of new social movements because of the importance of the competition for the working-class vote:

> In such a situation, the Social Democratic party has been relatively weak in electoral terms, and it has engaged in a contest with the Communist party for the hegemony on the left. This contest has above all been a contest for the working class vote, which means that the traditional class conflict between labor and capital and the concomitant marxist ideology have always played an important role in the strategy not only of the Communist party, but also of the Social Democrats. . . . In such a context one can expect the Social Democrats to subordinate their support of NSMs [new social movements], which characteristically have a new middle class core, to their struggle for hegemony in the left. (1991, p. 18)

On the other hand, one could hypothesize that the communist parties—being "movement" parties and more to the left of the spectrum—are more open to protest. Tarrow argued, for instance, that the Italian Communist Party acted as "off-stage but creative prompters in the origins, the dynamics, and the ultimate institutionalization of the new movements" (1990, p. 254).

Regarding Italy and West Germany, we deal with relatively clear-cut Communist and Social Democratic parties (which is graphically shown in Figures 3 and 4; the PCI is always more to the left than the SPD). The Italian Communist Party in the 1960s and 1970s still strove for a fundamental change of society, promoted a class struggle discourse, was supported mainly by the working class, and was still rooted in a subcultural milieu. The Social Democratic Party in Germany aimed at only partial reforms, promoted a pluralist ideology, and—besides its traditional yet weakened ties to the working class—increasingly appealed to the new middle class. These differences notwithstanding, both types of left-wing parties dramatically changed their position toward the new social movements, resulting in different effects on the behavior of the movements. We think, however, that the two types of left-wing parties helped to foster a different version of left-libertarian movements, usually termed new social movements. We hypothesize that *a strong communist party induces the rise of a significant New Left and restricts the evolution of independent new social movements, whereas a strong social democratic party, having lost its class character and become a catch-all party, leaves room for movements that are ideologically and organizationally distinct from both the Old and the New Left.*

With respect to these differences, we argue that a hegemonic Communist Party on the left side of the Italian party system has contributed to the salience of the traditional left-right cleavage, also perpetuated by the existence of an organized and radical right. As a result of this situation, the independent left-libertarian groups (including New Left parties) kept their strong affinity to the Communist Party and its related organizations, sharing the class struggle discourse and also trying to appeal to the working class. This situation caused strong competition for the same resources within the leftist spectrum without, however, resulting in a wide gap between the Old and the New Left groups. They considered themselves "natural" allies. This picture applies by and large to the first period in Italy (1967–76). In Germany, the hegemony of the Social Democratic Party in the 1970s reduced the opportunities of the New Left but allowed for the formation of heterogeneous autonomous movements that were only marginally influenced by a class struggle discourse. The Social Democrats and the autonomous movements sometimes acted in an implicit division of labor, but they hardly perceived themselves as "natural" allies. This development eventually led to the establishment of the Green Party, which, among other factors, contributed to the moderation of the new social movements.

The striking parallels of moderate left-libertarian social movements in the two countries after the early 1980s can be partly explained by the gradual "social democratization" of the Italian Communist Party. While opening up space for new social movements, including the Greens, this change of character reduced the competitive attitudes toward the left-libertarian movements, but also indirectly curtailed the influence of the New Left strand.

The Impact of Independent Variables

So far we have focused on the role of conflict and alliance systems as variables to explain shifts in social movement behaviors. We found empirical evidence that these variables have a considerable explanatory power but are not enough to completely determine the dynamics of social movements. Although investigating the relevance of all other variables that come into play is beyond the scope of this essay, we want to illustrate briefly the impact of some other variables we have presented in our explanatory model.

Nondomestic Factors.   We have emphasized striking cross-national parallels in issues addressed by the movements and in the timing of the related social and political conflicts. Obviously, these features cannot be sufficiently explained by parallels in national power constellations. Rather, *we would attribute overall similarities in issue conflicts to international processes and events and to phenomena of cross- national diffusion.* The constant flow of information via modern mass media and other means of communication contributes to the blurring of national specificities as well as to the diffusion of general moods, perceptions of problems, arguments, action repertoires, and so on. We see this, for example, in changing levels of expectation in the broader population, whereby the optimism exhibited in the first and the last phases in both countries appears to be associated with varying perceptions of the economic future. These perceptions are relatively independent of short-term and often national-based business cycles. Indeed, we assume a strong impact from the expectations about the medium- and long-term economic developments that depend largely on international economic parameters. Supposedly, the period of sustained economic growth of the 1960s created an overall climate of optimism and facilitated the orientation toward reform in most advanced capitalist countries; conversely, the long crisis and growing unemployment after the mid-1970s contributed to a climate of pessimism (Brand 1990, pp. 30–31). Together, these changes in the climate were reflected in the attitudes of the conflict and alliance systems, and in the overall dynamics and issues of left-libertarian movements in Italy and West Germany. Also, the direct communication between social movements from different countries (including such factors as cross-national organizational ties, personal friendships, international congresses, distribution of pamphlets and other literature), contributes to converging movement patterns in different countries. For instance, many parallels can be found in the dynamics of the student revolt and conflicts over abortion, nuclear power, and the deployment of Cruise missiles in the two countries.

Long-Term Cultural and Institutional Changes.   Beyond the inherent dynamics of a single social movement cycle, the trend toward more pragmatism that we have found in the 1980s seems to be fostered also by a long-term evolution of the political culture in recent decades. We see indicators of the opening of the decision-making system for such nonestablished actors as social movements and of an increased sensitivity toward demands for citizen participation in dominant policy styles. This tendency affects even ideologically "straight" actors such as the Communist Party as we described it earlier. In Italy and Germany, convergences appear to derive from the similarities between these countries (i.e., as advanced Western European capitalist societies), and these similarities are enhanced by the aforementioned international structures and cross-national diffusion. Thus we argue that *the presence of channels of formal and informal access to political power has a moderating effect on the behavior of social movements.* Checking the potential relevance of other independent variables discussed in the literature under the label of the openness of the institutional structure (Tarrow 1983; Kriesi 1991), we found in our cases virtually no empirical support for the relevance of our dependent variable of factors such as degree of centralization, (functional) concentration of state power, coherence of public administration in terms of internal coordination and professionalization, and institutionalization of direct democratic procedures. The same applies to the capacity of the administrations to implement their policies (Kitschelt 1986; Kriesi 1991). By and large, all these factors did not significantly change over time in our two cases, while the behavior of the social movements underwent quite impressive changes.

Levels of the Welfare State and Class Conflict.   We think that two other factors mentioned in the literature (Brand 1985, p. 319) have some importance for our study. These are the level of the welfare state and the degree to which the (economic) class conflict is institutionalized and pacified. In general, we assume that *the left-libertarian movements tend to deradicalize with the development of the welfare state and the institutionalization of the class conflict.* This assumption seems to be quite evident in the case of outspoken New Left movements that are oriented to the working class. We think, however, that it also applies to progressive movements that basically focus on issues other than those of the more traditional Old and New Left. This can be illustrated by Italy in the first period we have described. Because the New Left and the emerging new social movements still perceived the workers' organizations as their allies, they also were affected by the class-struggle concept, and aimed at relating their concerns to this issue. In this situation, both the Old and the New Left groupings tended toward radical forms of action. Moreover, conservative forces, feeling challenged by such a (potential) alliance, reacted with conflictive and even repressive strategies, thus supporting the spiral of conflict. In Italy, this could be seen both in terrorism and in broader social movement activities.

Gradually, with the increase of the welfare state and the institutionalization of the class conflict in Italy in the 1980s, the social movements' behavior became more moderate. In West Germany, where the class conflict was already institutionalized when the student movement emerged, the few occasional alliances with the working class never had a radicalizing effect on the social movements. Thus the movements in the two countries ended up with a very similar position: the dominance of nonradical strategies. We found no clear evidence, however, for the assumption that left-libertarian parties and movements are more likely to grow in corporatist welfare states (Kitschelt 1990, p. 182). Though the German system in the 1970s would support this thesis, the later periods in Germany do not. Also, we found that a noncorporatist system (such as the Italian) is not necessarily unfavorable to new movements and Green parties. In general, we would argue therefore that it is not so much the corporatist system[17] per se that is supportive of new movements but rather the degree to which the class conflict is institutionalized.

Internal Factors for the Institutionalization of Social Movements.   One striking feature in our comparison was the similarity in the life cycles of the individual movements in the two countries (see Figure 2). Because these life cycles transcend the developmental phases we have identified, we hypothesize that some of these similarities are mainly a result of internal properties of the movements. These, as we mentioned in explaining our model, are in part influenced by the structural context. In general, we observed that in a first prepolitical phase new issues were forged in small intellectual circles that served as forums for discussion. Aggressive interactions between movements and institutions are not likely to occur at the emergence of a new issue. In the incubation phase, the movement is preoccupied with collecting information, forming a collective identity, and creating networks. In the second phase, social movement mobilization occurs during campaigns and open political confrontation. When the movement challenges the political system through mass protest, the members of the polity (Tilly 1978) first attempt to

resist changes and thus provoke further radicalization. When mass mobilization declines, we also observed that a minority tends to radicalize substantially and attempts to dramatize and moralize the situation. In the long run,
however, individual movements and movement families as a whole tend toward more pragmatic and cooperative strategies. Once violent actions have
been used without significant success during or after the peak of the conflict,
the more professional and moderate movement organizations prevail.

When the issue has by and large lost its mobilizing capacity, or compromises between the conflict partners are reached, the social movements do
not disappear. Organizations and personal networks survive, keeping the social movement identity alive during a state of low activity or latency. Alternat-
ing between visibility and latency (Melucci 1989, pp. 70–73), most of the individual social movements continue to be part of a social movement family,
mobilizing for single-issue campaigns or—together with other social movements—broader cycles of protest.[18] We can conclude that *once a movement
has reached a certain organizational level, it tends to survive despite changes
and even unfavorable conditions in its environment. This situation increases the
trend toward institutionalization of the movements' infrastructure, which in
turn facilitates contacts with policy makers and allies and ultimately moderates
the movements' behavior.*

Conclusion

The aim of this essay was, first, to develop an explanatory model by identifying the main factors that account for differential behaviors of social movement families. This model was based on two sets of independent variables (internal factors and the structural context) and a set of intervening variables.
The latter have been conceptualized as the behaviors of the conflict and alliance systems interacting with a social movement family. Second, we described similarities and differences between the left-libertarian movement
families in Italy and West Germany with special emphasis on their behavioral
changes over time. Although we were not able to weigh the relative influence
of so many variables on the behavior of the left-libertarian movements, we
nevertheless ended up with several substantiated hypotheses.

Regarding the context structure, we think that striking parallels in the timing of various issue conflicts are largely influenced by the cross-national diffusion of themes, frames, action repertoires, and so on. Both mass media and
direct communication between movements from different countries play an
important role in this cross-national transfer. In addition, we found that the

better the challengers' access to political power and the more class conflicts are smoothed over, the more the behavior of left-libertarian movements tends to deradicalize. Internal variables such as organizational and cultural resources of the social movements appear to influence the trend toward the survival of movements even under unfavorable external conditions and, in the long run, toward more pragmatic attitudes and protest activities.

Our main emphasis, however, was on the role of the alliance and conflict systems in shaping the prevailing social movements' behavior over time. In contrast to other authors, who generally characterize social movements in a given country as either moderate or radical, we found significant changes in the degree of radicality of the same movement family. Obviously, these changes have to be explained by factors that, in turn, change over time.[19] We found evidence that the single most relevant factor is the attitude of the major left-wing party toward the left-libertarian movements regardless of whether this party is in power. The more confrontational the party's position toward the left-libertarian social movements, the more the latter will radicalize. Thus the crucial point is whether the major party joins the conflict system or the alliance system. Also, gradual ideological changes in the major left-wing party, for example the "social democratization" of the Communist Party in Italy, have an effect on a social movement's behavior, insofar as these changes create room for new social movements at the expense of both Old and New Left groups.

Admittedly, these are findings based on preliminary comparative observations in only two countries. We are still at the beginning of more refined conceptual elaboration and closer empirical studies. We think, however, that our analysis provides a basis to move a step further, either in broadening the cross-national and cross-temporal perspective, or, based on a low number of countries, deepening by the use of more systematically collected data. Of course, a combined research strategy would be ideal, though it does not seem to be realistic.

Notes

A first version of this paper was presented at the workshop Social Movements: Framing Processes and Opportunity Structures held at the Wissenschaftszentrum Berlin fur Sozialforschung (WZB) July 5–7, 1990. We are grateful to Mario Diani, Doug McAdam, Roland Roth, Sidney Tarrow, and the colleagues of our research unit at the WZB for useful comments on previous drafts.

1. This has been demonstrated in a comparison of the changing strategies of antinuclear movements in the United States, France, and West Germany (Rucht 1990a).

2. This model has some parallels to the "political process model of movement emer-

gence" presented by McAdam (1982, p. 51). His variables—"broad socioeconomic processes," "indigenous organizational strength," and "expanding political opportunities"—correspond by and large to our "structural context," "internal factors," and "intervening factors" respectively. We did not, however, integrate the additional "cognitive liberation" factor emphasized by McAdam. This factor supposedly is relevant for the emergence but not for later phases of a movement.

3. We also disagree with Garner and Zald's definition of a social movement, on which their concept of social movement sector is based. If a social movement is "any sentiment and activity shared by two or more people oriented towards changes in social relations or in the social system" (1985, p. 129), there would be no criteria to exclude parties, governments, international agencies, etc., from a social movement, and consequently from the social movement sector. For terminological reasons, we hesitate to use the term *sector*, which usually refers to a part of a larger entity comprising other similarly structured sectors. For the social movement sector, however, it is not clear how to distinguish the whole cake from its pieces nor to what degree various pieces of the same cake resemble each other. Analogous to the scientific literature on political parties, we would suggest calling the whole cake the *social movement system*—that is, the totality of coexisting social movement families in a given society or country, no matter their relationship to each other.

4. It is important to stress that the idea of a social movement family and a social movement system should not be equated with the sum of protest actions in a given society. Though protest, particularly in its more radical and disruptive forms, is an activity of social movements, protest is by no means restricted to movements. Other social actors, such as conventional parties and pressure groups, may also use protest actions, and sometimes even ally themselves with social movements in order to carry out common protest campaigns. We should therefore separate the idea of a protest cycle as defined by Tarrow (1989a, pp. 13–14; 1989b, pp. 41–56) from the cycle that a social movement family is undergoing. Our analytical focus is on the latter aspect, though there may be an empirical overlap between movement cycles and protest cycles. We use the term *cycle* in a loose sense, referring to the pattern of the growth, peak, and decline of social movements' protest activities. Our notion of a movement's cycle necessarily implies neither a symmetry of growth and decline nor a regular repetition of cycles over time.

5. *Strategy* "refers to a conscious, long-range, planned and integrated general conception of an actor's conflict behavior based on the overall context (including third parties and potential allies), and with special emphasis on the inherent strengths and weaknesses of the major opponent" (Rucht 1990b, p. 161). With regard to social movement families, we were initially tempted to use the term *strategy* instead of *behavior*. As a result of a critique made by William Gamson—who expressed doubts about the extent of coordination within a movement family, and even within a single movement—we chose *behavior*, which is more open and better suited for what we have in mind.

6. It is beyond the range of this paper to assess the extent to which the various collective actors were directed by strategic choices.

7. As Klandermans observed, this is a fluid model; boundaries between the two systems remain vague and may change in the course of events: "Specific organizations that try to remain aloof from the controversy may be forced to take sides. Parts of the political system (political parties, elites, governmental institutions) can coalesce with SMOs [social movement organizations] and join the alliance system. Coalitions can fall apart, and previous allies can become part of the conflict system" (1989b, p. 302). While Klandermans developed these observations in respect to social movement organizations, our work on social movement families prompted us to favor a looser definition of the organizational field: the

contacts we examined, and found significant, are not always meant as "concrete" organizational exchanges.

8. Some authors have chosen a twofold categorization. For example, Kitschelt (1986, p. 67) distinguished between confrontative and assimilative strategies of social movements. Kriesi (1989b, p. 296) classified the system's reactions to challengers as either integration or repression. We think that our categories have the advantage of taking into account the specificities of relationships between social movement families on the one hand and alliance or conflict systems on the other.

9. After a complex sequence of alliances and divisions, three main New Left groups survived the decline of mobilization: Lotta Continua, Avanguardia Operaia, and Manifesto-Partito di Unita Popolare. Active in the phase of high mobilization, these groups had a large number of members: around 3,000 for Avanguardia Operaia, 10,000–30,000 for Lotta Continua, and 5,000–6,000 for Il Manifesto (Monicelli 1978, pp. 47–49; for the history of Lotta Continua, see Bobbio 1988).

10. For much of our information on this period, we rely on the research directed by Melucci on the social movement sector in Milan (Melucci 1984).

11. A few autonomous initiatives—such as magazines, cafés, and bookstores—offered sporadic occasions for contact, but nobody tried to coordinate the various activities.

12. 1981–83 were the years of high visibility for the peace movement; 500,000 people participated in protest marches in Rome in 1981 and 1983.

13. Judith Adler Hellman analyzed the complex relationships of the feminist movement with the Unione Donne Italiane (UDI), controlled by the PCI (1987, pp. 40–54, 215–22), and with the trade unions (1987, pp. 208–11). On feminism and UDI, see also Beckwith (1985).

14. Since 1983, membership in the ecological groups has increased dramatically. For instance, the membership of the conservationist World Wildlife Fund grew from 30,000 in 1983 to 120,000 in 1987; that of the political ecologist Lega per l'Ambiente went from 15,000 in 1983 to 100,000 in 1986. After a few experiences at the local level beginning in 1980, the first significant electoral campaign took place in 1985: there were 150 Green lists in the local and regional elections, and they won 600,000 votes (2.1 percent of the total). Two years later they received 1 million votes in the 1987 national election (see Diani 1988, pp. 56–86).

15. It must also be recalled that votes for the Greens came from voters of different parties; among them were 22.9 percent from the centrist Republican Party and 16.7 percent from the Socialist Party (Diani 1988, p. 186; see also Biorcio 1988).

16. Kriesi deals with four variables, positing the following hypotheses: "The relative strength of the left is of crucial importance for the mobilizing capacity, and the chances of success of nsms [new social movements]. A hegemonic Social Democratic party which is open to the claims made by the nsms may assure their success before they even start building up a mobilization campaign. A hegemonic or dominant Social-Democratic party which is closed to the claims made by the nsms may cause them to found their own party. . . . Second, fragmentation of the left can be expected to provide favorable preconditions for the mobilization of nsms—if the Communist party is not very powerful. Fragmentation implies the presence of more homogenous, smaller leftist parties, with a more radical stance, and, correspondingly, with a greater inclination to mobilize new potentials critical of existing power relations. Third, the stronger the Communist party in a political system, the greater the salience of traditional class conflicts, and the less pacified these conflicts tend to be. . . . Finally, left-wing parties in the opposition will find it much more attractive and easier to make promises to nsms than left-wing parties in government which have to fulfil such promises" (1989b, pp. 296–97).

17. Frank Wilson (1990, pp. 73ff.) also expresses doubts about the relation of the incidence of new social movements to the extent of corporatism.

18. Of course, this inherent tendency toward organizational maintenance does not guarantee a movement's survival. Internal factors can be overruled by powerful external factors. The student movement practically disappeared as a coherent movement—quickly in West Germany, slowly in Italy—though conflicts within the university system also arose in later periods. Likewise, the peace movement weakened rapidly, while the women's and ecological movements kept up a high level of activity.

19. In purely logical terms, behavioral changes can also occur if, or even because, context variables do not change. For instance, people who are deprived may first patiently wait for an amelioration of their situation. After a while, and because things are not changing, people start to revolt. Empirically, however, we found much more evidence to attribute behavioral changes to changing opportunities.

Part IV

The State and Movement Outcomes: System Transformations and Political Reform

Chapter 10

The Success of Political Movements: A Bargaining Perspective

Paul Burstein, Rachel L. Einwohner, and Jocelyn A. Hollander

"The interest of many scholars in social movements stems from their belief that movements represent an important force for social change," write McAdam, McCarthy, and Zald in the *Handbook of Sociology* (1988, p. 727). This belief, in fact, has provided an indispensable justification for the studies of social movements conducted since the field was revitalized in the 1970s. At the heart of Gamson's pathbreaking work, *The Strategy of Social Protest* (1990 [1975]), is the claim that movement participation should be viewed as a rational way to achieve political goals, riskier than more conventional types of political action (such as voting), but reasonable for those unable to exert influence through conventional, institutionalized means (Jenkins 1983a).

The claim that movement participation is rational has credibility only if participation can lead to success; that is, for participation to be interpreted as rational, social movements must succeed fairly often, and their achievements must depend at least partly on factors subject to participants' control. Gamson therefore began his empirical work by showing that movements often achieve some success, and he devoted most of *The Strategy of Social Protest* to showing how success is influenced by factors potentially affected by participants, including the challenging group's goals, size, organization, provision of incentives to members, and use of violence.

Although they were influential, Gamson's conclusions were highly preliminary because there was so little precedent for what he did. Earlier studies of social movements focused on one or at most a handful of movements, nearly always those deemed especially consequential. Because of the focus on small numbers of successful movements, it was impossible to determine how often movements succeeded or what distinguished those that succeeded from those that failed. What was needed, Gamson concluded, was systematic comparative research. This meant analyzing a relatively large random sample of movements and operationalizing crucial variables (such as success) so that objective descriptions and comparisons of movements were possible.

Gamson emphasized that the very originality of his work required many of his contributions to be relatively simple attempts to deal with complex problems. Thus, for example, examining a relatively large sample of movements enabled him to generalize on a sounder basis than earlier researchers had, but resource constraints limited the amount of information he could gather on each movement. His definitions of crucial concepts (such as success) and his statistical analyses were admittedly simple and amenable to refinement.

A few researchers extended or challenged Gamson's work, and some of the exchanges showed how stimulating his approach could be (see, for example, Gamson's debates with Goldstone and others in Gamson 1990). Nevertheless, subsequent work failed to follow up on many of his advances; in fact, Gamson's book is still identified as "perhaps the most systematic attempt to isolate the effects of organized social movements" (McAdam, McCarthy, and Zald 1988, p. 727). The field of social movements grew tremendously in the 1970s and 1980s, but the study of movement outcomes did not; indeed, McAdam, McCarthy, and Zald devote less than a page and a half of their forty-two-page review to outcomes.

Thus, we still know little about the impact of social movements on social change. Partly this is because it is so difficult to demonstrate that social movements cause social change and to attribute whatever effect they have to particular characteristics of the movement (Gamson 1990; Huberts 1989; McAdam, McCarthy, and Zald 1988, p. 727). Another contributing factor may be that, despite great theoretical advances in the area as a whole, we still lack an overall theory of movement success. Yet the many studies of movement emergence, participation, and maintenance done since the 1970s mean little if movements never effect social change or if their successes are beyond participants' control.

It is therefore essential to refocus social movements research onto movement outcomes. This chapter reviews what we have learned since the mid-1970s about such outcomes and identifies gaps in our knowledge. Our focus will be on *political* movements, those seeking to influence government institutions, because recent work concentrates on them (Gamson 1990; McAdam, McCarthy, and Zald 1988; Tilly 1984) and it is impractical to review work on all types of movements in a single chapter.

The concept of bargaining provides our framework. We view movement outcomes not as simply the product of movement characteristics and activities, but as the result of interactions among movement organizations, the organizations whose behavior they are trying to change, and relevant actors in the broader environment, all struggling to acquire resources and use them to their best advantage vis-à-vis the others. This bargaining perspective suggests that the dependence of movement targets on other actors is a critical factor in movement success. As we discuss later, this framework shares many features with resource mobilization theory, notably a focus on resources and their use. We believe it expands upon the resource mobilization model however, in ways that will deepen our ability to understand movement outcomes. We begin by defining what a movement is and go on to define success, categorize its possible causes, and review what is known about the impact of movements. We then discuss the implications of the review for our understanding of political movements and for future work.

Political Movement: A Definition

Virtually everyone writing about social movements agrees that they have two defining characteristics: they demand social and political change, and they are outside established political institutions (e.g., McCarthy and Zald 1977, p. 1217; Freeman 1975, pp. 46–47; McAdam 1982, p. 25; Tilly 1984, p. 306). But it is really "outsider" status that distinguishes social movements from mainstream institutions—almost every group involved in politics, including political parties and organizations such as the Chamber of Commerce, wants change.

There is considerable disagreement, however, about what aspect of outsider status is most crucial. Gamson (1990, p. 16) focuses on mobilization: challenging groups are outsiders largely because they seek to represent a constituency not previously mobilized to participate in politics. Tilly (1984, p. 306) sees representation as crucial: the constituencies of social movements are outsiders because they lack formal representation in government decision making. McAdam (1982, p. 25) focuses on tactics: movements involve "noninstitutional forms of political participation."

Gamson's and Tilly's approaches create an ironic problem for those who analyze movement outcomes. Both suggest that once a movement begins to succeed—by mobilizing its constituency or gaining formal representation—it ceases to be a movement, even if its goals, membership, and tactics do not change. Researchers who adopt these approaches seemingly have to choose between studying political change and studying social movements. Studying political change requires examining how movement goals influence government even after constituencies mobilize and gain representation, but the Gamson and Tilly approaches require abandoning the study of movements at this point.

In addition, what Tilly means by "formal representation" is unclear. In the United States, the only groups formally represented under the Constitution are geographical constituencies—states and congressional districts. If Tilly means something less formal—for example, regularly being invited to testify before congressional committees or respond to proposed federal regulations—then many groups typically considered social movement organizations (SMOs), such as the NAACP, have had formal representation for 50 years, beginning well before the peak of movement activity. Yet no one would propose that the NAACP or other civil rights organizations were not SMOs in the 1960s.

McAdam's approach is more useful. From his point of view, outsider status is defined by a willingness to use noninstitutionalized tactics. Groups willing to do so must see themselves as less committed to institutionalized forms of behavior, and thus define themselves as outsiders. Movements should not be thought of as utilizing *only* noninstitutionalized tactics, however. Although McAdam is not explicit on this point, many efforts to bring about social or political change involve both institutionalized and noninstitutionalized tactics. For example, the civil rights movement engaged in both sit-ins and litigation, and the environmental movement both lobbies members of Congress and disrupts logging in the Northwest (cf. Burstein 1991).

How should *noninstitutionalized* be defined? Noninstitutionalized tactics customarily have two defining characteristics: they involve activities that (1) are not part of the formal political process and (2) are intended to be disruptive (whether they are legal or illegal). Sit-ins, mass marches, and boycotts are examples. Not included are legally regulated components of the political process such as voting and lobbying; unregulated but nondisruptive tactics such as letter-writing campaigns; and sometimes disruptive but institutionalized forms of participation such as continuous court challenges to proposed regulations (a tactic often employed by environmentalists, for example).

Thus, we define social movements as organized, collective efforts to achieve social change that use noninstitutionalized tactics at least part of the time. Political movements, the focus of this chapter, are social movements directed at formal government institutions.

Conceptual Framework

Although many scholars have analyzed movement outcomes, it can be argued that we still lack a conceptual framework that can explain how multiple factors interact to produce success or failure. Thus, for example, although numerous studies attempt to gauge the impact of violence on movement success independent of other factors, we know very little about how violence interacts with other factors, such as movement organization or public opinion. Some research suggests that interactions are important without making them an explicit focus. For example, Mueller (1978) notes that riot violence in 1967–68 was significantly more likely to evoke policy responsiveness immediately after the assassination of Martin Luther King Jr. than at other times, suggesting an interaction between violence and dramatic historical events.

For conclusions like Mueller's to be truly useful, however, we need a broad conceptualization of how such specific hypotheses and findings fit into the larger process of movement mobilization. We suggest that the concept of *bargaining* can provide the basis for such a conceptualization. Although some social movement researchers found the concept of bargaining useful in the 1960s (see, for example, J. Q. Wilson 1961; Lipsky 1968), it has been largely ignored in more recent work (with the partial exception of McAdam 1982). We believe, however, that it can provide a framework useful for analyzing social movement outcomes.

According to J. Q. Wilson, bargaining describes "any situation in which two or more parties seek conflicting ends through the exchange of compensations. . . . The essential element in bargaining is that concessions are rewarded. The task is to find a mutually agreeable ratio for the exchange of those rewards" (1961, p. 291). Thus, we may conceive of SMOs as trying to bargain with the targets of their actions (here, government agencies) to achieve their ends.

Initially, however, SMOs cannot bargain as other organizations do, because they are powerless outsiders: "bargaining is not available because the excluded group has nothing the others desire, either in relation to the issue in point or to any future issue which might arise" (J.Q. Wilson 1961, p. 292). SMOs must therefore increase their bargaining power through protest or other means if they are to succeed. One common way outsider groups "can 'create' bargaining resources," according to Lipsky (1968, p. 1145), is "to activate 'third parties' to enter the implicit or explicit bargaining arena in ways favorable to the protesters" (cf. Schattschneider 1960; Jenkins 1983a; Jenkins and Perrow 1977).

The power that SMOs must achieve to bargain effectively must be seen in the context of other groups—specifically, their targets and relevant third parties. As Gurr argues, "the resources, interests, and dynamics of the other party to the conflict have as much bearing on the outcomes . . . as do characteristics of the challengers" (1980, p. 244). The "tactics and power of the countermovement," if there is one, are likely to have a critical effect on movement outcomes (Colby 1985, p. 582). The resources and behaviors that empower SMOs in one relationship may have no effect on a different target group, and these effects may change, depending on the resources and behavior of other third parties.

A bargaining perspective thus suggests, in line with social exchange theory (Emerson 1972a, 1972b; Blau 1964), that the outcome of bargaining is not the result of the characteristics of either party, but rather is a function of their resources relative to each other, their relationships with third parties, and other factors in the environment. Analyses of movement success must consider interactions among (1) characteristics of the SMOs, (2) characteristics of the target (here, typically a government agency), and (3) characteristics of the environment, especially the actions of third parties and factors that affect the availability of resources to those involved (cf. Jenkins 1983a; McAdam 1982).

Bargaining theory thus directs our attention to the interdependence of movement and target: "The upshot of bargaining activity is that each party receives some outcome. And it is a critical characteristic of bargaining activity that these outcomes be interdependent. Thus, each party must, at least in part, be dependent on the other for the quality of the outcomes which he, himself, receives" (Rubin and Brown 1975, p. 10). Exchange theory extends this idea by suggesting that each party's bargaining power is a function of the other's dependence (Emerson 1972b, p. 64). For SMOs, this dependence need not be direct; although protesters themselves may not have resources sufficient to sway policy makers, their protests may win the support of other groups upon whom the target is dependent. We suggest that the concept of dependence is critical to understanding movement success, and that it can bring coherence to seemingly disparate findings on movement outcomes.

There are obvious similarities between the resource mobilization model advanced by McCarthy and Zald (1977), Jenkins (1983a), and others, and what we are calling the bargaining perspective. The two models agree on the importance of resources and the need for strategic mobilization of them. We believe, however, that the bargaining perspective extends resource mobilization theory in several ways that make it more useful for the study of social movement outcomes.

First, the bargaining perspective broadens resource mobilization's conceptualization of resources. While resource mobilization theory focuses on resources as the property of a protest group or sponsor, the bargaining model focuses not on the possession of resources but on their value to the group relative to other groups in a given situation. This approach introduces two new concepts: an emphasis on the interactive and dynamic context of social movements rather than the static properties of involved groups; and a distinction between resources per se and their value in a bargaining situation—between resources and resources *in use*. Resources can empower a movement organization in different ways, depending on the situation and the groups involved. Moreover, shifts in the resources of other groups or in the political context can change the value of a movement organization's resources, entirely independent of any variation in the resources themselves.

Second, the bargaining model expands our understanding of the use of resources and the creation of bargaining power. As McAdam (1982, p. 30) points out, resource mobilization theorists typically focus on resources used as positive inducements, particularly the support of elites and conscience constituents, as factors creating political power. Although positive inducements are often undeniably important, however, negative inducements (such as violence or the threat of violence) can also be critical to successful movement outcomes. Here again the distinction between resources and their use or value in a given situation is fundamental. Not only may the value of an organization's resources depend on the circumstances, but these resources may also be used in different ways. The same resource could be used either as a reward for pro-movement policies, or as a threat aimed at preventing undesirable behavior.

Defining Success

Assessing a movement's success involves determining whether it has achieved its goals. But what are its goals? Any social movement has a multiplicity of participants and of observers, each of whom may view movement goals differently. Furthermore, movements often involve many SMOs, which may disagree with each other about goals. Should we use as our measure of organizational goals the sentiments of rank and file participants, the media-reported demands of social movement leaders, or the perceptions of movement targets or observers? Moreover, social movements are dynamic; if goals change over the course of a movement's activities, which set of goals should we consider in deciding if success has been achieved (see discussions in Tilly 1978; Gurr 1980; Webb et al. 1983; Mueller 1978)?

Here we define goals as the formally stated objectives of political movement organizations: those goals publicly presented in speech or writing to nonmovement actors such as movement targets, the media, or bystander publics. This approach takes an intermediate position between a subjective measurement of movement goals based on the views of individual participants and an approach based on outsiders' opinions of what the movement is attempting to accomplish.

We have chosen this definition for several reasons. First, it is used by a majority of researchers, facilitating comparisons of goals and the determinants of outcomes across studies, organizations, and movements. Second, formalized objectives lend themselves to measurement by researchers; such objectives are often reported in the mass media or elsewhere (for example, in organizational publications), making it possible to ascertain goals at specific times and to track changes over time. In addition, there is likely to be intraorganizational agreement on formalized goals; although internal dissension may exist, it is likely that only a single set of objectives will be formalized through public demands (although of course extreme dissensus may lead to the breakup of a movement organization and the formation of new ones). Finally, it is more often the formalized goals of an SMO, rather than internally discussed or individual goals, that elicit responses from movement targets or bystander publics.

What constitutes a successful movement outcome? Intuitively, movements may be considered successful to the extent that they achieve their formally stated goals. But this definition does not get us very far. Movements have many goals; if we want to compare them and to seek the general conditions for success, we must categorize goals in ways that make comparison possible across movements and over time.

The best-known attempt to do this is Gamson's. He focused on two critical aspects of success: the *acceptance* of a challenging group by its antagonists as a valid representative for a legitimate set of interests, and the winning of *new advantages* for the group's beneficiary (1990, pp. 28–29). This categorization proved very useful, but for those focusing on political movements, it leaves out something critical: the political process occurring between the initial challenge and potential substantive political changes.

Here Schumaker's work (1975, pp. 494–95) is helpful. He argues that success should be defined in terms of the political system's responsiveness to

SMO demands, and he sees potential responsiveness occurring in five stages: *access responsiveness*, the willingness of the target to hear the concerns of the movement organization (similar to Gamson's "acceptance"); *agenda responsiveness*, the target's willingness to place the movement's demands on the political agenda; *policy responsiveness*, the target's adoption of new policies (particularly legislation) congruent with the manifest demands of protest groups (which Gamson would consider a new advantage); *output responsiveness*, the target's effective implementation of its new policies; and *impact responsiveness*, the "degree to which the actions of the political system succeed in alleviating the grievances of the protest group."

Schumaker's typology highlights aspects of the political process not explicitly analyzed by Gamson. It can be made even more useful by supplementing it with an aspect of political change often important to social movements: what Kitschelt (1986, p. 67) calls "structural impacts" involving "a transformation of the political structures themselves." That is, movements may try to change political structures and rules that influence political outcomes for everyone, not only themselves. For example, eliminating literacy tests used to prevent blacks from voting made it easier for less-educated whites as well as blacks to vote; and changes in the concept of legal standing brought about by some groups made it easier for many SMOs to sue their targets in federal court (Bosso 1987, chapter 2).

Analyzing movement success in achieving the six types of government responsiveness (summarized in Table 1) enables us to distinguish between movements that really produce social change and those that win only symbolic victories (such as gaining the passage of legislation that is not subsequently enforced). We should also be able to determine whether factors that affect success at one level (for example, gaining access) are same as those that influence success at another (for example, winning the passage of legislation).

There remains the problem of gauging responsiveness. Because previous work provided Gamson with little guidance in comparing groups with varied goals, he felt forced to measure acceptance and the winning of new advantages as simple dichotomies, while expressing the hope that future work would lead to more refined measures (see also Webb et al. 1983; Burstein and Monaghan 1986). Recent research tends to focus on single movements, however, rather than adopting Gamson's comparative approach, so little progress has been made in refining general measures of success. For this review, then, we must rely on the measures already employed, and try to provide rough comparability ourselves.

Table 1. Types of policy responsiveness

Type	Examples
Access	Movement participants testify at congressional hearing; submit amicus brief in court
Agenda	Desired bill introduced in Senate or House
Policy	Desired legislation adopted
Output	Legislation enforced as movement desired
Impact	Legislation has intended consequences
Structural	System changed to increase opportunities for movement influence

Arguably, the six types of responsiveness represent increasing success (with structural responsiveness being somewhat different than the others), and it seems plausible that success will require greater resources at each succeeding stage. But success is not simply a matter of the quantity of resources (assuming a single metric could be devised); particular resources and strategies are likely to be more effective with regard to some kinds of responsiveness than others.

Mueller's (1978) findings suggest, for example, that violent protest tactics gain more symbolic reassurances (which we would categorize as access responsiveness) than actual change. According to her analysis, violence provides an SMO with enough resources to bargain for access but not enough to achieve policy, output, or impact responsiveness. Similarly, disruptive tactics may help an SMO win a place on the political agenda or even the adoption of legislation, but ensuring that the legislation is enforced may require the development of legal and technical expertise and the capacity to monitor the activities of enforcement agencies (Sabatier 1975).

The Correlates of Success

The bargaining perspective suggests that SMO success depends on interactions among SMOs, their targets, and the political context. Unfortunately, most research fails to take all of these interactions into account systematically, instead trying to generalize about the impact of particular factors taken out of context. Some researchers have identified the importance of a single interaction; Klandermans (1989a), for instance, calls attention to the interaction between movements and their environments. Research has not yet examined movement outcomes in terms of interactions among all three variables, however, which limits our understanding of the determinants of movement success. In this section, we draw as much as possible from prior work (whatever model of movement activity it relies on) in order to summarize findings on SMO success and indicate how they may aid the development of a bargaining model of social movements.

The first thing to note about recent work is that it focuses on some types of responsiveness while virtually ignoring others. Most studies focus on policy responsiveness, fewer on access responsiveness, and very few on the political agenda, outputs, policy impact, or structural change (cf. McAdam, McCarthy, and Zald 1988, pp. 727–28). Those studying social movements have paid little attention to how SMOs get their demands onto the formal political agenda, and almost none to how successful SMOs have been at ameliorating the conditions that originally motivated their activities.

Logically, past work should be reviewed in terms of the stages of responsiveness just described. Practically, however, most stages have been studied little, and it makes more sense first to review work on the one most intensely studied: policy responsiveness. Because some studies analyze policy and output responsiveness together, we will do so here as well. And because so many studies treat characteristics of SMOs, their targets, and the environment independently, we must often do so, even though the bargaining perspective suggests that the focus should properly be on the interactions among them. We will try, however, to interpret the findings from the bargaining perspective as much as possible.

Policy and Output Responsiveness

What factors increase an SMO's ability to bargain for what it wants? SMO organization, including professionalization, formalization, centralization, and bureaucratization, contributes to the capacity to affect policy (Staggenborg 1989; Gamson 1975; Mirowsky and Ross 1981). SMOs that provide selective incentives to members are more likely to succeed than those that do not, while factionalization seems to reduce the likelihood of success (Gamson 1975). Organization, in turn, may be influenced by SMO ideology (which may have its own effect on policy responsiveness; see Staggenborg 1989).

More directly relevant to the bargaining framework, Colby (1985, p. 592) claims that the importance of the SMO to the "normal functioning of the target institution" strongly affects success, as does its electoral power, especially on issues subject to elite control. Steedly and Foley, using Gamson's data, find that alliances with other groups contribute substantially to SMO success (1990, pp. 191–92, 195).

SMO organization is likely to affect success through its impact on SMO actions, of course, and some scholars have considered how tactics influence policy responsiveness. Violence is the tactic most frequently studied, and also the one leading to the most contradictory findings. Gamson (1975), Colby (1982), and Piven and Cloward (1977, 1979) all suggest that violent tactics may help SMOs achieve their goals. Other researchers, however, argue that violence may have the opposite effect, perhaps because it reduces third-party support (Schumaker 1975) or leads to an especially strong reaction by the target (Colby 1985). Still others posit that violence has no independent effect on policy responsiveness (Mirowsky and Ross 1981; Hahn 1970; Steedly and Foley 1990). The nature of the issue itself may affect tactics' success: attempting to publicize an issue and mobilize the general public may be more effective for domestic than for foreign policy (Metz 1986), while direct lobbying may be more effective when issues are defined narrowly than when they are very broad (Milbrath 1970). It is in the face of such contradictory findings that the bargaining perspective may prove especially useful. Gamson (1990), Garrow (1978), and Burstein (1985) all suggest, for example, that the impact of violent tactics depends very heavily on the relative strength of perpetrators and victims and on whether it succeeds in bringing third parties into the conflict on the side of the victims. Other researchers (e.g., Schumaker 1980; Gurr 1980; Button 1989, p. 184) suggest that the effectiveness of violent tactics may depend on other factors, such as their novelty, economic and political pressures from third parties, preexisting policy, or public opinion.

SMO violence may also affect output responsiveness. For example, riots have been associated with increases in welfare payments and urban expenditures (Colby 1975; Welch 1975; Isaac and Kelly 1981; but Colby later [1985, p. 588] argues that riots are "at best ineffective and at worst counterproductive"). Isaac and Kelly (1981) claim that it is the frequency rather than the severity of riots that affected welfare increases.

Researchers are also divided on the effectiveness of nonviolent protest techniques, such as sit-ins and boycotts. Colby (1982) first concluded that nonviolent protest had more impact on changes in welfare policy than riots or electoral power, but later decided that nonviolent protest, like violence, does not help SMOs (1985, p. 588). Schumaker (1980, p. 138) cautiously suggests that there is a curvilinear relationship between the unconventionality of protest techniques and policy success, such that "nonviolent direct-action techniques" are actually less effective in achieving policy success than either conventional techniques (such as negotiation, public hearings, or petitions) or violent unconventional ones. Again, these findings might be clarified if the context in which action occurs and the characteristics of those against whom actions are taken were taken into consideration; unfortunately, the available data do not permit this kind of reanalysis.

Characteristics of SMO goals are also said to affect success. Groups that want to displace those in power or make broad structural changes in the political system are seldom successful (Gamson 1990; Mirowsky and Ross 1981; Steedly and Foley 1990). The scope of goals may also be important; SMOs with narrow goals may be more successful than those with broad goals (Gamson 1990; Barkan 1984; Steedly and Foley 1990), though Gamson finds that scope is unimportant once the intent to displace is controlled. Hahn (1970, p. 104) claims that the more intense the movement's grievance (as categorized by the Kerner Commission), the more likely a community is to respond, while Milbrath (1970) and Fowler and Shaiko (1987) contend that characteristics of the issue itself—such as its salience to the SMO and the general public, or its scope—can affect policy responsiveness.

The bargaining perspective suggests that the actions and resources of the SMO's target affect the SMO's ability to bring about change. Unfortunately, we know much less about how the target's characteristics affect movement outcomes than we know about SMO characteristics. Some evidence points to the ability of the target to affect movement success. Turk and Zucker (1984), for example, suggest that the more organized the target, the lower the likelihood of SMO success (cf. Isaac and Kelly 1981). Barkan (1984) notes the importance of white response to black civil rights activities in the South. His examination of protest campaigns in five southern U.S. cities finds that SMOs achieved their goals (usually desegregation) where whites responded violently, especially when the violence was reported nationally (e.g., in Birmingham and Selma). Where whites employed legal tactics (such as prohibiting demonstrations) rather than violence, protest efforts were less successful.

Barkan presents precisely the type of research suggested by the bargaining perspective, where interactions between SMO and target affect movement success. We may think of the effectiveness of resources deployed by the SMO (including its tactics) as dependent on the resources and responses of the target as well as those of the movement itself. Thus, for example, tactical mistakes in planning routine activities or responding to protest may weaken a target or cause it to lose support from third parties, increasing the likelihood of movement success (see, for example, Walsh and Cable 1986 on the antinuclear movement, and also Walsh 1986; cf. Nelkin and Poulkin 1990). Along these lines, McAdam (1983) notes the importance of the interaction between movement tactics and the target's responses; the latter often force the SMO to innovate tactically in order to succeed.

The impact on bargaining of the environment surrounding SMOs—including the political opportunity structure, culture, third parties, and the circumstances of particular protests—is the focus of increasing attention (see Klandermans 1989b, p. 388). One major factor that contributes to movement success is the "political opportunity structure," which Eisinger describes as "the openings, weak spots, barriers, and resources of the political system itself" (1973, pp. 11–12). Kitschelt writes that "political opportunity structures function as 'filters' between the mobilization of the movement and its choice of strategies and capacity to change the social environment" (1986, p. 59).

One particularly important dimension of the political opportunity structure is the openness of the policy-making system; SMOs are likely to take advantage of political structures that afford citizens a great deal of access to political institutions (Eisinger 1973; Tarrow 1983; Kitschelt 1986). Tarrow notes that reform is most likely when the political regime is unstable, for at such times powerful parties are likely to permit reform out of fear of losing power, while opposition parties will support new causes in order to gain power. McAdam (1982) argues that the structure of political opportunities may provide protest groups with expanded political access and the incentive to act collectively; these in turn may increase their bargaining power and render repression more costly.

The political culture surrounding a social movement may affect people's notions of what constitutes acceptable reform and thus affect a movement's ability to achieve policy responsiveness. Few studies adequately operationalize "culture," so conclusions about its impact must be treated very cautiously; nevertheless, the general logic of the argument is clear (see, for example, McAdam 1983; Button 1989; Taylor 1989). Nagel also notes the importance of ideology in policy change. In her examination of federal Indian policy, she suggests that a change from termination (ending the special treaties between the government and Indian tribes) to self-determination (returning some power to the tribes and committing the government to cultural pluralism) was partly the result of ideological change linked to traditional American values. She writes: "The delegitimation of colonialism with its racist . . . ideological foundations and the popularity of the concept of self-determination were both factors in the ideological 'resonance' of Self-Determination policy and its overthrow of Termination" (1990, p. 18).

As both the bargaining perspective and resource mobilization theory predict, third parties are also important for success. For instance, Schumaker

(1975) finds that the public attention given a social movement can aid its cause (see also Milbrath 1970; cf. Schattschneider 1960). In fact, he concludes that the "environment of social support" (particularly the support of officials) is more important than protester-controlled variables in explaining movement outcomes. Support from other movements may also further movement goals (Gamson 1990; Schumaker 1975; Tarrow 1983), while well-organized countermovements may prevent SMOs from succeeding, especially when they are supported by government.

Special attention should be paid to the relationship between social movements and political parties. As the most important nongovernmental political organizations in modern states, parties play a critical role in all aspects of political change. In fact, many parties developed out of social movements—including, arguably, the Democratic and Republican parties in the United States —and relationships between movements and parties are central to many analyses of European politics (e.g., Tarrow 1989a). Winning the support of a major political party should have a major impact on movement success.

Assessing the impact of movement-party relationships on political change in the United States is difficult, however. Traditional scholarship on American parties suggests that movements have strongly influenced them at times of crisis, pressuring the two major parties to adopt new policy stands while threatening to challenge their hold on power by creating new parties (Sundquist 1983). And research on specific issues argues that movements can help determine which issues win a place on party platforms, which policy options will be considered, which candidates will win election, and which policies will be enacted (e.g., Lo 1990 on the "tax revolt" and Carmines and Stimson 1989 on civil rights).

Unfortunately, neither the relationship between movements and parties nor their joint impact on policy has been studied very much. Disciplinary boundaries are partly to blame; sociologists primarily concerned with social movements pay little attention to political parties, and political scientists studying parties seldom devote much effort to examining movements (while sometimes acknowledging their importance—e.g., Carmines and Stimson 1989, p. 189). The neglect of movement-party relationships also seems attributable to the difficulty of studying them in the American context. American parties are much less organized and centralized than most parties elsewhere; they have porous boundaries, broad and amorphous demographic bases, and relatively vague ideologies (see, for example, Epstein 1986). It is therefore often unclear to SMO and party leaders which party a particular movement might successfully look to for support; the alliances that occur often appear to have been impossible to predict (even though, once made, they may have major impacts on policy—see, for example, Lo 1990; Carmines and Stimson 1989). Movement participants sometimes try to gain access to party resources by running for office in party primaries—the openness of which is uniquely American—thereby trying to influence parties from within (Epstein 1986, pp. 129–30, 345). Finally, the election of candidates widely seen to represent particular movements may affect movement-party relationships, and should be investigated.

The circumstances in which movement activities occur may also affect their consequences. Mueller (1978) argues that particular circumstances may create public support for movements and offset generally unfavorable public reactions to the use of violence. SMOs may also be more successful in achieving policy responsiveness during periods perceived as crises (Gamson 1975; Goldstone 1980; see also McAdam 1983; Button 1989; Nagel 1990). Sometimes protests themselves create a sense of crisis. Jenkins and Brent argue that the passage of the 1935 Social Security Act resulted in part from "a series of sustained protests combined with growing electoral instability [which created] a sense of political crisis among elites, thereby placing major reform proposals on the political agenda" (1989, p. 894).

Other environmental factors may affect output responsiveness as well. Swank (1983), for instance, has shown that electoral competitiveness is associated with increased welfare spending; city government structure may also affect SMO success (Hahn 1970; Welch 1975; Schumaker 1980).

Thus, the broader environment clearly influences SMO success. To better understand how this occurs, however, we must examine how third-party support and other factors interact with characteristics of SMOs and their targets to affect success.

Access and Agenda Responsiveness

Most research on SMOs focuses on policy responsiveness, but there is a fair amount of work on access responsiveness as well. For the most part, the factors associated with access responsiveness are the same as those associated with policy responsiveness. This suggests that there is little point in analyzing the two separately, but such a conclusion would be misleading. In order to achieve policy responsiveness, an SMO must first gain access to the political arena; thus an attempt to determine what factors contribute primarily to winning access will be confounded by the inclusion of groups that have achieved both.

Some factors do appear to help SMOs win access without having much effect on policy responsiveness, however, including violence (at least according to Mueller 1978) and group size (Gamson 1990). The extent to which winning access requires different, or fewer, resources than gaining policy responsiveness is not clear. A bargaining perspective suggests that there should be differences; but to determine what they are requires that more research be done following Gamson's model, clearly distinguishing between access and policy responsiveness (as well as other types of responsiveness) and analyzing them separately.

Impact Responsiveness and Structural Change

As important as the steps leading to policy responsiveness are those occurring subsequently. The question then becomes: will SMO activity have its intended impact on people's lives?

According to the bargaining perspective, there is a clear conceptual division between agenda, policy, and output responsiveness on the one hand and impact responsiveness and structural change on the other—that is, between the bargaining process itself and the consequences of that process. As noted earlier, however, very few studies of social movements systematically assess movement impact. There seem to be two reasons for this, one conceptual and the other methodological. Conceptually, many of those studying social movements find themselves in a trap of their own devising: once an SMO has gained regular access to political decision makers, it is considered an "insider" group or a lobby rather than a true SMO, and social movement researchers lose interest in it. Methodologically, as McAdam, McCarthy, and Zald note, it is difficult to study movement impact: "demonstrating the independent effect of collective action on social change is difficult"; there are "evidentiary requirements . . . generally beyond the means of most researchers" (1988, p. 727).

A few scholars who consider themselves part of the social movements field have analyzed movement impact, most often by examining how movements that achieve policy responsivess continue to pursue their goals in administrative agencies and the courts (e.g., Handler 1978; Sabatier 1975; Burstein 1985; Burstein 1991). They show that movements may bring about policy change but confront many barriers to having an impact. From a bargaining perspective, it is apparent that the kinds of resources needed to achieve impact responsiveness often differ from those needed to win the passage of legislation. Success after passage often depends on having the legal and technical expertise needed to monitor enforcement, for example. At the same time, some types of resources, including money and bureaucratic organization, are helpful to SMOs both before and after passage of legislation.

Although few social movement scholars have formally analyzed movement impact, other researchers have conducted studies of potential interest to those concerned about movement impact. Many political scientists and economists have analyzed the adoption, implementation, and consequences of public policies, including policies focusing on the environment (e.g., Bosso 1987), equal employment opportunity (Leonard 1986), working conditions (Steinberg 1982), and divorce (Jacob 1988). Social movement scholars could use such studies as a basis for their own work, adding social movement activity to the frameworks provided by others or even, in some instances, reinterpreting others' work from a social movements perspective.

Like impact responsiveness, structural change has been studied relatively infrequently by social movement scholars, but relevant research has been conducted by researchers in other fields. Gale (1986) presents a schematic model for the stages in relationships between a social movement, its countermovement, and government agencies. He notes that the creation of a new agency may constitute a movement victory; and if creating a new agency alters the rules for political participation and protest, this may be thought of as structural change. Kitschelt suggests that movement activity in closed political opportunity structures will produce strong structural pressures sometimes leading to system change, because "the less innovative and the more immobile and political [the] regime, the greater the risk that this inflexibility itself will trigger demands that go beyond the immediate policy issue to one threatening the legitimacy of the regime" (1986, p. 82).

Political scientists have often examined attempts to bring about structural change (e.g., Garrow 1978), and recent years have seen a rebirth of theoretical and empirical work on change in political institutions (e.g., March and Olsen 1989). Sociologists, too, have done substantial work on structural change; little of this has been incorporated into work on social movements, but it certainly could be, since a great deal focuses on the forces affecting suffrage, citizenship, and the openness of government to societal influences (e.g., Lipset and Rokkan 1967; Thomas et al. 1987). Links could be strengthened between work on social movements and studies of revolution, following Tilly's (1978) lead; certainly the downfall of communist regimes in Eastern Europe would offer a fruitful opportunity to analyze the relationship between movement activities and structural change.

Conclusions and Implications

Do political movements represent an important force for social change? And if they do, is their success at least partly a result of factors under their participants' control? As Gamson argued, studying movements as forms of political action makes little sense unless these questions can be answered in the affirmative. Why study phenomena with no significant consequences, or activities with no predictable impact on their goals? By providing systematic evidence that SMOs often succeed, partly as a result of actions planned by their leaders, Gamson provided a justification for continuing study of social movements.

Since the 1970s, many of Gamson's conclusions have been buttressed by further research, particularly work on policy responsiveness, suggesting that SMOs often affect policy. It helps to be well organized and to have delimited goals; it helps if the target is relatively weak or disorganized; and some environments are more conducive to success than others. It is, however, difficult to sort out the consequences of choosing some tactics (especially violence) rather than others.

Nevertheless, our understanding of movement outcomes has not increased as rapidly as our understanding of movement emergence or participation (as reflected in McAdam, McCarthy, and Zald 1988). There has been much less research on agenda, impact, and structural responsiveness than on access, policy, and output responsiveness; consequently, we know little about how movements get their demands on the formal political agenda or, most critically, about the ultimate impact of movement activities on people's lives.

The work of the 1970s and 1980s clearly points to a deeper understanding of movements and their consequences. To build on past work, however, more systematic attention must be paid to overcoming some of its weaknesses, particularly failures to examine the behavior of SMOs once they gain regular access to political institutions, and to surmounting the methodological difficulties involved in separating SMO impact from the effects of other forces. Finally, we need a theoretical framework capable of making sense out of the many disparate findings described in prior work.

Here the bargaining perspective, and especially its concept of dependence, may be particularly useful. Essentially, the more dependent the target is on the SMO, the more power the SMO has over the target, and the more likely it is to succeed. A central task for any protest group, then, is to increase the target's dependence, directly or indirectly.

This concept has the potential to explain a wide range of disparate findings as manifestations of one underlying process, and thus to make sense out of many of the seemingly fragmented research findings discussed here. For example, Colby (1985, p. 592) suggests that groups pivotal to the normal functioning of the target are likely to achieve policy success no matter what tactics they use. This is a straightforward example of dependence; the more dependent the target is on the SMO, the more bargaining power the SMO has and the more likely it is to succeed.

More complex examples of dependence are provided by the involvement of third parties. One of the most consistent findings described here is that third-party support for an SMO—particularly the support of officials and other elites, but also that of other SMOs and the general public—has a positive effect on policy and outcome success (e.g., Schumaker 1975; Milbrath 1970; Gamson 1990; cf. Tarrow 1983). The support of any of these third parties may raise the dependence of the target on the movement; for example, the target may be dependent on officials and other elites for financial and political support, and on the general public for electoral support. To the extent that the protest group has allied itself with groups that are important to the target, then, the target is forced to heed the SMO's demands. The bargaining perspective suggests that third-party support will be particularly effective when the group is important to the target; to test this hypothesis, researchers must pay attention to the role played by third parties in the movement-target relationship.

The bargaining perspective also has the potential to explain some of the contradictory findings on violence described here. To provide just one example, Button (1989) suggests that violent protest is more effective when it presents an economic threat—for example, when business is disrupted. The bargaining perspective suggests that this effectiveness may be a result of the fact that business leaders have economic power that they can use to pressure government leaders to respond to protesters' demands. If key elites are not threatened, however, this pressure may not exist, and target response may be slower. This perspective suggests a need to reanalyze data on violence focusing on its context, and particularly to consider whose interests are threatened.

Finally, Tarrow's (1983) finding that unstable regimes are conducive to reform efforts also lends itself to bargaining analysis; at times of regime instability, political parties and leaders are particularly dependent upon the electorate for support, and therefore the electorate has more influence.

These examples represent findings from diverse areas of social movement research. Nonetheless, the bargaining perspective enables us to see them as instances of the same underlying mechanism: it is the dependence, direct or indirect, of the target on the SMO that allows the SMO to achieve its goals. These conclusions are necessarily post hoc, but they demonstrate the potential utility of the bargaining perspective for integrating widely varied findings. Future research on movement outcomes should be designed to take into account the bargaining among SMOs, their targets, and important organizations in the wider environment. Doing so may revitalize the study of movement outcomes and direct our attention once again to the most basic concern of social movements: bringing about social change.

Note

We would like to thank William Gamson and Pamela Oliver for helpful comments. An earlier version of this essay was presented at the annual meeting of the American Sociological Association in Cincinnati, August 27, 1991. Jocelyn Hollander's work on this article was supported by a National Science Foundation Graduate Fellowship.

Chapter 11

Strategies of Partisan Influence: West European Environmental Groups

Russell J. Dalton

Nearly two decades ago, a new policy controversy emerged on the political agenda of advanced industrial societies—environmental quality. The significance of the environmental issue involves more than just the emergence of new policy interests, however. These interests led to the creation of a new environmental movement and a renewal of the earlier nature conservation movement. By many accounts, membership in these groups now exceeds formal political party membership in many European democracies. Moreover, the environmental movement has become a very visible and contentious new actor in the policy process of most West European democracies. The American sociologist Robert Nisbit has observed that "it is entirely possible that when the history of the twentieth century is finally written, the single most important social movement of the period will be judged to be environmentalism" (1982, p. 101).

The emergence of this active Green movement has spawned considerable scholarly debate about the social and political implications of environmentalism. Much of this debate has revolved around the theory that environmental groups typify the "new social movements"—including women's groups, the peace movement, and self-help groups—that underlie the new political style of advanced industrial democracies (Brand, Büsser, and Rucht 1983; Klandermans, ed. 1989; Dalton and Kuechler 1990; Rucht 1992; Dalton forthcoming). Environmentalism is often cited as an example of the noneconomic, quality-of-life issues that typify these new movements. Green issues are creating new bases of political cleavage that challenge long-standing political alignments. These movements also supposedly follow a decentralized structure and a participatory style of decision making that differs from the neocorporatist style of European interest groups. Theory holds that these new movements are changing the style of interest representation, placing greater reliance on protests and unconventional political activities.

One of the central questions of the new social movement debate involves the partisan implications of the environmental movement. The importance of this question partially derives from the centrality of political parties in most Western democratic systems. Political parties provide the primary method of selecting political elites; they largely determine the content of the electoral and legislative agendas; and the parliamentary structure of most European governments converts partisan majorities into control of the institutions of governance. Discussions of interest group politics thus almost inevitably must consider the relationship between interest groups and the parties because of the parties' predominant role as institutions of interest articulation and aggregation. An additional source of interest in the partisan implications of new social movements is the political volatility that most European party systems have experienced over the past decade (Dalton, Beck, and Flanigan 1984; Franklin et al. 1992). Many party systems have become more fractionalized, and fluctuations in voting results have increased at the aggregate and individual levels. Many factors account for this new wave of partisan instability, but the possible contribution of environmentalism and other new social movements is prominent in explanations of these trends.

The extensive discussion in the literature, and in this volume, on the partisan consequences of the environmental movement attests to the significance of the movement-party relationship. This essay addresses this question by studying the partisan orientations and behaviors of environmental interest groups in ten West European nations. My research is guided by two goals. First, I want to determine how central actors in the Green movement, environmental interest groups, actually view political parties and partisan activities. There is a large body of literature on the Green movement and political parties in Europe, but this literature provides an uncertain basis for generalization because it is seldom based on systematic, cross-national research. Seldom is hard empirical evidence available on the actual political views and behavior of movement actors. I will provide evidence on these points.

My second concern touches on this volume's interest in the importance of political opportunity structures in shaping the behavior of social movement organizations. Much of the literature on opportunity structures is cast in terms of general patterns of political action and general features of the political system (Kitschelt 1986; Tarrow 1983). There is, in addition, a hypothesized linkage between explicitly partisan opportunity structures and partisan activity (e.g., Kriesi, chapter 7 in this volume; Kitschelt 1989). I will argue that this emphasis on political opportunity structures is overdrawn, but it is a research question that deserves attention. By drawing on the diversity of political structures in the ten nations, I can provide systematic evidence on the role of political opportunity structures in guiding the behavior of environmental groups.

The basis of my analysis is a comparative study of environmental interest groups in Western Europe (Dalton forthcoming). Interviews with representatives from leading environmental groups in ten West European democracies were part of a larger study of the structure, goals, and policy activities of the environmental movement. In addition to the topics just listed, the interviews probed into the group representatives' views of partisan politics: perceptions of the parties' performance on environmental issues, policy agreement with the parties, and contact with the parties. I believe that a study of environmental groups provides an important basis for examining the possible impact of environmentalism on European party systems. These groups are the institutional base for environmentalism, representing Green interests within the policy process and mobilizing the public on these issues. In pursuing their activities, these groups make decisions about the agenda and political direction of the Green movement, and they furnish the public with political cues on which policies are important and which strategies—including partisan alliances—should be adopted. In addition, for parties seeking to establish their environmental credentials, these groups afford an institutionalized link to the movement and its goals. While few formal ties now exist between the parties and environmental groups, the partisan perceptions of environmental groups and their informal party contacts indicate the latent partisan tendencies of the movement, which may eventually produce more enduring partisan alignments. In short, environmental interest groups can play a primary role in defining the partisan meaning of the movement.

Research Base

The collection of detailed information from a cross-national set of environmental groups is a major research undertaking (Dalton forthcoming). During the summer and fall of 1985, the leading five or ten national environmental groups in each of the ten member states of the European Community were contacted; the core of this list was drawn from the membership of the European Environmental Bureau in Brussels (Lowe and Goyder 1983, chapter 10). In November 1985 a research team traveled to Europe to interview group representatives; interviewing was completed in spring 1986. The interviews lasted approximately ninety minutes, based on a common survey questionnaire adapted to the national context.

A total of sixty-nine environmental groups were surveyed, including most of the major environmental groups in Western Europe (see Table 1). Our intent was to study ongoing, national, multi-issue groups that represent the diversity of the European environmental movement, ranging from large established groups to student-run activist groups, from traditional wildlife protection groups to critics of advanced industrialism, from amenity societies to *Alternativebewegungen*. I feel that the surveyed groups fulfill this objective. The sample includes forty-seven mass membership groups, thirteen national "umbrella" organizations, six research or educational institutions, and three "by invitation only" groups of environmental elites.

Research on the environmental movement frequently focuses on unconventional groups: Friends of the Earth (FoE), Greenpeace, and other New Left groups such as the BBU and Robinwood in Germany and NOAH in Denmark. We adopted a broader definition of the environmental movement because ecologists, conservationists, wildlife groups, and other environmental groups often have common interests in specific environmental issues, as well as a partially overlapping membership and financial base. This research strategy allows us to examine the pattern of movement-party relations across the environmental spectrum.

The diversity of the environmental groups in our survey also enables us to examine the new social movement thesis in a more focused way by comparing the behavior of the "old" and "new" components of the environmental movement. Drawing upon similar distinctions made by Lowe and Goyder (1983), Cotgrove (1982), and Rucht (1988), we distinguished between *conservation* groups and the new *ecologist* component of the environmental movement. The conservation groups largely consist of nature conservation organizations and other groups that address the consensual issues of environmental policy, such as protection of wildlife, nature conservation, and amenity societies.[1] These groups also tend to be conservative in their political philosophy and adopt conventional policy styles.[2] Within this group, for example, we include the national bird protection associations, the World Wildlife Fund, and other nature conservation groups. These groups are marked by a plus sign in Table 1.

The focus of attention in environmentalism lies, however, in the views and actions of ecology groups. Ecology groups are more likely to question the dominant social paradigm of industrial society and endorse what has been called the "new environmental paradigm" (Milbrath 1984; Dunlap and Van

Table 1. European environmental groups (an asterisk represents conservation groups; a plus sign, ecology groups)

Belgium
*Les Amis de la Terre
Bond Beter Leefmilieu
*Greenpeace
+Inter-environment Wallonie
+National Union for Conservation
Raad Leefmilieu te Brussel
+Reserves Ornitologiques
+Stichting Leefmilieu
+World Wildlife Fund

Denmark
+Friluftrådet
+GENDAN
*Greenpeace
+Naturfrednings Forening (DN)
*NOAH
+Ornitologisk Forening (DOF)

France
*Les Amis de la Terre
+COLINE
CREPAN
+FFSPN
*Greenpeace
+Inst. European Environmental Policy
+Journalists and the Environment

Nature and Progress
+Society for the Protection of Nature
+World Wildlife Fund

Great Britain
+Civic Trust
+Council Environmental Conservation
*Conservation Society
+Council Protect Rural England
+Fauna and Flora Society
*Friends of the Earth (FoE)
Green Alliance
*Greenpeace
+Royal Society for the Protection of Birds (RSPB)
+Town and Country Planning Association

Greece
Ellinike Etairia
+EREYA
*Friends of the Earth
+Friends of the Trees
+HSPN
PAKOE

Key (Note that when a name appears in quotation marks the official English name of the organization is used.)
Belgium: Les Amis de la Terre; Bond Beter Leefmilieu, coordinating organization for local environmental action groups; Raad Leefmilieu te Brussel, the Brussels department of Bond Beter Leefmilieu; Stichting Leefmilieu, about the same as Institution for environmental education in the Netherlands (information center, documentation center, etc.). Denmark: Friluftrådet, private association for environmental conservation; GENDAN, recycling company; Naturfrednings Forening (DN), private association for environmental conservation; NOAH, private association for environmental conservation; Ornitologisk Forening, association for the protection of birds. France: Les Amis de la Terre; COLINE, private association for environmental conservation; CREPAN, "Comité régional d'études pour l'amenagement et la protection de la nature" (local committee for the studies of the design and the protection of nature); FFSPN, Federation nationale des sociétés de protection de la nature (national federation of conservation associations"). Greece: Ellinike Etairia/HSPN, "Hellenic Society for the Protection of Nature," established in 1951 (a preservation-conservation society that has succeeded in pressuring the government to create national parks; conducts excursions and sensitizes citizens on issues concerning the protection of nature; conducts scientific studies and collaborates with similar international groups); EREYA, "Society for Research and Monitoring of Air, Water, and Soil Pollution." In the 1970s it published a series of small volumes on pollution problems in Greece; PAKOE, "Panhellenic Center for Ecological Research." Employs scientific personnel and conducts studies on pollution for individuals and social groups.

Table 1. (*continued*) European environmental groups (an asterisk represents conservation groups; a plus sign, ecology groups)

Ireland
+An Taisce
+Wildlife Federation

Italy
+Agriturist
*Amici della Terra
+Fondo per l'Ambiente Italiano
+Italia Nostra
*Lega per l'Ambiente Arci
*Lega per l'Abolizione Caccia
+Lega Protezione Uccelli (LIPU)
+World Wildlife Fund

Luxembourg
*Mouvement Ecologique
+Natura

Netherlands
*Greenpeace
+IVN
*Stichting Milieu-educatie (SME)

*Stichting Mondiaal Alternatief
+Stichting Natuur en Milieu (SNM)
*Vereniging Milieudefensie (VMD)
+Vereniging van Vogels
Vereniging Waddenzee

West Germany
*BBU
BUND
+Bund für Vogelschutz
+Deutscher Naturschutzring
*Greenpeace
*Robinwood
+Schutzgemeinschaft Deutscher Wald
+World Wildlife Fund

Key (Note that when a name appears in quotation marks the official English name of the organization is used.)
Italy: Agriturist, an association that moves in between agriculture and tourism, "agri-tourism," "Green" tourism; they have a list of camping sites, "agrirestaurants," etc.; Fondo per l'Ambiente Italiano, foundation for the Italian environment; Italia Nostra, Our Italy, association for environmental conservation; Lega per l'Ambiente Arci, league for the environment, of the association Arci, which is more or less linked to the PDS, a left-wing political party; Arci has several branches in which it is active; Lega per l'Abolizione Caccia, league for the ban of hunting; Lega Protezione Uccelli (LIPU), league for the protection of birds. Luxembourg: Mouvement Ecologique, ecological movement; Natura, association for environmental conservation. Netherlands: IVN, Vereniging voor Natuur en Milieu Educatie (Institution for Environmental Education); Stichting Milieu Educatie, Environmental Education; Stichting Mondiaal Alternatief, Foundation for Ecodevelopment; Stichting Natuur en Milieu, "The Netherlands Society for Nature and Environment"; Vereniging Milieudefensie, "Friends of the Earth Netherlands"; Vereniging van Vogels, "Nederlandse Vereniging tot Bescherming van Vogels" (Dutch association for the protection of birds); Vereniging Waddenzee, "Landelijke Vereniging tot Behoud van de Waddenzee" ("Dutch Society for the Preservation of Wadden Sea"). Germany: BBU, Bundesverband Burgerinitiativen Umweltschutz (Federal association for civilian initiatives for environmental conservation); BUND, "Bund für Umwelt und Naturschutz Deutschland" (association for the environment and conservation Germany); Bund für Vogelschutz, federation for the protection of birds; Deutscher Naturschutzring, German association for environmental protection; Schutzgemeinschaft Deutscher Wald, association for the protection of the German forest.

Liere 1978). These groups advocate significant reforms in the economic or political systems, such as creation of a sustainable society or the restriction of capitalist market forces. These political orientations are often combined with an unconventional style based on protests and other direct-action techniques. Friends of the Earth, Greenpeace, and student groups such as Robinwood and NOAH best illustrate the ecologist component of the movement. Ecology groups are denoted by an asterisk in the table.

A comparison of these different environmental organizations illustrates the diversity that exists within the rainbow of Green groups. More important, it provides a stronger reference point for testing the new social movement thesis by comparing traditional conservation groups to the vanguard of the environmental movement.

A Choice of Three Models

Embedded in the research on political opportunity structures is the assumption that social movement organizations have opportunities. The ability of a social movement to develop partisan ties presumes the availability of potential alliance partners (Tarrow 1989a; Klandermans 1990). The potential partisan allies of the Green movement, however—if there are true allies—remains a matter of much speculation. The recent history of European party systems makes it difficult, if not impossible, to identify a systematic pattern in the relationship between Green groups and parties that transcends national boundaries. Many political parties remain skeptical of environmentalists and the policy reforms they offer; other established parties, of all political colors, are courting Green voters with claims of a new environmental awareness. And everywhere, it seems, a plethora of New Left and Green parties are enticing voters with their environmental programs. Where, one might ask, are the real opportunities for partisan alliance that might structure political action?

This diversity in European party experience contains three basic models of the potential alliance pattern between environmental groups and political parties. Each is somewhat visible in the relationship between environmental groups and political parties, though varying in frequency across nations and time. Each model also leads to somewhat different predictions about the long-term implications of the environmental movement.

One pattern of opportunity would involve *alliances with one of the existing political parties*. Because of the rigid structure of European party systems, there are good reasons to presume that the existing parties would eventually incorporate any significant new political interest. The political parties have historically integrated new social forces into the political system, leading to the formation of agrarian parties, religious parties, and labor parties. Indeed, Rudolf Heberle, an early scholar of social movements, concludes that "in order to enter into political action, social movements must, in the modern state, either organize themselves as a political party or enter into a close relationship with political parties" (1951, pp. 150–51).[3] Given enough time, therefore, environmentalism and other new social movements might be integrated into the dominant partisan framework of most European political systems. Tarrow (1989a) makes this argument for new social movements in Italy, and the refrain has been shared by others (Kriesi and van Praag 1987; Klandermans 1990).

In actual fact, however, the European environmental movement has had a tempestuous relationship with the major established parties on both the left and the right. During the mobilization phase of the environmental movement in the 1960s and early 1970s, many of the existing political parties quickly developed environmental programs. Partisan support for environmental reform waned in the later 1970s and early 1980s, however, as worldwide recession shifted the parties' attention to other political agendas. Conflicts over policies to address these economic problems also highlighted inherent tensions between environmentalists and the traditional support groups of social democratic (labor-oriented) and conservative (business-oriented) parties. Even if the established parties supported environmental issues while they were in opposition, they often proved to be unreliable allies once they were elected to office, since the party leadership was primarily attuned to the policy demands of their dominant labor or business supporters.

As public support for environmental reform has grown over the past decade, several established parties have displayed a renewed concern for environmental issues. Leftist parties often have taken the initiative in attracting environmentalists into their progressive coalition. The French Socialists, for example, have tried to develop their environmental credentials since the late 1970s (Ladrech 1989; Rohrschneider 1993). Similarly, one of the most assertive groups in Italy, Lega per l'Ambiente Arci, was formed in the early 1980s by intellectuals from the Italian Communist Party (PCI), and until 1985 received financial support from the PCI's cultural organization. The Dutch Labor Party (PvdA) has been one of the most progressive parties in Europe on issues of environmental reform (Kriesi, chapter 7 in this volume; Jamison et al. 1990). The left-wing parties in Denmark, especially the small Socialist People's Party (SF) and Radical Venstre, have competed in placing Green programs before the voters (Jamison et al. 1990).

The depth and persistence of leftist support for a Green agenda remains uncertain, however. Hanspeter Kriesi (chapter 7 in this volume), for instance, points out that the French Socialists drew voting support from the Green movement and then failed to deliver on campaign promises. Donatella della Porta and Dieter Rucht (chapter 9 in this volume) observe that the German Social Democratic Party (SPD) recently adopted a progressive environmental program, but only after it was forced from government. When the SPD was in the government, it was less supportive of environmental reform than its successors. The Greek Socialists' commitment to their environmental supporters lasted about as long as it took to count the votes for Papandreou's victory in 1981.

Furthermore, environmentalism is not synonymous with the left; parties spanning the entire left-right spectrum have attempted to capture (or deny) the environmental label. In a theoretical discussion, Claus Offe (1985b) has discussed the potential alliance options of the environmental movement with both established leftist and rightist parties. There is some evidence to support this argument. For example, after the Christian Democrats' (CDU) election victory in Germany in 1983, Chancellor Helmut Kohl moved aggressively to deal with acid rain, establishing new regulations for automobile emissions and pressing the European Community to establish Europe-wide regulations (Patterson 1989). The British Liberal Party and Liberal/Social Democratic (SDP) alliance were advocates of environmental protection, although the institutional links to the Green movement remained weak. Even Margaret Thatcher claimed to be a born-again environmentalist in 1988, although this was unconvincing to most Britons (Flynn and Lowe 1992). While Thatcher at least attempted to court environmentalists, the British Labor Party seemed unreceptive to Green thought. Temporary alliances occasionally formed between Green groups and the Labour Party, but they were short-lived and were followed by feelings of incompatibility on both sides.[4]

In short, it is unclear how the Green movement relates to the ideological spectrum of established European political parties—that is, whether and where the movement can find potential partisan allies. While it might be natural for a new political movement to seek alliances with one of the established actors in the party system, the actual experiences of the Green movement make it unclear whether environmentalists see clear and dependable allies among these parties. The commitment of the established parties to environmental reform is secondary to their primary founding principles of representing other socioeconomic groups; once a party is in power, its Green promises often fade. There is also a stylistic tension between the Green movement and the bureaucratic and administrative style of most established parties. Consequently, whether environmentalists see the potential for a systematic pattern of alliances with one or more of the established parties is an open question.

Because of this history of difficulties with the established parties, many Green activists (and activists in other new social movements) claim that their greatest opportunity for action is *working with a new political party* that explicitly advocates Green and other New Left issues (Müller-Rommel 1989). This option assumes that environmentalists will be drawn into partisan politics because of the centrality of party government to policy making. Rather than working through the existing parties, however, new social movements will create new political parties in their own image. Jonathan Porritt, former head of Friends of the Earth, explains his own activity in the British Ecology Party in these terms:

> It is my contention that party political activity will always remain an essential part of that development [of Green ideas in this country]; for better or worse, the Ecology party is the only organization prepared to take on that role to the fullest extent. But even as a political party, we have no illusions about the fact that our primary function is still an educative one, the spreading of green politics to as wide an electorate as possible. (1984, p. 9)

Green parties are not new just in chronological terms, they also represent parties of a new type, most visibly exemplified by the German Greens (Kitschelt 1989; Kitschelt and Hellemans 1990; Müller-Rommel 1989). Green parties base their appeals on environmental issues and other new social movement goals, so they are not cross-pressured by the traditional social group interests of the established parties. Researchers find that the Greens and other New Left parties attract a distinct electoral clientele, which increases electoral volatility and changes voting patterns by enticing individuals to cross traditional party lines (Müller-Rommel 1985; Rüdig and Franklin 1992).

Environmentalists and even environmental interest groups have frequently played an active role in the formation of new Green parties. An association of several environmental groups, headed by Amis de la Terre (AdlT), was instrumental in the creation of the French Ecology Party in 1978. The Belgian Amis de la Terre was equally active in the creation of Ecolo, providing resources for the party and guiding its programmatic development. Friends of the Earth activists were instrumental in creating the British Ecology Party (now the Green Party), and a strong personal network still links Friends of the Earth and the present British Green Party (Porritt 1984). The

Italian AdIT assisted in the formation of the Italian Green Party in the late 1980s. In other nations, environmental interest groups have avoided the organizational problems of creating a new party by working with existing New Left parties, such as the PPR in Holland or the Socialist People's Party in Denmark. By the end of the 1980s, Green parties or their New Left supporters had seats in the national or European parliament in most West European nations.[5]

Finally, others have argued that neither of these patterns—working with the established parties or a new Green party—represents a viable political strategy for the environmental movement. The *apartisan* model argues that environmentalists cannot (or should not) develop alliances with political parties, and instead should work outside of the established channels of partisan politics. Many environmentalists are hostile to political parties because they see parties as pursuing different goals and functioning on the basis of a different philosophy. In addition, environmentalists often view the parties as uninterested in true environmental reform. Even the relationships between the environmentalists and political parties described in the preceding paragraphs often were temporary, contentious affairs. It is difficult to identify ongoing, formalized ties between the movement and political parties; often relationships are informal and based at a personal level. Lowe and Goyder (1983, p. 72) quote one British environmental leader as saying, "There's nothing to choose between them [parties]. Thank God the environment is not a matter of party politics." This refrain, in some form, appears to be part of the ethos of the Green movement.

The apartisan model thus holds that environmentalists do not see viable opportunities for formal alliances with political parties. Environmental interest groups therefore may insulate themselves from partisan politics, even when Green parties are involved. They also may attempt to maximize their political influence by presenting themselves as a broad public interest group, without ties to any specific party.

In summary, these three models present much different descriptions of the opportunity structures as perceived by the environmental movement. Moreover, the existing literature provides an uncertain basis for deciding between the alternatives outlined here. Hard empirical evidence on the partisan affinities of the environmental movement is extremely rare. Analyses are often based on a subjective reading of party actions and electoral outcomes, or other information in the published record, without directly assessing the perceptual map of environmentalists. As I have noted, the lessons from this published record are uncertain as well as implicit. Despite academic speculation and insider accounts, we have precious little systematic evidence on the actual ties between environmental interest groups and the political parties in cross-national terms, nor do we know how these groups view partisan politics and the respective political parties in each nation. This survey of environmental organizations provides some initial evidence to determine how environmentalists view the options available to the movement.

Partisan Friends and Foes

The first step in this analysis is to determine how environmentalists perceive the potential for partisan alliance. As a precondition for partisan action, environmental groups must be able to identify potential allies with whom they might cooperate.

In order to approach the question of partisan allies in terms as neutral as possible, we asked the representative of each group, "Which political party comes closest in representing the interests of [your group]?" The question does not inquire about party endorsements or group activity on behalf of a party, but simply asks whether one or more political parties espouse policies close to those of the group. Table 2 presents the results from this question, cumulated across all nations to determine whether there is a general pattern of partisan alliances that transcends national borders. Reflecting the strong apartisan norms of the movement, the majority of groups initially reacted by stressing the apolitical nature of their organization. Even with a modest level of encouragement from the interviewer to name specific parties, and the assurance that we were not asking about formal ties but only shared interests, almost a third of our respondents could not (or would not) identify a single partisan ally of their group. These responses were commonly explained in terms of the explicitly nonpartisan nature of the group; there was a hesitancy to discuss partisan politics in any way, since the question did not ask about group endorsements, but only for an evaluation of party policies. In other instances, group officials stated that support for any one party might alienate the supporters of other parties among their membership; thus any appearance of partisan preferences was avoided.

While the apartisan norms of the movement are certainly strong, Table 2 also illustrates that most environmental elites can identify sympathetic parties when they are pressed to do so. Among those who named a specific party, the preference for leftist parties is overwhelming. At the time of our survey, viable Green parties existed in only three nations (Germany, Belgium, and France); within these three nations, nearly all the environmental

Table 2. Parties representing interests of environmental groups by group type

Party type	Type of group (in %)			Total (%)
	Conservation	Mixed	Ecology	
Green parties	19	25	24	21
New Left	24	13	71	38
Communist	5	13	5	8
Socialist/labor	24	25	38	29
Liberal	22	25	37	30
Conservative	3	0	0	2
Other party	0	0	5	2
All parties	8	13	5	8
No party/don't know	32	38	0	23
Refused	5	0	10	6
Total responses (%)	142	152	195	167
(N)	(37)	(8)	(21)	(66)

Note: Table entries are the distribution of responses to the question "Which political parties come closest in representing the interests of the group?" The percentages add to more than 100 percent because multiple responses were possible.

groups saw the Greens as supportive of their cause. Various small New Left parties exist in almost every nation, making these parties the most frequently mentioned partisan allies of the movement across Europe as a whole (38 percent). A number of environmentalists also cite socialist/labor parties and liberal parties as potential supporters, although we will shortly see that the evaluations of these parties vary widely across national boundaries. The conservative parties are the obvious void in the alliance network of the environmental movement. From all the groups surveyed, spanning ten nations and a range of environmental orientations, there was only a single mention of a major conservative party as representing a group's interests. Although several conservative party officials have attempted to redress their parties' negative policy image, environmentalists fail to see these parties as supporting their interests.

The other dimension of opportunity structures involves perceptions of potential partisan opponents. Again reflecting a tendency to avoid expressions of partisan sentiments, nearly half of the groups surveyed declined to mention any specific party that was seen as uninterested in or hostile to the

Table 3. Parties opposing interests of environmental groups by group type

Party type	Type of Group (in %)			
	Conservation	Mixed	Ecology	Total (%)
Green parties	3	0	0	2
New Left	0	0	0	0
Communist	5	13	10	8
Socialist/labor	0	13	5	5
Liberal	8	25	33	18
Conservative	19	63	57	36
Other parties	3	0	5	3
All parties	8	8	0	6
No party/don't know	57	13	29	42
Refused	3	0	14	6
Total responses (%)	106	135	153	126
(N)	(37)	(8)	(21)	(66)

Note: Table entries are the distribution of responses to the question of which parties were seen as uninterested in or even hostile to the group's cause. The percentages add to more than 100 percent because multiple responses were possible.

group's cause (Table 3). When a potential partisan opponent was named, perceived opposition from leftist parties was very scarce and opposition was concentrated among the major conservative parties. In broad cross-national terms, therefore, the environmental movement seems to be loosely integrated into the traditional left-right framework of European party systems, identifying more positive links to leftist parties and more opposition from rightist parties.

The survey included a wide range of environmental groups, and I have elsewhere argued that differences in the environmental orientations of groups are extremely important in structuring political action (Dalton forthcoming). This also should be the case for partisan action. Prior theorizing on new social movements holds that *ecology* groups typify the new ideological perspective and political style of the modern environmental movement, while *conservation* groups represent a more traditional and less politically challenging shade of Green activism. Ecology groups are often described as the vanguard of the movement: more willing to engage in unconventional action, more willing to criticize political authorities, and more likely to criticize existing political procedures. Thus, we might assume that ecologists will be more likely to hold apartisan orientations or at least be more critical of the established parties.

In terms of their basic orientation toward partisan politics, we find that ecology groups are actually less likely to take an apartisan stance. Most ecology groups (85 percent) identify at least one specific partisan ally that represents the group's interests, and most also name a potential partisan opponent (57 percent). In contrast, barely half (55 percent) of the conservation groups mention a specific party that represents their interests, and less than half note a partisan opponent.

Ecology groups most often find their partisan representatives outside the circle of established political parties. Ecologists primarily see their support as coming from the small Green and New Left parties.[6] Similarly, ecology groups are more positive than conservation groups in evaluating the environmental performance of Green and New Left parties, and they are also comparatively more critical in judging the performance of socialist, liberal, and conservative parties.[7] Thus ecology groups perceive a greater alliance potential with new political parties, while generally criticizing the established parties.

Environmental Performance

A similar cross-national pattern is obtained by asking group representatives to judge the environmental policy performance of political parties. Environmental leaders were presented with a list of social and political organizations—including the major political parties—and asked to evaluate how good a job each organization was doing in addressing the environmental problems in their nation.[8] Not surprisingly, we found that Green parties and small Green-oriented New Left parties receive the highest overall environmental scores averaged across all nations (mean score = 3.05). The established parties generally receive negative ratings, and only modest differences emerge between the major party groups. The "family" of European socialist parties receive a 2.02 rating on average, compared to 1.66 among liberal parties, and 1.55 for conservative parties. The differences across these three established party groups thus barely span a half-point on a four-point scale, short of the point-or-more difference separating Green and New Left parties from the three groups of established parties.

The pattern of party images inevitably becomes more complex when we examine national differences in party evaluations separately. Figure 1 pre-

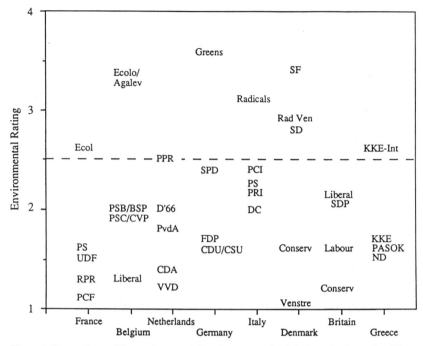

Figure 1. Perceptions of the environmental performance of political parties by nation. Figure entries are mean scores from evaluations of each party's environmental performance: 4 = excellent, 3 = good, 2 = fair, and 1 = poor.

sents the average performance rating of specific parties in each nation. The reader is cautioned that these comparisons are based on a small number of groups within each nation, and only one spokesperson was interviewed from each group (Ireland and Luxembourg are not presented because only two groups were contacted in each of those nations). Still, relative party rankings are fairly consistent across groups with different ideologies and policy interests. Furthermore, these groups are not a sample, they nearly comprise the relevant population of national environmental interest groups in each country.

The data in Figure 1 highlight environmentalists' broad criticism of the major established European parties; only the Danish Social Democrats are rated above the midpoint on the environmental performance scale, while twenty-six other established parties are rated below the midpoint. Only Green and New Left parties systematically receive positive policy endorsements from environmentalists. Figure 1 also illustrates the extent to which environmental policy is seen as cutting across the traditional left-right dimension of European party systems. The perceived differences across the established parties are generally quite modest—and the gap between the Green or New Left party and the nearest established party is generally larger by comparison. In other words, the major environmental cleavage runs between the Green and New Left parties and *all the other* parties.

Even among the established parties, the rankings seldom conform exactly to a traditional left-right party ordering. French environmental elites, for example, give the lowest rating to the Communists (PCF), even below the conservative RPR and UDF. This is because the Communists' pro-growth philosophy has led the party to oppose strict environmental protection as a threat to the economic interests of the working class. The environmental ratings given to European liberal parties frequently violate the presumption that these parties are political centrists. In Britain, the Liberals are more positively evaluated than any of the other established parties. Yet the liberal parties in Belgium (Liberal), the Netherlands (VVD), Denmark (Venstre), and West Germany (FDP) receive lower environmental ratings than most other parties. The conservative business and agricultural orientations of these parties, and their narrow electoral bases, often lead them to become prime critics of the environmental movement. These same political tendencies exist within the major conservative parties, but they are partially moderated by the broad catch-all nature of these larger parties.

The potential for environmentalism to build alliances among the established parties is probably greatest for the social democratic parties of Europe. Leftist parties are the normal electoral outlet for new progressive movements, and most European socialist parties are developing an interest in the issues raised by the environmental movement—if for no other reason than that Green and New Left parties are often making inroads into the socialists' electoral support among young, university-educated, postmaterial voters. Still, environmental elites generally do not give social democratic parties high marks for their policy performance. In France, Belgium, and Greece, the rating of the socialist party is virtually indistinguishable from that of its conservative party rival. Only in Denmark and West Germany do the socialist parties emerge with relatively good environmental ratings that are clearly better than those of the other established parties. Across the map of Europe, the social democratic left is not perceived as the obvious and strong ally of the movement.

In summary, the leaders of the groups who were interviewed do not see that the environmental issue is producing clear and consistent alliance options among the established political parties. Choosing an ally from among the established parties is like choosing the best from among the worst. Thus, from the perspective of the movement, the opportunities to establish clear and enduring alliances with any of the established parties are relatively limited. At the same time, it may be premature to accept the apartisan label for the movement, even though many environmentalists are quick to vocalize such sentiments. Representatives of ecology groups were the most likely to initially proclaim their apartisan tendencies during the interviews, but these protestations were then followed with specific evaluations of which parties represented their group's interests and which did not. In fact, most environmental elites can identify some ally among the parties competing in their nation, and in the majority of cases the ally is a Green or New Left party. From the perspective of the movement, the primary partisan opportunity for environmentalism occurs outside the structure of the major established parties.

Working with the Parties

The evaluations of political parties discussed in the previous section illustrate the political sympathies of environmental interest groups. In order for these sentiments to have an impact on party alignments, however, they must be carried into action. Are environmental groups actually working with and through parties to represent their interests, establishing the relationships that provide clear political cues for the public and might lead to the type of alliance pattern that exists between parties and economic interests such as labor unions, business associations, and agricultural lobbies? Or has the apartisan rhetoric of the environmental movement precluded direct party contact, at least for the present?

The question of the partisan activity of environmental groups is a central concern of the new social movement literature. While research on traditional interest groups emphasizes the corporatist tendencies of contemporary Western democracies, many new social movement theorists maintain that environmental groups try to remain outside the institutional framework of policy making and partisan politics (Brand, Büsser, and Rucht 1986). Alberto Melucci (1980) and Claus Offe (1985b, p. 830) extend this argument to suggest that new social movements do not participate in normal electoral politics because they command no resources that would attract party support; thus these movements must resort to unconventional methods of political persuasion. This literature is counterbalanced by other research citing the evolving ties between new social movements and political parties in Europe (Kriesi, chapter 7 in this volume; Tarrow 1989a; Rohrschneider 1993).

Our study of the activities of environmental groups can provide direct evidence on the partisan activities of these Green actors. Within the larger survey, we presented group representatives with a list of various activities and asked how regularly their organization used each method (Table 4). Despite the supposedly antiestablishment image of the environmental movement, most of the environmental groups surveyed are in direct contact with government policy makers. Over 50 percent of the groups surveyed maintain frequent formal or informal contacts with government officials and parliamentary committees dealing with environmental issues. In addition, over 40 percent of the groups we surveyed often participate in government commissions and advisory committees—the epitome of corporatist politics (Dalton forthcoming, chapter 8).

Against this backdrop of substantial interaction between environmental groups and the institutions of government, the low level of partisan activity stands out sharply. Contact with political parties is the activity cited by the fewest number of groups, even less frequently than unconventional tactics such as protests or blocking actions, or any of the conventional activities on the list. Barely one group out of ten claims that it often has contact with party leaders. Similarly, an open-ended question about each group's specific political activities over the preceding year displays an equal sparsity of party contacts; only 6 percent of all groups mention party contacts in connection with their major policy initiative. These findings present what we feel is the strongest evidence of the apartisan nature of the environmental movement: even though environmental groups can identify potential partisan allies (and foes), they nevertheless shun direct party contact.

The findings shown in Table 4 appear to lend credence to the new social movement theorists who stress the apartisan or antipartisan tendencies within the Green movement, yet the pattern of partisan contact across environmental groups partially contradicts this conclusion. The new social movement literature suggests that partisan activity would be least likely among ecology groups, because they oppose the structured, bureaucratic style of politics represented by the established political parties. In contrast to these expectations, ecology groups are slightly *more likely* to work with the parties. Only 6 percent of conservation groups often contact party leaders, compared to 20 percent of ecology groups (r = .13).[9] Many ecologists remain sharply opposed to partisan activity, and these sentiments are common within several Greenpeace organizations and some of the more decentralized and unconventional ecology groups. At the same time, the most visible examples of formal working relationships between the environmental movement and political parties have often involved ecology groups. In most of these instances,

Table 4. Methods of political action

Activity	Percent of groups that "often" participate
Contacts with people in the media	86
Mobilize public opinion	72
Informal contacts with civil servants or ministers	53
Contacts with MPs/parliamentary committees	53
Contacts with local government	45
Participation in government commissions and advisory committees	41
Formal meetings with civil servants or ministers	36
Demonstrations, protests, or other direct action	25
Legal recourse through the courts or other judicial bodies	20
Blocking undesired policies by refusing to cooperate with the government and bureaucracy	13
Contacts with party leaders	11

ecology organizations have focused on supporting Green or New Left parties, such as Friends of the Earth's involvement with several of these parties across Europe. In overall terms, however, the differences between ecology and conservation groups are modest in comparison to the general tendency of all groups to avoid partisan contact.

A more convincing explanation of the apartisan behavior of Green groups lies in their general evaluation of partisan activity as a method of political influence. Environmentalists of all colors have open doubts about the effectiveness of party work. We heard repeated tales of the unreliability of party promises and the futility of past partisan activities. Virtually all of the groups that once had been involved in electoral politics recounted negative experiences. The established parties too often are unreliable political allies, and the Green and New Left parties are difficult to work with and have limited electoral appeal. Even as a more general observation on partisan politics, environmentalists doubted the efficacy and reliability of partisan representation of their views. French and Greek environmentalists, for instance, were alienated by their past support of the socialists and the policies that Mitterrand and Papandreou actually implemented when they were elected (e.g., Hatch 1986, chapter 6; Stevis 1993). Dutch groups illustrated their skepticism of parties with similar stories of PvdA and D'66. Environmental groups have learned that they can influence parties and trust party pronouncements only until the ballots are counted.

These impressions were substantiated by questions in the survey that asked how effective each group found various methods of influencing government policy. A majority of groups (55 percent) declared that working with parties is *rarely or never* an effective method of policy influence.[10] Furthermore, the perceived effectiveness of party activity is substantially below other policy activities such as working with the media, the environmental ministry, or governmental commissions (Dalton forthcoming, chapter 8).

Opportunity Structures and Partisan Action

Resource mobilization research has emphasized institutional context as an important factor guiding the type of political behavior that we are studying (McAdam 1983; Tarrow 1989a; Klandermans, Kriesi, and Tarrow 1988). Since resource mobilization theorists view social movement organizations as rational actors responding to opportunities as they arise, they assume that the structure of these opportunities will influence the strategies chosen by social movement organizations. For instance, if neocorporatist activities represent a real opportunity for influence, the sensible organization will use these methods; if conventional lobbying is more effective, then this will be a preferred mode of activity.

Opportunity structures also are an important theme in research on new social movements. In a provocative article, Herbert Kitschelt (1986) mapped the action modes of anti-nuclear-power groups in four nations as a function of the political structures of each nation; he then extended this analysis of the political environment in his work on Green parties in Germany and Belgium (Kitschelt 1989; Kitschelt and Hellmans 1990). In chapter 7 of this volume Kriesi builds upon this model, though elsewhere he suggests that environmental groups may be less affected by political opportunity structures (Kriesi and van Praag 1987). Similarly, Joyce Gelb (1989) emphasizes the political opportunity structure as a major factor determining the particular style of national women's movements. The importance of these environmental factors is also discussed in research on the peace movement (Klandermans 1990; Kriesi 1985; Rochon 1988). Indeed, the logic that political organizations should respond to the structure of political competition seems to be a very reasonable assumption, and one that is advocated by others in this volume.

Despite the apparent logic behind research on political opportunity structures, there is countervailing evidence that questions this structural approach. For example, Dieter Rucht (1990a) has criticized Kitschelt's emphasis on national opportunity structures for ignoring the temporal variations in political strategies used by antinuclear groups even while opportunity structures remain constant. Furthermore, in most applications of the opportunity structure model, the test is based on subjective readings of the historical evidence for a preselected set of cases rather than on hard empirical analyses for a generalizable empirical base. Thus separate analyses can disagree on fundamental questions of interpretation and evidence, since the evidence is subjective.

Our experience with environmental interest groups highlighted another weakness of descriptive accounts of movement strategies. Such evidence is normally based on published accounts of movement activities, which yields a very biased sample of actual movement activities. The popular media, for example, are drawn to events they deem newsworthy rather than reporting on the mundane, ongoing political activities of social movements. Even insider accounts often focus on the unusual, spectacular campaign rather than on what happens in the offices and hallways of the organization and the government. We found, for instance, that some of the most active protest groups were equally active in informal lobbying activities, but kept these efforts out of the public view.

An even more basic weakness of the political opportunity structure approach is that it focuses on modal patterns of action for an entire movement in a nation while ignoring the substantial variation that exists among organizations within a social movement. In the larger study from this project (Dalton forthcoming), I argue that the political identities of social movement organizations have a much more direct impact on their behavior, in part because these identities create their own opportunity structures (and resources). This framework of ideologically structured action maintains, for example, that even though the Royal Society for the Protection of Birds (RSPB) and Greenpeace are both concerned with wildlife issues, their different political identities lead to large and predictable differences in the political opportunities and behaviors of these two groups. While the RSPB may be able to develop political alliances with an established political party, such political options do not exist for Greenpeace. These *within-movement* differences in political activities as a function of group identities appear much greater than cross-national differences that can be traced to institutional structures.

The importance of political identity has attracted growing attention from social movement scholars. Snow and Benford (1988) refer to this as prognostic framing: a group's identity defines the opportunity structures it faces, and its decision on how to respond to these opportunities (also Klandermans 1991). Similarly, Edward Walsh (1983) found that the tactics of American antinuclear-power groups were influenced by the broader political values and ideology of each group. From this perspective, national political structures should have only a modest impact on the behavior of movement organizations when considerable diversity in political identities exists within a movement.

We have assembled the data to demonstrate the limited importance of national political opportunity structures on the partisan activities of environmental interest groups. One might begin by assuming that the existence of a potential partisan ally is the first prerequisite for partisan action. We therefore identified those nations with a viable Green party or New Left party or both, expecting that partisan activity would be higher in nations where such alliance potentials existed. Analysts have also discussed the role of the major leftist party in stimulating new social movement activity. Kriesi suggests in chapter 7 that a leftist government will decrease the general political mobilization of new social movements because they will establish political alliances with the leftist party in government and win policy reforms. Others suggest, as della Porta and Rucht do in chapter 9, the opposite: that major leftist parties are more responsive to new social movements when they are outside of government, and thus do not have to deliver on their promises for policy reform. We can test the validity of these rival claims. Finally, there has been a general presumption in the political opportunity structure literature that alliances between new social movements and established political channels are more likely to develop in "open" political systems than in systems with closed corporatist structures (Kitschelt 1986; Kriesi and van Praag 1987).[11] While it is not directly linked to partisan activity, this assumption can easily be extended to contact with the established political parties; in open systems, one or more of the established parties is likely to develop ties to new contenders, such as environmentalists or women's groups.

Table 5 examines whether these features of the national political structure influence partisan activity. The availability of viable partisan allies does not increase party activity by environmental groups. In fact, the relationships are in the opposite direction to what political opportunity structure theory would suggest (though they are statistically insignificant). Frequent party contact was slightly lower (12 percent) in the three nations with a viable Green party at the time of our survey than in nations without a Green party. There is also a weak negative relationship between the presence of a New Left party in a nation and partisan activity by environmental groups. Leftist control of the national government similarly seems to discourage partisan activity by environmental groups. This latter relationship might be a result of the specific set of

Table 5. National opportunity structures and the frequency of partisan contact

National opportunity structure	Pearson correlation coefficient
Viable Green party	–.09
Viable New Left party	–.16
Left party in government	–.22*
Corporatism	–.09
System openness	.07

• Statistically significant at the .10 level.

nations that had leftist governments in 1985–86 (France, Greece, and Ireland). The interviews, however, uncovered a common feeling that leftist parties are more willing to work with environmental groups when they occupy the opposition benches.

Finally, the broader opportunity structures of a nation—represented by the extent of corporatist policy making and an open policy style—have a negligible impact on partisan activity.[12] Indeed, from our perspective of thinking about political tactics as the choice of individual social movement organizations, such broad national attributes should have little bearing on these choices because national structures do not reflect the opportunities that individual groups actually face.

All of the relationships shown in Table 5 are weak, and they suggest that even when environmental groups have access to sympathetic political parties or function within an open political system, they remain outside the sphere of partisan politics. Thus, the lesson to be learned from these analyses is that a group's willingness to participate in partisan politics is relatively unaffected by the external context. Avoiding partisan politics is apparently a pervasive attitude shared by Green interest groups. Environmentalists say that the parties operate under a weltanschauung that prevents close group-party ties. The spokesperson for one Greenpeace organization, for example, states that "the philosophy of the parties is totally different, they have only a short-term, pragmatic perspective." Sentiments of this sort are interspersed throughout our interviews. Environmentalists feel that parties prefer to deal with Green issues in an incremental way and want to avoid the fundamental questions raised by environmentalists—especially ecology groups. Thus parties become part of the problem rather than the solution. Other respondents complain that electoral politics and the logic of party competition encourage parties to water down their issue positions and concentrate their efforts on mobilizing potential voters. A member of a German group expressed this view; he maintained that the political parties do not want to support the environmental movement, but instead attempt to coerce environmentalists into supporting the party. Group representatives believe that they exercise a political role that partially conflicts with the norms of partisan politics. Furthermore, because these views reflect a common belief among environmentalists, the structure of short-term political opportunities has very little impact on the potential for partisan action.

The Green Movement and Partisan Politics

I began this inquiry by outlining three alternative partisan strategies that European environmental groups might pursue: working with the existing political parties, forming new Green parties, or remaining aloof from partisan politics. In different ways, the findings provide some evidence in support of each pattern.

Instead of uncovering clear partisan tendencies within the environmental movement, the research underscores the diversity of the movement's partisan orientations. Various elements of the movement see allies among Green and New Left parties, Old Left parties, liberal parties, or no parties at all. The partisan tendencies of the movement interact with the partisan choices available, yielding a different potential for partisan alliances in each party system. Moreover, differences in attraction to the established parties are often fairly minor, not the type of clear partisan choices necessary to produce major electoral change. Despite the attention to environmental issues displayed by the established parties in recent years, we doubt that the patterns we uncovered have changed substantially. The lack of a consistent fit between the environmental issue and existing partisan alignments thus mitigates the potential that the environmental issue presently can generate a systematic, broad-scale realignment among the established European political parties.

The uncertain partisan orientations of the Green movement in Europe are further attenuated by the pattern of interaction between the movement and the parties. While most environmental interest groups can identify potential partisan friends and foes, they nevertheless adhere to their apartisan rhetoric in avoiding formal association or direct contact with party elites. Environmental groups inevitably deal with party leaders in their official positions as legislators or government officials, but direct contact with the parties per se is frequently considered contradictory to the goals of the movement—even, to a degree, formal contact with Green or New Left parties. This is a much different picture than the one that emerges from other recent research on new social movements because of the nature of our evidence. Rather than simply asking about the partisan loyalties of individual movement supporters (e.g., Kriesi and van Praag 1987; Klandermans 1990) or looking at the attempts of parties to develop policies that appeal to movement supporters (Tarrow 1989a; Maguire, chapter 8, and Kriesi, chapter 7, in this volume), we took the perspective of the movement itself. Are movement organizations developing the type of formalized, institutionalized ties that characterize the developmental pattern of earlier social movements? When we focus on this key question, it is clear that such ties have not developed in a broadly consistent cross-national pattern. Consequently, the partisan tendencies existing within the Green movement remain ambiguous and latent.

If there is a potential for the environmental movement to develop partisan alliances, it is perhaps greatest in the case of Green and New Left parties. First, surveys generally indicate widespread popular support for strict environmental policies and, in principle, substantial support for environmental parties (Dalton forthcoming, chapter 3; Inglehart 1990a, p. 266). Second, the major line of partisan cleavage on environmental issues runs between Green and New Left parties and all other parties. Despite these factors, the potential electoral appeal of Green parties is lessened by their unconventional style and often extremist views. In addition, the apartisan tendencies of the movement weaken the electoral potential of even the moderate Green parties. Environmental groups are almost uniformly hesitant to establish firm and direct ties to any political party. In his study of this relationship from the perspective of the Green parties in West Germany and Belgium, Herbert Kitschelt reaches a similar conclusion. Unless environmental groups break from their aversion to party contact, their partisan impact is likely to remain fluid and uncertain.

Even if alliances were possible with political parties, environmentalists are skeptical about whether this would enhance their political influence. Group leaders maintain that too close an identification with any one party would undermine their influence as a public interest group. They worry that the parties would co-opt them and they would lose their clout as a single-issue lobby; experience tends to confirm these views. In addition, environmentalists feel that partisan allies would inevitably create partisan enemies. The gain of influence when one's preferred party was in power would not compensate for the lack of influence when that party sat on the opposition benches.

Environmentalists believe their strength lies in the popular base of the movement and the ability to pressure governments of all colors. Partisan politics would only narrow public support for environmental groups and restrict their access to decision makers. The head of one British environmental group illustrated this point by explaining how they would pursue issues that were attractive to Tory voters (e.g., the Channel Tunnel and countryside protection) when the Conservatives were in power and another agenda (e.g., worker exposure to toxins, urban decay) if the Labour Party assumed office. They can mobilize public support for these campaigns only by appearing to remain above partisan politics and representing the "public interest" before both parties. To stay above partisan politics is thus an advantage for broad-based public interest groups.

If the Green movement fails to establish clear partisan ties, it is still possible that the environmental cleavage will be integrated into partisan politics by the actions of the political parties. For instance, the head of one British group, who stood for Parliament in 1987, acknowledged the hesitancy of the movement to engage in electoral politics and said that his party (the Social Democratic Party) would therefore have to "capture of flag of environmentalism" on its own. Certainly, many of the established parties in Europe have worked to develop Green credentials as voter interest in these issues has increased. These efforts often display the internal tensions that environmental issues evoke within the established parties, however, leading the parties to advocate an ambivalent mix of environmental policies. And voters were understandably skeptical when Margaret Thatcher and George Bush declared that they are environmentalists.

To some extent, the patterns described here may be a unique feature of the environmental movement, reflecting the broad popular base of the movement and the noneconomic, collective nature of the environmental issue. Yet these findings also illustrate a pattern of fluidity and diversity that appears to characterize the style of citizen politics in advanced industrial societies (Dalton, Beck, and Flanagan 1984, chapter 15; Dalton 1988). Furthermore, this ambiguous pattern of partisan interaction has been found in studies of the European peace movement and women's movement. Contemporary politics is becoming less structured as long-term, social-group-based politics gives way to the more fluid, issue-based politics that environmentalism exemplifies. The movement organizations and citizen interest groups that represent these new concerns at present avoid entangling partisan attachments in most European states. As representatives of collective public interests, these movements are consciously hesitant to develop firm party ties that limit their potential membership or political access. Thus, the long-term impact of the environmental issue may be less in creating a new stable base of partisan alignments than in contributing to a more fluid system of interest representation in advanced industrial societies.

Notes

Support for this research was provided by a grant from the National Science Foundation (SES 85–10989) and the Council on Research and Creativity, Florida State University.

1. Lowe and Goyder refer to these organizations as "emphasis" groups, "by which we mean groups whose aims do not conflict in any clear-cut way with widely held social goals or values" (1983, p. 35).

2. These groups also display systematic differences in terms of their longevity, internal structure, and characteristics of their leadership; see Dalton (forthcoming, chapters 4 and 6).

3. For another example of this same logic see Kelly (1984).

4. Lowe and Goyder (1983, p. 128) recount the tale of how Friends of the Earth in Britain felt that they had been unfairly used after supporting the Labour Party in the 1973 Greater London Council elections and shunned further partisan ties. Our respondent recounted a similar story of FoE's negative experience in supporting some Labour candidates in 1979—with an even stronger vow to avoid direct party ties in the future.

5. At the end of the 1980s, Green parties had won seats in the national parliament of all the nations studied except Britain (because of its electoral system) and Greece (for lack of electoral support).

6. The relatively infrequent mention of Green parties occurs because at the time of the study, only three viable parties existed: the West German Greens, the Belgian Ecolo/ Agalev, and the French Ecologists.

7. The tau-c correlation between an ecologist orientation and the party environmental ratings displayed in Figure 1 are as follows: Green/New Left party, .20*; socialist party, -.09; liberal party, -.13; conservative party, -.23*. Coefficients marked by an asterisk are significant at the .10 level.

8. The question reads: "Now we'd like to get your ideas about how well various institutions are addressing the important environmental issues facing [your nation] today. Would you indicate whether you think each of the groups I list is doing an excellent, good, fair, or poor job on these issues?" For these analyses the response categories are coded (1) poor, (2) fair, (3) good, and (4) excellent.

9. There is also a slight, though statistically insignificant, tendency for ecology groups to rate party activities as more effective in influencing policy.

10. There is a .30 tau-c correlation between perceptions of the effectiveness of party work and actual contact with a party.

11. The states coded as corporatist were Belgium, the Netherlands, West Germany, Luxembourg, and Denmark. System openness is a subjective judgment of the author that is intended to distinguish between systems that are willing to interact with citizen groups versus those that have closed bureaucratic structures or are hostile to new interests; the open systems were the Netherlands, Luxembourg, and Denmark.

12. Dalton (forthcoming, chapter 7) also finds that such opportunity structures have only a minor influence on the use of other political tactics, ranging from the use of conventional lobbying activities to protest and other forms of direct action.

Chapter 12

Starting from Scratch Is Not Always the Same: The Politics of Protest and the Postcommunist Transitions in Poland and Hungary

Bronislaw Misztal and J. Craig Jenkins

Communism was a system of incomplete social change. Originally launched in East Central Europe as a utopian project to overcome the problems of economic scarcity and class inequality in relatively backward societies, it proved unable to meet the challenge of competition with Western capitalism. Although it succeeded in creating an industrial base in societies that had been largely agricultural, it failed to generate a mechanism for sustained economic and technological progress. Despite significant advances in education and public health, the polity remained a restrictive system of controlled participation and opportunistic political activism that generated considerable alienation, especially among the industrial workers who were supposed to be its primary beneficiaries. By the mid-1980s, the communist sytem confronted a series of social, economic, and political crises that eventually culminated in the collapse of the system, heralding a "postcommunist" age, or an "end to history" (Malia 1991a, 1991b).

In the aftermath of this collapse, scholars have addressed two major issues: the causes of the system's failure, and the directions of the postcommunist transition. These two issues are intimately related because explanations of the collapse inform how we interpret the nature of the postcommunist societies and their prospects. This essay addresses both questions through a comparative analysis of the collapse and the postcommunist transition in Poland and Hungary. The basic argument is that, although communism (or state socialism)[1] was an international system that collapsed simultaneously, the processes by which it collapsed and the resulting outcomes varied in particular states. The Polish state was the least reconstructed of the communist states and responded to social unrest with political concessions, thus producing a concerted political opposition and, after the transition, a hyperpoliticized society. The Hungarian state, in contrast, responded with economic concessions, thereby creating an independent "second economy" that eventually created a basis for capitalist development and democratization.

This argument departs from the standard interpretations of the collapse of communism. One view, popular among East European scholars, is that the communist states in East Central Europe had reached the limits of their capacity to change and, as a consequence, became ungovernable and spontaneously collapsed (Burawoy and Krotov 1992; Stark 1990; Misztal 1990; Hankis 1988, 1991; Geremek 1991). This is too simple because it misses the central role of political protest in this transition. Although not all of the communist states experienced large-scale protests, protest destabilized the weakest regimes and, combined with the Soviet decision to refrain from military intervention, forced the collapse of the communist system. A second international contagion argument sees political conflict as the central factor spreading from the center to the peripheries of the communist system in the same way that cultural innovations are diffused (Rosenau 1990). While this correctly points to the international aspect of the disintegration and the importance of protest, it misses the domestic origins of these conflicts and mistakenly assumes that the protests began in the core of the system, namely, the Soviet Union, rather than among the more vulnerable peripheries like Poland and Czechoslovakia that were more integrated with the West. A third view treats the postcommunist transitions as similar to those in Latin America, arguing that mass democratization movements plus elite negotiation of a mutual nonagression compact led to democratization (Diamond, Linz, and Lipset 1990; O'Donnell and Schmitter 1986). While this captures the interaction of elites and masses, it neglects the international aspect of this transition and the distinctive nature of protest in communist states.

We advance instead a political economy interpretation that emphasizes the domestic class struggles and international dependencies of these states. First, we examine the contending classes and political groups that played a central role in the collapse of the communist states. There were different groups at play in these states, producing a differential disintegration of the communist system. The system did not collapse spontaneously, but because of political challenge. This challenge was not evenly spread, however, but was stronger in particular states. Poland, as the least reconstructed and most Western of these states, became the weak point in the communist system and was the first to collapse as a result of domestic challenge.

Second, we analyze the international nature of the communist system and how this structured the transition. From the outset, the communist system was an international system that depended on the political leadership and military power of the Soviet Union. The Soviet Union's finding itself militarily overextended created political opportunities for revolt in the periphery that eventually generated a collapse of the system.

This analysis also borrows on political process and statecentric theories of political opportunities. These theories, however, are premised on a capitalist political economy in which the state and civil society are distinct. In communist societies, the state organizes the economy, and civil society is weak or nonexistent. Hence the social bases for mobilization are much weaker and the political opportunities more episodic and tied to short-term leadership and policy changes. Protest cycles are more erratic and shorter, producing protest waves that emerge suddenly and then subside (Zhou 1993). Second, the nature of dissent is different, independent economic actions constituting a form of political challenge. Third, state actions are decisive in defining the goals of dissidence and the post-transition outcome. The Polish state attempted to control unrest by political concessions, thereby creating a political movement and a hyperpoliticized society, while Hungary, which responded with economic reforms, channeled dissent into independent economic production and a moderate capitalist system. Fourth, extending the idea that elite realignments structure political opportunities, we advance an international opportunities argument in terms of instability in international alignments. Specifically, the Soviet Union's refusal to intervene militarily on behalf of communist regimes created new opportunities for an international social movement against the communist system.

First we discuss the crisis of communism, which created social unrest throughout the communist system. Second we look at the response of particular states to these strains. In Poland, the government adopted political concessions, eventually creating a political challenge. In Hungary, economic liberalization channeled dissent into autonomous economic activity that created a "second economy" parallel to the official state-controlled economy. Third, we show how this produced distinctive postcommunist outcomes, a highly politicized system in Poland with little economic reorganization versus a decentralized market system and constitutional state in Hungary. In both, the transition required a wholesale reorganization of basic political and economic institutions. Yet these two societies took qualitatively different tacks. Hence the theme of this essay: starting from scratch is not always the same.

Dismantling the Old System: The Crisis of Communism and the Paths of Dissidence in Poland and Hungary

By comparative standards the communist states have been relatively stable (Hibbs 1973; Gurr 1989). In large part, this is because of the system of political controls established by the communist regimes, chiefly party-controlled "transmission belts" in the form of sports teams, unions, and social clubs, and the controlled social mobility opportunities in the new state-owned industrial sector made available to the ideologically loyal. Reinforced by party control over the mass media, the educational system, and the strategic sectors of the economy, these states have been largely immune to large-scale disorders and independent oppositions. They were also highly traditional societies with a large peasantry and a weak heritage of independent political action (Schopflin 1991, pp. 80–86). Yet there were still periodic crises and protest waves, especially in the communist states installed by Soviet force in Eastern Europe at the end of World War II. In these states, legitimacy has never been high and the system has been incomplete and contradictory, creating periodic political explosions, typically in response to suddenly imposed economic austerity, which has alternated with reform and repression by the regimes. East Germany in 1953, Poland in 1956, 1968, and 1981, Hungary in 1956, and Czechoslovakia in 1968 experienced protest explosions that required repression combined with selective reforms designed to restore order. In each, Soviet troops provided critical reinforcement.

What was different in the late 1980s was the expansion of this unrest combined with the sudden withdrawal of the Soviet military protector. First, let us look at the Soviet withdrawal. As an international system, communism rested on an alliance among states sharing common ideology and organizational features. In the face of domestic opposition, the core of the communist system— the Soviet Union—had traditionally guaranteed sufficient military force to preserve domestic order. With the withdrawal from Afghanistan and the initiation of arms negotiations in 1988, however, the Soviet Union tacitly abandoned this policy, leaving the client states to fend for themselves. Hence, when protests developed in the late 1980s, first in Poland and then in Czechoslovakia and East Germany, it soon became apparent that the military protector was no longer available. This created international opportunities in the sense that the central military protector of the system was neutralized.

How was this rooted in the deeper communist crisis? Over the past two decades, all of the communist states have experienced a loss of legitimacy and declining capacity for internal reform. Innumerable studies have documented the trends of declining work morale, decreased authority of communist institutions and leaders, reduced and segmented political participation, and an overall shift from political concerns to the issues of morality and purely pragmatic economic concerns.[2] Accompanying these trends has been a steady decline in economic growth, growing external indebtedness, rising inflation, and lowered living standards. As Parkin (1976) has argued, state control over the economy immediately politicizes these grievances, leading citizens to blame the state for their problems. In large part, this social unrest stemmed from the failures of communist social and economic reconstruction, specifically:

1. The proletarianization of a previously peasant society produced a working class with no specific "socialist" form of consciousness or loyalty to the system.

2. The creation of a class of industrial managers to run the new state-owned enterprises produced a "new class" characterized by opportunistic and technocratic attitudes rather than a new type of socialist leadership or a new entrepreneurial class that would stimulate further economic growth.

3. The middle classes, including small proprietors in selected industries, found themselves threatened by unpredictable and exploitative tax rates.

4. The failure to professionalize the intelligentsia left this class only partly autonomous from the state and sufficiently alienated that it served as a radical critic of the system.

As a consequence, over the past two decades the communist states have faced growing political discontent and episodic explosions of protest typically triggered by economic austerity measures, followed by attempts to relegitimize the regimes through repression combined with social spending or temporary tolerance for cultural diversity or both. None of these incidents, however, addressed underlying structural problems or restored economic growth. As a result, the communist regimes found it increasingly difficult to compete internationally with the West. As the political center of this system, the Soviet Union found these costs an increasing burden, eventually compelling it to withdraw from its international commitments.

What form did this political discontent take? Instead of a generalized opposition, the form depended on the specific conditions in particular countries. Poland and Hungary contained significant niches of autonomous groups and institutions that created a basis for dissent. In Poland, the persistence of private peasant farming, the autonomy of the Catholic Church, and the independence and Western ties of the intelligentsia created multiple bases for opposition. Even Communist Party tutelage was limited by the persistence of formally distinct parties. In the early 1980s, the regime responded to the Solidarity-led industrial protests with political concessions, mainly increased influence of the coalitional parties, provision for independent but decentralized unions, and the reintroduction of worker self-management (Kolankiewicz 1973; Mason 1989). Researchers discovered a "second society" project in which alternative political values prevailed among significant segments of the population (Gadomska 1984; Nowak 1989; Hankis 1988). Opposition, then, took on a political form. In Hungary, the government responded to the protests in 1956 with a series of economic concessions that allowed independent petit bourgeois production and private ownership of housing. By the 1970s, this "second economy" project had created a new petite bourgeoisie and growing inconsistency between personal norms and the public norms of the socialist system (Marody 1991; Schopflin 1991, pp. 78–79).

By contrast, the other communist states were able to normalize the situtation by short-term fiscal concessions (as in Czechoslovakia after 1968); by temporizing tolerance for marginal cultural dissent (like acceptance of the rock group Plastic People of the Universe in Czechoslovakia in 1977); or by co-opting youth and intellectuals (as in the East German-sponsored sport and scientific or cultural activities). In still others, repression and strong party controls were sufficient to keep growing unrest at least temporarily in check.

Crisis and Political Dissent in Poland

The vulnerabilities of the communist state in Poland stemmed in part from the incomplete form of the postwar reconstruction. Because of its weak base of support, the postwar communist state left intact private peasant agriculture, an independent nationalistic Catholic church, and a semi-independent intelligentsia. This created significant basis for opposition, providing organizing space and resources for potential opposition. The strongest base of opposition came, however, from the industrial working class that was proclaimed as the major beneficiary of the new regime. The communist government assumed that industrial growth coupled with controlled upward mobility from the peasantry into the working class would generate incremental affluence and loyalty among a new working class (Morawski 1980; Wasilewski 1988). The results, however, were quite different. Instead of becoming urbanized and proletarianized, the new working class became the bearer of nonurban and nonproletarian values with considerable egalitarian content.[3] Because the communist regime decided not to impose massive collectivization but to leave agriculture largely in peasant hands, urban workers maintained strong social and cultural ties to the countryside. Many peasants migrated seasonally to the cities as a way of preserving their peasant households, and others viewed industrial jobs as a way station on the road back to their farms (Nagengast 1991, p. 19). This produced a split labor market: the industrial workforce consisted of the new urban working class, who had recently moved from the country to the city, and the peasant-workers, whose dwellings were in the villages but who sold their labor in the cities in the winter season or part time. Both groups of workers held dissident attitudes, and the latter had strong ties to the peasantry.

In addition, working-class and popular aspirations were increasingly defined by comparison to the affluent West rather than the poor economic standards of the immediate postwar period. With increasing international trade and cultural exchange, the Polish working class increasingly adopted Western standards as their reference group (Marody et al. 1981, pp. 317–18). There was also the rapidly accelerating decremental deprivation produced by the ongoing economic crisis of the 1980s. Compared to those in other countries in the region, living conditions in Poland deteriorated earlier and more rapidly, magnifying the feeling of relative deprivation. The people felt that they were not getting as much as they should have because an allegedly omnipotent actor ("the state") was diverting the flow of produced goods and circumventing the volume of the existing freedoms so that neither were available to the rank and file members of society. This focused blame on the state, especially for its failure to address the economic problem.

Finally, the intellectual community became radicalized, first by becoming concerned with the living conditions of the workers, then in response to governmental repression of working-class activists. Becoming involved in underground education and publication activities through the Solidarity movement in the late 1970s, radical intellectuals formed an alliance with working-class activists and the Catholic Church, developing a new consciousness of common oppression by the state. By the time of the Gdansk strikes in the summer of 1980, working-class protesters had adopted intellectual demands for abolishing censorship, free access to information, and questioning the legitimacy of the Party (Goodwyn 1991; Mason 1989). In an unusual display of interclass solidarity, striking workers expressed their concern about the deprivations of other segments of society: intellectuals, office workers, students, and peasants (Nowak 1991; Kuczynski and Nowak 1988). By the late 1970s, this consciousness of oppression by the state had spread to the general populace; less than 18 percent of the population expressed general support for the system. Increasingly, the system as a whole was judged by how the state treated the people as citizens—negatively (Mach 1990, p. 202; Frentzel 1990, p. 763).

Tarrow (1988, p. 430) argues that one needs to distinguish the objective existence of political opportunities from their subjective recognition. The growing three-way partnership between the radical intelligentsia, the working class, and the Catholic Church brought these groups together in a set of movement organizations, especially the Committee of Workers' Defense (KOR) and the informal but highly effective ombudsman of human rights, and eventually the Solidarity movement. In addition to generating political consciousness of oppression by the state, this partnership provided a communication network of underground publications that spread dissident attitudes and awareness of political opportunities revealed by collective testing actions. First in the industrial strikes in 1980–81 and then in a more concerted manner in 1987–88, these movements fused into a broad-based oppositional challenge to the communist state.

This challenge was sparked by the failure of the Rokowski government to control inflation, including its defeat in the November 1987 popular referendum on lifting price controls and freezing wages, and a resulting wave of industrial strikes. Unlike the 1980–81 strikes, these were largely spontaneous, organized by plant-level strike committees that were loosely coordinated by the underground Solidarity movement but largely led by a new generation of younger, more radical activists (Zubek 1991). By conceding a series of wage hikes, the government created hyperinflation, finally forcing the government to enter into a series of Roundtable negotiations (named for the building in which the negotiations were conducted) with the previously outlawed Solidarity movement in February 1989. In a historic accord, the Communists agreed to open elections for the Senate and 35 percent of the seats in the Sejm (parliament), effectively opening the way for a transitional government. In June 1989, Solidarity overwhelmingly won the elections, drawing support from a broad cross section of industrial workers, peasants, the urban middle class, and Catholics (Heynes and Bialecki 1991; Milanovic 1992). The industrial working class, which had been the official base of the regime, had become its leading opponent.

Embourgeoisement and Economic Dissent in Hungary

The vulnerabilities of the Hungarian regime were different, stemming in large part from the government's privatization measures in the late 1950s. Following the 1956 Soviet intervention, the communist regime adopted a policy of economic liberalization, gradually widening the sphere of independent economic activities but without granting political rights. This prevented groups from organizing politically, producing a "hybridic social reality" (Hankis 1991, p. 177) that combined incompatible organizational principles of autonomy and dependence. Social unrest, however, remained relatively low because of the stability of personal leadership, economic prosperity, and limited ties to the West. The long tenure of Janos Kadar created diffuse paternalistic support for the ruling elite despite weak support for the communist system itself. Citizens judged the system from the vantage point of its effectiveness in protecting their economic interests. Insofar as economic liberalization allowed improved standards of living, most felt that some cooperation with the regime was functional and constructive. By 1982, one-third of the Hungarian population perceived their material situation as very good, and two-thirds saw their material situation as being better than during their childhood (Hankis 1991, pp. 170–71). The Hungarians also had less contact with the West, hence restricting their comparative aspirations.

The regime's economic concessions opened the way for, instead of a political challenge, economic dissent in the "second economy." First, the regime authorized small-scale private production in services and agriculture. Second, state workers were allowed to work in their off hours in the state-owned enterprises, supplementing their meager official wages with private earnings. In effect, they could "moonlight," more than doubling their incomes by working for themselves after hours and using physical capital provided by the state. Third, the regime created private housing, encouraging a private construction industry, private investment in personal housing, and extensive speculation in the private housing market.

The "second economy" was at least temporarily a success: "It kept the Hungarian system afloat, the political system (quasi-) legitimate, and society content" (Kornai 1990, p. 264; see also Stark 1990, p. 356). It also effectively defused chances for political mobilization and coalition between various segments of the society, keeping workers involved in their off hours and pursuing private advantage. At the same time that the Polish working class was concerned more with trade unions, plant meetings, and workplace democracy, Hungarian workers were hard at work earning a livelihood by moonlighting. This system also created increased investment and private accumulation, reestablishing elementary forms of economic and social capital and autonomous lifestyles.

In the long run, however, it also created cultural contradictions, economic inefficiency, and growing worker power against state management. The populace found themselves confronting contradictory roles and logics of action, sometimes pursuing private advantage while at other times submitting blindly to the state. This created confusion as to roles and logics of behavior, so that people frequently had difficulty comporting themselves and interacting with other people. There was also ambiguity regarding legitimate codes of conduct. Was it "socialist man" or individual financial merit that counted (Beskid et al. 1986)? It also created inefficient capital and labor markets, since the same principles did not govern both sectors and resources could not easily flow between the sectors. Because not all state workers were able to engage in extra employment, a segmented labor market emerged: a privileged sector where opportunities were available and a secondary sector that lacked them. Third, the "second economy" gave workers greater bargaining leverage against state managers and the ability to reduce their work commitments to the state sector while investing more of their time in the private sector (Burawoy 1985, p. 192; Hankis 1991, p. 181).

Alongside this "second economy" for the working class was the emergence of a genuine bourgeoisie. First, there were a significant number of *Besitzburgertum* (propertied bourgeoisie) who managed to persist in the agricultural sector. Many had family ties and private property dating back to the pre-World War II period when Hungary had been a center of export-oriented capitalist agriculture. Having succeeded in holding onto their private holdings, these "new" entrepreneurs also encouraged petit bourgeois attitudes among the smallholder peasantry (Szelenyi 1988, pp. 40–41). Second, the Party cadre elite entered the private market, first through consumerism and travel tied to Western international trade and later through investment in private housing. With the opening of Western international trade in the 1970s, Party officials and state managers became involved in conspicuous consumption of Western goods and travel abroad. The most irreversible change came with the privatization of housing in 1975. While workers and the middle class were involved, the communist officials were the primary actors, building detached private housing and then, through real estate speculation, accumulating assets that were often invested in country estates (Manchin and Szelenyi 1985, p. 259; Szelenyi 1988, 1990). What had once been a central provision of collective consumption was now seized upon as a lifetime opportunity for enrichment by the cadre elite.

These structural processes yielded four types of class actors (Mizstal 1990; Tosics 1987; Pickvance 1988; Konrad and Szelenyi 1990):

1. the newly bourgeois workers, who increasingly adopted a petit bourgeois way of life;

2. the *Besitzburgertum*, who constituted an authentic entrepreneurial class;

3. the bourgeoisified cadre elite of the communist system, who lacked entrepreneurial skills but were oriented toward enriching themselves with private consumer assets and speculation in the private housing market; and

4. the intelligentsia, who, especially over the past two decades, became assimilated into the cadre elite.

Despite these contending interests, the regime remained entrenched and able to prevent opposition. The main political actors were in "parking orbits" (Konrad and Szelenyi 1990, p. 8), that is, they were politically latent and concerned with their private economic interests. Until the Soviet collapse, no counterelite or mass movement emerged to contest power. Potentially, however, this was an explosive situation with increasing commitment by all classes to a private economy and declining commitments to the old political economy. All that was needed was the recognition that alternatives were possible and that the Soviet military would not intervene to block a shift.

Two Postcommunist Revolutions: Hyperpoliticization versus Westernization

The revolutions in Poland and Hungary came about in different ways and produced societies with distinctly different prospects. Both experienced a standard revolutionary cycle: initial protest interacting with expanded opportunities, followed by a transitional regime with maneuvering coalitions and heightened popular mobilization, and finally a conservative consolidation with significant demobilization. In Poland, the Solidarity movement prevailed, mounting a broad political challenge that forced the regime into negotiations and, without Soviet protection, to concede power. The Solidarity movement, however, factionalized and failed to create a plan for economic reconstruction, producing an eclectic mixture of inefficient worker-controlled state enterprises, petit bourgeois farms, and a handful of foreign-owned firms. Because of a weak election law and the plurality of political actors that brought about the revolution, there was no political center aside from Lech Walesa and the Catholic Church (which refused to rule directly) that could claim authority to enforce binding decisions. By contrast, the "negotiated revolution" in Hungary created a more limited number of contenders and a more gradual reform process that emphasized legal measures. The legacy was a stronger state and better economic prospects.

The Organizational Decay of the Polish Democracy Movement

In Poland, significant mobilization potential provided the basis for widespread protest and a frontal challenge to the state. In the winter of 1989, the Communists confronted an inflationary wage-price spiral, escalating strikes, and the political challenge by the Solidarity movement, finally proposing the Roundtable elections to bring the opposition in the government. Because Solidarity had been an underground movement, it was a loosely structured network of local committees dominated by the urban intellectuals surrounding the Temporary National Committee. At this point, Solidarity split into three factions: (1) a "realist" group centered among the intellectuals and older activists who favored negotiations with the Communists and a vague type of democratic socialism; (2) a younger generation of "radicals," typically workers mobilized by the 1987–88 strikes, who opposed any type of dialogue in the name of worker control and pure communism; and (3) the "compromisers," who did not foresee the possibility of a transition. Despite dissension, the realists prevailed and entered into negotiations, accepting a weak election law that provided for proportional representation with no minimum ceiling, open elections for the Senate and 35 percent of the Sejm, and a power-sharing arrangement in which the Solidarity activists would control key cabinet seats to gain governmental experience. General Jaruzelski retained the presidency, giving the security apparatus a claim to power. Although the election law did not initially present a problem because of the broad popular support for Solidarity, it later encouraged a proliferation of parties and an ineffective Parliament.

During the Roundtable elections, Solidarity concealed factional divisions by avoiding detailed discussions of reform proposals and appealing to anti-regime sentiments. While this prevented factional struggles, it also steered the movement away from its historical union base. The pro-Walesa faction launched a series of local citizens committees to mobilize support throughout the country, bringing the movement into contact with the peasants and urban middle classes. The radicals formed an anti-incorporative Solidarity '80 union opposing the power-sharing arrangments and favoring worker control. In the parliamentary elections, Solidarity shifted from an industrial worker base to an intellectual-peasant and Catholic coalition, receiving its strongest support in the rural districts of the southeast (Heynes and Bialecki 1991). Meanwhile, the Communists factionalized, failing to generate an alternative and losing all of the openly contested seats.

The new government adopted a set of contradictory economic policies. On the one hand, it reorganized state and industrial finance, thus allowing foreign and private investment and currency convertibility, and eliminating food subsidies and other austerity measures. This created escalating unemployment, which further weakened the Solidarity unions and created worker alienation. On the other hand, it was reluctant to privatize or reorganize state enterprise because of the threat of unemployment and further economic hardship. Thus inefficient state firms kept workers regardless of efficiency or market demand, creating a pileup in certain commodities and scarcities in others, along with inefficiency and inflation. This temporarily satisfied the international banking community but no one else. Private investors refused to invest, perceiving an undisciplined workforce, weak domestic demand, and inflation that would erode export earnings. The workers councils strengthened their control over the state enterprises, continuing to overemploy inefficient workers producing products with no market. Inflation eroded earnings, discouraging investment and efficient work.

At this point, Jaruzelski announced his resignation and scheduled a presidential election for December 1990. The remaining Solidarity factions then split into two: a conservative intellectual-peasant faction known as the Citizens Movement-Democratic Action (ROAD) led by Tadeusz Mazowiecki, and a vaguely populist Center Agreement (PC) led by Lech Walesa. Appealing to economic resentments, Walesa campaigned on a program of relaxed monetarism and accelerated decommunization while Mazowiecki defended his gradualist promarket policies. Meanwhile, the Solidarity unions were further weakened by competition from the former communist union and the Solidarity '80 group. Since there were few actual policy differences between the candidates, the campaign was waged largely on personal attacks, producing a dismal turnout and an indecisive Walesa victory. Solidarity then dissolved in a series of secondary political struggles, losing support among youth and the peasants and its ties to the Citizens' Committees that had provided the parliamentary victory. The popular feeling was that the former communist cadre had somehow transformed itself into a "new bourgeoisie" that was enriching itself despite the fact that there were no legal foundations for privatization. The former human rights opposition penetrated the defense and state security apparatus, gradually taking it over and deprofessionalizing it.

In this context, the new government formed by Jan Bielecki further weakened the Solidarity trade unions. The government's central agenda was deficit reduction, privatization, and further austerity. Bielecki's new political party, the Congress of Liberal Democrats (KLD), drew its support increasingly from a group of entrepreneurs in Gdansk and the petit bourgeois peasants. The intellectuals withdrew from Solidarity, leaving it a hollow shell. The parliamentary elections in October 1991 were also indecisive. Religious and nationalistic themes became prominent, the centrist coalitions split, and the peasants and workers movements became defensive, attempting to protect their short-term economic interests. More than eighty parties qualified for parliamentary seats, creating an unwieldly legislature. The neocommunists returned as a strong opposition party, and the Solidarity '80 group found itself in an odd alliance with them.

The upshot was a conservative regime influenced by a handful of entrepreneurs, the petite bourgeoisie, and the Catholic Church but without the legitimacy to reorganize the economy. The social movement that had created these changes demobilized, losing so much support that its leaders allied with antiworker forces. Paradoxically, the most proworker politicians were intellectuals who had lost their popular following. The workers focused on protecting their control over the state enterprises but found themselves under attack by the government. In two consecutive governments, the minority parties managed to control the agenda, attacking welfare measures. Democratic socialism and Western social democratic ideas both went into eclipse. An immobilized economy was matched by a stalemated and defensive polity.

The Formation of a Democracy Movement in Hungary

The Hungarian situation was qualitatively different because, for the past two decades, the country lacked an organized opposition and the Party remained in firm control.[4] A small entrepreneurial class existed in the countryside and petit bourgeois consciousness was common among the cadre and intellectual elites as well as among the newly bourgeois workers. Instead of collapsing under pressure from popular mobilization, the Communist Party splintered, pressured by international events and the declining power of the Soviet Union. This created the opportunity for the formation of a new set of inde-

pendent parties—the Smallholders' Party, the People's Party, and the Social
Democrats—that focused on citizenship rights, a constitution, privatization,
and economic reform. The result was a greater opportunity for initiating economic reforms and building a sustained democratic movement.[5]

From the spring through the autumn of 1989, the opposition groups negotiated with the Communists about a prospective transition. In October 1989,
the new constitution was unveiled and, the following April, a president was
elected with a strong parliamentary majority. Based on a more solid election
law, the number of parties was limited and created a strong centrist government. The ruling coalition—based on a centrist coalition of bourgeois, petit
bourgeois, and reform-minded intellectuals—provided a sufficiently strong
government for effective development and implementation of policies. Although many of the same social and economic problems that existed in
Poland also confronted the Hungarian government, it was better positioned
to address them. Moreover, petit bourgeois values and habits were more
widespread, offering a more fertile ground for privatization. And, perhaps
most critical of all, instead of rushing to dismantle the communist state and
turn state enterprise over to the workers, the opposition forces focused on establishing a new constitution and a strong government that could carry
through economic and political reforms.

Conclusions: Starting from Scratch Differently

In these two countries that "started from scratch," postcommunist reforms
were more constructive where they started later and were preceded by the
formation of new classes and political parties and by legal reform. Where political reorganization itself became the central issue, the reforms were inconsistent, legally vague, and economically ineffective. While these countries
shared common starting points—a crisis of the communist system, a weakening Soviet protector, and increasing ties to the West—their paths to this
point were different. Communist Poland had a strong political opposition,
having retained a strong peasant sector, an independent Catholic Church and
intelligentsia, and strong unions. This created a frontal political challenge
that succeeded in dismantling the communist state but did little to build new
legal institutions or reorganize the economy. Communist Hungary, by contrast, combined an entrepreneurial and petit bourgeois class with a bourgeois
working class. International pressure played a stronger role in the transition,
allowing a more gradual transition and a greater focus on building new legal
institutions and reforming the economy.

In Poland, the Solidarity leaders overlooked the fact that political free-doms are embedded in a social and economic framework. Instead of address-ing economic problems, they focused on democratizing the polity and assum-ing that some spontaneous mechanism would stimulate the economy. Since there was no bourgeois sector and individual enterprise was weak among the peasantry and the working class, there was no constituency to press for pri-vatization. As one observer put it, the postcommunist regime found itself "the administrators of social and economic catastrophe rather than the champions of freedom and prosperity" (Ekiert 1991). After repeated failures to address economic problems, the government finally turned to a proposal for "popular capitalism" in which the state would distribute public assets free of charge to citizens in the form of private stock (Poznanski 1992, p. 92). This stock could be traded on the stock market, which ensured some responsiveness to mar-ket forces. But there was no provision for reorganizing the management of former state enterprises or ensuring the short-term reallocation of invest-ment to new enterprises. Nor was the political situation more favorable. A fac-tionalized parliament held together by the paternalistic symbol of Lech Walesa provided a weak state that was unable to develop or implement effec-tive policies. The democracy movement had won a hollow victory.

In Hungary, a new set of economic classes formed before the political tran-sition, allowing a more gradual transition in which legal reforms prepared the way for subsequent political mobilization. Although the former Party cadres turned out to be a major element in the new bourgeoisie, the institutional set-ting was far more conducive to lasting change. A strong constitutional state that offered the possibility of gradual democratization was created. This also provided the political foundation for a market economy and thereby a mecha-nism for promoting economic growth.

The comparison between Poland and Hungary has significant implications for the politics of economic development. Many have noted the general asso-ciation between capitalist development and political democratization and as-sumed that the former must occur prior to or at least alongside the latter. These postcommunist transitions suggest other options. Poland took the route of political democratization without privatization, producing a stale-mated economy that frustrated the ideals of the reformers. The key obstacle was the creation of worker-controlled state enterprises that defensively op-posed market forces. Nor, because of the antistatist attitudes of Solidarity, was an effective state established. It was difficult to initiate further economic reforms. Hungary took the route of instituting a strong democratic state that promoted petit bourgeois as well as capitalist enterprise. It remains unclear whether the country will move toward a more centralized industrial economy or remain a largely petit bourgeois economy, but the transition created a stronger state that offered greater promise for economic growth and stable democratization.

Notes

This paper benefited greatly from comments by Bert Klandermans and Brian Martin, who loaned copies of his dissertation in progress on Polish strikes. Charles Tilly, Slawomir Magala, and Janusz Mucha pointed to problems in interpreting East European stratification.

1. Many scholars prefer "state socialism" to "communism" because it emphasizes the central institution—state ownership of the means of production—and to emphasize the distinction from democratic socialism. We use "communism" out of conventional usage to emphasize societies dominated by communist parties.

2. For evidence, see Rychard and Sulek 1988, Zaslavskaya 1990, Misztal 1978, Wasilewski 1990, Mucha et al. 1991, Szelenyi 1987.

3. What made people believe in socialist transformation was their opinion about equal opportunities. People expected that everybody can accomplish everything and that everything is due to every member of society (Marody 1991, pp. 30–31).

4. The following is a synthesis of Bozoki 1990; Staniszkis 1988, 1992; Feher and Heller 1990; and Misztal 1992.

5. The following draws on Friszke 1990 and Bozoki 1990.

Bibliography

Adler Hellman, Judith. 1987. *Journeys Among Women: Feminism in Five Italian Cities.* New York: Oxford University Press.

Agulhon, Maurice. 1970. *La vie sociale en Provence intérieure au lendemain de la Révolution.* Paris: Société des Etudes Robespierristes.

————. 1982. *The Republic in the Village.* Cambridge: Cambridge University Press.

————. 1983. *The Republican Experiment, 1848–1852.* Cambridge: Cambridge University Press.

————. 1984. "Working Class and Sociability in France before 1848." In *The Power of the Past*, edited by Pat Thane, Geoffrey Crossick, and Roderick Floud, 37–66. Cambridge: Cambridge University Press.

Ajzen, Icek, and Martin Fishbein. 1980. *Understanding Attitudes and Predicting Social Behavior.* Englewood Cliffs, N.J.: Prentice-Hall.

Alford, Robert, and Roger Friedland. 1985. *The Powers of Theory.* New York: Cambridge University Press.

Alger, Chadwick. 1990. "Actual and Potential Roles for NGOs in Worldwide Movements for the Attainment of Human Rights." Unpublished paper. Columbus: Department of Political Science, Ohio State University.

Allison, Paul D. 1978. "Measures of Inequality." *American Sociological Review* 43: 865–80.

Allum, Percy A. 1979. "Italy." In *Political Parties in the European Community*, edited by Stanley Henig, 135–69. London: Allen & Unwin.

Almond, Gabriel, and G. Bingham Powell. 1966. *Comparative Politics.* Boston: Little, Brown.

Amman, Peter. 1975. *Revolution and Mass Democracy.* Princeton, N.J.: Princeton University Press.

Amyot, Grant. 1981. *The Italian Communist Party.* London: Croom Helm.

Arian, Asher. 1985. *Politics in Israel: The Second Generation.* Chatham, N.J.: Chatham House.

Arian, Asher, and Michal Shamir. 1983. "The Primarily Political Function of the Left-Right Continuum." *Comparative Politics* 15: 138–58.

Aronoff, Myron J. 1989. *Israeli Visions and Division.* New Brunswick, N.J.: Transaction.

Arrighi, Giovani, Terence K. Hopkins, and Immanuel Wallerstein. 1989. *Antisystemic Movements.* London: Verso.

Baker, Keith Michael. 1987. "Representation." In *The Political Culture of the Old Regime*, edited by Keith Michael Baker, 469–91. Oxford: Pergamon.

Barbagli, M., and P. Corbetta. 1978. "Partito e movimento. Aspetti di rinnovamento nel PCI." *Inchiesta* 2:46.

Barbagli, M., P. Corbetta, and S. Sechi. 1979. *Dentro il PCI*. Bologna: Il Mulino.

Barkan, Steven. 1984. "Legal Control of the Southern Civil Rights Movement." *American Sociological Review* 49: 552–65.

Barley, Karen. 1991. "Rebellious Alliances: The State and Peasant Unrest in Early Seventeenth-Century France and the Ottoman Empire." *American Sociological Review* 56: 699–715.

Barnes, Samuel, and Max Kaase. 1979. *Political Action*. Newbury Park, Calif.: Sage.

Barnes, Samuel H., et al. 1979. *Political Action: Mass Participation in Five Western Democracies*. Beverly Hills, Calif., and London: Sage.

Bastid, Paul. 1954. *Les institutions politiques de la monarchie parlementaire française (1814–1848)*. Paris: Recueil Sirey.

Beckwith, Karen. 1985. "Feminism and Leftist Politics in Italy: The Case of UDI-PCI Relations." *West European Politics* 8: 19–37.

Bell, Daniel. 1977. *The Cultural Contradictions of Capitalism*. New York: Basic Books.

Belsley, David A., Edwin Kuh, and Roy E. Welsch. 1980. *Regression Diagnostics: Identifying Influential Data and Sources of Collinearity*. New York: Wiley.

Berenson, Edward. 1984. *Populist Religion and Left-Wing Politics in France 1830–1852*. Princeton, N.J.: Princeton University Press.

Berger, Peter. 1986. *The Capitalist Revolution*. New York: Basic Books.

Berry, Jeffrey. 1984. *The Interest Group Society*. Boston: Little, Brown.

Beskid, Lidia, et al. 1986. "Deprywacje materialnych warunkow zycia w Polsce i na Wegrzech" (Deprivations of material living conditions in Poland and Hungary). *Studia Socjologiczne* 3: 131–53.

Biorcio, Roberto. 1988. "L'elettorato verde." In *Lasfida verde*, edited by Roberto Biorcio and Giovanni Lodi. Padua: Liviana.

Birch, Anthony H. 1971. *Representation*. New York: Praeger.

Birnbaum, Pierre. 1988. *States and Collective Action*. New York: Cambridge University Press.

Blackmer, Donald M. 1975. "Postwar Italian Communism." In *Communism in Italy and France*, edited by Donald M. Blackmer and Sidney Tarrow, 21–68. Princeton, N.J.: Princeton University Press.

Blau, Peter M. 1964. *Exchange and Power in Social Life*. New York: Wiley.

Block, Fred. 1987. *Revising State Theory*. Philadelphia: Temple University Press.

Bobbio, Luigi. 1988. *Storia di Lotta continua*. Milan: Feltrinelli.

Bornschier, Volker. 1988. *Westliche Gesellschaft im Wandel*. Frankfurt and New York: Campus.

Bornschier, Volker, and Peter Heintz. 1979. *Compendium of Data for World System Analysis*. Zurich: Sociological Institute.

Bosso, Christopher. 1987. *Pesticides and Politics*. Pittsburgh: University of Pittsburgh Press.

Boswell, Terry, and William J. Dixon. 1990. "Dependency and Rebellion." *American Sociological Review* 55: 540–59.

Bozoki, Andras. 1990. "Negotiated Revolution: Constitutional Change and Political Transition in Hungary." Unpublished manuscript.

Brand, Karl-Werner. 1985. "Vergleichendes Resümee." In *Neue soziale Bewegungen in Westeuropa und den USA: Ein internationaler Vergleich*, edited by Karl-Werner Brand, 306–34. Frankfurt: Campus.

———. 1990. "Cyclical Aspects of New Social Movements: Waves of Cultural Criticism and Mobilization Cycles of New Middle Class Radicals." In *Challenging the Political Order: New Social Movements in Western Democracies*, edited by Russell J. Dalton and Manfred Kuechler, 23–42. Cambridge: Polity Press.

Brand, Karl-Werner, Detlef Büsser, and Dieter Rucht. 1983. *Aufbruch in eine andere Gesellschaft: Neue soziale Bewegungen in der Bundesrepublik*. Frankfurt: Campus.

Braun, Dietmar. 1989. *Grenzen politischer Regulierung: Der Weg in die Massenarbeitslosigkeit am Beispiel der Niederlande*. Wiesbaden: Deutscher Universitäts Verlag.

Braungart, Richard, and Mary Braungart. 1986. "Life-Course and Generational Politics." *Annual Review of Sociology* 12: 205–31.

Brint, Steven. 1984. "'New Class' and Cumulative Trend Explanations of the Liberal Political Attitudes of Professionals." *American Journal of Sociology* 90: 30–70.

———. 1985. "The Political Attitudes of Professionals." *Annual Review of Sociology* 11: 389–414.

Budge, Ian. 1981. "Review of 'Political Action,'" *American Political Science Review* 75: 337–50.

Burawoy, Michael. 1985. *The Politics of Production*. London: Verso.

Burawoy, Michael, and Pavel Krotov. 1992. "The Soviet Transition from Socialism to Capitalism: Worker Control and Economic Bargaining in the Wood Industry." *American Sociological Review* 57 (1): 16–38.

Burstein, Paul. 1985. *Discrimination, Jobs, and Politics*. Chicago: University of Chicago Press.

———. 1991. "Legal Mobilization as a Social Movement Tactic." *American Journal of Sociology* 96: 1201–25.

Burstein, Paul, and Kathleen Monaghan. 1986. "Equal Employment Opportunity and the Mobilization of Law." *Law and Society Review* 20: 355–88.

Button, James. 1989. *Blacks and Social Change*. Princeton, N.J.: Princeton University Press.

Byrne, Paul. 1988. *The Campaign for Nuclear Disarmament*. London: Croom Helm.

Calhoun, Craig. 1991. "The Problem of Identity in Collective Action." In *The Micro-Macro Linkage in Sociology*, edited by Joan Huber. Beverly Hills, Calif.: Sage.

———. 1993. "New Social Movements of the Early 19th Century." *Social Science History* 17: 385–427.

Cameron, David. 1978. "The Expansion of the Public Economy: A Comparative Analysis." *American Political Science Review* 72: 1243–61.

Cameron, David. 1984. "Social Democracy, Corporatism, Labor Quiescence, and the Representation of Economic Interests in Advanced Capitalist Societies." In *Order and Conflict in Contemporary Capitalism: Studies in the Political Economy of West European Nations*, edited by John H. Goldthorpe, 143–78. Oxford: Oxford University Press.

Campbell, Angus, et al. 1960. *The American Voter*. New York: Wiley.

Canosa, Romano. 1976. *La polizia in Italia*. Bologna: Il Mulino.

Cardoso, Fernando Henrique, and Enzo Faletto. 1979. *Dependency and Development in Latin America*. Berkeley: University of California Press.

Carmines, Edward G., and James A. Stimson. 1989. *Issue Evolution: Race and the Transformation of American Politics*. Princeton, N.J.: Princeton University Press.

Carnoy, Martin. 1982. *The State and Political Theory*. Princeton, N.J.: Princeton University Press.

Carter, April. 1974. *Direct Action and Liberal Democracy*. New York: Harper.

Castells, Manuel. 1983. *The City and the Grassroots.* Berkeley: University of California Press.

Chong, Dennis. 1991. *Collective Action and the Civil Rights Movement.* Chicago: University of Chicago Press.

CIED (Centro de Informacion, Estudio y Documentacion). 1980. *¿El Voto Perdido? Critica y autocritica de la Izquierda en la Campaña Electoral de 1980.* Lima: CIED.

Clark, Peter B., and James Q. Wilson. 1961. "Incentive Systems: A Theory of Organizations." *Administrative Science Quarterly* 6: 129–66.

Clawson, Mary Ann. 1989. *Constructing Brotherhood.* Princeton, N.J.: Princeton University Press.

Coates, David. 1975. *The Labour Party and the Struggle for Socialism.* Cambridge: Cambridge University Press.

Colby, David. 1975. "The Effects of Riots on Public Policy: Exploratory Note." *International Journal of Group Tensions* 5: 156–62.

———. 1982. "A Test of the Relative Efficacy of Political Tactics." *American Journal of Political Science* 26: 741–53.

———. 1985. "Black Power, White Resistance, and Public Policy." *Journal of Politics* 47: 579–95.

Conover, Pamela Johnston, and Stanley Feldman. 1981. "The Origins and Meaning of Liberal/Conservative Self-Identification." *American Journal of Political Science* 25: 617–45.

Converse, Philip E. 1964. "The Nature of Belief Systems in Mass Publics." In *Ideology and Discontent,* edited by David E. Apter, 209–61. Glencoe, Ill.: Free Press.

Cook, R. Dennis, and Sanford Weisberg. 1982. "Criticism and Influence Analysis in Regression." In *Sociological Methodology 1982,* edited by Samuel Leinhardt, 313–61. San Francisco: Jossey-Bass.

Coser, Lewis A. 1956. *The Social Functions of Conflict.* New York: Free Press.

Cotgrove, Stephen. 1982. *Catastrophe or Cornucopia.* New York: Wiley.

Cramer, Jacqueline. 1989. *De Groene Golf: Geschiedenis en Toekomst van de Milieubeweging.* Utrecht: Jan van Arkel.

Crouch, Colin. 1985. "Conditions for Trade Union Wage Restraint." In *The Politics of Inflation and Economic Stagnation,* edited by Leon N. Lindberg and Charles S. Maier, 105–39. Washington, D.C.: Brookings Institution.

Crozier, Michael J., Samuel P. Huntington, and Joji Watanubi. 1975. *The Crisis of Democracy.* New York: New York University Press.

Czada, Roland. 1983. "Konsensbedingungen und Auswirkungen neokorporatistischer Politikentwicklung." *Journal für Sozialforschung* 23: 421–39.

Dahl, Robert. 1967. *Pluralist Democracy in the United States.* New York: Rand McNally.

Dalton, Russell. 1988. *Citizen Politics in Western Democracies.* Chatham, N.J.: Chatham Publishers.

———. Forthcoming. *The Green Rainbow: Environmental Action in Western Europe.* New Haven, Conn.: Yale University Press.

Dalton, Russell, Paul Allen Beck, and Scott C. Flanagan, eds. 1984. *Electoral Change in Advanced Industrial Democracies.* Princeton, N.J.: Princeton University Press.

Dalton, Russell, and Manfred Kuechler, eds. 1990. *Challenging the Political Order.* New York: Oxford University Press.

Dauphinais, Pat D., Steven E. Barkan, and Steven F. Cohn. 1992. "Predictors of Rank-and-File Feminist Activism." *Social Problems* 39: 332–44.

della Porta, Donatella. 1989. "Anti-Terrorist Policies in Italy." Paper presented at the International Conference on Terrorism and European Integration. Leiden.

———. 1990. *Il terrorismo di sinistra.* Bologna: Il Mulino.

————. 1991. "Die Spirale der Gewalt und Gegengewalt: Lebensberichte von Links- und Rechtsradikalen in Italien." *Forschungsjournal Neue Soziale Bewegungen* 42: 53–62.

della Porta, Donatella, and Sidney Tarrow. 1986. "Unwanted Children: Political Violence and Cycle of Protest in Italy." *European Journal of Political Research* 14: 607–32.

Deutsch, Karl. 1961. *The Nerves of Government*. New York: McGraw-Hill.

Diamond, Larry, Juan Linz, and Seymour Martin Lipset, eds. 1990. *Democracy in Developing Countries*. Boulder, Colo.: Lynne Rienner.

Diani, Mario. 1988. *Isole nell'arcipelago. Il movimento ecologista in Italia*. Bologna: Il Mulino.

————. 1990. "The Network Structure of the Italian Ecology Movement." *Social Science Information* 29: 5–31.

Dietz, Henry A. 1980. *Poverty and Problem Solving Under Military Rule: The Urban Poor in Lima, Peru*. Austin: University of Texas Press.

————. 1986–87. "Aspects of Peruvian Politics: Electoral Politics in Peru, 1978–86." *Journal of Interamerican Studies* 28: 139–64.

Downs, Anthony. 1957. *An Economic Theory of Democracy*. New York: Harper & Row.

Dryzek, John. 1978. "Politics, Economics and Inequality: A Cross-National Analysis." *European Journal of Political Research* 6: 399–410.

Dubuc, Andre. 1948. "Frederic Deschamps, Commissaire de la République en Seine-Inférieure (Février-Mai 1848)." In *Actes du Congrès Historique du Centenaire de la Révolution de 1848*, 388–92. Paris: Congrès Historique du Centenaire.

Dunlap, R. E., and K. Van Liere. 1978. "The New Environmental Paradigm." *Journal of Environmental Education* 9: 10–19.

Durkheim, Emile. 1986 [1893]. *De la division du travail social*. Paris: Quadrige.

Duverger, Maurice. 1963. *Political Parties*. New York: Wiley.

Duverger, Maurice. 1967 [1954]. *Political Parties*. New York: Science Editions.

Duyvendak, Jan Willem. 1990a. "The Development of the French Gay Movement 1975–89." Unpublished manuscript. University of Amsterdam.

————. 1990b. "Profiles and Trajectories of Five Social Movements." Unpublished paper. University of Amsterdam.

Duyvendak, Jan Willem, and Ruud Koopmans. 1989. "Structures politiques, processus interactifs et le développement des mouvements écologiques." Presentation for the seminar Political Ecologism: Its Constants and Differences in Europe, European Consortium of Political Research joint workshops. Paris.

Edwards, Stewart. 1973. *The Paris Commune 1871*. New York: Quadrangle.

Ehrenreich, John, and Barbara Ehrenreich. 1977. "The Professional-Managerial Class." *Radical America* 11: 7–31.

Eisinger, Peter K. 1973. "The Conditions of Protest Behavior in American Cities." *American Political Science Review* 67: 11–28.

Ekiert, Grzegorz. 1991. "Democratization Processes in East Central Europe: A Theoretical Reconsideration." *British Journal of Political Science* 21: 285–313.

Emerson, Richard M. 1972a. "Exchange Theory, Part I: A Psychological Basis for Social Exchange." In *Sociological Theories in Progress*, vol. 2, edited by J. Berger, M. Zelditch Jr., and B. Anderson, 38–57. New York: Houghton Mifflin.

————. 1972b. "Exchange Theory, Part II: Exchange Relations and Network Structures." In *Sociological Theories in Progress*, vol. 2, edited by J. Berger, M. Zelditch Jr., and B. Anderson, 58–87. New York: Houghton Mifflin.

Epple, Ruedi. 1988. *Friedensbewegung und direkte Demokratie in der Schweiz*. Frankfurt: Haag und Herchen.

Epstein, Leon. 1967. *Political Parties in Western Democracies*. New York: Praeger.

———. 1986. *Political Parties in the American Mold.* Madison: University of Wisconsin Press.

Ergas, Yasmine. 1982. "1968–1979: Feminism and the Italian Party System: Women's Politics in a Decade of Turmoil." *Comparative Politics* 14: 253–79.

———. 1986. *Nelle maglia della politica: Femminismo, istituzioni e politiche sociali nell'Italia degli anni '70.* Milan: Angeli.

Esping-Andersen, Gosta. 1985. *Politics against Markets.* Princeton, N.J.: Princeton University Press.

———. 1990. *The Three Worlds of Welfare Capitalism.* Princeton, N.J.: Princeton University Press.

Esping-Andersen, Gosta, and Kees van Kersbergen. 1992. "Contemporary Research on Social Democracy." *Annual Review of Sociology,* 161–86.

Etzioni-Halevy, Eva. 1989. *Fragile Democracy.* New Brunswick, N.J.: Transaction.

Evans, Peter, Dietrich Rueschemeyer, and Theda Skocpol, eds. 1985. *Bringing the State Back In.* New York: Cambridge University Press.

Fach, Wolfgang, and Georg Simonis. 1987. *Die Stärke des Staates im Atomkonflikt: Frankreich und die Bundesrepublik im Vergleich.* Frankfurt: Campus.

Feather, N. 1982. *Expectations and Actions: Expectancy-Value Models in Psychology.* Hillsdale, N.J.: Erlbaum.

Feher, Ferenc, and Agnes Heller. 1990. "From Totalitarian Dictatorship through 'Rechtsstaat' to Democracy." *Thesis Eleven* 26: 719.

Ferree, Myra Marx. 1987. "Equality and Autonomy." In *The Women's Movements of the United States and Western Europe,* edited by Mary Katzenstein and Carol Mueller. Philadelphia: Temple University Press.

Ferree, Myra Marx, and Frederick D. Miller. 1985. "Mobilization and Meaning: Towards an Integration of Psychological and Resource Perspectives on Social Movements." *Sociological Inquiry* 55: 38–61.

Finkel, Steven E., Edward N. Muller, and Karl-Dieter Opp. 1989. "Personal Influence, Collective Rationality, and Mass Political Action." *American Political Science Review* 83: 885–903.

Finkel, Steven E., and Karl-Dieter Opp. 1991. "Party Identification and Participation in Collective Political Action." *Journal of Politics* 53: 339–71.

Finlay, David J., Douglas W. Simon, and L. A. Wilson II. 1974. "The Concept of Left and Right in Cross-National Research." *Comparative Political Studies* 7: 209–22.

Fireman, Bruce, and William Gamson. 1979. "Utilitarian Logic in the Resource Mobilization Perspective." In *The Dynamics of Social Movements,* edited by Mayer N. Zald and John D. McCarthy, 8–44. Cambridge, Mass.: Winthrop.

Flanigan, William H., and Edwin Fogelman. 1970. "Pattern of Political Violence in Comparative Historical Perspective." *Comparative Politics* 3: 1–20.

Flynn, Andrew, and Philip Lowe. 1992. "The Greening of the Tories." In *Green Politics Two,* edited by Wolfgang Rüdig. Edinburgh: University of Edinburgh Press.

Forstenzer, Thomas. 1981. *French Provincial Police and the Fall of the Second Republic.* Princeton, N.J.: Princeton University Press.

Fowler, Linda L., and Ronald G. Shaiko. 1987. "The Grass Roots Connection: Environmental Activists and Senate Roll Calls." *American Journal of Political Science* 31: 484–510.

Franklin, Mark, et. al. 1992. *Social Structure and Party Choice.* Cambridge: Cambridge University Press.

Freeman, Jo. 1975. *The Politics of Women's Liberation.* New York: Longman.

Frentzel, Janina. 1990. "Civil Society in Poland and Hungary." *Soviet Studies* 40 (4): 759–77.

Friszke, Andrzej. 1990. "The Polish Political Scene." *East European Politics and Societies* 4 (2): 305–41.

Fuchs, Dieter. 1990. "The Normalization of the Unconventional. Forms of Political Action and New Social Movements." Discussion Paper FS III 90–203. Wissenschaftszentrum Berlin.

Fuchs, Dieter, and Hans-Dieter Klingemann. 1990. "The Left-Right Schema." In *Continuities in Political Action*, edited by M. Kent Jennings et al., 203–34. Berlin and New York: De Gruyter.

Gadomska, Magdalena. 1984. "Przemiany w percepcji podzialow spolecznych" (Transformations in the perception of social problems). In *Spoleczenstwo polskie czasu kryzysu: Przeobrazenia swiadomosci i warianty zachowan* (Polish society at the time of the crisis: Transformations in social consciousness and the variants of behavior), edited by Stefan Nowak, 150–61. Warsawa: University of Warsaw.

Gaillard, Jeanne. 1971. *Communes de province, commune de Paris 1870–1871*. Paris: Flammarion.

Gale, Richard P. 1986. "Social Movements and the State: The Environmental Movement, Countermovement, and Government Agencies." *Sociological Perspectives* 29: 202–40.

Gallie, Duncan. 1983. *Social Inequality and Class Radicalism in France and Britain*. Cambridge: Cambridge University Press.

Gambetta, Leon. 1882. "Speech of October 9, 1877." In *Discours et plaidoyers politiques de M. Gambetta*, vol. 7, edited by Joseph Reinach. Paris: Charpentier.

Gamble, Andrew. 1986. *Britain in Decline*. London: Macmillan.

Gamson, William A. 1975. *The Strategy of Social Protest*. Homewood, Ill.: Dorsey.

———. 1990. *The Strategy of Social Protest*. 2d ed. Belmont, Calif.: Wadsworth.

Garner, Roberta Ash, and Mayer N. Zald. 1987. "The Political Economy of Social Movement Sectors." In *Social Movements in an Organizational Society*, edited by Mayer N. Zald and John McCarthy, 293–318. New Brunswick, N.J.: Transactions.

Garrow, David J. 1978. *Protest at Selma*. New Haven, Conn.: Yale University Press.

Gelb, Joyce. 1989. *Feminism and Politics*. Berkeley: University of California Press.

Gelb, Joyce, and Marian Lief Palley. 1981. *Women and Public Policy*. Princeton, N.J.: Princeton University Press.

Geremek, Bronislaw. 1991. "Between Hope and Despair." In *East Europe . . . Central Europe . . . Europe*, edited by Stephen R. Graubard, 95–115. Boulder, Colo.: Westview.

Gerhards, Jürgen. 1991. "Die Mobilisierung gegen die IWF- und Weltbanktagung in Berlin: Gruppen, Veranstaltungen, Diskurse." In *Neuesoziale Bewegungen in der Bundesrepublik Deutschland*, edited by Roland Roth and Dieter Rucht. Bonn: Bundeszentrale für politische Bildung.

Gerhards, Jürgen, and Dieter Rucht. 1991. "Mesomobilization Contexts: Organizing and Framing in Two Protest Campaigns in West Germany." Discussion Paper FS III 91–101. Wissenschaftszentrum Berlin.

Ginsborg, Paul. 1989. *Storia d'Italia dal dopoguerra adoggi*. 2 vols. Turin: Einaudi.

Giugni, Marco, and Hanspeter Kriesi. 1990. "Nouveaux mouvements sociaux dans les années 80: Évolution et perspectives." *Annuaire Suisse de Science Politique* 30.

Golden, Miriam. 1986. "Interest Representation, Party Systems, and the State." *Comparative Politics* April: 279–302.

Goldstein, Robert J. 1983. *Political Repression in 19th Century Europe*. London: Croom Helm.

Goldstone, Jack. 1980. "The Weakness of Organization: A New Look at Gamson's 'The Strategy of Social Protest.'" *American Journal of Sociology* 85: 1017–42, 1426–32.

Goodwin, J., and Theda Skocpol. 1989. "Explaining Revolutions in the Contemporary Third World." *Politics and Society* 17: 489–509.

Goodwyn, Lawrence. 1991. *Breaking the Barrier: The Rise of Solidarity in Poland.* New York: Oxford University Press.

Gossez, Remi. 1956. "Diversité des antagonismes sociaux vers le milieu du XIXe siècle." *Revue Économique* 6: 439–58.

Gouldner, Alvin W. 1961. "The Norm of Reciprocity." *American Sociological Review* 25: 161–79.

———. 1979. *The Future of Intellectuals and the Rise of the New Class.* New York: Oxford University Press.

Grundy, Kenneth W., and Michael A. Weinstein. 1974. *The Ideologies of Violence.* Columbus: Merrill.

Gurr, Ted R. 1970. *Why Men Rebel.* Princeton, N.J.: Princeton University Press.

———. 1980. "On the Outcomes of Violent Conflict." In *Handbook of Political Conflict*, edited by T. Gurr, 238–94. New York: Free Press.

———. 1989. "Protest and Rebellion in the 1960s: The United States in World Perspective." In *Violence in America*, edited by T. R. Gurr, 101–30. Beverly Hills, Calif.: Sage.

Habermas, Jürgen. 1973. *Legitimationsprobleme im Spätkapitalismus.* Frankfurt: Suhrkamp.

Hahn, Harlan. 1970. "Civic Responses to Riots: A Reappraisal of Kerner Commission Data." *Public Opinion Quarterly* 34: 101–7.

Haines, Herbert. 1986. *Black Radicals and the Civil Rights Mainstream, 1954–1970.* Knoxville: University of Tennessee Press.

Halebsky, Sandor. 1976. *Mass Society and Political Conflict.* New York: Cambridge University Press.

Halevi, Ran. 1985. "Modalités, participation, et luttes electorales en France sous l'Ancien Regime." In *Explication du Vote: Un bilan des études électorales en France*, edited by Daniel Gaxie, 85–105. Paris: Presses de la Fondation Nationale des Sciences Politiques.

Hall, Robert L., Mark Rodeghier, and Bert Useem. 1986. "Effects of Education on Attitude to Protest." *American Sociological Review* 51: 564–73.

Handler, Joel. 1978. *Social Movements and the Legal System.* New York: Academic Press.

Hankis, Elemer. 1988. "The Second Society: Is There an Alternative Social Model Emerging in Contemporary Hungary?" *Social Research* 55 (12): 13–43.

———. 1991. "In Search of a Paradigm." In *East Europe . . . Central Europe . . . Europe*, edited by Stephen R. Graubard, 165–97. Boulder, Colo.: Westview.

Hanushek, Eric A., and John Jackson. 1977. *Statistical Methods for Social Scientists.* New York: Academic Press.

Hatch, Michael. 1986. *Politics and Nuclear Power.* Lexington: University of Kentucky Press.

Helander, Voitto. 1982. "A Liberal-Corporatist Sub-System in Action: The Incomes Policy System in Finland." In *Patterns of Corporatist Policy-Making*, edited by Gerhard Lehmbruch and Philippe C. Schmitter, 163–87. London: Sage.

Heberle, Rudolf. 1951. *Social Movements.* New York: Appleton-Century-Crofts.

Herring, Cedric. 1989. *Splitting the Middle.* New York: Praeger.

Hewitt, Christopher. 1977. "The Effect of Political Democracy on Equality in Industrial Societies." *American Sociological Review* 42: 450–64.

Heynes, Barbara, and Ireneusz Bialecki. 1991. "Solidarność: Reluctant Vanguard or Makeshift Coalition?" *American Political Science Review* 85: 851–74.

Hibbs, Douglas A. 1973. *Mass Political Violence: A Cross-National Causal Analysis.* New York: Wiley.

———. 1977. "Political Parties and Macroeconomic Policy." *American Political Science Review* 71: 1467–87.

Higley, John, and Lowell Field. 1979. *Elitism*. London: Routledge.

Hinton, James. 1989. *Protests and Visions: Peace Politics in Twentieth-Century Britain*. London: Hutchinson Radius.

Hintze, Otto. 1975. *The Historical Essays of Otto Hintze*, edited by Felix Gilbert. New York: Oxford University Press.

Hirschman, Albert O. 1973. "The Changing Tolerance for Income Inequality in the Course of Economic Development." *Quarterly Journal of Economics* 87: 544–66.

Hobson, John A. 1961 [1902]. *Imperialism: A Study*. 3d ed. London: Allen & Unwin.

Huard, Raymond. 1978. "La genèse des partis démocratiques modernes en France." *La Pensée* 201: 96–119.

———. 1982. *La préhistoire des partis: Le mouvement républicain en Bas-Languedoc*. Paris: Presses de la Fondation Nationale des Sciences Politiques.

———. 1985. "Comment apprivoiser le suffrage universal?" In *Explication du Vote: Un bilan des études électorales en France*, edited by Daniel Gaxie, 126–48. Paris: Presses de la Fondation Nationale des Sciences Politiques.

Huberts, Leo W. 1989. "The Influence of Social Movements on Government Policy." *International Social Movements Research* 2: 395–426.

Hülsberg, Werner. 1988. *The German Greens*. London: Verso.

Huntington, Samuel P. 1968. *Political Order in Changing Societies*. New Haven, Conn.: Yale University Press.

———. 1982. *American Politics*. Cambridge, Mass.: Harvard University Press.

Inglehart, Ronald. 1977. *The Silent Revolution: Changing Values and Political Styles Among Western Publics*. Princeton, N.J.: Princeton University Press.

———. 1979. "The Impact of Values, Cognitive Level, and Social Background." In *Political Action: Mass Participation in Five Western Democracies*, edited by Samuel H. Barnes and Max Kaase, 343–80. Beverly Hills, Calif.: Sage.

———. 1990a. *Culture Shift in Advanced Industrial Society*. Princeton, N.J.: Princeton University Press.

———. 1990b. "Political Value Orientations." In *Continuities in Political Action*, edited by M. Kent Jennings and J. W. van Deth, 67–102. New York: De Gruyter.

Inglehart, Ronald, and Hans Klingemann. 1976. "Party Identification, Ideological Preference and the Left-Right Dimension among Western Mass Publics." In *Party Identification and Beyond: Representations of Voting and Party Competition*, edited by Ian Budge, Ivor Crewe, and Dennis Farlie, 243–73. London and New York: Wiley.

———. 1979. "Ideological Conceptualization and Value Priorities." In *Political Action: Mass Participation in Five Western Democracies*, edited by Samuel H. Barnes, and Max Kaase, 203–13. Beverly Hills, Calif.: Sage.

International Labor Organization. 1977. *ILO Yearbook*. Geneva, Switzerland: ILO.

Isaac, Larry, and William R. Kelly. 1981. "Racial Insurgency, the State, and Welfare Expansion." *American Journal of Sociology* 86: 1348–86.

Isaac, Larry, Elizabeth Mutran, and Sheldon Stryker. 1980. "Political Protest Orientations among Black and White Adults." *American Sociological Review* 45: 191–213.

Jackman, Robert W. 1975. *Politics and Social Equality: A Comparative Analysis*. New York: Wiley.

Jacob, Herbert. 1988. *The Silent Revolution*. Chicago: University of Chicago Press.

Jagodzinski, Wolfgang. 1983. "Oekonomische Entwicklung und politische Protestverhalten 1920–1973." In *Politische Stabilität und Konflikt*, special issue 14 of *Politische Vierteljahresschrift*, edited by Wolf-Dieter Eberwein, 18–23. Opladen: Westdeutscher.

Jamison, Andrew, et al. 1990. *The Making of the New Environmental Consciousness: A Comparative Study of Environmental Movements in Sweden, Denmark and the Netherlands.* Edinburgh: University of Edinburgh Press.

Jenkins, J. Craig. 1977. "Radical Transformation of Organizational Goals." *Administrative Science Quarterly* 22: 568–85.

———. 1981. "Sociopolitical Movements." In *Handbook of Political Behavior*, vol. 4, edited by Samuel L. Long, 81–153. New York and London: Plenum.

———. 1983a. "Resource Mobilization Theory and the Study of Social Movements." *Annual Review of Sociology* 9: 527–53.

———. 1983b. "The Transformation of a Constituency into a Movement." In *Social Movements of the Sixties and Seventies*, edited by Jo Freeman, 52–70. New York: Longman.

———. 1985. *The Politics of Insurgency.* New York: Columbia University Press.

———. 1987. "Interpreting the Stormy Sixties: Three Theories in Search of a Political Age." *Research in Political Sociology* 3: 269–303.

Jenkins, J. Craig, and Barbara Brent. 1989. "Social Protest, Hegemonic Competition, and Social Reform." *American Sociological Review* 54: 891–909.

Jenkins, J. Craig, and Craig Eckert. 1986. "Elite Patronage and the Channeling of Social Protest." *American Sociological Review* 51: 812–29.

Jenkins, J. Craig, and Augustine Kposowa. 1990. "Military Coups in Black Africa." *American Sociological Review* 55: 861–75.

Jenkins, J. Craig, and Charles Perrow. 1977. "Insurgency of the Powerless." *American Sociological Review* 42: 249–68.

Jenkins, J. Craig, and Kurt Schock. 1992. "Global Structures and Political Processes in the Study of Domestic Political Conflict." *Annual Review of Sociology* 18: 161–85.

Jenkins, J. Craig, and Michael Wallace. 1995. "The New Class and the Structure of Contemporary Dissidence." *Research in Social Movements, Conflict and Change* 18.

Jennings, M. Kent. 1987. "Residues of a Movement: The Aging of the American Protest Movement." *American Political Science Review* 81: 367–82.

Jennings, M. Kent, and Richard C. Niemi. 1981. *Generations and Politics.* Princeton, N.J.: Princeton University Press.

Jennings, M. Kent, and Jan W. van Deth, eds. 1990. *Continuities in Political Action.* New York: De Gruyter.

Jessop, Bob. 1979. "Corporatism, Parliamentarism and Social Democracy." In *Trends Toward Corporatist Intermediation*, edited by Philippe C. Schmitter and Gerhard Lehmbruch, 185–212. Beverly Hills, Calif., and London: Sage.

Jung, Otmar. 1990. "Direkte Demokratie: Forschungsstand und Aufgaben." *Zeitschrift für Parlamentsfragen* 21 (3): 491–504.

Kaase, Max. 1990a. "Mass Participation." In *Continuities in Political Action*, edited by M. K. Jennings and J. W. van Deth, 23–64. New York: De Gruyter.

Kaase, Max. 1990b. "The Cumulativeness and Dimensionality of the Participation Scales." In *Continuities in Political Action*, edited by M. K. Jennings and J. W. van Deth, 393–95. New York: De Gruyter.

Karstedt-Henke, Suzanne. 1980. "Theorien zur Erklärung terroristischer Bewegungen." In *Politik der inneren Sicherheit*, edited by E. Blankenburg, 198–234. Frankfurt: Suhrkamp.

Katzenstein, Peter J. 1985. *Small States in World Markets: Industrial Policy in Europe.* Ithaca, N.Y.: Cornell University Press.

Kelly, Petra. 1984. *Fighting for Hope.* Boston: South End.

Kesselman, Mark, et al. 1987. *European Politics in Transition.* London: Heath.

Kilpatrick, Franklin P., and Hadley Cantril. 1960. "Self-Anchoring Scaling: A Measure of Individuals' Unique Reality Worlds." *Journal of Individual Psychology* 16: 158–73.
Kitschelt, Herbert P. 1986. "Political Opportunity Structures and Political Protest: Anti-Nuclear Movements in Four Democracies." *British Journal of Political Science* 16: 57–95.
———. 1988. "Left-Libertarian Parties: Explaining Innovation in Comparative Party Systems." *World Politics* 40: 194–234.
———. 1989. *The Logics of Party Formation.* Ithaca, N.Y.: Cornell University Press.
———. 1990. "New Social Movements and the Decline of Party Organization." In *Challenging the Political Order: New Social and Political Movements in Western Democracies,*
edited by Russell J. Dalton and Manfred Kuechler, 179–208. Oxford: Polity Press.
Kitschelt, Herbert, and Staf Hellemans. 1990. *Beyond the European Left.* Durham, N.C.:
Duke University Press.
Klandermans, Bert. 1984. "Social Psychological Expansions of Resource Mobilization Theory." *American Sociological Review* 49: 583–600.
Klandermans, Bert. 1989a. "Introduction: Organizational Effectiveness." *International So-
cial Movements Research* 2: 383–94.
———. 1989b. Introduction: Social Movement Organizations and the Study of Social
Movements. In *Organizing for Change: Social Movement Organizations in Europe and
United States,* edited by Bert Klandermans, 1–17. Greenwich, Conn.: JAI.
———. 1990. "Linking the 'Old' and 'New': Movement Networks in the Netherlands." In
Challenging the Political Order: New Social Movements in Western Democracies, edited
by Russell J. Dalton and Manfred Kuechler, 122–36. Cambridge: Polity Press.
———. 1991. "The Peace Movement and Social Movement Theory." In *Peace Movements
in Western European and the United States,* edited by Bert Klandermans. Greenwich,
Conn.: JAI.
———. 1992. "Peace Movements in Europe and the U.S." *International Review of Social
Movements Research* 3: 1–57.
Klandermans, Bert, ed. 1989. *Organizing for Change: Social Movement Organizations across
Cultures.* Greenwich, Conn.: JAI.
Klandermans, Bert, and Dirk Oegama. 1987. "Potentials, Networks, Motivations and Barri-
ers: Steps Towards Participation in Social Movements." *American Sociological Review*
52: 519–31.
Klandermans, Bert, and Sidney Tarrow. 1988. Introduction to *From Structure to Action:
Comparing Movement Participation across Cultures,* edited by Bert Klandermans,
Hanspeter Kriesi, and Sidney Tarrow. Greenwich, Conn.: JAI.
Klandermans, Bert, Hanspeter Kriesi, and Sidney Tarrow, eds. 1988. *From Structure to Ac-
tion.* Greenwich, Conn.: JAI.
Klein, Ethyl. 1984. *Gender Politics.* Cambridge, Mass.: Harvard University Press.
Klingemann, Hans D. 1972. "Testing the Left-Right Continuum on a Sample of German Vot-
ers." *Comparative Political Studies* 5: 93–106.
———. 1979a. "The Background of Ideological Conceptualization." In *Political Action:
Mass Participation in Five Western Democracies,* edited by Samuel H. Barnes and Max
Kaase, 255–77. Beverly Hills, Calif.: Sage.
———. 1979b. "Ideological Conceptualization and Political Action." In *Political Action:
Mass Participation in Five Western Democracies,* edited by Samuel H. Barnes and Max
Kaase, 279–303. Beverly Hills, Calif.: Sage.
———. 1979c. "Measuring Ideological Conceptualization." In *Political Action: Mass Participation in Five Western Democracies,* edited by Samuel H. Barnes and Max Kaase,
215–54. Beverly Hills, Calif.: Sage.

Knoke, David. 1988. "Incentives in Collective Action Organizations." *American Sociological Review* 53: 311–29.

Kohn, Melvin. 1989. *Cross-National Research in Sociology*. Newbury Park, Calif.: Sage.

Kolankiewicz, George. 1973. "The Working Class." In *Social Groups in Polish Society*, edited by David Lane and George Kolankiewicz, 88–151. New York: Columbia University Press.

Konrad, George, and Ivan Szelenyi. 1990. "Intellectuals and Domination in Post-Communist Societies." Unpublished manuscript. Budapest.

Koopmans, Ruud. 1990a. *Bridging the Gap: The Missing Link between Political Opportunity Structure and Movement Action*. Paper presented at the International Sociological Association congress. Madrid.

———. 1990b. *Patterns of Unruliness: The Interactive Dynamics of Protest Waves*. Unpublished manuscript. University of Amsterdam.

Kornai, Janos. 1990. "Socialist Transformation and Privatization: Shifting from a Socialist System." *East European Politics and Societies* 4 (2): 255–304.

Kornhauser, William. 1959. *The Politics of Mass Society*. Glencoe, Ill.: Free Press.

Korpi, Walter. 1983. *The Democratic Class Struggle*. London: Routledge.

———. 1985. "Economic Growth and the Welfare State: Leaky Bucket or Irrigation System?" *European Sociological Review* 1: 97–118.

Korpi, Walter, and Michael Shalev. 1979. "Strikes, Industrial Relations and Class Conflict in Capitalist Societies." *British Journal of Sociology* 30: 164–87.

Kretschmer, Winfried, and Dieter Rucht. 1987. "Beispiel Wackersdorf: Die Protestbewegung gegen die Wiederaufbereitungsanlage." In *Neue soziale Bewegungen in der Bundesrepublik Deutschland*, edited by Roland Roth and Dieter Rucht, 134–63. Frankfurt: Campus.

Krieger, Joel. 1986. *Reagan, Thatcher, and the Politics of Decline*. New York: Oxford University Press.

Kriesi, Hanspeter. 1984. *Die Zürcher Bewegung: Bilder, Interaktionen, Zusammenhänge*. Frankfurt: Campus.

———. 1989a. "New Social Movements and the New Class in the Netherlands." *American Journal of Sociology* 94: 1078–116.

———. 1989b. "The Political Opportunity Structure of the Dutch Peace Movement." *West European Politics* 12: 295–312.

———. 1989c. "Politische Randbedingungen der Entwicklung neuer sozialer Bewegungen." In *Westliche Demokratien und Interessenvermittlung: Beiträge zur aktuellen Entwicklung nationaler Parteien- und Verbandssysteme*, edited by Ralf Kleinfeld and Wolfgang Luthardt, 104–21. Fernuniversität-Gesamthochschule Hagen.

———. 1990. "Federalism and Pillarization: The Netherlands and Switzerland Compared." *Acta Politica* 25: 433–50.

———. 1991. "The Political Opportunity Structure of New Social Movements." Discussion Paper FS III 91–103. Wissenschaftszentrum Berlin.

Kriesi, Hanspeter, ed. 1985. *Bewegungen in der Schweizer Politik*. Frankfurt: Campus.

Kriesi, Hanspeter, et al. 1981. *Politische Aktivierung in der Schweiz, 1945–1978*. Diessenhofen: Rüegger.

Kriesi, Hanspeter, et al. 1992. "New Social Movements and Political Opportunities in Western Europe." *European Review of Political Research* 22: 219–44.

Kriesi, Hanspeter, and Philip van Praag Jr. 1987. "Old and New Politics: The Dutch Peace Movement and the Traditional Political Organizations." *European Journal of Political Science* 15: 319–46.

Kuczynski, Pawel, and Krzysztof Nowak. 1988. "The Solidarity Movement in Relation to Society and the State." *Research in Social Movements, Conflicts and Change* 10: 127–47.

Kuznets, Simon. 1955. "Economic Growth and Income Inequality." *American Economic Review* 45: 1–28.

Ladd, Everett. 1979. "Pursuing the New Class: Social Theory and Survey Data." In *The New Class?* edited by B. Bruce- Briggs, 101–22. New Brunswick, N.J.: Transaction.

Ladner, Andreas. 1989. "Green and Alternative Parties in Switzerland." *New Politics in Western Europe*, edited by Ferdinand Müller-Rommel. London: Westview.

Ladrech, Robert. 1989. "Social Movements and Party Systems: The French Socialist Party and New Social Movements." *West European Politics* 12: 262–79.

Lang, Kurt, and Gladys Lang. 1961. *Collective Dynamics*. New York: Crowell.

Lange, Peter. 1984. "Unions, Workers, and Wage Regulation: The Rational Bases of Consent." In *Order and Conflict in Contemporary Capitalism*, edited by John H. Goldthorpe, 98–123. Oxford: Clarendon.

Lange, Peter, Sidney Tarrow, and Cynthia Irvin. 1990. "Mobilization, Social Movements and Party Recruitment: The Italian Communist Party since the 1960s." *British Journal of Political Science* 20: 15–42.

Langguth, Gerd. 1983. *Protestbewegung. Entwicklung, Niedergang. Renaissance*. Cologne: Wissenschaft und Gesellschaft.

LaPalombara, Joseph, and Myron Weiner. 1966. "The Origin and Development of Political Parties." In *Political Parties and Political Development*, edited by J. LaPalombara and M. Weiner, 3–42. Princeton, N.J.: Princeton University Press.

Laponce, J. A. 1970. "Note on the Use of the Left-Right Dimension." *Comparative Political Studies* 2: 481–502.

Latta, Claude. 1980. *Un républicain méconnu: Martin Bernard*. Saint-Etienne: Centre d'Etudes Foreziennes.

Lawson, Kay. 1988. "Linkage Politics." In *When Parties Fail*, edited by Peter Merkl and Kay Lawson. Princeton, N.J.: Princeton University Press.

Lehman-Wilzig, Sam N. 1990. *Stiff-Necked People, Bottle-Necked System*. Bloomington: Indiana University Press.

Lehmbruch, Gerhard. 1977. "Liberal Corporatism and Party Government." *Comparative Political Studies* 10: 91–126.

———. 1984. "Concertation and the Structure of Corporatist Networks." In *Order and Conflict in Contemporary Capitalism*, edited by John H. Goldthorpe, 60–80. New York: Oxford University Press.

———. 1985. "Neocorporatism in Western Europe: A Reassessment of the Concept in Cross-National Perspective." Paper presented to the International Political Science Association, 13th World Congress. Paris.

Leif, Thomas. 1990. *Die strategische (Ohn-)Macht der Friedensbewegung*. Opladen: Westdeutscher.

Leonard, Jonathan. 1986. "What Was Affirmative Action?" *American Economic Review* (papers and proceedings) 76: 359–63.

Lequin, Yves. 1984. *Les citoyens et la démocratie*. Paris: Armand Colin.

Lewis, Steven C., and Srenella Sferza. 1987. "Les socialistes français entre l'Etat et la Société: De la construction du parti à la conquëete du pouvoir." In *L'Expérience Mitterrand*, edited by Stanley Hoffmann and George Ross, 132–51. Paris: Presses Universitaires de France.

Lijphart, Arend. 1974. "Consociational Democracy." In *Consociational Democracy: Political Accommodation in Segmented Societies*, edited by K. McRae, 70–89. Toronto: McClelland and Stewart.

Lipset, Seymour M. 1960. *Political Man: The Social Bases of Politics*. Garden City, N.Y.: Doubleday.

Lipset, S. M. 1981. *Political Man*. Expanded ed. Baltimore: Johns Hopkins University Press.

Lipset, Seymour M., and Ralph Bendix. 1959. *Social Mobility in Industrial Society*. Berkeley: University of California Press.

Lipset, Seymour Martin, and Stein Rokkan. 1967. "Cleavage Structures, Party Systems, and Voter Alignments." In *Party Systems and Voter Alignments*, edited by S. M. Lipset and S. Rokkan, 1–64. New York: Free Press.

Lipset, Seymour M., and Stein Rokkan. 1985 [1967]. "Cleavage Structures, Party Systems, and Voter Alignments." In *Consensus and Conflict. Essays in Political Sociology*, edited by S. M. Lipset, 113–85. New Brunswick, N.J.: Transaction.

Lipsky, Michael. 1968. "Protest as a Political Resource." *American Political Science Review* 62: 1144–58.

Lo, Clarence. 1990. *Small Property versus Big Government: Social Origins of the Property Tax Revolt*. Berkeley: University of California Press.

Lodi, Giovanni. 1984. *Uniti e diversi: Le mobilitazioni per la pace nell'Italia degli anni '80*. Milan: Unicopli.

Lowe, Philip, and Jane Goyder. 1983. *Environmental Groups in Politics*. London: Allen & Unwin.

Mach, Bogdan W. 1990. "Autoidentyfikacja a samowiedza spolecz na" (Self-identification and self-knowledge of society). In *Grupy i Wiezi Spoleczne w Systemie Monocentrycznym* (Social groups and social bonds in the monocentric social system), edited by Edmund WnukLipinski. Warsaw: Polska Akademia Nauk (Polish Academy).

Macy, Michael. 1988. "New Class Dissent among Socio-Cultural Specialists." *Sociological Forum* 3: 325–56.

Major, J. Russell. 1960. *The Deputies to the Estates General of Renaissance France*. Madison: University of Wisconsin Press.

Malia, Martin. 1991a. "The August Revolution." *New York Review of Books* 26: 22–28.

———. 1991b. "To the Stalin Mausoleum." In *East Europe . . . Central Europe . . . Europe*, edited by Stephen R. Graubard. Boulder, Colo.: Westview.

Manchin, Robert, and Ivan Szelenyi. 1985. "Eastern Europe in the 'Crisis of Transition.'" In *Poland after Solidarity*, edited by Bronislaw Misztal, 87–102. New Brunswick, N.J.: Transaction.

Mann, Michael. 1988. *States, War and Capitalism*. New York: Basil Blackwell.

Mansbridge, Jane. 1980. *Beyond Adversarial Democracy*. New York: Basic Books.

Marasa, Bruno. 1986. *Gli Anni di Comiso, 1981–1984*. Palermo: Istituto Gramsci Siciliano.

March, James G., and Johan Olsen. 1989. *Rediscovering Institutions: The Organizational Basis of Politics*. New York: Free Press.

Marody, Miroslawa. 1991. "Miec aby byc" (To have in order to be). In *Spoleczenstwo polskie u progu przemian* (Polish society on the verge of change), edited by Janusz Mucha et al. Wroclaw: Ossolineum.

Marody, Miroslawa, ed. 1991. *Co nam zostalo z tych lat: Spoleczenstwo polskie u progu zmiany systemowej* (What is left from those years: Polish society at the brink of systemic change). London: Aneks.

Marody, Miroslawa, et al. 1981. *Polacy 1980*. Warsaw: University of Warsaw Press.

Mason, David S. 1989. "Solidarity as a New Social Movement." *Political Science Quarterly* 104 (1): 41–58.

Mauss, Marcel. 1969. *The Gift: Forms and Functions of Exchange in Archaic Societies*. London: Routledge & Kegan Paul.

McAdam, Doug. 1982. *Political Process and the Development of Black Insurgency 1930–1970*. Chicago: University of Chicago Press.

———. 1983. "Tactical Innovation and the Pace of Insurgency." *American Sociological Review* 48: 735–54.

McAdam, Doug, John D. McCarthy, and Mayer N. Zald. 1988. "Social Movements." In *Handbook of Sociology*, edited by Neil Smelser, 695–737. Beverly Hills, Calif.: Sage.

McCarthy, John, and Mayer Zald. 1973. *The Trend of Social Movements in America*. Morristown, N.J.: General Learning.

———. 1977. "Resource Mobilization and Social Movements." *American Journal of Sociology* 82: 1212–41.

McCarthy, John, David W. Britt, and Mark Wolfson. 1991. "The Institutional Channeling of Social Movements by the State in the United States." *Research in Social Movements, Conflicts and Change* 13: 45–76.

Melucci, Alberto. 1980. "The New Social Movements: A Theoretical Approach." *Social Science Information* 19: 199–226.

———. 1981. "Ten Hypotheses in the Analysis of New Movements." In *Contemporary Italian Sociology*, edited by Diana Pinto, 173–94. Cambridge: Cambridge University Press.

———. 1984. "La sfida della pace." Introduction to Giovanni Lodi, *Uniti e diversi: Le mobilitazioni per la pace nell'Italia degli anni '80*. Milan: Unicopli.

———. 1989. *Nomads of the Present: Social Movements and Individual Needs in Contemporary Society*, edited by John Keane and Paul Mier. Philadelphia: Temple University Press.

Melucci, Alberto, ed. 1984. *Altri codici*. Bologna: Il Mulino.

Memoria. Rivista di storia delle donne. 1986. Donne insieme. I gruppi degli anni Ottanta. No. 13.

Merriman, John. 1978. *The Agony of the Republic*. New Haven, Conn.: Yale University Press.

Metz, Steven. 1986. "The Anti-Apartheid Movement and the Populist Instinct in American Politics." *Political Science Quarterly* 101: 379–95.

Meyer, David. 1990. *A Winter of Discontent: The Nuclear Freeze and American Politics*. New York: Praeger.

———. 1993. "Protest Cycles and Political Process: American Peace Movements in the Nuclear Age." *Political Research Quarterly* 47: 451–79.

Migdal, Joel. 1988. *Strong Societies and Weak States*. Princeton, N.J.: Princeton University Press.

Milanovic, Branko. 1992. "Poland's Quest for Economic Stabilization, 1988–1991." *Soviet Studies* 44: 511–32.

Milbrath, Lester. 1970. "The Impact of Lobbying on Governmental Decisions." In *Policy Analysis in Political Science*, edited by I. Sharansky, 360–82. Chicago: Markham.

———. 1984. *Environmentalists: Vanguard for a New Future*. Buffalo: State University of New York Press.

Miliband, Ralph. 1961. *Parliamentary Socialism*. London: Allen & Unwin.

Mirowsky, John, and Catherine E. Ross. 1981. "Protest Group Success: The Impact of Group Characteristics, Social Control, and Context." *Sociological Focus* 14: 177–92.

Misztal, Bronislaw. 1978. *Zagadnienia Spolecznego uczestnictwa i wspoldzialania* (Problems of social participation and cooperation). Wroclaw. Ossolineum.

———. 1990. "The Commodification of Housing under the State Socialism: Welfare Policies in Poland." In *International Handbook of Housing*, edited by Willem Van Vliet. Greenwood, Conn.: Greenwood.

————. 1992. "Between the State and Solidarity. One Movement, Two Interpretations: The Orange Alternative Movement in Poland." *British Journal of Sociology* 43 (1): 55–78.

Monicelli, Mino. 1978. *L'ultrasinistra in Italia 1968–1978*. Bari: La Terza.

Moore, Barrington Jr. 1966. *The Social Origins of Democracy and Dictatorship*. Boston: Beacon.

Moore, Barrington Jr. 1978. *Injustice: The Social Bases of Obedience and Revolt*. White Plains, N.Y.: Sharpe.

Morawski, Witold. 1980. "Society and Strategy of Imposed Industrialization." *Polish Sociological Bulletin* 4: 52.

Moss, Bernard. 1976. "Producers' Associations and the Origins of French Socialism: Ideology from Below." *Journal of Modern History* 48: 69–89.

Mucha, Janusz, et al., eds. 1991. *Spoleczenstwo polskie u progu przemian* (Polish society on the verge of change). Wroclaw: Ossolineum.

Mueller, Carol McClurg. 1978. "Riot Violence and Protest Outcomes." *Journal of Political and Military Sociology* 6: 49–63.

Muller, Edward N. 1979. *Aggressive Political Participation*. Princeton, N.J.: Princeton University Press.

————. 1982. "An Explanatory Model for Differing Types of Participation." *European Journal of Political Research* 10: 1–16.

————. 1985. "Income Inequality, Regime Repressiveness, and Political Violence." *American Sociological Review* 50: 47–61.

Muller, Edward N., Henry A. Dietz, and Steven E. Finkel. 1991. "Discontent and the Expected Utility of Rebellion: The Case of Peru." *American Political Science Review* 85: 1261–82.

Muller, Edward N., and R. Kenneth Godwin. 1984. "Democratic and Aggressive Political Participation: Estimation of a Nonrecursive Model." *Political Behavior* 6: 129–46.

Muller, Edward N., and Karl-Dieter Opp. 1986. "Rational Choice and Rebellious Collective Action." *American Political Science Review* 80: 471–89.

Muller, Edward N., and Mitchell A. Seligson. 1987. "Inequality and Insurgency." *American Political Science Review* 81: 425–51.

Müller-Rommel, Ferdinand. 1985. "New Social Movements and Smaller Parties: A Comparative Perspective." *West European Politics* 8: 41–54.

Müller-Rommel, Ferdinand, ed. 1989. *New Politics in Western Europe: The Rise and Success of Green Parties and Alternative Lists*. London: Westview.

Müller-Rommel, Ferdinand, and Thomas Poguntke. 1989. "The Unharmonious Family: Green Parties in Western Europe." In *The Greens in West Germany*, edited by Eva Kolinsky, 11–29. Oxford: Berg.

Municipal Archives of Saint-Etienne: 7 K 1.

Nagel, Joane. 1990. "Cycles of Protest and Cycles of Reform: From Termination to Self-Determination in Federal Indian Policy." Paper presented to the annual meeting of the American Sociological Association. Washington, D.C.

Nagengast, Carole. 1991. *Reluctant Socialists, Rural Entrepreneurs: Class, Culture and the Polish State*. Boulder, Colo.: Westview.

National Archives of France: BB30 365, BB18 1766.

Neidhardt, Friedhelm. 1989. "Gewalt und Gegengewalt. Steigt die Bereitschaft zu Gewaltaktionen mit zunehmenderstaatlicher Kontrolle und Repression." In *Jugend-Staat-Gewalt*, edited by Wilhelm Heitmeyer, Kurt Moeller, and Heinz Suenker, 233–43. Weinheim and Munich: Juventa.

Nelkin, Dorothy, and Jane Poulkin. 1990. "When Do Social Movements Win? Three Campaigns against Animal Experiments." Paper presented to the annual meeting of the American Sociological Association. Washington, D.C.

Nicolet, Claude. 1982. *L'idée républicaine en France*. Paris: Gallimard.

Nisbit, Robert. 1982. *Prejudices: A Philosophical Dictionary*. Cambridge, Mass.: Harvard University Press.

Nollert, Michael. 1990. "Social Inequality in the World System: An Assessment." In *World Society Studies*, vol. 1, edited by Volker Bornschier and Peter Lengyel, 17–54. Frankfurt: Campus.

———. 1991. "Zwischen Konvergenz und Variation: Zur Berufsmobiliät im internationalen Vergleich." In *Das Ende der sozialen Schichtung?* edited by Volker Bornschier, 154–86. Zurich: Seismo.

———. 1992. *Interessenvermittlung und sozialer Konflikt*. Pfaffenweiler: Centaurus.

Nowak, Krzysztof. 1991. "Dekompozycja i rekompozycja dzialan zbiorowych a systemu dominacji: Polska lat osiemdzie siatych" (Decomposition and recomposition of collective action and the transformation of the system of domination in Poland in the 1980s). In *Spoleczenstwo polskie u progu przemian* (Polish society on the verge of change), edited by Janusz Mucha et al. Wroclaw: Ossolineum.

Nowak, Stefan. 1989. "The Attitudes, Values and Aspirations of Polish Society." *Sociological Studies* 5: 133–63.

Oberschall, Anthony. 1973. *Social Conflict and Social Movements*. Englewood Cliffs, N.J.: Prentice-Hall.

———. 1978. "Theories of Social Conflict." *Annual Review of Sociology* 4: 291–315.

O'Connor, James. 1973. *The Fiscal Crisis of the State*. New York: St. Martin's.

O'Donnell, Guillermo. 1979. "Tensions in the Bureaucratic-Authoritarian State and the Question of Democracy." In *The New Authoritarianism in Latin America*, 285–318. Princeton, N.J.: Princeton University Press.

O'Donnell, Guillermo, and Philippe C. Schmitter. 1986. *Transitions from Authoritarian Rule*. Baltimore: Johns Hopkins University Press.

Offe, Claus. 1981. "The Attribution of Public Status to Interest Groups." In *Organizing Interests in Western Europe*, edited by S. Berger, 123–58. New York: Cambridge University Press.

———. 1985a. "Legitimation through Majority Rule?" In *Disorganized Capitalism*, edited by John Keane, 259–99. Cambridge, Mass.: MIT Press.

———. 1985b. "New Social Movements: Challenging the Boundaries of Institutional Politics." *Social Research* 52: 817–68.

Oliver, Pamela. 1984. "If You Don't Do It, Nobody Else Will." *American Sociological Review* 49: 601–10.

Oliver, Pamela, and Gerald Marwell. 1988. "The Paradox of Group Size in Collective Action." *American Journal of Sociology* 88: 1–8.

Olson, Mancur. 1965. *The Logic of Collective Action*. Cambridge, Mass.: Harvard University Press.

———. 1982. *The Rise and Decline of Nations*. New Haven, Conn.: Yale University Press.

Olszak, Norbert. 1987. "Les conseils de prud'hommes: Un archetype judiciaire pour le mouvement ouvrier?" *Le Mouvement Social* 141: 101–19.

Opp, Karl-Dieter. 1985. "Konventionelle und unkonventionelle politische Partizipation." *Zeitschrift für Soziologie* 14: 282–96.

Opp, Karl-Dieter, in collaboration with Peter and Petra Hartmann. 1989. *The Rationality of Political Protest: A Comparative Analysis of Rational Choice Theory*. Boulder, Colo.: Westview.

Otto, Karl O. 1977. *Vom Ostermarsch zur APO*. Frankfurt: Campus.
Paige, Jeffrey. 1975. *Agrarian Revolution*. New York: Free Press.
Panitch, Leo. 1979. "The Development of Corporatism in Liberal Democracies." In *Trends Toward Corporatist Intermediation*, edited by Philippe C. Schmitter and Gerhard Lehmbruch, 119–46. Beverly Hills, Calif., and London: Sage.
———. 1986. *Working Class Politics in Crisis*. London: New Left Books.
Papadakis, Elim. 1984. *The Green Movement in West Germany*. London: Croom Helm and St. Martin's.
Pappi, Franz U. 1989. "Die Anhänger der neuen sozialen Bewegungen im Parteiensystem der Bundesrepublik." *Aus Politik und Zeitgeschichte*, no. 26: 17–27.
Parkin, Frank. 1972. *Class Inequality and Political Order*. London: Paladin.
———. 1976. "System Contradiction and Political Transformation: The Comparative Study of Industrial Societies." In *Power and Control*, edited by Tom R. Burns and Walter Buckley, 127–46. Beverly Hills, Calif.: Sage.
———. 1979. *Marxism and Class Theory: A Bourgeois Critique*. New York: Columbia University Press.
Parvin, Manoucher. 1973. "Economic Determinants of Political Unrest." *Journal of Conflict Resolution* 17: 271–96.
Patterson, William. 1989. "Environmental Politics." In *Developments in West German Politics*, edited by Gordon Smith et al. London: Macmillan.
Payne, Howard. 1966. *The Police State of Louis Napoleon Bonaparte*. Seattle: University of Washington Press.
Pelinka, Anton. 1981. *Modellfall Oesterreich? Möglichkeiten und Grenzen der Sozialpartnerschaft*. Vienna: Wilhelm Braumüller.
Pempel, T. J., and Keiichi Tsunekawa. 1979. "Corporatism without Labor? The Japanese Anomaly." In *Trends Toward Corporatist Intermediation*, edited by Philippe C. Schmitter and Gerhard Lehmbruch, 185–212. Beverly Hills, Calif., and London: Sage.
Pickvance, Chris G. 1988. "Employers, Labour Markets and Redistribution under State Socialism: An Interpretation of Housing Policy in Hungary." *Sociology* 22 (2): 193–214.
Piven, Frances, and Richard Cloward. 1971. *Regulating the Poor*. New York: Pantheon.
———. 1977. *Poor People's Movements: How They Succeed, Why They Fail*. New York: Vintage.
———. 1979. "Electoral Instability, Civil Disorder, and Relief Rises." *American Political Science Review* 73: 1012–19.
———. 1992. "Collective Protest." In *Frontiers in Social Movement Theory*, edited by Aldon Morris and Carol Mueller, 301–25. New Haven, Conn.: Yale University Press.
Pizzorno, Alessandro. 1978. "Political Exchange and Collective Identity in Industrial Conflict." In *The Resurgence of Class Conflict in Western Europe Since 1968*, edited by Colin Crouch and Alessandro Pizzorno, 278ff. London: Macmillan.
Plutzer, Eric. 1988. "Work Life, Family Life, and Women's Support of Feminism." *American Sociological Review* 53: 640–49.
Ponteil, Felix. 1968. *Les classes bourgeoises et l'avenement de la démocratie, 1815–1914*. Paris: Albin Michel.
Porritt, Jonathan. 1984. *Seeing Green*. London: Blackwell.
Poulantzas, Nicos. 1973. *Political Power and Social Classes*. London: New Left Books.
———. 1975. *Classes in Contemporary Capitalism*. New York: New Left Books.
Powell, G. Bingham. 1982. *Contemporary Democracies*. Cambridge, Mass.: Harvard University Press.
Poznanski, Kazimierz, ed. 1992. *Constructing Capitalism: The Reemergence of Civil Society and Liberal Economy in the Post-Communist World*. Boulder, Colo.: Westview.

Praag, Philip van Jr., and Kees Brants. 1980. "Depillarization and Factionalism: The Case of the Dutch Labour Party." Paper presented at the European Consortium of Political Research workshop Factionalism and the Political Parties in Western Europe. Florence.

Przeworski, Adam. 1989. *Capitalism and Social Democracy.* New York: Cambridge University Press.

Przeworski, Adam, and John Sprague. 1986. *Paper Stones: A History of Electoral Socialism.* Chicago: University of Chicago Press.

Przeworski, Adam, and Michael Wallerstein. 1982. "The Structure of Class Conflict in Democratic Capitalist Societies." *American Political Science Review* 76: 215–38.

Redding, Kent. 1992. "Failed Populism: Movement-Party Disjuncture in North Carolina, 1890–1900." *American Sociological Review* 57: 340–52.

Reddy, William. 1984. *The Rise of Market Culture.* Cambridge: Cambridge University Press.

Rochon, Thomas R. 1988. *Mobilizing for Peace: The Antinuclear Movements in Western Europe.* Princeton, N.J.: Princeton University Press.

——. 1990a. *Mobilizing for Peace.* Princeton, N.J.: Princeton University Press.

——. 1990b. "The West European Peace Movement and the Theory of New Social Movements." In *Challenging the Political Order,* edited by Russell J. Dalton and Manfred Kuechler, 105–21. Oxford: Polity.

Rohrschneider, Robert. 1993a. "Impact of Social Movements on European Party Systems." *Annals of the American Academy of Political and Social Science* 528: 157–70.

Rolke, Lothar. 1987. *Protestbewegungen in der Bundesrepublik.* Opladen: Westdeutscher.

Rosenau, James. 1990. *Turbulence in World Politics.* Princeton, N.J.: Princeton University Press.

Roth, Roland. 1985. "Neue soziale Bewegungen in der politischen Kultur der Bundesrepublik—eine vorläufige Skizze." In *Neue soziale Bewegungen in Westeuropa und in den USA,* edited by Karl-Werner Brand, 20–82. Frankfurt: Campus.

——. 1987. "Kommunikationsstrukturen und Vernetzungen in neue sozialen Bewegungen." In *Neue soziale Bewegungen in der Bundesrepublik Deutschland,* edited by Roland Roth and Dieter Rucht, 68–88. Frankfurt and New York: Campus.

——. 1988. *Entgrenzung von Politik? Zur Bilanzierung der institutionellen Effekte neuer sozialer Bewegungen.* Deutsche Verein Politik Wissenschaft-Kongress. Darmstadt.

Roth, Roland, and Dieter Rucht. 1991. "Die Veralltäglichung des Protests." In *Neue soziale Bewegungen in der Bundesrepublik Deutschland,* edited by Roland Roth and Dieter Rucht. Revised and enlarged edition. Bonn: Bundeszentrale für politische Bildung.

Rubin, Jeffrey Z., and Bert R. Brown. 1975. *The Social Psychology of Bargaining and Negotiation.* New York: Academic Press.

Rucht, Dieter. 1988. Environmental Movement Organizations in West Germany and France. In *Organizing for Change,* edited by Bert Klandermans. Greenwich, Conn.: JAI.

——. 1989. "Vorschläge zur Konzeptualisierung von Kontextstrukturen sozialer Bewegungen." Contribution to the workshop "Vergleichende Analysen sozialer Bewegungen." Wissenschaftszentrum Berlin.

——. 1990a. "Campaigns, Skirmishes and Battles: Anti-Nuclear Movements in the USA, France and West Germany." *Industrial Crisis Quarterly* 4: 193–222.

——. 1990b. "The Strategies and Action Repertoire of New Movements." In *Challenging the Political Order: New Social Movements in Western Democracies,* edited by Russell J. Dalton and Manfred Kuechler, 156–75. Cambridge: Polity.

——. 1991. "Social Movement Sectors in France and West Germany Since 1968." In *New Social Movements: European and American Traditions,* edited by Margit Mayer. London: Unwin Hyman.

Rucht, Dieter, ed. 1992. *Research on Social Movements: The State of the Art in Western Europe and the USA*. Frankfurt: Campus.

Rüdig, Wolfgang, and Mark Franklin. 1992. "Green Prospects: The Future of Green Parties in Britain, France and Germany." In *Green Politics Two*, edited by Wolfgang Rüdig. Edinburgh: University of Edinburgh Press.

Rueschemeyer, Dietrich, and Peter Evans. 1985. "The State and Economic Transformation." In *Bringing the State Back In*, edited by Peter Evans, Dietrich Rueschemeyer, and Theda Skocpol, 44–77. New York: Cambridge University Press.

Russell, D. H. 1974. *Rebellion, Revolution and Armed Force*. New York: Academic Press.

Russett, Bruce M. 1964. "Inequality and Instability: The Relation of Land Tenure to Politics." *World Politics* 16: 442–54.

Rychard, Andrzej, and Antoni Sulek. 1988. *Legitymacja: Klasyczne teorie i polskie doswiadczenia* (Legitimacy: Classical theories and the Polish experience). Warsaw: PTS and University of Warsaw.

Sabatier, Paul. 1975. "Social Movements and Regulatory Agencies." *Policy Sciences* 6: 301–42.

Sartori, Giovanni. 1976. *Parties and Party Systems*. Cambridge: Cambridge University Press.

Sawyer, Malcolm. 1976. Income Distribution in OECD Countries. *OECD Economic Outlook, Occasional Studies* July: 3–36.

Scharpf, Fritz W. 1984. "Economic and Institutional Constraints of Full Employment Strategies: Sweden, Austria and West-Germany, 1973–82." In *Order and Conflict in Contemporary Capitalism: Studies in the Political Economy of West European Nations*, edited by John H. Goldthorpe, 257–90. Oxford: Oxford University Press.

Schattschneider, E. E. 1960. *The Semisovereign People*. New York: Holt.

Schmid, Gerhard. 1986. "Demokratisch-soziale Partei (DSP) Basel-Stadt—Ablauf und Bedeutung einer Parteispaltung." *Annuaire Suisse de Science Politique* 26: 89–106.

Schmidt, Manfred G. 1986. "Politische Bedingungen erfolgreicher Wirtschaftspolitik." *Journal für Sozialforschung* 26: 251–73.

Schmitt, Rüdiger. 1991. *Die Friedensbewegung in der Bundesrepublik Deutschland*. Opladen: Westdeutscher.

Schmitter, Philippe C. 1974. "Still the Century of Corporatism?" *Review of Politics* 36: 85–131.

———. 1981. "Interest Intermediation and Regime Governability in Contemporary Western Europe and North America." In *Organizing Interests in Western Europe*, edited by Suzanne Berger, 287–327. Cambridge: Cambridge University Press.

———. 1982. "Reflections on Where the Theory of Neo-Corporatism Has Gone and Where the Praxis of Neo-Corporatism May Be Going." In *Patterns of Corporatist Policy-Making*, edited by G. Lehmbruch and P. C. Schmitter, 259–80. London: Sage.

Schopflin, George. 1991. "The Political Traditions of Eastern Europe." In *East Europe . . . Central Europe . . . Europe*, edited by Stephen R. Graubard, 59–95. Boulder, Colo.: Westview.

Schumaker, Paul. 1975. "Policy Responsiveness to Protest Group Demands." *Journal of Politics* 37: 488–521.

———. 1978. "The Scope of Political Conflict and the Effectiveness of Constraints in Contemporary Urban Protest." *Sociological Quarterly* 19: 168–84.

———. 1980. "The Effectiveness of Militant Tactics in Contemporary Urban Protest." *Journal of Voluntary Action Research* 9: 131–48.

Schwartz, Michael. 1976. *Radical Protest and Social Structure*. New York: Academic Press.

Seidelman, Raymond. 1984. "Protest Theories and Left in Power: Italian Cities under Communist Rule." *West European Politics* 7: 43–63.

Selznick, Philippe 1953. *TVA and the Grass Roots: A Study in the Sociology of Formal Organizations.* Berkeley: University of California Press.

Seyd, Patrick. 1987. *The Rise and Fall of the Labour Left.* London: Macmillan.

Sigelman, Lee, and Miles Simpson. 1977. "A Cross-National Test of the Linkage Between Economic Inequality and Political Violence." *Journal of Conflict Resolution* 21: 105–22.

Sinden, Peter G. 1979. "Inequality and Political Conflicts." *Comparative Social Research* 2: 303–20.

Skocpol, Theda. 1979. *States and Social Revolution.* New York: Cambridge University Press.

Smelser, Neil. 1963. *The Theory of Collective Behavior.* New York: Free Press.

Snow, David, and Robert Benford. 1988. "Ideology, Frame Resonance, and Participant Mobilization." In *From Structure to Action,* edited by Bert Klandermans et al. Greenwich, Conn.: JAI.

Snow, David A., et al. 1988. "Frame Alignment Processes, Micromobilization, and Movement Participation." *American Sociological Review* 51: 464–81.

Soboul, Albert. 1975. *The French Revolution 1787–1799.* Translated by Alan Forrest and Colin Jones. New York: Vintage.

Sorlini, Claudia, ed. 1978. *Centri sociali autogestiti e circoli giovanili. Un'indagine sulle strutture associative a Milano.* Milan: Feltrinelli.

Soule, Claude. 1962. "La notion historique de répresentation politique." *Politique* 6: 17–32.

———. 1968. *Les Etats Généraux de France.* Heule: USA.

Sprinzak, Ehud. 1991. *The Ascendence of Israel's Radical Right.* New York: Oxford University Press.

Stack, Steven. 1979. "The Effect of Political Participation and Socialist Party Strength on the Degree of Income Inequality: A Cross-National Study." *American Sociological Review* 44: 168–71.

Staggenborg, Suzanne. 1989. "Stability and Innovation in the Women's Movement." *Social Problems* 36: 75–92.

Staniszkis, Jadwiga. 1988. "Stabilizacja bez uprawomocnienia" (Stability without legitimacy). In *Legitymacja: Klasyczne Teorie i Polskie Doswiadczenia* (Legitimacy: Classical theories and the Polish experience), edited by Andrezej Rychard and Antoni Sulek, 215–39. Warsaw: Polish Sociological Association and University of Warsaw.

———. 1992. "Main Paradoxes of the Democratic Change in Eastern Europe." In *Constructing Capitalism: The Reemergence of Civil Society and Liberal Economy in the Post-Communist World,* edited by Kazimierz Poznanski, 179–99. Boulder, Colo.: Westview.

Stark, David. 1990. "Privatization in Hungary: From Plan to Market or from Plan to Clan?" *East European Politics and Society* 4 (3): 351–92.

Steedly, Homer R., and John W. Foley. 1979. "The Success of Protest Groups: Multivariate Analyses." *Social Science Research* 8: 1–15.

Steinberg, Ronnie. 1982. *Wages and Hours.* New Brunswick, N.J.: Rutgers University Press.

Stephens, John. 1989. "Democratic Transition and Breakdown in Western Europe." *American Journal of Sociology* 94: 1019–77.

Stevis, Dimitris. 1993. "Political Ecology in the Semi-Periphery: Lessons from Greece." *International Journal of Urban and Regional Movements* 17: 85–97.

Sundquist, James. 1983. *Dynamics of the Party System.* Washington, D.C.: Brookings.

Swank, Duane H. 1983. "Between Incrementalism and Revolution: Group Protest and the Growth of the Welfare State." *American Behavioral Scientist* 26: 311–31.

Szelenyi, Ivan. 1987. "The Prospects and the Limits of the East European New Class Project: An Autocritical Reflection on the Intellectuals on the Road to Power." *Politics and
Society* 15: 103–42.
———. 1988. *Socialist Entrepreneurs: Embourgeoisement in Rural Hungary.* Madison: Uni-
versity of Wisconsin Press.
———. 1990. "Hungary 1989." *East European Politics and Societies* 4 (2): 208–11.
Szelenyi, Ivan, and Robert Manchin. 1987. "Social Policy and State Socialism." In *Renewal
in Social Policy,* edited by Gosta Esping-Andersen, Lee Rainwater, and Martin Ragleds.
New York: Sharpe.
Tarrow, Sidney. 1983. "Struggling to Reform: Social Movement and Policy Change During
Cycles of Protest." Western Societies Program. Occasional paper no. 15. Ithaca, N.Y.:
Cornell University.
———. 1988. "National Politics and Collective Action." *Annual Review of Sociology* 14:
421–40.
———. 1989a. *Democracy and Disorder: Protest and Politics in Italy 1965–1975.* Oxford:
Clarendon.
———. 1989b. "Struggle, Politics, and Reform: Collective Action, Social Movements, and
Cycles of Protest. Western Societies Program." Occasional paper no. 21. Ithaca, N.Y.:
Cornell University.
Tarrow, Sidney. 1990. "The Phantom at the Opera: Political Parties and Social Movements
of the 1960s and the 1970s in Italy." In *Challenging the Political Order: New Social Movements in Western Democracies,* edited by Russell J. Dalton and Manfred Kuechler,
251–73. Cambridge: Polity.
———. 1993a. "Modular Collective Action and the Rise of the Social Movement." *Politics
and Society* 21: 69–90.
———. 1993b. "States and Opportunities." Unpublished paper. Ithaca, N.Y.: Department
of Government, Cornell University.
Taylor, Charles L. 1985. *World Handbook of Political and Social Indicators III.* Cologne: Zen-
tralarchiv für Empirische Sozialforschung.
Taylor, Charles L., and David A. Jodice. 1983. *The World Handbook of Political and Social
Indicators.* New Haven, Conn.: Yale University Press.
Taylor, Verta. 1989. "Social Movement Continuity: The Women's Movement in Abeyance."
American Sociologial Review 54: 761–75.
Therborne, Goran. 1977. "The Rule of Capital and the Rise of Democracy." *New Left Review*
103: 3–41.
Thomas, George M., et al. 1987. *Institutional Structure.* Newbury Park, Calif.: Sage.
Tilly, Charles. 1964. *The Vendée.* Cambridge, Mass.: Harvard University Press.
———. 1978. *From Mobilization to Revolution.* Reading, Mass.: Addison-Wesley.
———. 1984. "Social Movements and National Politics." In *Statemaking and Social Move-
ments,* edited by C. Bright and S. Harding, 297–317. Ann Arbor: University of Michigan
Press.
———. 1988. *The Contentious French.* Cambridge, Mass.: Harvard University Press.
Tilly, Charles, Richard Tilly, and Louise Tilly. 1975. *The Rebellious Century, 1830–1930.*
Cambridge, Mass: Harvard University Press.
Timberlake, Michael, and Kirk Williams. 1984. "Dependence, Political Exclusion and Gov-
ernment Repression." *American Sociological Review* 49: 141–46.
Tosics, Ivan. 1987. "Privatization in Housing Policy: The Case of Western Countries and
That of Hungary." *International Journal of Urban and Regional Research* 11: 61–87.
Touraine, Alain. 1969. *The Post-Industrial Society.* New York: Knopf.
———. 1981. *The Voice and the Eye.* New York: Cambridge University Press.

Traugott, Mark. 1978. "Reconceiving Social Movements." *Social Problems* 26: 38–49.

Tudesq, A. J. 1964. *Les Grands notables en France*, vol. 2. Paris: Presses Universitaires de France.

Tullock, Gordon. 1974. *The Social Dilemma*. Blacksburg, Va.: University Publications.

Turk, Herman, and Lynne G. Zucker. 1984. "Majority and Organized Opposition: On Effects of Social Movements." *Research in Social Movements, Conflict, and Change* 6: 249–69.

Turner, Ralph H., and Lewis M. Killian. 1987. *Collective Behavior.* 3d ed. Englewood Cliffs, N.J.: Prentice-Hall.

UNESCO. 1977. *UNESCO Statistical Yearbook*. Geneva, Switzerland: UNESCO.

United Nations. 1977. *Compendium of Social Statistics*. Geneva, Switzerland: United Nations.

Valenzuela, J. S. 1989. "Labor Movements in Transition to Democracy." *Comparative Politics* 21: 445–72.

Verba, Sidney, Norman H. Nie, and Jae-On Kim. 1978. *Participation and Political Equality: A Seven-Country Comparison*. New York: Cambridge University Press.

Vigier, Philippe. 1973. "Elections municipales et prise de conscience politique sous la monarchie de Juillet." In *La France au XIXe siècle: Etudes historiques*, 276–86. Paris: University of Paris.

Visser, Jelle. 1987. *In Search of Inclusive Unionism: A Comparative Analysis*. Amsterdam: University of Amsterdam.

von Oppeln, Sabine. 1989. *Die Linke im Kernenergiekonflikt: Deutschland und Frankreich im Vergleich*. Frankfurt: Campus.

Wallace, Michael, and Ronald L. Jepperson. 1986. "Class Structure and Political Culture." *Research in Social Stratification and Mobility* 5: 321–61.

Wallerstein, Immanuel. 1979. *The Capitalist-World System*. New York: Cambridge University Press.

———. 1980. *The Modern World System*, vol. 2. San Diego, Calif.: Academic Press.

Walsh, Edward J. 1981. "Resource Mobilization and Citizen Protest in Communities around Three Mile Island." *Social Problems* 29: 1–21.

———. 1983. *Democracy in the Shadows*. Boulder, Colo.: Greenwood.

———. 1986. "The Role of Target Vulnerabilities in High-Technology Protest Movements." *Sociological Forum* 1: 199–218.

Walsh, Edward J., and Sherry Cable. 1986. "Litigation and Citizen Protest after the Three Mile Island Accident." *Research in Political Sociology* 2: 293–316.

Walsh, Edward J., and Rex H. Warland. 1983. "Social Movement Involvement in the Wake of a Nuclear Accident." *American Sociological Review* 48: 764–80.

Wasilewski, Jacek. 1988. "Spoleczenstwo polskie, spoleczenstwo chlopskie" (The Polish society as a peasant society). *Studia Socjologiczne* 1.

———. 1990. "Bureaucratic Elite Recruitment in Poland." *Soviet Studies* 42 (4): 743–57.

Webb, Keith, et al. 1983. "Etiology and Outcomes of Protest: New European Perspectives." *American Behavioral Scientist* 26: 291–310.

Weber, Max. 1947. *From Max Weber*, edited by Hans Gerth and C. Wright Mills. New York: Oxford University Press.

Weill, Georges. 1928. *Histoire du parti républicain en France*. Paris: Resources.

Welch, Susan. 1975. "The Impact of Urban Riots on Urban Expenditures." *American Journal of Political Science* 19: 741–60.

Williams, Kirk R., and Michael Timberlake. 1984. "Structured Inequality, Conflict, and Control: A Cross-National Test of the Threat Hypothesis." *Social Forces* 63: 414–32.

Willetts, Peter. 1982. *Pressure Groups in the Global System*. London: Pinter.

Wilson, Frank L. 1987. *Interest-Group Politics in France*. Cambridge: Cambridge University Press.

———. 1990. "Neo-Corporatism and the Rise of New Social Movements." In *Challenging the Political Order: New Social Movements in Western Democracies*, edited by Russell J. Dalton and Manfred Kuechler, 67–83. Cambridge: Polity.

Wilson, James Q. 1961. "The Strategy of Protest." *Journal of Conflict Resolution* 5: 291–303.

———. 1973. *Political Organizations*. New York: Basic Books.

Wilson, John. 1973. *Introduction to Social Movements*. New York: Basic Books.

———. 1977. "Social Protest and Social Control." *Social Problems* 24: 469–81.

Winkler, Jack T. 1976. "Corporatism." *European Journal of Sociology* 17: 100–136.

Wolf, Eric. 1969. *The Peasant Wars of the Twentieth Century*. New York: Harper.

Wolfsfeld, Gadi. 1988. *The Politics of Provocation: Participation and Protest in Israel*. Albany: State University of New York Press.

———. Forthcoming. "The Politics of Provocation Revisited: Participation and Protest in Israel." In *Israel: Democracy under Stress*, edited by L. Diamond and E. Sprinzak.

Wolfsfeld, Gadi, et al. Forthcoming. "The Structure of Political Action: A Cross-Cultural Analysis." *Social Science Quarterly*.

Wright, Erik Olin. 1979. *Class, Crisis and the State*. London: New Left Books.

———. 1985. *Classes*. London: Verso.

Zahn, Ernst. 1984. *Das unbekannte Holland. Regenten, Rebellen und Reformatoren*. Berlin: Siedler.

Zaslavskaya, Tatyana. 1990. *The Second Socialist Revolution: An Alternative Socialist Strategy*. London: Tauris.

Zevaes, Alexandre. 1927. "La lutte des classes à Rouen en Avril 1848." *La Révolution de 1848* 24: 214–15.

Zhou, Xueguang. 1993. "Unorganized Interests and Collective Action in Communist China." *American Sociological Review* 58: 54–73.

Zimmermann, Ekkart. 1985. "The 1930s World Economic Crisis in Six European Countries: A First Report on Causes of Political Instability and Reaction to Crisis." In *Rhythms in Politics and Economics*, edited by Paul M. Johnson and William R. Thompson, 84–127. New York: Praeger.

Zipp, John F. 1986. "Social Class and Social Liberalism." *Sociological Forum* 1: 301–29.

Zubek, Voytek. 1991. "The Threshold of Poland's Transition." *Studies in Comparative Communism* 24: 355–76.

Zwicky, Heinz. 1989. "Income Inequality and Violent Conflict in Developing Countries." *Research in Inequality and Social Conflict* 1: 67–93.

Zwicky, Heinz, and Peter Heintz. 1982. "Soziale Ungleichheit, Legitimationsanforderung und Konflikt." *Zeitschrift für Soziologie* 11: 268–78.

Zysman, John. 1983. *Governments, Markets, and Growth*. Ithaca, N.Y.: Cornell University Press.

Contributors

Ronald Aminzade is professor of sociology at the University of Minnesota. His research focused on the social and political consequences of early industrialization in Western Europe and the social origins of democratic institutions. His most recent book is *Ballots and Barricades* (1993).

Paul Burstein is professor of sociology and adjunct professor of political science at the University of Washington. Author of "Legal Mobilization as a Social Movement Tactic" (*American Journal of Sociology*, 1991) and "Policy Domains: Organization, Culture, and Policy Outcomes" (*Annual Review of Sociology*, 1991), he is interested in how social movements influence democratic politics.

Russell J. Dalton is professor of political science at the University of California, Irvine, where he is director of the Research Program on Democratization. His scholarly interests include comparative political behavior, political parties, and political change in advanced industrial societies. He is author of *The Green Rainbow* (forthcoming), *Politics in Germany* (1992), and *Citizen Politics in Western Democracies* (1988); coauthor of *Germany Transformed* (1981); and editor of *Electoral Change in Advanced Industrial Democracies* (1984), *Challenging the Political Order: New Social and Political Movements in Western Democracies* (1990), and *Germany Votes 1990* (1992).

Donatella della Porta is professor of local government in the department of political science and political sociology of the University of Florence, Italy. Her main research fields are social movements, political violence, political corruption, and the police. She is the author of *Il terrorismo di sinistra* (1990) and *Lo scambio occulto: Casi di corruzione politica in Italia* (1992); and editor of *Terrorismi in Italia* (1984) and *Social Movements and Political Violence* (1992).

Henry A. Dietz is associate professor in the department of government and associate dean of the College of Liberal Arts at the University of Texas in Austin. His major areas of interest include political participation, urbanization, electoral politics, and civil-military relations in the Third World, especially in Latin America. He has written or edited three books as well as articles in *American Political Science Review, American Journal of Political Science, Comparative Political Studies, Social Science Quarterly,* and other academic journals. He has received grants from the National Science Foundation, the Tinker Foundation, the Heinz Foundation, Ford-Rockefeller Foundation, the Social Science Research Council, and the American Philosophical Society.

Rachel L. Einwohner is a Ph.D. candidate in sociology at the University of Washington. Her research interests, including political sociology and social movements, center on the efficacy of protest. Her current work is a study of the effectiveness of campaigns within the U.S. animal rights movement.

Steven E. Finkel is associate professor of government and foreign affairs at the University of Virginia. His areas of specialization include political participation, electoral behavior, and research methodology. Professor Finkel is the author of numerous articles on these topics in such journals as *American Political Science Review, American Review of Political Science,* and the *Journal of Politics*. He is currently writing a manuscript with Edward Moller and Karl-Dieter Opp entitled *Collective Political Action,* and is completing a monograph on *Causal Analysis with Panel Data* for the Sage Series on Quantitative Applications in the Social Sciences.

Jerrold D. Green is corporate research manager and head of the department of international policy at RAND. He has conducted extensive research in the Middle East, and his work has appeared in such journals as *World Politics, Comparative Studies in Society and History, Comparative Politics,* and *Ethics and International Affairs*. His current research is focused on the relationship between ideology and practice in the Middle East.

Jocelyn A. Hollander is a doctoral candidate in sociology at the University of Washington. Her most recent research examined the effects of antiabortion protest on the U. S. abortion rate after *Roe v. Wade*. Her current interests include gender, violence, and political discourse.

J. Craig Jenkins is professor of sociology and fellow at the Mershon Center, Ohio State University. Author of *The Politics of Insurgency: The Farm Worker Movement of the 1960's* and the forthcoming *Patrons of Social Reform: Foundation Funding of Contemporary Movements*, he has contributed extensively to studies of social movements and comparative studies of protest and political violence. In addition to being deputy editor of *American Sociological Review*, he has held appointments at the Center for Policy Research, New York, and the Program on Non-Profit Organizations at Yale University.

Bert Klandermans is professor of applied social psychology at Free University in Amsterdam, the Netherlands. He has published widely on social movements in journals such as *American Sociological Review, Sociological Forum*, and *European Journal of Social Psychology*. He was editor of the International Social Movement Research series for JAI Press and is the editor of the Social Movements, Protest, and Contention series for the University of Minnesota Press. He is currently engaged in research on farmers' protest in the Netherlands and Spain and on the social psychological consequences of the political changes in South Africa.

Hanspeter Kriesi is professor of political science at the University of Geneva. He has taught on the faculty of political and social-cultural sciences at the University of Amsterdam and participated in a number of studies on the motivation of social movements in Western Europe. His earlier work has mainly been concerned with the structure and decision-making process of the Swiss political system.

Diarmuid Maguire is lecturer in European and international politics in the government department at the University of Sydney. The author of a number of articles on protest movements, he is currently writing a book on the British Campaign for Nuclear Disarmament.

Bronislaw Misztal is professor of sociology at Indiana University at Fort Wayne. Born and educated in Poland, he specializes in social movements research with special focus on East Central Europe. His work has appeared in

British Journal of Sociology, International Journal of Comparative Sociology, and *Politics and Society.* His most recent work is *Religion and Politics in Comparative Perspective: Revival of Religious Fundamentalism East and West* (1992, with Anson Shupe). He is currently working on a comparative study of social movements: *Social Movements at the Turn of Century* (forthcoming).

Edward N. Muller taught political science at the State University of New York at Stony Brook and has been professor of political science at the University of Arizona since 1979. He also has been a visiting professor at the University of Mannheim, the European University Institute in Florence, and the University of Hamburg. His research on causes of political instability and violence, democratization, and income inequality has been supported by numerous grants from the National Science Foundation. He is the author of *Aggressive Political Participation* (1979) and is author or coauthor of numerous articles, many of which have appeared in *American Political Science Review* and *American Sociological Review.*

Michael Nollert was assistant teacher in the sociology department at Zurich University from 1987 to 1993. He has studied the causes and consequences of neocorporatism and currently is doing research at the University of Trier in Germany on European interest intermediation.

Karl-Dieter Opp is professor of sociology at the University of Leipzig. His research focuses on rational choice theory, philosophy of the social sciences, and collective political action. He is coauthor (with Peter Voß and Christiane Gern) of a forthcoming book on the East German revolution and is currently conducting a panel study of the effects of participating in the Leipzig protests of 1989 and the subsequent changes in the lives of the respondents on present political attitudes and political action.

Dieter Rucht is senior fellow at the Wissenschaftszentrum Berlin. His research interests include modernization processes in a comparative perspective, social movements, and political protest. He is editor of *Research on Social Movements: The State of the Art in Western Europe and the USA* (1991).

Michael Wallace is professor of sociology at Indiana University. His interests in social movements include historical and contemporary studies of the U. S. labor movement and the politics of the working class. He is also interested in the consequences of technological change in the workplace and in the restructuring of the American economy. His recent publications have appeared in *American Sociological Review, American Journal of Sociology, Social Forces, Sociological Quarterly,* and *Work and Occupations.*

Gadi Wolfsfeld is senior lecturer at the Hebrew University of Jerusalem with a joint appointment in political science and communication. His primary research interests are in political communication and political behavior. His most recent publication is a volume he edited with Akiba Cohen entitled *Framing the Intifada: People and Media.*

Author Index

Subject Index

access responsiveness, 283, 290
agenda responsiveness, 283, 290
alliance system, 4, 11, 25, 32, 34, 230, 235, 239, 242
alternative movement, 31-32
alternative parties, 219
Austria, 63, 96, 142, 175, 190
Autonomen, 253

bargaining, 12, 22, 50, 109, 160, 235, 244, 277-93
Besitzburgertum, 333
Bielecki, Jan, 337
bloc recruitment, 43
Brandt, Willy, 249
British Labour Party, 207, 208, 210, 218
British Liberal Party, 304f.
Bush, George, 322

Campaign for Nuclear Disarmanent (CND), 211-19, 227, 247
capitalism, 19, 29, 127, 138, 160, 324
Catholic Church, 190, 223, 329, 330, 335
Catholics, 9, 110, 116
Christian Democrats, 28, 112, 188, 218, 245, 329
Christlich Demokratische Union/Christian Democratic Party (CDU), 73, 241, 247
Citizens Movement-Democratic Action (ROAD), 336
civil disobedience, 101f.
class conflict, 27-31, 105, 181, 190, 237, 238

class indentification, 109, 116, 118
class ideology, 192
class oganization, 99, 105, 191, 192
class structure, 97, 105, 118, 127
class voting, 108
collective action, 66, 87, 291
collective goods problem, 20
collective protest, 68, 72, 146, 149
Communist Party, 73, 174, 184, 189, 237, 337
competition, 28, 162, 184, 189, 235
concertation, 141, 143
configuration of power, 10, 168, 169, 170, 180, 181, 188, 193, 196
conflict, 23, 40, 41, 167, 242, 245, 280
conflict system, 4, 11, 22, 34, 230-39
confrontation, 40, 56, 235
Congress of Liberal Democrats (KLD), 337
conjectural/linear new social movment, 192, 193
conservation groups, 299
Conservative Party, 248
constituency resource, 204, 217
contention for power, 42, 50, 60
cooperation, 235
corporatism, 140, 190
countercultural/instrumental movements, 178, 192, 193
countermovement, 236
Cox, John, 215
Cruise missiles, 177, 188, 210-19, 240, 241
cultural resource, 203, 208
Czechoslovakia, 325, 329